REPRESENTATIONS OF BLACKNESS AND THE PERFORMANCE OF IDENTITIES

Edited by
JEAN MUTEBA RAHIER

BERGIN & GARVEY
Westport, Connecticut • London

Library of Congress Cataloging-in-Publication Data

Representations of blackness and the performance of identities /
    edited by Jean Muteba Rahier.
        p.   cm.
    Includes bibliographical references and index.
    ISBN 0–89789–606–8 (alk. paper).—ISBN 0–89789–607–6 (pbk. :
alk. paper)
    1. Blacks—Race identity.   2. African diaspora.   3. Race
relations.   I. Rahier, Jean, 1959–   .
    GN645.R47   1999
    305.896—dc21   98–41382

British Library Cataloguing in Publication Data is available.

Library of Congress Catalog Card Number: 98–41382
ISBN: 0–89789–606–8
        0–89789–607–6 (pbk.)

First published in 1999

Bergin & Garvey, 88 Post Road West, Westport, CT 06881
An imprint of Greenwood Publishing Group, Inc.
www.greenwood.com

Printed in the United States of America

The paper used in this book complies with the
Permanent Paper Standard issued by the National
Information Standards Organization (Z39.48–1984).

10 9 8 7 6 5 4 3 2 1

To the most important people in my life:
My wife Kelly, who always supports me unconditionally;
our daughters Nadège Marguerite, the most precious little flower I have
ever seen,
and Simone Esmeralda, suddenly born after the recent passage of
hurricane Georges;
and my mother, Muswamba, who has endured so much pain.

To Nina de Friedemann,
who dedicated her professional life
to the study of the African diaspora in Colombia,
and who suddenly passed away at the end of 1998.

Contents

Figures ix

Preface and Acknowledgments xi

Introduction xiii

I. CELEBRATIONS

1. Festive Rituals, Religious Associations, and Ethnic
   Reaffirmation of Black Andalusians: Antecedents of the Black
   Confraternities and Cabildos in the Americas 3
   Isidoro Moreno

2. Presence of Blackness and Representations of Jewishness in the
   Afro-Esmeraldian Celebrations of the Semana Santa (Ecuador) 19
   Jean Muteba Rahier

3. Re-/Presenting Black Female Identity in Brazil: "Filhas
   d'Oxum" in Bahia Carnival 49
   Carole Boyce Davies

4. Samba Schools: The Logic of Orgy and Blackness in Rio de
   Janeiro 69
   Myrian Sepúlveda dos Santos

5. On the Apparent Carnivalization of Literature from the French
    Caribbean   91
    Maryse Condé

II. SOCIAL ARENAS

6. Kwanzaa and the U.S. Ethnic Mosaic   101
    Ariana Hernandez-Reguant

7. Identity, Arena, and Performance: Being West Indian in the
    San Francisco Bay Area   123
    Percy C. Hintzen

8. Uptown Ladies and Downtown Women: Female
    Representations of Class and Color in Jamaica   147
    Gina Ulysse

9. Representations of Blackness in Colombian Popular Music   173
    Peter Wade

III. AFRICAN AND NATIVE AMERICAN PERSPECTIVES

10. In Memory of the Slaves: An African View of the Diaspora in
    the Americas   195
    Peter Sutherland

11. Imagery of "Blackness" in Indigenous Myth, Discourse, and
    Ritual   213
    Norman E. Whitten, Jr., and Rachel Corr

Bibliography   235

Index   255

About the Contributors   261

Figures

2.1. The Two Traditional Black Regions of Ecuador   20

2.2. Longino with his spear, guided by a Roman soldier in front of
the Monte del Calvario   29

2.3. Jesus Christ carrying his cross during Good Friday procession,
surrounded by Roman soldiers   31

2.4. Barabbas during Good Friday procession   32

2.5. A frontal view of a Jew in the church during the Tres Horas
ceremony   33

2.6. A view of the back side of a Jew running in the church
during the Tres Horas ceremony   34

2.7. Jesus during one of the fourteen stations of the Cross in the
church   36

3.1. Filho de Gandhi member in costume   54

3.2. The offering of flowers and perfume to Oxum at Lake Abaete   58

3.3. *Lavagem*: Washing the heads of participants and the
community at Lake Abaete   59

3.4. A Filhas d'Oxum member overpowered at the Lake Abaete
Despatch ceremony   60

3.5.   Young girl participants in Filhas d'Oxum   61

3.6.   Offering at the crossroads in the center of Pelourinho   64

4.1.   Comissão de frente (front line) showing well-dressed leaders
       of samba schools in 1966   72

4.2.   Costume paraders in 1997   73

4.3.   *Porta-bandeira* (flag bearer) and *mestre-sala* (master of
       ceremony) in the royal eighteenth-century attire   77

4.4.   Baiana   82

4.5.   *Baterista* (drum player)   83

10.1. Mural inside Hounon palace, Whydah, showing lineage
       ancestors of Daagbo Hounon   199

10.2. Street mural outside Hounon palace showing slaving
       encounter on Whydah Beach   203

10.3. Daagbo Hounon's prayers at the Whydah Festival, 1997   206

11.1. Indigenous Territories   217

11.2. *El Mestizaje* as Model of Hybridity, Mixture, and Racial
       Separation   226

11.3. An Ecuadorian Model of Counterhegemony   231

Preface and Acknowledgments

This volume emerged out of "Representations of Blackness in the Context of Festivity," a symposium I organized during the 49th International Congress of Americanists that took place in Quito, Ecuador, in July 1997. The objective was to compare various festive performances that represent, in one way or another, different constructs of blackness in the Americas. The flyer distributed to scholars of the Americas inviting them to participate indicated that the festivities of interest could be performed both by blacks and non-blacks: indigenous groups, mestizos or ladinos, and even whites or white-mestizos. The aim was that this comparative approach would provide the participants with the opportunity to debate, in addition to the performances themselves, a series of themes such as the similarities and differences among the various forms of blackness and black resistance in the Diaspora; the spatial dimensions of blackness; the relations among blackness, gender constructs, and social classes; indigenous and other non-black groups' views of blackness; self-images of blackness; the hypersexualization of blackness and so forth.

Once the symposium was over, and with the inclusion into the book project of scholars who did not participate in our discussions in Quito, it became clear that what we were looking at was performances of black identities in festivities as well as in daily life situations. That is why the title of the symposium was abandoned for the more generalizing book title, "Representations of Blackness and the Performance of Identities."

I would like to thank Daniel R. Weir, a Ph.D. student in geography at Louisiana State University, who assisted me in the preparation of this volume. Without his dedication and his clear mind, I would not have been able to finish this project. My gratitude goes as well to the Department of Geography & Anthropology at Louisiana State University, and especially to the chair, William Davidson, for funding the translation of Maryse Condé's and Isidoro Moreno's pieces, and my trip to Quito, Ecuador, to organize the symposium. Many thanks as well to Jane Garry and Rebecca Ardwin from Greenwood Press, who assured the professional quality of this book.

I could not end my acknowledgments without thanking the nineteen participants in the symposium for the depth of the discussions their presence allowed.

Introduction

Como ignorante que soy
me precisa preguntar
si el color blanco es virtud
para mandarme a blanquear.

El ser negro no es afrenta
ni color que quita fama,
porque de zapatos negros
se viste la mejor dama.
Las cejas y las pestañas
y su negra cabellera,
que lo analice cualquiera
que interrogando que estoy.
Me precisa preguntar
como ignorante que soy.

Pregunto sin vacilar
que ésto no comprendo yo;
si el Sabio que hizo la tierra
de que color la dejó?
De que pasta le formó
a nuestro padre Adán?
Y el que me quiera tachar
que me sepa contestar.
Como ignorante que soy,
me precisa preguntar.

Because I'm an ignorant
I need to inquire
if the white color is virtue
to decide if I get myself whitened.

To be black is not an affront
nor a color that takes fame away,
because black shoes
are used by the best lady.
The eyebrows and the eyelashes
and her black hair,
can be analyzed by anybody
because I am asking.
I need to inquire
because I'm an ignorant.

I ask without hesitation
because I don't understand that;
the Sage who made the earth
what color did He give to it?
What material did He use
to make our father Adam?
And if somebody wants to cross me out
he must answer my question.
Because I'm an ignorant,
I need to inquire.

Pregunto porque me conviene,	It pleases me to ask,
si ser negro es un delito.	if to be black is a crime.
Desde que nací a este mundo	Since the day I was born
letras blancas yo no he visto.	I've not seen white letters.
Negra fue la cruz de Cristo	Black was Christ's cross
donde murió el Redentor.	whereon died the Redeemer.
De negro vistió María	Mary dressed in black
viendo morir a Jesús.	when she saw Jesus dying.
Me precisa preguntar	I need to inquire
si el color blanco es virtud?	if the white color is virtue?

El negro con su color	The black person with his color
y el blanco con su blancura,	and the white with his whiteness,
todos vamos a quedar	everyone will end up
en la negra sepultura.	in the black grave.
Se acaban las hermosuras	Good-bye to the beauty
de las blancas señoritas,	of the white young ladies,
se acaba el que más critica	even the one with the biggest mouth will die
y el del color sin igual.	and also the one with incomparable color.
Y si el color blanco es virtud	And if the white color is virtue
para mandarme a blanquear.	I'll have to get myself whitened.

(Décima—Afro-Esmeraldian oral poem [Ecuador]
—*La Pregunta del Negro* [see Rahier 1987: 123–124])

The essays gathered in this volume deal with representations of blackness and the performance of black identities in various historically determined societal contexts of the Americas, Benin (Sutherland), and Spain (Moreno). The first portion of the book's title evokes the general premise that there is no such thing as a world "out there" that would exist independently of the discourses of representation. Representations constitute, in part, the world in which we live. As Michel Foucault explained, discursive formations, modes of thought, or modes of representation are used by people for conceptualizing the world, their existence, and the existence of Others. Dominant groups produce and re-produce representations of themselves and of Others that justify their position at the apex of racial/spatial orders and the subjugation of the negatively de-picted Others. This volume shows an important aspect of the struggles of dominated people who—more or less overtly—challenge, manipulate, combat, negate, and sometimes invert representations of themselves that are repro-duced in the dominant discourse of their national society, and/or of the soci-ety in which they live. In effect, as Stuart Hall puts it, racism should be seen as a "structure of knowledge and representations," with a symbolic and nar-rative energy and work that aims to secure "us" over here and the Others over there, down there, fixing each in its "appointed species place" (Hall 1992: 16). Most of the contributions to this book focus on oppositional rep-resentations of blackness imagined from somewhat subaltern socioeconomic and political positionalities, that is to say, they focus on representations—imagined and performed by black peoples.

The second portion of the book's title, "the performance of identities," underlines the contributors' shared understanding of cultural, and/or ethnic, and/or racial identities within the fluctuation of political, economic, and social processes embedded in particular time/space contexts, which are constituted within local, regional, national, and transnational dimensions. Identities, whatever they may be, cannot be defined once and for all, in fixed or essentialist terms, as if they were unchanging, frozen, as it were, in time and space. The premise here is that if identities are more fluid, or much less fixed, than previously thought, it is because they are constantly enacted and reenacted, performed and performed anew, within specific situations, and within changing socioeconomic and political contexts that provide sites for their negotiations and renegotiations, their definitions and redefinitions. Cultural and identity politics are obviously at the core of our endeavor.

AFRICAN DIASPORA IDENTITIES, "CULTURE," PLACE, AND SPACE

At this time of the 50th anniversary of the creation of the Program of African Studies at Northwestern University by Melville Herskovits in 1948, it is timely to contrast the orientation taken by the following essays with the most visible characteristics of the Herskovitsian approach. Indeed, Herskovits, an anthropologist, is considered by many—in various disciplines—as the founder, in the 1920s, of systematic research on African diaspora communities. To appreciate Herskovits' approach, it is necessary to go back, briefly, to the history of (English-speaking) anthropology and the definitions given to "culture."

The definitions the concept of culture received throughout the history of anthropology explain why the concepts of place and space have not attracted, until recently, the theoretical attention of the discipline. Edward Burnet Tylor and his American counterpart Louis Morgan thought that the dynamics of culture lay in what they called the "laws of thought." They established culture (and cultural identity) as an important, and in many ways politically neutral property of people everywhere. "Since people everywhere had culture, and since culture was a product of thinking, the specific places societies inhabited had little bearing on general cultural development" (Richardson 1989: 142–145). Thus, the concept of culture as Tylor understood it, was place free. Such it remained with Franz Boas, who conceived of anthropology as a descriptive and historical science, whose goal was to study the development of cultures within their singular and immediate past. These multiple histories of cultures justified the concept of culture area, or "the study of the spatial distribution of cultures."

Under the prevailing notions of scientific rigor, cultures were conceived as reducible to a series of observable units, or traits. This objectified enumeration permitted the tracing of individual traits, or larger trait-complexes, across space. The observed clustering of traits in a contiguous geographical area allowed the designation of that region as a culture area. In sum, although the concept of culture area produced regions of cultural uniqueness, the concept had little similarity with the more place-oriented *genre de vie* of Vidal de la Blache. The concept was a purely cultural one and again, in essence, place free. (Richardson 1989: 143)

In the work of two of the most famous of Boas' students, Alfred Kroeber and Robert Lowie, culture clearly appeared as a coherent totality, a " 'superorganic' collectivity that transcended the actions of individual human beings. This was a powerful and, as it turned out, an influential talisman: hence, presumably, Karl Sauer's (Kroeber and Lowie's student) belief that human geography 'is a science that has nothing to do with individuals but only with . . . cultures.' It continued to be an article of faith for many decades" (Gregory 1989; see also Stocking 1966; Richardson 1989).

Melville Herskovits, another student of Boas, defined the research project of African-Americanist anthropology exclusively in terms of cultural continuity, even if he sometimes wrote about his research as falling within the scope of what he called "acculturation studies." Obviously, he had inherited the Boasian understanding of "culture," which identified the concept with a *burden* "that was seen as functional to the continuing daily existence of individuals" (Stocking 1966: 878). For Herskovits, the cultures of the African diaspora in the Americas were nothing but, in final analysis, some sort of emigrated African cultures. The obsession of his work for the study and/or discovery of "africanisms," "African retentions," and "cultural reinterpretations" that allowed Africa to survive in the Americas are well known. Logically, his work was grounded on the idea that Afro-Americans are not an object of study for americanists but for africanists. He wrote in 1938:

In the organization of our scientific endeavor, it is important to consider the geographical divisions as well as the political borders as simple titles of chapters that are useful for the classification of data and for the organization of our research. But if the data that we possess do not agree with these categories, we have to follow them where they lead us. This is the reason why we have to acknowledge in our research that the numerous black populations of the New World, African in origin, African in various degrees in their physical types and, much more than we thought so far, African in their traditions, must be considered an integral part of the field of study of Africanists. (Herskovits 1938b: 66)

He concluded the same article with:

Thus, it is both because of the contribution that the Africanist may bring to the study of the Blacks of the New World and because of the advantages that these studies may procure to the Africanist, that we are in the obligation to conclude that the geographically distinct regions of Occidental Africa and the Americas must be considered as a same unity from the point of view of the scientific problems they present. (Herskovits 1938b: 88)[1]

His spaceless conception of African diaspora cultures could not be better illustrated. In his interpretations, he actually denied any real importance of the socioeconomic histories, political processes, and the geographies of the Americas.

In various texts, he went to the point of proposing a "scale of intensity of New World africanisms":

It is quite possible on the basis of our present knowledge to make a kind of chart indicating the extent to which the descendants of Africans brought to the New World have retained Africanisms in their cultural behavior. If we consider the intensity of African cultural elements in the various regions north of Brazil . . . , we may say that after Africa itself it is the Bush Negroes of Suriname who exhibit a civilization which is the most African. As a matter of fact, unless the observer omitted to take their language into consideration, and unless he were familiar with small elements obtained from the whites with whom these people were in contact while they were in slavery and the Indians whom they drove out of the Guiana bush, he would assume, at first glance, that their culture was wholly African. Next to them, on our scale, would be placed their Negro neighbors on the coastal plains of the Guianas, who, in spite of centuries of close association with the whites, have retained an amazing amount of their aboriginal African traditions, many of which are combined in curious fashion with the traditions of the dominant group.

And he continues his description until the last category—which has not drawn his attention: "Finally, we should come to a group where, to all intents and purposes, there is nothing of the African tradition left, and which consists of people of varying degrees of Negroid physical type, who only differ from their white neighbors in the fact that they have more pigmentation in their skins (Herskovits 1938b). In "Problem, Method and Theory in Afroamerican Studies," he presents a scale of intensity of africanisms which takes into consideration twenty-one African diaspora communities from Guiana, Haiti, Brazil, Cuba, Jamaica, Honduras, Trinidad, Mexico, Colombia, and the United States. He then evaluates various cultural aspects of these communities: technology, economy, social organization, non-kinship institutions, religion, magics, art, folklore, music, and language by assigning to each one of them, by community, a letter (or grade) from "a" to "e": "a" meaning "very African"; "b," "quite African"; "c," "somewhat African"; "d," "little African"; and "e," "vague traces of African customs, or no trace at all." That is how the blacks from the Guaianese forest receive mostly "a" and "b" evaluations, while blacks from Colombia (Chocó) get only "d"s and "e"s (Herskovits 1966).

In "The African Heritage in the Caribbean," M. G. Smith criticized the way Herskovits conceived the study of acculturation. Herskovits' "acculturation studies," wrote Smith, consisted of nothing more than putting the cart before the horse, that is, focusing exclusively on cultural data at the expense of other

aspects of reality, and proceeding by deduction, instead of actually conducting
serious ethnohistorical research in available archives. When studying processes
of acculturation, Smith insisted, one should keep in mind that:

the study of acculturation or cultural change cannot be completed without parallel study
of social change; that acculturation studies include studies of assimilation; that encultur-
ation is an aspect of socialization, or vice versa. If this is so, it follows that the study of
African heritage [in the New World] in purely cultural terms is not adequately conceived
and cannot by itself reveal the processes and conditions of acculturation. Thus, if acculturation, rather than the simple identification of elements as African or other, is the aim
of such study, we must study the relevant social conditions equally and simultaneously.
(Smith 1957: 38)

Faced with the relative instability of cultural traits, the diversity of African cultures, and
the relative lack of historical records detailing the processes of transmission of African
culture in the New World, we are unavoidably committed in the study of this heritage
to put the cart before the horse and to start with end-effects, real or assumed, and then
try to work back through their hypothetical processes of persistence, development, or
change to some particular tribal culture or to some undifferentiated "African" culture.
In an enquiry of this type, it is therefore especially urgent that we should distinguish as
sharply as possible between precise and indefinite forms and between specific and indeterminate attributions. The alternative is simply to perpetuate a wayward enquiry based
on poor methodology and to invite the substitution of speculative derivation by the
multiplication of indeterminate concepts and hypotheses in place of the search for de-
monstrable relations. (Smith 1957: 40)

Herskovits' studies of acculturation do not compare to, for instance, the detailed
ethnohistorical research conducted by George Brandon for the writing of his
Santeria: From Africa to the New World (Brandon 1993). They are silent as
well about the cultural processes referred to by the authors of *créolité* (Bernabé
1993), and by the valuable work of Edouard Glissant on creolization (Glissant
1990).

Herskovits' approach provoked a malaise among African-Americanist scholars. Many, influenced by the British school of social anthropology, walked away
from his model and concepts (Whitten 1970: 28–29). One of them, Norman
Whitten (a contributor to this volume), conducted research in the 1960s and
1970s in the Ecuadorian province of Esmeraldas. His research denotes an awareness of the embeddedness of the socioeconomic and political reality lived by
Afro-Esmeraldians and their cultural traditions within regional and national
dimensions. He approached Afro-Esmeraldians in terms of their economic marginality (Whitten 1965; Whitten 1974). It is on the grounds of this economic
marginality, he explained, that social relations are established with members of
the kin group, friends and any "exploitable companion." The black lower class,
so called according to national standards, is situated within the wider, stratified
entity, composed of the different classes or sectors (national white and white-

mestizo elites, local white and white-mestizo elites, local class of professionals, etc.) engaged in the political and economic life of the province of Esmeraldas. The focus of Whitten's work was on the ability of Afro-Esmeraldians to adapt to a situation of economic deprivation. He proposed a model of adaptive mobility for the Pacific Lowlands of Colombia and Ecuador (Whitten 1965; Whitten 1970).[2] In the 1990s, Peter Wade, another contributor to this volume, underlines the impossibility of understanding blackness without considering the specific racial order in which it is located. Blackness, he continues, may not be understood but locally, without downplaying the existence of regional, national, and international ensembles. Studying black migrations in Colombia, he understands that society produces spatial arrangements that act as constraint on, as well as a set of resources for, further development. Once social relations have a given spatial form, this affects the way those relations can change and develop. In this view, society is broken up into interdependent "locales" and regions. The locales and regions are interconnected and their interconnectedness gives shape to the spatial constitution of society. In his recently published book, *Race and Ethnicity in Latin America* (Wade 1997), he presents a brief history of African diaspora and Native American studies, and lists several consequences that Michel Foucault, Jacques Derrida, and Jean-François Lyotard's works, among others, have had on postmodern thinking about race, ethnicity and identity:

First, the constructedness of identity has become even more important. . . . Identity is seen as constructed through complex processes of relationality and representation; it is a process, not a thing, and it is constantly under renegotiation. . . . Second . . . the reification and essentialisation of identity has been challenged more intensively—the idea is no longer acceptable that a given person or group might have a basic identity that could be characterised in terms of a core, defining essence; groups and indeed individuals are "decentred," they have no single identity. . . . Third, multiple identities and the challenge to metanarratives both imply that the seemingly "big question" of the primacy of race/ethnicity *versus* class has become less of an issue. Fourth, culture, or more accurately, the politics of culture, became a central focus. Anthropologists at least had always been concerned with culture . . . but now culture was not something that groups just "had," it was a discursive construct that was lived, but was also open to different readings. (Wade 1997: 81–82)

The awareness of the spatial constitution of societies, and of blackness in particular, as expressed in Whitten's publications and further developed by Wade, announce both a departure from Herskovits' spaceless model, as well as one of the major orientations taken by the scholars who have contributed to this volume. The following essays present analyses of representations and performances of blackness in which emerge the importance and singularity of specific places which are relocated by the authors' interpretations within regional, national, and transnational spatial structures. This orientation follows relatively recent research by human geographers (Massey 1985; Giddens 1985; Gregory 1985, 1989; Sayer 1985; Agnew 1989; Robinson 1989; Duncan 1993; Keith

1993), as well as by other anthropologists and cultural studies scholars (see, among others, Whitten & Whitten 1993; Hill 1996; the special issue of *Cultural Anthropology* entitled "Space, Identity, and the Politics of Difference," 7 (1) (1992); Feld and Basso 1996). In recent articles, J. Streicker and Cecilia McCallun, for example, both demonstrate respectively Afro-Colombian and Afro-Brazilian local communities' awareness of spatial structures' importance in political processes of domination (McCallum 1996; Streicker 1997; see also Rahier 1998). In a video recently released, "Race: The Floating Signifier" (Hall 1996a), Stuart Hall explains that "race"—just like words in Saussurian theory—is a signifier because it is relational and not essential. It can never be finally fixed and, on the contrary, is subjected to constant processes of redefinition and appropriation, to the loosening of old meanings and the appropriation and collection of nuances, to the endless process of being constantly resignified, made to mean something different in different cultures, in different historical formations, at different moments in time. In an essay in which he recounts the creation of cultural studies in England, Hall confesses that what

cultural studies has taught me is, indeed, the importance of historical specificity, of the specificity of each cultural configuration and pattern. There may undoubtedly be, and I think there are, general mechanisms in common across the globe that are associated with the practices of racism. But in each society, racism has a specific history that presents itself in specific, particular, and unique ways, and these specificities influence its dynamic and have real effects that differ from one society to another. One thing that cultural studies has taught me is, indeed, not to speak of racism in the singular, but of *racisms* in the plural. (Hall 1992: 12–13)

The importance of space is also convincingly made evident by another contributor to this volume, Carole Boyce Davies, in the lecture "Beyond Unicentricity: Transcultural Black Intellectual Presences" given in December 1997 at the conference celebrating the fiftieth anniversary of the journal *Presence Africaine* in Paris. She criticizes the unicentricity or logic of one-centeredness she finds in both eurocentrism and (Molefi Asante's kind of) afrocentrism, the latter following the former "in the sense that it too assumes the existence of irreducibly distinct cultural invariants that shape historical paths of different people." She writes, having in mind the suggestion of a new multicentered paradigm for black intellectuals in the twenty-first century:

A fully international "Africana Studies" paradigm, in my view, has to pursue and account for a range of relations of African peoples internationally as they interact with a variety of cultural spaces. In this connection, the logic of diaspora guides as it identifies as many locations as are available where African peoples reside, and tries to understand and account for their existence in these locations. . . . Cross-cultural Africana discourses, as I define them, speak to the variety of movements ushered in by migrations and the consistent reproduction of different modes of being in the world. Rather than a giant, monolithic traditional African culture, then, we can assert multiple, trans-cultural presences within and outside Africa. Thus they are Transformational Discourses (''New World Discourses'') central to diaspora. Examinations of the relationships between aspects of African cultures and [Native American] and Western cultures as imbricated histories and the range of colliding and collaborating relationships are similarly critical. In other words, here we actualize the idea of related spheres (Boyce Davies December 1997: 20).[3]

That is exactly what Whitten and Rachel Corr are pointing to in the last essay of this collection when they write that they ''deviate substantially from vulgar ethnic categorization and assume that all culture is interethnic, and that all ethnicity is intercultural.'' This orientation characterizes this collection.

PLACE AND SPACE IN THIS VOLUME

The particularities of given places within specific societal and/or transnational spaces are underlined in the essays making up this volume. Isidoro Moreno's chapter deals with the fifteenth–eighteenth-century black brotherhoods of Seville, Spain, and their participation in the celebration of the Semana Santa, Holy Week. To the black Andalusians—in Seville and elsewhere—located at the bottom of the racial order, the confraternities or *cabildos* gave the only opportunity to organize. They integrated blacks within the central ideological mold of the society of the time (Catholic religion) and provided the Spanish elites with a tool to control them. Moreno shows how at a certain time the presence of Seville's black brotherhood was tolerated within the white-controlled space of celebrations, while at other times it was contested and rejected; Afro-Andalusians' parading being then relegated to peripheral areas of the city. This change came along as a consequence of the transformation of Spanish representations of blacks as unthreatening child-like people, to one of relatively dangerous predators.

My essay on the ''presence'' of blackness and the representations of Jewishness in the Afro-Esmeraldian celebration of the Semana Santa focuses on ceremonies that have for public transcript the reenactment of the Passion of Christ. I argue that, beyond this reenactment of the suffering of Jesus lies an expression of Afro-Esmeraldian resistance to the Ecuadorian racial/spatial order—in the form of manipulations of anti-Semitic images of the ''white people who killed the Christ.'' Taking as a departure point the village of Selva Alegre's local perspective, I interpret the performative representations of demonic Jews as a metaphor for the white and white-mestizo urban elites who dominate Ecuadorian society.

Boyce Davies' chapter studies the participation of the all-female *afoxé* Filhas d'Oxum in Brazil's Bahia Carnival. After differentiating Bahia's carnival from Rio's, she explores questions of gender and the performative, memory, ritual and cultural re-invention. She shows that Filhas d'Oxum's performances challenge the popular stereotypic, exotic representations of black women by putting in their place a carnival of beauty and joy in femininity that emanates from the orisha Oxum. Her argumentation, which underlines the importance of Candomblé religion in Bahia's carnival, dialogues in an interesting and multidimensional way with Sepúlveda dos Santos' analysis of the logic of orgy and blackness in the Rio de Janeiro's samba school parade. Myrian Sepúlveda dos Santos' objective is to show how much the embodied practices performed during this parade have maintained "many features linked to black culture that expand the perceptions of the participants' bodies and feelings and increase the scope of their freedom." Her intent is to underline the structures and values that have survived, although rewritten and modernized, remaining identifiably black. After recounting past initiatives by Rio's elites to contain poor blacks' presence to black ghettos, she focuses upon Afro-Brazilians' struggle to remain included in the festivities, despite the attempts of Brazilian elites to "steal carnival" and tune down their visibility within it (see also Sheriff, unpublished manuscript).

Maryse Condé's contribution focuses on what Bakhtin has called "the carnivalization of literature" in the texts of two contemporary Martinican authors: Raphaël Confiant and Patrick Chamoiseau. She suggests that these two novelists—who are the proponents of the concept of *créolité* with Jean Bernabé (Bernabé 1993)—have advanced a definition of "authentic," that is, fixed, Caribbean blackness that is in many ways oppressive. Furthermore, the carnivalization of their texts exoticizes the Martinican Other for the French market. Although créolité or "creoleness" was at first defined in opposition to Western, especially French, identity and culture, "carnivalized" créolité novels could be seen as having been written for nobody but French readers. Maryse Condé writes: "Doesn't this extravagance, this tumultuous representation of Antillean sexuality with the added spice of Creole satisfy a need—that of the Other? He is the one transported to an exotic locale. It is through his eyes that Antillean sexuality becomes mouth-watering, burlesque, almost folksy . . . [Confiant and Chamoiseau] flatter the taste for the diverse, for the different exhibited in French culture." Condé's text must be read in parallel with Percy Hintzen's (see below).

Ariana Hernandez-Reguant's contribution on Kwanzaa replaces this "new tradition of blackness" within the relatively recent development of multiculturalism in America. She emphasizes how contemporary mass media representations of Kwanzaa have popularized this cultural trend within the revolutionary black power movement of the 1960s and early 1970s as a reaffirmation of middle-class values and American citizenship, by presenting blackness as one additional, "neutral," ethnic identity within the American cultural mosaic. Kwanzaa is now visible in "respectable" places and media, such as presidential addresses, mainstream corporate advertisement of toothpaste and cars; middle-class restaurants with new "traditional African" culinary recipes, libraries and museums, community organizations, churches and middle-class homes, the *Washington Post* and the *New York Times*.

Hintzen's study of West Indian identity in the San Francisco Bay area shows how different local contexts provide sites wherein specialized and class-based,

boundary-defining performances of identity that underline different aspects of
"West Indianness" take place: the San Francisco Carnival, Caribbean restaurants and bars, cricket matches, open house events, clubs and associations, university groups, the military, house parties, and soccer games. Hintzen
emphasizes the particularity of West Indian presence in the Bay Area, in contrast
with the situation of West Indians in New York (see Kasinitz 1992). While in
certain situations, West Indians in the Bay Area assert their racial identity as
black to gain access to resources of upward mobility reserved to U.S.-born
African Americans; in other situations, they exploit exoticized images of difference to separate themselves from the terms of American racial discourse and,
especially, from African Americans. At the same time, West Indians work to
assert their status as "model minority" in rituals of self-representations. "The
contradictions between exoticized images of West Indian difference and mainstream images of success associated with model minority status are managed
through the practice of separation. Exoticized images of West Indianness are
displayed most evidently in public (or semipublic) sites and arenas. The display
of model minority status is reserved for the private spaces of the home or for
semiprivate activities open exclusively to the West Indian middle class."

Gina Ulysse's essay deals with the Jamaican dichotomy between the class-
based concepts of *lady* and *woman*: "[two] oppositional racial and color categories that affect the lives of all females, and those of black females in
particular." She shows how this dichotomy developed during colonialism by
desexualizing and idealizing white females, while hypersexualizing and deni-
grating African females, reinforcing the racially coded white Madonna/black
whore polarity. She then demonstrates how after Independence the latter evolved
into the current brown/black opposition. She focuses on the way this brown
lady/black woman dichotomy is embedded within Jamaican economic history
and the racial/spatial order (uptown versus downtown), and how it is played out
in specific arenas: beauty contests, dancehalls, fashion clashes, funerals of public
personalities, and popular songs. Transnational dimensions are included in the
analysis through her focus on both Afro-Jamaican women who travel to New
York and back as informal, commercial importers, and the influence on dancehall developments played by Jamaican disc jockeys residing in the United States.

Peter Wade's contribution on the representations of blackness in Colombian
popular music looks at types of black music that "derived from the way black
people used and adapted various musical styles to create cultural forms that
could be seen as an expression of their own identities." He explains how these
musical forms initially associated with blackness have become through time
symbols of national Colombian identity. His analysis encompasses the dimensions of time and space. He goes back to the colonial cabildos, the world of the
bogas that originated in the Caribbean coast during the colonial period, the
migration of *costeño* blacks in the Andean interior, the foreign musical influences from other regions of the Americas and the Caribbean, the relatively recent

processes of commercialization of music as a commodity, and so on.

Peter Sutherland's essay analyzes the recently invented Whydah (Benin) vodun festival of the tenth of January, which celebrates the memory of the African peoples who were shipped as slaves via Gorée Island in Senegal to the "land of the whites" between the 1640s and the 1860s. Sutherland's analysis underlines how that festival, organized by the traditionalist faction of priests and kings, "develops the concept of diaspora consciousness to challenge the Benin government's neocolonial values that undermine the traditional authority of priests and kings." He interprets the festival within Beninian cultural politics and provides an interesting look at aspects and processes of the Black Atlantic untouched by Paul Gilroy (Gilroy 1993).

Whitten and Corr's contribution on the imagery of blackness in indigenous myth, discourse, and ritual begins by deploring the questionable and enduring separation between the fields of African diaspora and Native American studies. The roots of this separation, they write, go back to the fifteenth century and the European imperial enterprises. Assuming that "all culture is interethnic, and that all ethnicity is intercultural," they examine texts and images drawn from mythology and festivity, from discourses on shamanism, and from public performances wherein indigenous people from Panama, Venezuela, Colombia, and Ecuador reflect upon various forms of blackness. In the last section of their chapter, they conclude that "the African diaspora is one of intertwined traditions that continue to span Africa, Europe, and the Americas. And it became most apparent that representations of power in the African diaspora are not confined to people with a particular skin color or other physical features. Blackness has to do with spirituality, with forces, with the known and the unknown, with history and historicity, with cultural transformation and endurance."

BLACK IDENTITIES AND THE DIVERSITY OF BLACK RESISTANCE

Black identities cannot be defined once and for all by pointing to—more or less vaguely—their "origin," as some sort of immutable entities, in what Gilroy has called "ethnic absolutist" terms (Gilroy 1993, 1995). Black identities are defined and redefined, imagined and re-imagined, performed and performed again within the flux of history and within specific, changing, spatially determined societal structures.

In addition of providing a good opportunity to reflect upon the importance of "place" and "space" for African diaspora studies, the contributions to this volume raise a series of different issues: the similarities and differences between the various forms of blackness in the diaspora and between the various shapes taken by black resistance; blackness and gender constructs (especially Boyce Davies, Sepúlveda dos Santos, and Ulysse); indigenous and other non-black groups' views of blackness (Whitten and Corr, Wade); self-representations of blackness (Hernandez-Reguant, Boyce Davies, Rahier, Hintzen, and Ulysse);

and the political role taken by representations of the African diaspora in African politics (Sutherland).

Because of the limited space allocated to this introduction, I am not able to discuss all of these issues here. However, I would like to insist on what I see as one of the major teachings of this book: black resistances in the diaspora, just like black identities, cannot be essentialized. According to the specificities of the various time/space societal contexts in which they are living, and the places these contexts occupy within the globalized world, African diaspora communities develop different strategies for struggles against particular forms of racism, exclusion, and exploitation; some may also accommodate to the racial/ spatial order. While particular African diaspora communities can try to benefit from the racial orders as they exist (middle-class West Indians in San Francisco [Hintzen]; middle-class African-Americans in the United States [Hernandez-Reguant]; middle-class brown ladies in Jamaica [Ulysse]; etc.), others may engage more or less directly in challenges to these orders (Afro-Esmeraldians in Selva Alegre [Rahier]; all women afoxé in Bahia's carnival [Boyce Davies]; Afro-Jamaican women informal commercial importers [Ulysse]; etc.). The former as well as the latters may or may not refer to or use images of Africa and/or African cultural traditions in their endeavor. African diaspora resistance may happen without specific representations of Africa and African cultures.

The diversity of black resistance is well illustrated in the following pages. The obscenity strategy adopted by Ulysse's Afro-Jamaican women's informal commercial importers (ICI), for example, contrasts strikingly with Boyce Davies' all-female afoxé Filhas d'Oxum who managed to secure a place for themselves within Bahia's carnival, and who perform a decisively nonobscene female identity directly opposed to current images of Afro-Brazilian women as hypersexualized beings. The Afro-Jamaican ICI engaged in dancehall culture, on the contrary, use obscenity as a way to assert themselves and resist the moral code of uptown Kingston.

THE BOOK'S THREE SECTIONS

The essays that analyze representations of blackness and the performance of black identities in particular festivities were regrouped under the section titled "Celebrations." The term "celebrations" was chosen because it expresses well the nature of the performances under scrutiny by encompassing both the subversive quality of "plays," which suggest the possibility of reinterpreting and challenging the order of daily life (''anti-structure''), and the characteristics of "rituals," which on the contrary are usually normative and have as their objective to maintain or reinforce the relationships of the normal or nonliminal time (''structure'') (see Handelman 1977; Manning 1983: 3–32; Turner 1983).

The four papers included in the section "Social Arenas" analyze representations of blackness and the performance of black identities within more than one sociocultural, politic and economic situation. Their focus is not centered on a given festival, ritual, or celebration.

The two papers included in the last section, "African and Native American Perspectives," bring an interesting switch by presenting African representations of the African diaspora (Sutherland) and Native South American images of blackness into the discussion (Whitten and Corr). In so doing, they force us to reflect upon some assumptions which were common sense until recently in African diaspora studies. The symbolic use of the African diaspora by the Beninian traditionalist faction of kings and priests for their political benefit requires us to think about the link between Africa and its diaspora in a non-Herskovitsian way; while the images of blacks held by Native Americans help us to understand the arbitrariness of the separation drawn between the fields of African diaspora studies and Native American studies.

NOTES

1. These two quotations are my translation. The article was published in French.

2. Whitten has continued publishing about the African diaspora in Ecuador and elsewhere (see the bibliography at the end of this volume).

3. In this context, Boyce Davies uses "African" as synonymous of "black," in a Pan-African sense.

I

CELEBRATIONS

Festive Rituals, Religious Associations, and Ethnic Reaffirmation of Black Andalusians: Antecedents of the Black Confraternities and Cabildos in the Americas

Isidoro Moreno

CONFRATERNITIES AND ASSOCIATIONS OF BLACKS IN ANDALUSIA AND AMERICA

Very soon after the conquest, in the principal cities founded by the Spaniards in the Americas, there were confraternities of Negroes, just as there were of Spaniards and Indians. Some were of mixed groups. In Lima, for example, during the sixteenth and seventeenth centuries, there were groups dedicated to Nuestra Señora de los Reyes, San Benito, San Salvador, San Nicolás, Santa María de la Antigua, Santas Justa and Rufina, Nuestra Señora del Rosario and others (Celestino 1992). From the independence of Peru to the present, it is the confraternity of the Señor de los Milagros, with its annual festival centered on a famous procession, which constituted the group with which all blacks have identified. In Mexico City, on the continental and island coasts of the Caribbean, and in practically all places of any importance in colonial Spanish America in which there were African slaves, confraternities, brotherhoods, and cabildos allowed some of the most important, if not the very most important, manifestations of reaffirmation and reproduction of black collective ethnicity. These institutions and their ritual festivals were the principal loci, and in some periods the only ones, in which a type of associationism not tolerated by the authorities in other contexts could develop. Through these associations and their festivals, organized primarily around Catholic icons, individuals of the most despised and stigmatized ethnic group managed to integrate themselves symbolically into a strongly hierarchical society in which they occupied the lowest level, whether they were slaves or free.[1]

BLACKS IN SEVILLE AT THE END OF THE MIDDLE AGES:
THE HOSPITAL AND BROTHERHOOD OF THE VIRGEN
DE LOS REYES

In a short piece published more than fifteen years ago (Moreno 1981, 1985), I demonstrated how both the Indian and black brotherhoods and confraternities that existed in the American territories colonized by the Spaniards had their origin and direct precedent in Andalusian ethnic confraternities predating the conquest. Already at the end of the fourteenth century the Guadalquivir Valley area of Andalusia, which had been incorporated into the kingdom of Castile a century and a half before, was a multiethnic society with Jews, Moriscos, blacks, mulattos, and the beginnings of a small gypsy community. The slave population was composed primarily of Moriscos and blacks, the former as a result of the capture of prisoners in periodic wars between Castile and the Nazari kingdom of Granada—which was independent until 1492—and the latter as a result of Castilian incursions onto the coast of Africa and, especially, of an active slave trade that had its center in Lisbon (Franco 1979, 1985). Between 1393 and 1401 the Archbishop Don Gonzalo de Mena founded a brotherhood and a hospital for invalid blacks. The last decade of the century was a time of frequent famines, caused by loss of crops due to floods and other natural disasters, creating a very grave situation for the lower social classes. Male and female slaves who were domestic servants in Seville and other Andalusian cities were considered luxuries. When they fell ill or became a burden because of advanced age, their owners often dismissed them to fend for themselves. In response to this situation, the Archbishop de Mena created charitable institutions outside the city walls where also evolved a brotherhood that, over the centuries, would welcome black men and women, both slave and free (Moreno 1997).

During the same time period, that of the reign of Henry III of Castile, the situation of blacks was regulated, and some rights were granted, among them that of gathering on certain Sundays and feast days in the plaza of Santa María la Blanca, where dances were organized to the sound of tambourines, drums, and other instruments of autochthonous tradition. Ortiz de Zúñiga (1677: Chapter 10), in his *Anales*, points out that "in Seville the blacks were treated benevolently from the time of Henry III, being permitted to gather at their dances and festivals on holidays, so that they appeared more happily for work and better tolerated captivity." This concession set the precedent for those that were granted centuries later to blacks of diverse American cities and that would be preserved even during the nineteenth century in the Caribbean colonies. As the Cuban anthropologist Fernando Ortiz correctly observed, the African American cabildos of the island were assemblies or meetings centered on dance, similar to those which were organized centuries before in Seville and whose directors were, in the early years, blacks from Seville who had come with their masters to Cuba (Ortiz 1916; 1920–21).

In the previously mentioned years of transition from the fourteenth to the fifteenth century the minority ethnic groups of Andalusia, the Jews, Moriscos, and gypsies were perceived as threats to the dominant ethnic group, the Castilian, because their strong ethnic cohesion and their strong resistance to cultural assimilation, especially in the religious sphere. Consequently their rights were curtailed and a politics of ethnocide was carried out against them, a campaign of social and religious intolerance that would culminate later in the deportation of the first two groups, after numerous genocidal actions. The Jews were expelled at the end of the fifteenth century, during the reign of the so-called "Catholic Kings" and the Moriscos, after the bloody ethnic war of the Alpujarra in 1570 and, definitively, in 1609. In the case of the gypsies, practically up to present time, they have been regarded with suspicion, viewed as delinquents, and subjected to both social and legal discrimination. Blacks, on the other hand, lacked the socioeconomic power that might arouse envy, as in the case of the Jews; nor did they possess, like the Moriscos and the gypsies, a strong ethnic consciousness based on markers such as religious beliefs, kinship, or other factors that might serve as a basis of collective self affirmation in the face of the dominant society. Actually, blacks did not exist as an ethnic group except as a social construction of the dominant society that saw as defining "body marks" of the slave condition a few biological characteristics—skin color, nose shape, lips, or hair—which, moreover, were far from homogeneous. Although it was the Yoruba group that contributed the greatest number of slaves, various other ethnic groups from Western Africa, with different cultures were robbed of thousands of their women and men who not only lost their freedom and became slave labor, but who were also the object of a brutal process of loss of ethnic identity by becoming generic blacks. More than a process of acculturation, what they suffered was actually a process of forced deculturation and imposition of a series of traits that the dominant ethnic group defined as generically *Negro*. The superficiality of such traits and the very difficulty of forging bonds of collective solidarity as a result of their working conditions prevented the existence of a strong sense of identity and a consequent perception of blacks as a dangerous group. Unlike blacks who worked on American plantations centuries later, the blacks of Seville worked separately or in small groups for various masters during the period under consideration. The Castilian crown as well as the church hierarchy adopted an attitude of tolerance and even sympathy for the blacks, especially as their numbers were never very high and the intellectual as well as moral inferiority attributed to them was interpreted in terms of almost total infantilism and irrationality. Therefore, like children, innocents, or fools, the blacks could not be evil or dangerous—as long as they were kept under a paternalistic protectionism, fundamentally authoritarian and secondarily tolerant.

On the other hand, the encouragement of associationism in the dominated ethnic groups that were considered to be potentially assimilatable—as was the case with the Africans and their descendants subjected to domestic slavery—through their membership in religious brotherhoods, yielded important benefits to the dominant social sectors. For one thing, the socially marginalized were integrated into the central ideological mold of the global society of the period, favoring the interiorization of some beliefs and a worldview that constituted a common representational framework for masters and slaves. This framework was the Christian religion, whose beliefs, rituals, and institutions functioned as an area of consensus that was supposedly neutral and which provided an equalizing element among the ethnic groups and the classes that occupied different places in the social hierarchy. The conflicts that resulted from the asymmetrical power relations would be played out on a symbolic level, in ritual emulation or a struggle over rights and prerogatives in religious ceremonies, as we shall see.

The apparent atmosphere of consensus that religion supplied not only diminished awareness of inequality but also, at least in part, caused the slaves themselves to perceive their situation as one of equality in the symbolic ceremonial sphere, since their confraternity was one of many in the city and could even rival those of the upper classes and enjoy protection from some of them and from the church. Later, however, unmanageable situations would develop that would lead to open conflict.

The encouragement of religious associationism had the additional benefit of allowing the blacks not to feel necessarily isolated, irresponsible and dissolute, excluded and self-exiled from mainstream society, and therefore condemned to asocial, picaresque, or even delinquent existence, a situation that would clearly endanger social stability.

This danger began to be felt by the second half of the fifteenth century for two principal reasons. First, the increase in the number of blacks living in Seville, "due to frequent expeditions from the ports of Andalucía to the coasts of Africa and Guinea, from whence black slaves were taken" (Ortiz de Zúñiga 1677: Chapter 10). Second, there was the growing presence of free blacks, those who were granted their freedom on the death of their masters or who were born of free black women. It was very difficult for them to find honorable employment, and most were obliged to live on public charity or through robbery and other criminal activities.

The organization of blacks into brotherhoods had the effect of providing a means of symbolic integration into society and, on the individual level, of imposing responsibilities. Furthermore, their organization into an association that was carefully regulated and subjected to the authority of established powers—which had the right to approve or not its rules, to review its accounts, and even to dissolve it—facilitated political control over the ethnic group more effectively than if the individual members, especially the free ones, were dispersed and uncontrolled, associating among themselves in noninstitutionalized social gatherings. In order to facilitate this control, the kings named "overseers of the blacks" officials who represented the political authority to the ethnic collective, acting as justices of the peace, and who also functioned as representatives of the group before the public powers. The most famous overseer of the Sevillian blacks was the *Conde Negro*, Juan of Valladolid, Chamberlain of the Catholic Kings, named in 1475 by royal decree, due to:

the many excellent, and loyal, and significant services that you have rendered unto us, and continue to render every day, and because we know your qualities and capabilities, we name you Overseer and Judge of all the Negroes and *Loros* (mulattos), free or captive, that have been and are captive and *horros* (free), in the very noble and very loyal City of Seville, and in all of its archbishopric, and decree that the aforementioned black men and women, and mulatto men and women, may not celebrate any festivals or judgments among themselves, only before you, the aforementioned Juan of Valladolid, Negro, our Judge and Overseer of the said Negroes, male and female mulattos; and we order that you familiarize yourself with the debates and suits and marriages and other events that might take place among them, you alone, insofar as you are the appropriate person for that, or whomever you might delegate, and you know the laws and ordinances that they must have, and we are informed that you are of noble lineage among the said Negroes. (Ortiz de Zúñiga 1677)[2]

We have various examples of the power and influence of the Conde Negro on the individuals of his ethnic group and of his close collaboration with the civil and ecclesiastical authorities. For example, the black Sevillians appeared in July of 1477 in a festive and orderly manner to receive Queen Isabel at the port of Macarena and, like other civic groups, always participated in the Corpus Christi processions during those years. A deposition of 1497 required and regulated their presence in the great procession and provided a model followed, decades later, by the authorities of various cities in Spanish America, such as Havana in 1573. One of the Sevillian overseers at the beginning of the sixteenth century, Juan de Castilla, was even popularly known as "the king of the blacks," the same designation that chiefs of Afro-American groups in the Caribbean and other parts of America would use until the past century (Gestoso 1917: 101; Ortiz 1920–21: 1–6; Franco 1985: 109).

In addition to the confraternity of blacks of Seville, which has its origins, as we pointed out, in the last decade of the fourteenth century, other brotherhoods of blacks, and some of mulattos, appeared during the sixteenth century and at the beginning of the seventeenth in diverse Andalusian cities: among them, Cádiz, Jerez de la Frontera, El Puerto de Santa María, Huelva, Jaén, and even the Sevillian suburb of Triana. On this model confraternities were created in the principal cities of the Indies. The most common patron of the blacks was Nuestra Señora de los Reyes, although the brotherhood in Seville changed their advocate's name to that of Nuestra Señora de los Angeles in the middle of the sixteenth century, at the time of their transformation into the brotherhood "of blood and light" and the inauguration of a procession on the night of Holy Thursday with an image of Christ crucified and one of Our Lady of Sorrows.

The primitive title of Virgen de los Reyes—which we also find in the ex-Spanish colonies in the Americas—made reference to the mother of Jesus adored by the Magi. She was represented iconographically with the child Jesus in her arms and the three "kings" paying homage, according to the detailed description that we have of the image of the brotherhood of Jaén. This advocacy should not be surprising: only through the representation of the legendary "holy kings of the Orient'' could a black—in some places identified as Melchior, in others as Gaspar or as Balthazar—be adored by blacks without contradicting the Christian religion. Indeed, this selection was fostered by the church, which had already established the iconography of the three Magi in the twelfth century and had supported and popularized it during the time of the increase in numbers of oriental and African slaves in Europe as a means of symbolizing the unity of all the races in the common adoration of the Christian God. The Three Kings reflected perfectly the ''universal'' Christian Order. The attribution to them of the characteristics considered proper to the three races of the then-known continents, the European, the Asian, and the African, and of each of the three ages, youth, maturity, and old age, symbolized the fact that all humanity, without exception, regardless of physical and social differences, had as its destiny to follow the religion of the only true God, the Christian God. Of course the third variable that would be fundamental to a reflection of all of humanity was lacking, that of sex; but in that period and almost to the present day, woman is a sort of ''hidden face of the moon.''[3]

The identification of the blacks with a holy king was thus promoted by the late medieval church as one of the means of facilitating the integration of peoples of color into the Christian faith. And since the liturgical feast of the kings is January 6, the blacks in Seville and later, for centuries in Spanish America, held on that day their principal festival of the year. During the second half of the last century, the Afro-Cubans still elected their ''kings'' and ''queens'' on that date and took to the streets and celebrated dances to the sound of drums (Ortiz 1920–21: 45–46). In the Andalusian capital, the blacks danced the *zarabanda* or the *paracumbé*, as indicated by various dramatic works of the Golden Age of Spanish literature. In a short piece entitled ''Los Mirones,'' for example, attributed to Cervantes, the story is told of an event that takes place before the church of Santa María la Blanca, ''in whose small plaza customarily congregate scores of Negroes and Negresses.'' This piece features, for the first time in European literature, an ''expert on blacks'' who challenges the stereotypical images of his fellow blacks as disobedient, loquacious, irrational, infantile, passionate about dance, guitar, and drums, and ''exaggerated and funny in everything they think and say'' (Fra Molinero 1995).

During the aforementioned festival of Corpus Christi, there were also black dancers who were costumed as little devils, representing, like the dragon, disorder and the sin that the sacraments were established to redeem. At least twenty-one groups of black dancers are documented in Seville in the second half of the sixteenth and beginning of the seventeenth century. They had expressive names such as *"Negros," "Negros de Guinea," "Cachumba de negros," "Reyes negros,"* or *"Batalla de Guinea."* The latter, for example was composed of ''eight men and four women, and a drum and a guitar; four men with tambourines and timbrels and the other four with small kettledrums, and the four women with timbrels and flags'' (Sentaurens 1984).

The love of dance and timbrels endured for a long time among the black men and women of Seville, and these elements were even present in the religious confraternity itself, in spite of the vigilance of the clerics. Thus, in the account books of the groups from the seventeenth century there are several entries of expenses for purchase and repair of timbrels and for income collected at public dances.

PERSECUTION OF SEVILLIAN BLACKS AND THEIR CONFRATERNITY: THE NEGATIVE IMAGE OF BLACK ETHNICITY

The number of black men and women slaves had grown astronomically in Seville during the sixteenth century, paralleling the consolidation of the city as "port and gateway to the Indies" and the growing importance of this slave market, which served to supply the important families as well as the artisan class and to provide for trips to the New World. In 1565 there were some 7,000 slaves in the city and a total of 15,000 in the archbishopric. For that reason, it was by then known as the "chess board" (Cires and García 1997: 493–499). Shortly after this time there were two confraternities of blacks and one of mulattos in Seville. All three were ethnically closed. They were made up of both men and women, although the latter, whether slave or free, could not attend the council meetings and cabildos. All of the slaves had to present signed authorization of their masters in order to belong to the brotherhood. The three groups carried out processions of penitents during Holy Week. Their economic status was very precarious, and internal crises, for this and other reasons, were frequent.[4]

Because of their ever greater numbers, by the end of the sixteenth century the blacks were no longer viewed as an exotic curiosity to be protected, but rather as a potential, but necessary, danger. By the middle of the century, various ordinances obligated them to live outside the walls of the city, with the one exception of the male and female slaves who slept in the homes of their masters. And violence, symbolic as well as physical, against them began to be evident. This is reflected clearly in the long legal process, fortunately preserved in the archives of the archbishopric, which pitted the black confraternity of the Virgen de los Angeles against one of the most important brotherhoods of the city and which was aimed at the extinction of the former.

Already in previous decades, in spite of the regulation of the confraternity by statutes approved in 1554 and the installation in its chapel of the first parish of the outlying neighborhood of Puerta de Carmona, the black brotherhood of Nuestra Señora de los Angeles was not invited, as was the norm with the other brotherhoods of the city, to attend the general processions. It was not invited in 1579 on the occasion of the solemn transfer to its new place in the royal chapel of the cathedral of the body of the king who conquered the city, Fernando III of Castile—later canonized—and those of his wife, his son King Alfonso X, and other royal persons. Nor were they invited to the processions that were celebrated upon the publication of the bull of the Holy Crusade. However, the authorities could not prevent the presence of two black confraternities, those of Puerta de Carmona and Triana, on the occasion of the transfer of the body of the founder of the former, the archbishop Gonzalo de Mena, from the cathedral, where he had been buried, to the monastery of Cartuja, on the other side of the river, which had been established by him two centuries before.

The distrust on the part of the authorities, both civil and ecclesiastical, and on the part of the upper classes of the city toward the autonomous organization of the blacks, slave and free men and women, even though it was within the framework of religious association, increased with the increase of the number of blacks. It developed into a real persecution of the brotherhood of the Virgen de los Angeles, especially by the archbishops Fernando Niño de Guevara and Pedro de Castro, who controlled the See during the first decades of the seventeenth century. The date chosen for its prohibition was the year 1604. A diocesan synod was celebrated in which harsh criticism was directed against all the Holy Week confraternities in general—more than forty in all, that "hardly cease parading day and night, with great profanity and disruption of the population," according to the archbishop—and especially against those of blacks and mulattos:

which may cause many scandals, sins, and offenses against God for two reasons: first, as they are slaves and have no money or goods with which to buy wax, insignias and other costly objects for the procession, they steal from their masters during the year in order to obtain the money and goods that they require; and second, because, given their color they are very visible; during the time that the procession lasts the people who see them pass make fun of them, occasioning quarrels and turning the procession into a disgrace, which the representatives of the archbishopric are helpless to remedy. (Sánchez 1992: 487)

That same year of 1604 a violent event took place in the street that would be the immediate cause for the suspension of the brotherhood: at midnight on Holy Thursday the confraternity of the blacks and the royal confraternity of Nuestra Señora de la Antigua, Siete Dolores y Compasión, composed of nobles and other "important people" converged on the plaza in front of the Colegial del Salvador. Representatives of each group engaged in a discussion as to which had more right to parade first, and soon the dispute progressed from words to deeds, producing an altercation with several wounded on each side and the immediate denunciation of the blacks by the "principal" brotherhood. The declarations of witnesses whose testimony was sought in the lengthy process are of great interest. The majority of them were clearly hostile to the blacks. Their hostility reflected a high degree of racism that extended practically to all of the social sectors of the dominant ethnic group. The attorney for the accusing party affirmed that "as the confraternity of la Antigua del Salvador, arrived, with the green cross of the women, to Carpintería street, the already present confraternity of the blacks ran from Alfalfa down Confitería armed and determined; with great commotion they crossed through and broke up the aforementioned group of la Antigua, forcefully and against their will, hurling stones and striking the sisters of the Antigua and with arms wounding its brothers."[5] The majority of the witnesses supported this version, reflecting the generalized animosity that existed during this period toward the blacks who were stigmatized as *bozales* (savages) and individuals "without reason," "ridiculous people," "scandal-mongers," and "by nature inclined toward public dereliction." Even their ability to carry out religious acts is called into question since "although Our Lord Jesus Christ died on the cross for all and our mother church does not exclude them, among them there are orders and degrees as there are in Heaven." And it is affirmed that "it is against good order and natural reason that the brothers of the said confraternity compete with the other groups of white people, since the former are slaves and have been converted rather than descended from old Christians"; therefore the authorities are asked "not to allow the said confraternity to parade, nor to gather on the said Holy Saturday at night, and to take away their Rule and other related things upon grave penalty," or at least "order the said confraternity to parade on Holy Tuesday by day and to go with it to the Cruz del Campo, and to indicate to them an hour at which they will not coincide with brotherhoods of white people, in order to avoid scandals and uprisings with the aforementioned blacks" (Archivo Palacio Arzobispal de Sevilla). Thus, a call was issued for the dissolution of the brotherhood or the rescheduling of its procession to a day other than the procession days—which were at that time from Wednesday to Holy Friday—and to a place outside the city. For the social exclusion of the blacks there should be a corresponding temporal and spatial segregation.

The fact was that for some time the "state of penitence" of the confraternity was viewed with hostility, being the object of scoff and scorn not only by the other confraternities—which were increasingly strongly opposed to the blacks having a group like theirs, competing with the others in the symbolic-ceremonial sphere—but also on the part of the general public. Some witnesses acknowledge that, years before, they had observed how "as the procession of Nuestra Señora de los Angeles passed by the steps of the cathedral, a rock hit the Christ figure that they carried"; and others point out that "the people are waiting for them in order to laugh and make fun of them" in order to "whistle at them and make them the butt of jokes and scorn," calling them "drunkards and blacks," "insulting them and calling them names in the language of Guinea and some times provoking anger and other times laughter" and "sticking them with pins, which angers them and they call the whites Jews, as do the female blacks who accompany them" (Archivo Palacio Arzobispal de Sevilla).

Even for those who recognized that the blacks were the ones who first and most repeatedly received the provocations, the latter were condemned because, since the provocations and jokes could not be avoided, it was "shameful for our religion to have the said confraternity of blacks parade, and significantly scandalous and of great satisfaction for the heretics to see that the Christians, i.e., the whites—hold the said confraternity of blacks in such low esteem" (Archivo Palacio Arzobispal de Sevilla). Therefore, it would be necessary to eliminate the cause in order to avoid these effects, which was the path taken by the archbishopric, in spite of the fact that the brotherhood might cite "statutes approved by the Ordinary and even bulls from His Holiness" and its "antiquity, it being much older than Antigua" (Archivo Palacio Arzobispal de Sevilla). An act of prohibition was declared, under threat of excommunication, against all processions of confraternities of blacks and mulattos, and the members of the board of the brotherhood of los Angeles were sentenced to one hundred blows each. The act declared that "the aforementioned are the most rude and the most ignorant of religion, devotion and reverence that there might be in such processions; they do and say ridiculous things, causing the common people to lose respect for them, also because they are so ridiculous in their procession and it serves only to disturb and to interfere with the devotion of the faithful who are in the churches and streets through which they pass" (Archivo Palacio Arzobispal de Sevilla).

The offensive against the confraternities of blacks and mulattos culminated in the confiscation of their goods and even of some of their images and in an effort at their dissolution. King Philip III himself, to whose jurisdiction they had appealed for support, signed in 1614 a royal provision addressed to an official in Seville in which he orders: "Do not allow processions of blacks except with our express permission and order" (Farfan Ramos 1914: 40). With this, he clearly supported the efforts of the archbishopric.

Nevertheless, the brotherhood of the Virgen de los Angeles, undoubtedly having secured some support by taking advantage of the confrontation between the archbishop and the Sevillian cathedral chapter, managed in 1625 to have the pope himself, Urban VIII, in the bull *In Supremo Apostolice Dignitatis* confirm its statutes. Thus the group escaped the grave danger of being dissolved, although the normalization of its public life was a very slow process and required demonstrations of religious fervor that even included the extreme measure of having two free brothers auction their very freedom in order to obtain monies to fund solemn rites in honor of the Immaculate Conception in the context of what came to be known as the "Marian War," a controversy that pitted the Franciscans, supported by all strata of the city, against the Dominicans, who questioned the belief. According to documents of the period, these rites "totally amazed this city, because never has sumptuousness like this been seen; proof of the fervor of these men and of the devotion that they profess to the Great Queen and to her pure conception." (Ortiz de Zúñiga 1677) In this way, slowly, the confraternity that had changed the time of its procession to the morning of Holy Friday, on which fewer groups paraded than on the previous night, saw its antiquity recognized and, because of it, its right to preside over all of those of the city with the exception of Vera Cruz and Cristo de San Agustín, the only ones with an older date of foundation. But this did not happen definitively until the second half of the seventeenth century, when the presence of blacks in Seville had diminished considerably, as much because of consequences of the demographic catastrophe that the plague of 1649 produced—in which half of the total population of the city died—as to the closing of the principal slave route, that of Lisbon-Seville, after the war of independence of Portugal.

FROM "NEGROES" TO "NEGRITOS": THE NEW PROTECTIONISM OF BLACKS IN THE EIGHTEENTH CENTURY AND THE FESTIVAL OF THE "GOOSE RACE"

In the eighteenth century, the Sevillian blacks constitute a much smaller number than in the two preceding centuries and they are more culturally integrated, the majority of them being sons or grandsons of other black men and women, slave and free, residents of the city. For one reason or another the open hostility against them that had marked the first decades of the 1600s disappears and is even gradually converted into a kind of sympathy that is compassionate, protective, and philanthropic. The blacks are no longer perceived as a potential threat; they are docile and almost exotic. Therefore the higher strata of the city, especially, become interested in them and offer them charitable actions, creating a time of splendor for the confraternity, although in terms of numbers it was smaller than in other epochs.

The archbishops of Seville, beginning with Cardinal Francisco de Solís Fox de Cardona, became their protectors, accepting the title of Older Brother, a guarantee of significant charity; and not a few whites, although not eligible to be "brothers," acted also as benefactors. The blacks were no longer labeled bozales (savages), but rather, from the second half of the century were called *negritos*, a diminutive that expresses an attitude both tolerant and paternalistic that had begun to predominate in the rest of the Sevillian population, especially in the upper strata. For white Sevillians blacks had begun to be a potential object of the exercise of charity—although with no questioning of the legitimacy of slavery, which would not be definitively abolished legally until 1837. While there were still a certain number of male and female domestic slaves, one of the beneficiaries of that charity was an important black of the brotherhood, Salvador de la Cruz, who occupied for almost forty years the post of majordomo. He made at least two documented trips to America while a slave, carrying small banks in order to obtain charitable donations during the trip. There was consideration of making a declaration to honor him after his "saintly" death in 1775, in a manner similar to one honoring the Sicilian Benito de Palermo fifty years before.

What is most interesting about the brotherhood in the eighteenth century, however, is the analysis of the festival known as the "goose race," integrated into the Real Maestranza de Caballería (Royal Order of Equestrain Knights) in which several members of the Sevillian high nobility participated along with the black brothers. As Ricardo White (one of the brotherhood's eminent secretaries) wrote in 1798 in the book of activities of the brotherhood:

Since their introduction in Seville, blacks were allowed to hold certain public festival celebrations among themselves, and it is believed that their meetings and celebrations were probably held before our chapel . . . , and that certain Knights probably were in attendance. Precisely for this reason, the Nobilísimo Real Cuerpo de Maestrantes, once established, decided to sponsor the brothers in the goose race which is to this day held on the eve of Nuestra Señora de los Angeles, the first of August of every year, the cost being borne by the Señores Maestrantes.[6]

In the *Historial de Fiestas y Donativos* of the Real Maestranza one can also read:

One of the practices which appears from the beginning of the incorporation, which is mentioned as very ancient in the first printed Rule, and whose origin can not be precisely determined, is that of the race with the brothers of the black confraternity of Nuestra Señora de los Angeles that, since its beginnings, was esteemed by the Sevillian nobility which undoubtedly selected it as a means of putting into practice an act of Christian humility, perhaps motivated even more by a consideration of the general low esteem in which the poor brothers were held. (de León y Manjón 1909:74)

Although there is evident exaggeration in this description, particularly with respect to the assertion that the brotherhood was always viewed in a positive manner by the nobility, it is true that from the end of the century, which is when the knightly order was founded, the relationship of the latter to the former was evident, "as a means of putting into practice some act of Christian humility" on the part of the knights. In the new ordinances of the Real Maestranza of 1724, we read:

It is a praiseworthy custom to accompany the blacks of this place in a race for the geese which is run in front of their chapel, and we hope that this act of Christian humility may continue among us, encouraging the affectionate zeal and devotion of these brothers, and in order that it be accomplished the Representatives of our Order will inform all of the Maestrantes of this goal, and upon their arrival to the site first will pass the procession, each Maestrante accompanying a brother, and then the geese will be run at, and this festival is hereby declared irrevocable. (de León y Manjón 1909:74)

What, exactly, was this "goose race" that took place on the eve of the festival of the patron virgin of the black brotherhood? The treasurer of the Real Maestranza of that epoch provided the following brief but suggestive description of the festival:

They run with the blacks; the horse of the black with a fine saddle and bells and rider dressed in ruffled collar and, if there were sleeves, they would be of white gauze, and there would be feathers. The knights in large flat collars, ordinary hat, no bells, the horse with no ribbons, which are, rather, placed on the horse of the black. The first race is run, the black and his *padrino* paired, the protégé at the right side. And the geese, first the black alone, and then the *padrino*. And in order to grab well the head, the hand must be turned up, the little finger toward the body of the goose. (de León y Manjón 1909: 75)

As is clearly indicated in the text, the festival constituted a true ritual of symbolic inversion of social reality. The blacks, slave or free, but in any case belonging to the lowest social stratum, dressed in the ritual dress and accessories of the knight—hat with feather, ruff, and sleeves of white gauze—were riding on horses adorned with ribbons and bells on luxurious riding saddles. The knights, in contrast, although of the nobility, dressed more modestly and rode without saddle and ribbons and with ordinary hats. In the procession of several pairs of blacks and knights, the latter yielded to the former the right side, in recognition of his preeminence, and in the race for the geese the black was in first position. All of this clearly reflected a ritual symbolic inversion of the social hierarchy: everything happened contrary to daily reality. For the knights, it had the importance of carrying out an act of public humility, of expiation of guilt and pride, with their willing rejection of adornment and rights in favor of the blacks whom they sponsored. The latter, for their part, were decked out as knights. They were deferred to generously by true knights and participating along with nobles in a ritual honoring their titular virgin, internalized, albeit in an ambivalent manner, the ethnic pride of "not being lesser," upon feeling themselves recognized as part of society and accepted by the social order that kept them in its most marginalized position, by means of their grateful acknowledgment of their protectors and *padrinos*.

The festival was celebrated on the esplanade in front of the chapel and consisted, fundamentally, in a lively parade of six pairs of blacks and knights on horseback. Blacks and nobles took turns passing at a gallop beneath a rope from which were hung live geese, heads down. The object was to jerk their heads off, hands in the position described above. This practice, which today would be considered cruel to the animals, is still observed in a very few places in Spain, especially in Castile and the Basque area, with chickens in place of geese and, on some occasions, motorcycles in place of horses. It was formerly very common in popular festivals all over the peninsula, and the custom passed to Spanish America. We do not know whether, during the colonial period, this type of race was held in other continental cities, in the context of a major festival of blacks. It would be interesting to investigate other ritual celebrations in which a similar symbolic inversion of social roles took place.

The last time that blacks and Sevillian nobles celebrated the goose race was the year 1806, although by the end of the previous century the festival was suspended with some frequency, because of various circumstances that led the

Real Maestranza to substitute in its place an important charitable donation to the brotherhood.

DEMOGRAPHIC CRISIS AND DECADENCE: SEVILLIAN BLACKS IN THE NINETEENTH CENTURY

By the last two decades of the 1700s the record books of the brotherhood make note of the small number of brothers, a situation reflected also in a growing economic precariousness, in spite of financial aid from the Archbishopric, the Maestranza, and some important families of the city. The processions on the afternoon of Holy Friday, which had been very regular, especially during the midyears of the century and even into the decade of the 1770s, became more infrequent and virtually nonexistent after 1787. There are fewer and fewer black men and women in Seville, and this scarcity has a direct repercussion on the brotherhood of "los negritos" at the end of the century and, especially, during the nineteenth century. Nevertheless, the annual festival of the Virgen de los Angeles and the ceremonies of the first three days of August did not fail to take place and were well attended. General meetings were also held, although at times with fewer than a dozen attendees. Periods of resurgence alternate with others of less activity. At such times the procession is again observed during Holy Week: in 1849 on Holy Friday, preceding the then very famous brotherhood of the Holy Burial of Christ; and in 1867 and 1869, on the afternoon of Palm Sunday. On these last two occasions they carried the crucified Christ of the Foundation and the figure of the Virgin Dolorosa de los Angeles on the same float in order to reduce expenses.

In 1888 the brotherhood ceased to be ethnic, that is, exclusively for blacks, and became a modest neighborhood association governed by whites. Gone were the walls that defined as marginal that area of the city where in previous centuries blacks had built their humble chapel, around which a neighborhood primarily composed of modest families of workers formed. The last four blacks who governed the brotherhood, especially the one who had the title of major-domo, Camilo Lastre, fiercely opposed its ceasing to be property "of those of their race." Consequently, they had strong confrontations with the parish priest of San Roque, in whose jurisdiction the chapel was and is, and with the clerics to whom the archbishops delegated their authority. The paternalistic protectionism of a hundred years earlier was not exercised over these few blacks who defended their historic rights; they were not considered, for all practical purposes, as delinquents. Their small number made impossible the sense of an ethnic identity, and the social marginalization to which they were subjected condemned them to the lumpen proletariat. The comparison of the history of the Sevillian blacks during the 500 years from the end of the fourteenth century to the end of the nineteenth, studied through the documents of the only permanent association permitted to them and through other evidence, literary, religious, and so on, with the history of the black collectives of diverse cities and areas of the American continents, from their arrival as slaves to the present, would doubtlessly yield very interesting results. There would probably be a high degree of correspondence between the two processes, given the evidence of their connection. The task is open to anthropologists, historians, and investigators of ethnic realities from other disciplines.

NOTES

1. During the eighteenth century, the period of the Enlightenment, the so-called "caste system" was even "naturalized" and fixed in the collective imagination through the pictorial representations included in various collections of canvases and paintings on copper known as "Scenes of Mestizaje." There is a gradual "whitening" as a result of the unions between descendants of the Spaniards and black women, producing mulattos, Moriscos, and albinos in successive generations, which was interrupted at the fourth generation by the appearance of a "throwback" in spite of the fact that among the ancestors there were fifteen Spaniards for only one Negro. This did not occur with the descendants of the cross between Spaniards and Indian women and subsequent marriages with Spaniards, which produced mestizos, *castizos* and, in the third generation, again *"Spaniard,"* with seven Spanish ancestors and one Indian. See Isidoro Moreno, 1973.

2. For centuries a street behind the chapel of the brotherhood of the Negroes has been called "Conde Negro."

3. In Mexico the three kings would be replaced by the three Juans, pictured below the Virgin of Guadalupe, representing whites, Indians, and mestizos. And in Cuba, beneath the Virgin of the Caridad del Cobre, the three row the little boat.

4. Of these, that of Triana would disappear shortly after the middle of the seventeenth century, following the plague outbreak that reduced by almost half the total population of Seville; that of the mulattos processed for the last time in 1731. Only the brotherhood of the Virgen de los Angeles remained and still continues to exist, although now composed exclusively of whites. Until the late date of 1888 it was in the hands of the few blacks who continued to live in the city.

5. See Legajo 94, Sección Hermandades, Archivo del Palacio Arzobispal de Sevilla.

6. From the sixteenth century, according to the Rule, the secretary or scribe of the brotherhood must be a white person of some eminence, in order to guarantee attendance at the meetings and cabildos of someone who knew how to read and write. This was the only person foreign to the black ethnic group who had voice and vote.

2

Presence of Blackness and Representations of Jewishness in the Afro-Esmeraldian Celebrations of the Semana Santa (Ecuador)

Jean Muteba Rahier

El sol se vistió de luto,	The sun went into mourning,
la tierra se estremeció,	the Earth began to shake,
las piedras lloraron sangre	the stones cried tears of blood
cuando Jesús expiró.	When Jesus expired.

(Initial quatrain of the *Décima*—Afro-Esmeraldian
oral poem—"*La Pasión de Cristo*"; see Rahier 1987)

Unlike the other papers included in this volume which deal with representations of blackness and performances of black identities, this essay analyzes what I call the "presence" of blackness and Afro-Esmeraldian representations of Jewishness in the celebration of Semana Santa (Holy Week) in the village of Selva Alegre ("Happy Forest").[1] This small village of less than 400 inhabitants is located on the left bank of the Santiago River, in the remote forest of the northern Ecuadorian Province of Esmeraldas (see Figure 2.1). My preference for "presence" of blackness over "representation" of blackness is because blackness is actually not "re-presented" in the text of the celebrations under scrutiny here. In the Afro-Esmeraldian Holy Week, blackness is, as it were, a "given"; it is there in the disguised and nondisguised entirely black population of the village. All who attend, participate, and perform in the various ceremonies of the five-day Easter celebration (from Wednesday through Sunday) are black. These complex celebrations, whose overt objective is the reenactment of the Passion of Jesus, according to the Bible, are centered around the crucifixion of a white Christ. I argue that beyond the public transcript—the official story or

Figure 2.1
The Two Traditional Black Regions of Ecuador

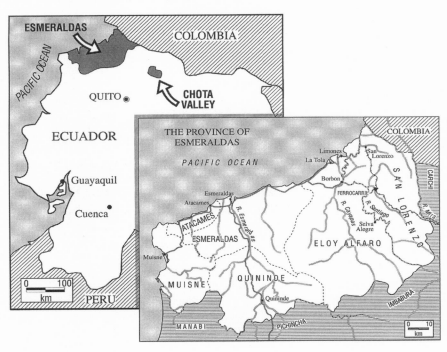

first layer of the performances—lies what James Scott has called a "hidden transcript" (a critique of power spoken behind the back of the dominant) (Scott 1990), an expression of Afro-Esmeraldian resistance to the Ecuadorian "racial"/ spatial order, in the form of manipulation of anti-Semitic images of the "people who killed the Christ." I show that by demonizing the Jews as a category of white people, Afro-Esmeraldians aim to reaffirm their respectability, symbolically challenging and denying the stereotypical and racist perceptions of blacks as backward, savage, and violent people deprived of culture, occupying the lowest position in the Ecuadorian racial order. In the context of the Semana Santa, Afro-Esmeraldian resistance does not involve any reference to Africa but, instead, representations of non-Africa centered reinterpretations of the Bible, Spanish folklore, and European anti-Semitic ideology—which undoubtedly dates back to the Spanish Renaissance, if not to the anti-Semitism that characterizes the entire history of Christianity.[2]

My principal premise is that the comprehension of festivities requires a detailed knowledge of the contexts in which they are inscribed, since festivities repeat or represent these contexts with a "critical distance" (Drewal 1992) and often provide the site wherein subordinate people produce a counterdiscourse that can project identities, blackness, and Jewishness for example, in a "subversive" fashion. In Selva Alegre, the subversive projection of blackness is indirect but obvious: blacks are not represented by disguised actors in the text of the celebrations, as are various white peoples such as Jesus Christ, Barabbas, Jews, and Romans. However, Afro-Esmeraldians are, behind the masks and in the audience, the people who reenact the various scenes that constitute Christ's Passion, an event in which black people did not participate—as they are prone to say: *los negros no estaban allí* ("black people were not there"). As Jacques Derrida, Michel Foucault, Gilles Deleuze, Edouard Glissant and others have shown: identities are constructed, and thus represented in their relation to difference(s), they are not just there, unproblematically, in a simple "presence." My approach relates the presence of blackness to the various white identities Afro-Esmeraldians represent in the reenactment of the Passion of Christ. The celebrations are analyzed within the context of the Ecuadorian racial/spatial order, in light of Afro-Esmeraldian cultural categories and processes.

THE VILLAGE OF SELVA ALEGRE AND THE RACIAL/SPATIAL ORDER

The Ecuadorian Racial/Spatial Order

In Ecuador, as elsewhere in Latin America, the official imagination of national identity has been constructed by the white and white-mestizo elites around the notion of *mestizaje* (race mixing). These elites have reproduced an "Ecuadorian ideology" of national identity that proclaims the mestizo (mixed-race individual who has both European [Spanish] and indigenous ancestry) as the prototype of modern Ecuadorian citizenship. This ideology is based on a belief in the indigenous population's inferiority, and an unconditional—although sometimes contradictory—admiration and identification with Occidental civilization (see Whitten 1981: Introduction; Stutzman 1981; Silva 1995).

Despite this obvious attempt at racial and ethnic homogenization, this Ecuadorian ideology of national identity results in a racist map of national territory: rural areas are places of racial inferiority, violence, backwardness, savagery, and cultural deprivation. These areas, mostly inhabited by non-whites or non-white-mestizos, are seen as representing major challenges to the full national development toward the ideals of modernity. In this way, Ecuador is quite similar to Colombia, as voiced by Peter Wade in his book *Blackness and Race Mixture*: "there is a distinctive spatial pattern to the overall structure of . . . nationhood and its racial order" (Wade 1993: 58). Furthermore, the editors of the recently published *Knowing Your Place: Rural Identity and Cultural Hierarchy* write in their introduction: "The utility of the countryside as a locus of national essence is more complicated in plural societies where rural populations are ethnically or racially marked, hence hardly a national unifier. In these cases, rural/urban differences often qualify ethnic and/or racial ones, demanding that all three be examined in tandem'' (Ching & Creed 1997: 25).

Mestizaje, as Norman Whitten explained, does not mean that the white indianizes himself but that, on the contrary, the Indian whitens himself "racially" and culturally. For him, the official imagination of Ecuadorian national identity "[is] an ideology of *blanqueamiento* (whitening) within the globalizing framework of *mestizaje*'' (personal communication).

In this official imagination of Ecuadorian-ness, there is logically no place for blacks: they must remain invisible. Afro-Ecuadorians—who represent around 5 percent of the national population[3]—constitute the ultimate Other, some sort of a historical accident, a noise in the ideological system of nationality, a pollution in the Ecuadorian genetic pool. The best example of "non-citizenship," "they are not part of *Mestizaje*'' (Stutzman 1981: 63).

The national development plans of the Ecuadorian elites see the cities (mainly Quito and Guayaquil) as the epicenters from which civilization radiates to the rural and frontier areas. Thus, Ecuadorian society, spatially constituted, is organized in a racial/spatial order within which the various ethnic and racial groups (indigenous peoples, blacks, mestizos, white-mestizos, and whites) occupy their "natural" places. Blacks and indigenous people are found at the bottom of the socioeconomic hierarchy and in the periphery of national space; and the two "traditional" regions of blackness (both developed during the colonial period), the Province of Esmeraldas and the Chota-Mira Valley, are looked down upon by the white and white mestizo urban citizenry.

The Esmeraldian Racial/Spatial Order

While 70 percent of the population of the Province of Esmeraldas are said to be blacks and mulattos, the Esmeraldian elites are mostly composed of white-mestizos and white-mulattos who either migrated from Colombia, the Ecuadorian Andes, or the province of Manabí. Their rule in the province relies on the hegemony of the national elites, who usually reside in Quito and Guayaquil (see Whitten 1974). Esmeraldian elites reproduce the national ideology of mestizaje at the provincial level and also apply a racist reading of the map of provincial territory. They consider the city of Esmeraldas as being the major, if not unique, center of culture and civilization, with secondary status given to the towns of Quinindé, Atacames, Muisne, and San Lorenzo (see Figure 2.1). The northern sector of the province, usually referred to as El Norte, the north, is seen as a place of backwardness and savagery. El Norte is the home of the *negros azules*, "the blue blacks," so called because of the darkness of their skin color (no race mixing). The "blue blacks" or Northerners are considered by the urban population of Esmeraldas as people without "culture," people untouched by modernity, who maintain traditions from another age, do not mind living amidst the dense rain forest, with no electricity or running water, with mosquitoes and wild animals, and who—when they come to town—have no manners and can sometimes behave as social predators. The village of Selva Alegre constitutes such a place of "blue blackness." There, subsistence economy still prevails: cultivated parcels in the forest, hunting, and fishing, along with a few other economic activities directed toward cash markets.

The city of Esmeraldas is Selva Alegre's polar opposite. Here, as elsewhere in Ecuador and in Latin America, the process of blanqueamiento (whitening) is the dominant theme of the social, economic, and racial fabric of life; this extends to the most intimate personal relationships (see Whitten 1974; Quiroga 1994). The popular expression *mejorar la raza*, "to improve the race," denotes blanqueamiento by pointing to the publicly acknowledged ideal followed by darker-skinned people to marry lighter-skinned individuals to secure upward mobility. Esmeraldas has a phenotypic typology that ranges from the most negative category to the most positive one. The bottom category is the blue blacks, the top is the whites, with a series of intermediary types such as, nonexhaustively: the *morados* (dark skinned individuals with "fair" [non-kinky] black hair), the mulattos (brown skinned with kinky hair), the *trigueños* (lighter skinned than the mulattos with softer dark hair), the *zambos* or *colorados* (light skinned persons with light and fair brown, red or even blond nappy hair), etc.

The (urban) Esmeraldian elites despise the black lower class, whom they see as repugnant, ignorant thieves. For example, my landlord throughout my six years stay in Esmeraldas—a white-mestizo—never really understood why I insisted on going back to the north to do research among the negros azules. He kept asking me if I was involved in the international trade of archeological artifacts from the famous site of La Tolita Pampa de Oro (near La Tola; see Figure 2.1). Despite my negative responses he was convinced that I had to be gathering some sort of wealth, probably illegally, from my numerous and long trips and persistently queried me on the matter. After several attempts, I gave up my desire to explain what I was really doing. It was incomprehensible to him that Afro-Esmeraldians, especially in the north, could have culture (*tener cultura*) worth discovering.

The economic history of the province of Esmeraldas is characterized by a succession of booms and busts (see West 1957; Whitten 1965, 1974; Rivera 1986; Jácome 1978, 1979; CONADE 1980). The northern sector of the province is in a period of economic depression that began in the 1960s. This situation has lead to processes of migration of northerners to the cities of Esmeraldas and, most importantly, Guayaquil. The celebration of the Semana Santa is one of the major occasions when Afro-Esmeraldian migrants make the costly and difficult trip to their home villages along the Santiago River and its affluents (Whitten and Quiroga 1995). The celebrations provide an opportunity to reaffirm the communal identity, the "local moral community" (Quiroga 1994). Semana Santa gives the urban migrants a chance to reconnect with family and friends. The youngest migrants who make the trip back to Selva Alegre are particularly interested in the dancing party, *baíle*, animated by a disc jockey, *discomóvil*, which ends the celebrations on Sunday afternoon. During the baíle, they can seduce a young male or female villager and expose exterior signs of wealth to impress the nonmigrants, justifying their decision to leave the village. Before one of my visits to Selva Alegre for Semana Santa, I witnessed the preparation of a Selva Alegreño, a young carpenter friend who resides in the city and planned to go back home for the celebrations. I was amazed by his preoccupation: he borrowed pieces of cloth, shoes, and golden jewelry from friends for the trip. When asked why he wanted to show off, he responded, "For Holy Week one has to dress sharp, to provoke respect."

ASPECTS OF THE TRADITIONAL AFRO-ESMERALDIAN WORLDVIEW AND THE LIMINAL TIME OF SEMANA SANTA

To understand the following brief descriptions of the Afro-Esmeraldian Semana Santa and make sense of the way time assumes a liminal quality during the celebrations, it is necessary to bear in mind basic elements of traditional Afro-Esmeraldian cosmology. Most Afro-Esmeraldians think of themselves as being Catholics, but their Catholicism has unique characteristics (see Whitten 1974; Quiroga 1994; Naranjo 1987; Barrero 1979a, 1979b; Speiser 1986, 1987). They believe that, "on the other side of the earth," there exist three worlds in the great beyond (see also Whitten 1974): la Gloria, Heaven, and el Purgatorio, Purgatory, which are in the sky; and el Infierno, Hell, which is underneath the sky but not necessarily underneath the earth. In Gloria live God, Jesus, virgins, saints and the *angelitos*, the souls of deceased children. In Purgatory, which is conceived of as a closed world (with no opening to Gloria), live most of the souls of deceased adults. The souls of adults who died in sin, the Devil (*el Diablo*), and other demons live in Hell, near the earth. In addition to these souls and beings there are a series of spirits or visions (*visiones*) living in the forest, in the rivers, and in the sea. The inhabited village area represents a communal place of relative security when opposed to the rest of the world, which is filled with dangers: the forest and the sea, but also urban areas with the capitalist system, racial hierarchy, and more individualist ways. Selva Alegreños have many stories to tell about their traveling in the outside world, their encounters with the Tunda, the Duende, the Riviel, the *Sirenas* (various spirits or visions), or witnessing surprising events which took place in the town of Borbón and in the city of Esmeraldas during a trip, all of which demonstrate the existence of evil forces. Indeed, for Northerners in general, traveling is a popular theme of conversation. It is emphasized as a necessary experience for young men to not only be able to find their way in the forest (and in the world), but also to gain reputation: *andar y conocer*, "to travel and to learn" (see Whitten 1974; see also Rahier 1987). Selva Alegreños, and Afro-Esmeraldians in general, have always traveled back and forth, since the end of the nineteenth century, between their villages and the surrounding towns, and even the city of Esmeraldas. It is in Borbón, Limones and Esmeraldas that they sell their agricultural surplus (bananas, *tagua*, nuts, and cacao) and purchase products that are unavailable in the villages.

Diego Quiroga has studied the Afro-Esmeraldian cosmology (Quiroga 1994). Although he conducted fieldwork in Muisne County, in the south of the province, his observations are nevertheless quite accurate and very helpful in describing the situation in the northern counties. His departure point is the traditional distinction made by Afro-Esmeraldians between the domain of the *humano* (human or profane) and the domain of the *divino* (divine or sacred). The divino basically refers to Gloria and its inhabitants: God, Jesus, virgins, saints, and angelitos. From them one seeks the protection and help necessary to find a husband, to have a good crop, to have a safe trip, to cure an illness, success in hunting, and so on. The space of the divino is juxtaposed to uncontrollable and threatening forces which constitute the domain of the humano. The humano "with its dreadful affective forces" is where one has "incongruous experiences of uncontrollable events" (Quiroga 1994: 129). Most of these events occur outside the village perimeter, in cities and towns or in forest areas abounding in mythical beings such as visiones and demons. There are moments or periods in the annual cycle when the relative security of the village is greatly diminished, and the dangers of the outside world are multiplied. That is true of the Semana Santa:

The *humano* is conceptualized in spatial and temporal terms. Temporally, there are periods during the annual cycle . . . when evil and disorder prevail. There are days of the year when the spirits of the *humano* wander among the living. Examples of such periods are the *día de los muertos* (All Saints Day) and Semana Santa (Easter). From the death of Christ until his resurrection, the forces of evil and disorder are ubiquitous, and devils and demons roam free on earth. In Muisne it is said that during this week *brujas*—women who have made pacts with Satan or who practice black magic—become *mulas*, mules, or *serpientes*, serpents. (Quiroga 1994: 130)

In Selva Alegre, the liminal time of Semana Santa officially begins on Thursday morning, with the ceremony called *encerrar la Gloria*, "to enclose or to seclude the Gloria." From then on, until Sunday, the last day of celebrations called *domingo de Gloria*, Sunday of Gloria, when the *Gloria entera* ceremony, "the ceremony of the full re-opening of Gloria," is performed, the divino remains closed, locked up as it were. It has become inaccessible. During these days the usual protection afforded by the positive forces of Gloria are unavailable. It is impossible to communicate with them. The reopening of Gloria at the end of the celebrations occurs progressively. It begins on Saturday with the Media Gloria ceremony, literally "Half Gloria," which is said to start the opening process that ends with Sunday's Gloria entera.

The liminality of Semana Santa time is accompanied by a series of prohibitions (see also Speiser 1987) that express an ambiance of imminent danger provoked by the closing of Gloria. From Thursday to Sunday, calm must reign in the village. Nobody may travel or work, and provisions for meals must have been made. Concepts of solidarity, equality, and community are emphasized. Money cannot change hands, and if necessity demands a purchase, the payment must be deferred until Sunday afternoon. If a parent wants to punish a child, the spanking waits until Sunday afternoon. No excess of any sort is allowed. One may eventually drink *aguardiente*, sugarcane alcohol, but with temperance. No music nor drums may be played. Running, making quick or strenuous movements such as hammering, breaking a coconut with a machete, and so on are forbidden. One may not bathe in deep water because sirenas (sirens) will pull under and drown the unfortunate bather. Bathing is allowed only in waist-deep water near the riverbank. Migrants returning to the village [4] for the celebrations make sure to arrive on Wednesday at the latest. Even saying the word ''Gloria'' is strictly prohibited. When the moment comes in a prayer or a song to pronounce ''Gloria,'' the word is replaced by the expression *de nuestro servicio, amén,* ''our service, amen.'' Indeed, Semana Santa time is a time characterized by a sudden and dangerous imbalance between two opposed forces, *lo humano* and *lo divino*: humans, spirits, and demons are left to themselves. It is a time of (possible) chaos, a necessary condition for the reenactment of the abominable act of the crucifixion of Christ by ''demonic Jews.'' There is no socioculturally active and visible Jewish community in the history of the Province of Esmeraldas. Jews—imaginary Others—play the role of expiatory victims. They are imagined as a cross between humans, demons, and beasts.

THE PRINCIPAL MASKED ACTORS

Although the Afro-Esmeraldian celebration of the Semana Santa is obviously inspired by passages of the Bible (''public transcript''), it also represents reinterpretations of the Bible that account for the local characteristics and meanings of the ceremonies (''hidden transcript''). The descriptions that follow have been made to serve my argument about the presence of blackness and the representations of Jewishness. The reading of my interpretive descriptions of the ceremonies requires first to learn about the various actors involved.

Los Santos Varones, ("The Saint Men")

Most villages along the Santiago river have their Santos Varones. They are usually four older men who are responsible for the organization of the various ceremonies of Semana Santa. They are in charge of transporting, hanging, and removing the big wooden crucifix to and from the Monte del Calvario, the ''Mount of Calvary.'' They organize the processions, read passages of sacred texts, and make sure that the *cantadoras*, women singers, are ready and present in the church at the right time and so on. They also handle the crucifix at other occasions: *Ascención*, and *Corpus Cristi*. They take care of the church throughout the year. During ceremonies, they collect small donations of money from the audience for the maintenance of the church, the purchase of a new crucifix, of candles, and so forth. This official responsibility for the village's church and its contents was probably entrusted upon them by itinerant Catholic priests who visit the villages of the river at most once a year. In 1991, the last time I attended the Semana Santa in Selva Alegre, they had not seen a priest for almost three years. In the northern sector of the province, Afro-Esmeraldians do not depend upon priests for the performance of their rituals. They recognize, for example, two kinds of baptism: the *bautismo de agua*, water baptism, and the *bautismo de oleos*, the oil baptism. The former does not require the presence of a priest. A *madrina*, godmother, and a *padrino*, godfather, are chosen by the parents of the child. While the godmother holds the child in her arms in the child's parents' house, the godfather spills some water on the child's forehead pronouncing: *En nombre del Padre, del Hijo y del Espíritu Santo, te bautizo*, "In the name of the Father, the Son and the Holy Spirit, I baptize you." The oil baptism is performed in the church by a priest who draws, with an oily thumb, a cross on the forehead of the individual being baptized, saying the same words as the padrino in the water baptism. Many Afro-Esmeraldians have not been baptized by a priest; the water baptism is seen as sufficiently valid by many.

In Selva Alegre, the Santos Varones do not wear specific clothing except, on Good Friday, a pair of black shorts over their pants. They take their role very seriously, particularly during the ceremonies. The four Santos Varones vaguely evoke the black brotherhoods of Seville described by Isidoro Moreno (this volume and also Moreno 1997). However, it would be impossible to try to contrast in the space allocated here the large black brotherhoods of Seville, Cuba (Ortiz 1960), and Peru (Celestino 1992) with the level of organization of the Santos Varones. The differences are many. Above and beyond the contextual dissimilarities, the size of the nonpermanent team of Santos Varones hardly compares to the size and the organizational complexity of the black *hermandades* (brotherhoods).

In Selva Alegre, the Santos Varones do not change their racial identity during the ceremonies as the actors representing Christ, Longino, the Roman soldiers, the Jews, and Barabbas do. Their individual identities are never concealed, their black faces always apparent. It is through them, in part, that blackness is made "present" on the scene of the performances. They are seen by the community as very knowledgeable about the tradition and the Bible. During the performances they are, in a way, the repositories of the respectability of blackness. In Wuimbí and Telembí, nearby Afro-Esmeraldian villages, the Santos Varones wear suits and ties and sometimes jackets during Semana Santa, despite the warm and humid climate.[5]

La Tropa ("The Troop [or Troops]") and Longino

The tropa is a group of ten to twenty young men armed with *escopetas* ("rifles"), machetes, knives, sticks, and so on. Most of them wear a sort of skirt made of long pieces of coco tree leaves. They are led by a middle-aged man, who is sometimes referred to as the *jefe de la tropa*, the "tropa's chief." They represent the Roman soldiers who arrested Jesus, led him to Pilate, and then to his crucifixion. This is probably a survival of Spanish folklore. Representations of Roman soldiers throughout the history of the Holy Week in Seville, Spain, are common (see Moreno 1982; Schrauf 1997).

The priest, Rafael Savoia, who lived in and visited many Afro-Esmeraldian villages, interprets—erroneously, I suggest—the patrolling of the tropa during the Semana Santa as the enactment of the formation of a maroon village (*palenque*):

The most dramatic ceremony in Esmeraldas Province is that of the *tropa* (the troop or troops). This is a forceful enactment of the formation of a *palenque*, which was a village established by black people (or indigenous people) fleeing bondage. Such people were known as *cimarrones*. *La tropa* is enacted at Easter. . . . [They enact] the bringing of the forest into the Catholic church of the *palenque*, the resurrection of Christ within the forest within the church, and the liberation of the people of the forest and of the church within the *palenque*. (Whitten and Quiroga 1995: 303)

Nothing in the actions of the tropa I had the pleasure to witness, nor in the interviews about the tropa with Selva Alegreños and other Afro-Esmeraldians, ever suggested any formation of a palenque. On the contrary, everybody agrees that the tropa represents the Roman soldiers who were patrolling the streets of Palestine.

As Romans, the tropa's soldiers are whites, although they do not cover their black faces as do other white Semana Santa characters. While they are patrolling, the actors representing the Roman soldiers suspend their normal interactions with the village population. They stop being themselves and become a soldier of the tropa, responsible only to their chief. In conversations about the tropa with young men who participate in it, as well as with village elders, my question about their racial identity always led to statements like: *Si son romanos, son italianos; y los italianos son blancos, pués,* "If they are Romans, they are Italians; and Italians are white!" During the celebrations, their most important role is to patrol the streets of the village and the church, looking for Christ, whom they want to arrest, marching or running with discipline, in two lines, at the rhythm of the loud orders of their chief: "One, two, one, two, . . ." overwhelming or muffling the sounds of the prayer being recited by the *rezanderas* (women who lead the prayers) and the audience.

The character named Longino represents the Roman centurion who stabbed Jesus with a spear. He strolls about with a long wooden spear back and forth in the church and surrounding streets. His most important role is to enact the stabbing during the ceremony of the Tres Horas, "the Three Hours," on Good Friday. Longino is a white man. The black skin of the actor is entirely covered by a white piece of cloth. His walk looks like the insecure sliding of a drunken man: he moves with the help of a undisguised young man who directs him on

Figure 2.2. Longino with his spear, guided by a Roman soldier in front of the Monte del Calvario.

the right path. According to tradition, he is blind. He does not talk but murmurs incomprehensible sounds from time to time. He appears with the tropa on Good Friday but acts independently from them (see Figure 2.2). Although the New Testament does not say much about the anonymous Roman official who stabbed Christ, European medieval iconography as well as European religious folklore is rich in images of the Christ bleeding from the wound (Moreno 1982). The text of the Siete Palabras, "the Seven Words," supposedly said by Christ before he died on the cross, which are read by a Santo Varón during the ceremony of the *Tres Horas* on Good Friday (see thereunder), informs us about Longino: "The Centurion, to demonstrate that the Savior had passed away, and that unjust people would be saved, seized a spear and stabbed the divine chest, opening the flank. Christ began bleeding. The blindness of Longino lifted: his face was washed with the water from the wound and his eyes could see."[6]

Jesucristo and Barabbas

Some of the ceremonies involve only the presence of Jesus as a big wooden crucifix. Others, on Good Friday, require a living Christ. On that day, another character is also enacted: Barabbas, the Jewish prisoner who, according to the Bible, had been convicted for murder during an insurrection, and who is liberated by Pilate while Jesus is sent to crucifixion. Both Jesus and Barabbas are represented as whites by two young men. Their black skin and faces are entirely covered with a white piece of cloth. Barabbas' disguise differs from Jesus' in that it includes a series of long leaves on the tunic and on the head, while Jesus has only a crown of thorns, which is sometimes replaced, if no thorns are available, by a crown of leaves. The leaves on Barabbas' tunic, although of a different kind and in a lesser quantity, recall the leaves on the Jews' bodies (see below). Neither Jesus nor Barabbas talk. They are silent throughout their entire performance (see Figures 2.3 and 2.4).

It is important to note here that this way of representing white people—Jesus Christ, Barabbas, and Longino—by covering the black skin of the "white character" with white cloth is also used in the Afro-Esmeraldian festival of the Kings, or Epiphany, by the white *cucuruchos*—who represent white people who have come from a faraway land to visit the village.[7] The white cucuruchos—who, unlike Jesus, Barabbas, and Longino, talk—also cover their bodies, from the belt down, with hanging leaves (see Rahier 1991; 1994).

Los Judíos ("The Jews")

The Jews appear in a group of three or four on Holy Thursday and Good Friday. On Wednesday, during the Primera Tiniebla ceremony, only one of them is present. Semiotically, their masks evoke a sort of intersection between whiteness and savagery, humanity and bestiality, whites and demons. They are dressed in a shirt, long pants, and boots. Their faces are covered with a piece of cardboard with holes for the eyes and mouth. From the head to the ankle they are covered with a bell-shaped structure made of tagua (a sort of palm tree) and coco tree leaves, with the leaves secured around their waists with a cord. Like Longino, they need the help of a young man, who serves as a guide, to run back and forth very quickly in the church. During their presence in the church, they do not talk but emit loud sounds such as "Mhu, hu, hu," like some savage and strange beasts. Their appearance is frightening. They inevitably scare the children (see Figures 2.5 and 2.6).

While the covering of their faces with cardboard and the presence of leaves on their bodies recall the way the white cucuruchos of the Afro-Esmeraldian Festival of the Kings are represented, their loud and grave screams, as well as the leaves, also evoke another character of the same festival: *el mono*, the monkey. In the Festival of the Kings, the white cucuruchos represent white people coming from faraway places; the monkey represents the irruption of the undomesticated and powerful forces of nature into the village (see Rahier 1994). Remote origin and bestiality are two characteristics that stand out in the performances of the Judíos, as well as in interviews about them with Selva Alegreños. Their whiteness is indubitable. All the interviewees identified, without hesitation, the Jews as being "a kind of white people."

Figure 2.3. Jesus Christ carrying his cross during Good Friday procession, surrounded by Roman soldiers.

Figure 2.4. Barabbas during Good Friday procession.

BRIEF DESCRIPTIONS OF THE CELEBRATIONS

This is a brief summary of the major activities of each day of celebration in a chronological order.

Wednesday: La Primera Tiniebla ("The First Obscurity")

On Wednesday, the last migrants who traveled back for the celebrations arrive. Men go, for the last time until the following Monday, to their cultivated parcels of land in the forest to bring back plantains, a variety of roots, and fruits for their family meals (see also Speiser 1987: 45).

In the evening, around five o'clock, the tropa begins to parade in the streets of the village. After three peals of the bell, people show up around seven o'clock at the village's church to attend the ceremony called la Primera Tiniebla, "the First Obscurity." During Semana Santa, there are three "Obscurities:" the first one on Wednesday evening, the second one on Thursday evening, and the last one on Friday evening. The third Tiniebla is the only one the Bible actually mentions. It refers to the darkness that fell on Earth when Jesus was dying on the cross lasting from noon to three o'clock (see Matthew 28:45; Mark 16:33; Luke 24:44).

With the progressive arrival of the village population into the church (fewer people attend the Primera Tiniebla than the ceremonies on the following days), the public take seats on the benches installed parallel to the sides of the church. The church consists mainly of one big room. Women, who are more numerous, are ac-

Figure 2.5. A frontal view of a Jew in the church during the Tres Horas ceremony.

companied by their young children. Songs and prayers are performed by the Santos Varones, cantadoras, ''women singers,'' and rezanderas, ''women who lead prayers,'' on the cement steps leading to the altar. The altar, with the crucifix above, is at the far end of the church. The public in attendance responds to the can-

Figure 2.6. A view of the back side of a Jew running in the church during the
Tres Horas ceremony.

tadoras and rezanderas. Because the benches are placed along the sides of the
church, the central area is left available for the coming events and representations.
Here is where, during the prayer, the tropa enters and walks about, back and forth,
to the cadence ''One, two, one, two,'' of its chief. The tropa is looking for Christ.

After the recitation of fifteen Padre Nuestros and fifteen Ave Marías—one for each of the fourteen *estaciones*, ''stations of the Cross,'' and one for the altar—the light is turned off by a Santo Varón, immersing the room in total darkness.[8] Suddenly, a Jew begins to run around and round in the central area of the church, and a Santo Varón closes the door behind him. Two lines of Roman soldiers, one on each side, separate the public from the Jew, who utters loud and grave sounds: ''Mhu, hu, hu . . .'' The children, who know a Jew has entered the church, scream in fear. The rezanderas and the audience pray loudly (Padre Nuestros) to counter the Jew's demonic presence. In Afro-Esmeraldian contexts, Padre Nuestro and Ave María, as sacred texts, are sometimes used to combat the negative influence or presence of visiones and demons.

Twenty minutes later, once the prayers are over, the Jew leaves the church and the light is turned back on. There are more songs and prayers for ten more minutes, before the doors are opened and the ceremony is ended.

Thursday: Encerrar la Gloria ("To Seclude the Gloria")

Around 8:30 in the morning, after the third bell call, people arrive at the church to perform the Encerrar la Gloria ceremony. The tropa is formed and begins to patrol again, as it did the previous evening: it is still looking for Christ inside and outside the church. For around forty minutes, inside the church, the Santos Varones, the rezanderas and cantadoras with the rest of the audience recite various prayers: Padre Nuestros, Ave Marías, the Oration of Via Crucis. After the singing of a few songs, the Gloria is considered *encerrada*, ''closed or secluded.''

The closing of Gloria is followed by the performance of the fourteen stations of the Cross in front of the fourteen frames which hang on the church's walls, and which represent one station each. A Santo Varón reads a hand-written text, copied from a Catholic missionary, which describes the successive stations of the Cross. A young man from the tropa impersonates Jesus (he is not disguised) and carries a cross on his shoulder. At the appropriate station, where Jesus is said to have fallen, the young man falls and stays on the floor until he is told by the Santo Varón to stand up, and so on until the last station. The other soldiers of the tropa also participate, as Roman troops, in the reenactment of the stations' scenes (see Figure 2.7). This means that during the performance of the fourteen stations, they do not patrol, and the church is therefore much quieter than when they do.

After the fourteen stations, everyone goes back home. Around two o'clock in the afternoon, the fourteen stations are performed again in the church.

La Segunda Tiniebla ("The Second Obscurity")

Around seven o'clock in the evening, after the third bell call, Selva Alegreños come back to the church for the Segunda Tiniebla. Usually, the attendance for

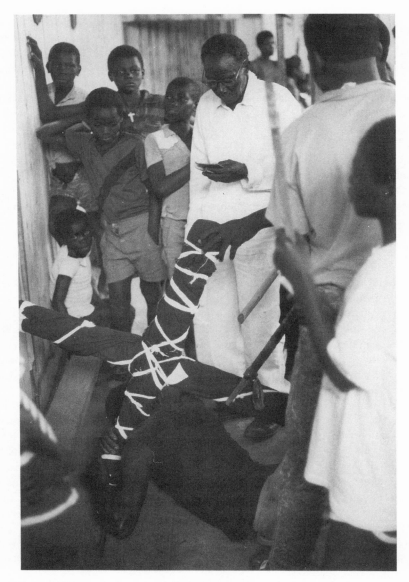

Figure 2.7. Jesus during one of the fourteen stations of the Cross in the church.
The old man dressed in white is a Santo Varón.

that ceremony is greater than the night before. The scenario of the tinieblas is
pretty much the same on all three days they are performed. The tropa patrols
with great noise. After the recitation of a few prayers and a few songs, the light
is again turned off, and this time three Jews begin to run around the central area

of the church, screaming loudly. Behind the two lines of Roman soldiers, the children react by screaming in fear. The rezanderas and the audience pray frantically. After about twenty minutes the light is turned back on, and the fourteen stations are performed anew. The Segunda Tiniebla ends with the recitation of the prayer called the "Twenty-four Pains," which lists the pains endured by Christ during the stations of the Cross. At around eight o'clock, everybody goes home for dinner.

El Alabado al Cristo ("The Alabado for Christ")

Around ten o'clock, people come back to the church to perform the *Alabado al Cristo*. Alabado is the name given to the funeral ritual performed for deceased adults. *Alabar* means "to praise" or "to laud." During the alabado the tropa does not patrol. The soldiers participate in the ritual, which consists mostly of singing. The alabado is supposed to last until dawn. Inevitably, some people—mostly young children and elders—fall asleep inside the church, where hammocks and blankets have been installed.

Around one o'clock in the morning, the tropa goes back to patrolling inside and outside the church. The tropa's noise usually attracts more people. The fourteen stations are performed again with the tropa participating, under the supervision of the Santos Varones. Once the estaciones are finished and after a few songs, the tropa proceeds under the leadership of its chief to *el levantamiento del Monte del Calvario*, "the raising of the Mount of Calvary." In Spanish, the term "monte" has two principal meanings; it can mean a "mount" (hill) or it can mean the "forest" (or "leaves"). In the Afro-Esmeraldian context of the Semana Santa, monte is understood in its second sense, "the forest and its numerous kinds of leaves." That is why, unlike in the Bible where the Mount of Calvary is described as a hill, Selva Alegreños represent the Monte del Calvario as a wall made of leaves, which they erect near the cement steps that lead to the altar inside the church. Here is where, on Good Friday, Jesus (the crucifix) and the two thieves will be hanging. After the levantamiento, which lasts for around an hour, songs are supposed to be sung until dawn. Very often, people get exhausted before dawn and go to sleep around four or five. When the alabado ends, the Santos Varones "steal" the body of Christ (the crucifix) and hide it in a house near the river.

Friday: El Crucifijo ("The Crucifix")

Good Friday is the most animated day of the Holy Week. The day begins with a set of performances called *El Crucifijo*, "the crucifix."

In the village school, a dozen women help two young men to dress: one as Christ and the other as Barabbas, who is also called *el Pícaro Fasineroso*, "the Uncontrollable Rascal." During the costuming, two tropas search noisily in the village for the Christ, who has disappeared since the night before. Then, Christ and Barabbas are found in the school. A procession begins with the women, Jesus and Barabbas, some Santos Varones and other villagers. Jesus carries his cross on his shoulder and performs the fourteen stations. The group goes progressively to the *malecón*, the street facing the river. There, the living Christ meets the crucifix, which had been stolen the night before by the Santos Varones.

After the meeting of the two Christs, the whole group—at that point almost the entire village—reforms in front of the church. There, the Santos Varones have installed a little table with a Bible. Passages of the Gospel are read by two Santos Varones. This is when the audience decides for the crucifixion of Christ and the freedom of Barabbas. As in the Bible, the same question is asked three times to the public by the Santo Varón who impersonates Pilate: "Whom do you want me to free: Jesus or Barabbas?" Three times the congregation responds: "Barabbas!" And when asked about the fate of Jesus, they respond: "*Crucifícalo!*," "Crucify him!" Then, in the midst of a great tumult, the tropa enters the church, where Christ is crucified. The living Christ and Barabbas undress, and attention now turns to the wooden crucifix.

The crucifixion of Christ consists of hanging the big wooden crucifix on the Monte del Calvario. The two thieves are crucified as well, one on each side of Jesus. Then, the estaciones are performed again. After the estaciones, everybody goes back home for lunch and rest before the ceremony of the *Tres Horas*, "the Three Hours," beginning around one o'clock.

Las Tres Horas ("The Three Hours")

The Tres Horas ceremony is also called Las Siete Palabras, "the seven words" that Jesus pronounced on the cross before expiring. The Tres Horas ceremony is the best attended and noisiest of all. When the people are assembled in the church, a Santo Varón reads the "Seven Words" from a board installed near the roof. He is therefore speaking from above, as if he were in the sky, in an off-stage voice. During the reading, the tropa continues patrolling tumultuously; Longino wanders around with his spear; four screaming Jews roam free in the center of the church, which seems to have been taken over by the ultimate chaos.

The Santo Varón reads: "The suffering of Jesus began at the first hour. Darkness invaded everything and the surroundings of the Cross became dense. There is absolute silence, one can only feel a profound withdrawal within weeping sadness . . . Now that the Mount of Calvary is surrounded, the noise and the jokes of the soldiers have stopped." (This is the *Primera Palabra*.) These sentences are said in the middle of a tremendous brouhaha.

Other passages of the "Seven Words" directly refer to the responsibility of the Jews for the crucifixion:

[Jesus] has been chased in the cities and in the country by the Jewish people with armed soldiers. (Primera Palabra).

The Jews have treated Him with extreme cruelty. They forced Him to carry on his shoulder the instrument of death. . . . Jews undressed Him in front of this aggressive people. This was the most excruciating pain for Jesus. This pain, He felt it through his entire sacred body. His wound is bleeding . . . (Segunda Palabra)

The pagans, the infidels, the Jews have blasphemed His sacred name. They have adored, paid tributes, honored false gods . . . Jesus predicted everywhere He went the example of His virtues, when the unfortunate Acaries was stoned to death by the Israelites. The sacred texts say that the entire population of Israel stoned Him . . . Even the children and the women participated in this barbaric punishment . . . Everyone who was involved in the stoning will have to experience the ultimate penalty in Hell. (Cuarta Palabra)

Crucify Him, crucify him screamed the Jewish people with enraged fervor . . . (Séptima Palabra)

At the end of each palabra, women behind the Monte del Calvario make sounds resembling the horn of a boat, like: "Boo, boo, boo . . ." with pieces of bamboo or rolls of newspapers placed on their mouths. At the end of the seventh palabra, when Christ expires, after Longino has pierced his flank, a din erupts from behind Mount Calvary: the women are now beating the cement steps with plates of zinc; a *camareta*, a big firecracker, explodes; rifles are fired in the air; and so on. This cacophony represents the earthquake that followed Christ's death. According to Matthew: "Then Jesus shouted again, dismissed his spirit, and died. And look! The curtain secluding the Holiest Place in the Temple was split apart from top to bottom; and the earth shook, and rocks broke, and tombs opened" (28: 50–52).

At this point, the Jews undress, and the tropa stays in the church for another performance of the fourteen stations of the cross. After the estaciones, everybody goes home. Around seven o'clock, the Tercera Tiniebla ceremony takes place, as on the night before. After the Tercera Tiniebla, the Jews disappear from the scene of the celebrations.

Alabado al Cristo ("Alabado for the Christ")

Around 10 o'clock, after the third bell call, people assemble in the church for the alabado of Good Friday. Like the alabado of the previous night, it consists of singing and praying. After midnight, the Santos Varones proceed to *desenclavar*, "to remove the nails from," the Christ. His body (the central part of the crucifix) is placed in a coffin laid on the cement steps. After more singing, a procession begins. It is led by the coffin, carried by the four Santos Varones. The coffin stops at every house in the village to collect a financial donation that will provide protection for the rest of the year. After the procession, the alabado inside the church continues. The soldiers of the tropa take the Monte del Calvario down, running out of the church with big branches and leaves. The singing continues until dawn.

Saturday: La Media Gloria ("The Half Gloria")

This ceremony is performed in the morning, around ten o'clock. It consists of praying and singing while the tropa parades back and forth in the church. The songs, unlike those of the previous days, are now accompanied by maracas (small dried squashes with little stones inside), *guazás* (identical to the maracas but from a piece of bamboo); and *cununos* and *bombos* (Afro-Esmeraldian percussion instruments). The joy and happiness that the instruments convey during the Media Gloria announce a joyful event: the resurrection of Christ on Sunday, domingo de Gloria, which will reopen access to the divino (see also Speiser 1987: 54). It lasts for around an hour. The rest of Saturday is dedicated to rest and preparation for the next and last day of celebration.

Sunday: La Gloria Entera ("The Entire Re-opening of Gloria")

Around ten o'clock in the morning, Selva Alegreños gather in the church for the last ceremony of Semana Santa: la Gloria Entera. Prayers, music, and songs are performed. The word "Gloria" can now be pronounced. Amidst the songs and music, the Santos Varones take the body of Christ out of the coffin, which had stayed in the church for the night, and dress him with a white robe, maintaining him straight, as if he were standing. After about an hour in the church, Gloria is said to be open and accessible again. Then the last procession begins in the main street of the village with the image of Christ first, followed by the statues of the three Marías, and the population of the village. Normal time has returned and the prohibitions of Holy Week have been put to an end. In the afternoon, a dance party with a disc jockey takes place in one of the houses of the village.

THE HIDDEN TRANSCRIPT

At first glance, it is obvious that the most visible objective of the Afro-Esmeraldian celebrations of Semana Santa is to reenact the Passion of Christ. However, if one wants to make sense of the way the liminal time of Semana Santa comes to be, the series of prohibitions that come along with it, the structure of the ceremonies, the semiotics of the masks, and the representations of Jews, one has no choice but to go beyond the Bible and take into consideration the various aspects of the local Afro-Esmeraldian perspective. The latter includes the traditional cosmology, the concept of the Devil, the position of Selva Alegre within the Ecuadorian racial/spatial order, the frequent travels between the village and surrounding towns and far away cities. The bestial and demonic appearances of the Judíos, for example, do not make sense except as an embodiment of the demons that come from faraway places and roam freely on earth when Gloria is secluded during Semana Santa time. Indeed, Afro-

Esmeraldian representations of Jews during Holy Week probably constitute the most challenging aspect of the celebrations to analyze. Some have walked away from the challenge. Miguel Ramos and Rafael Savoia, for instance, two Combonian[9] missionaries, published a book called *Semana Santa de las Comunidades Negras* (Ramos & Savoia 1993). This book mixes a selection of traditions of the Afro-Esmeraldian Holy Week with a variety of Semana Santa traditions from the Chota Valley[10]—which are, by the way, quite different. They make no reference whatsoever to the presence of masked characters representing the Judíos in Esmeraldas. Actually, their book/manual aims to teach Afro-Ecuadorian community leaders how to ''properly'' celebrate Semana Santa, by correcting ''wrong ways.'' I suspect that the silence about the Judíos is the consequence of the unease that the authors must have felt when witnessing these powerful and quite caricatured representations of demonic Jews. The Judíos must have reminded them of the anti-Semitism of medieval, Christian Europe. They certainly feel that these anti-Semitic representations should be suppressed.

If one adopts an outsider's perspective when reading the text of Semana Santa in Selva Alegre, the celebrations appear as a sometimes strange reenactment of the Passion of Christ; nothing more. If, on the contrary, one is interested in trying to discover the meanings they have for the people involved, it is necessary to adopt, or approximate, a local perspective. This viewpoint sees Semana Santa as an opportunity for the local community to reassert its worldview in opposition to the dominant discourses of (urban and white-mestizo) Ecuadorian society. In this worldview, stories about the Devil are central to the construction of local identity in contrast to the white and white-mestizo Other.

The spatial categories at work in the celebrations are various. The domain of the divino is closed, demons and spirits are free to travel and to act; and within the domain of the humano, there is a clear opposition between the village community and the rest of the world. That opposition, which exists all year long, is at the center of what the hidden transcript actually says. As Quiroga writes for Muisne, ''[spaces outside the local community] are areas where people have experienced uncontrollable forces, and are accordingly feared. Narratives about these beings and the spaces in which they often appear act as powerful moral statements and mediate oppositions such as local/foreign, Christian/wild, domestic livelihood/capitalist economy, female/male . . . Satan is associated with untamed nature, and syntagmatically related to the *tunda, riviel, brujas* and other *visiones*'' (Quiroga 1994: 143). The Devil is also particularly associated with cities, which are, from the local perspective, ''alienating, confusing, exploitative yet exciting and alluring places'' (ibid.). The Devil is said to own cities, where he takes people with whom he has signed a pact. It is in cities that most of the money, so necessary to participate in the market economy, is found. Socioeconomic and political powers are located in cities, where white and white-mestizo people rule. It is from cities that technological change comes. It is in cities that intrusions of the capitalist system are planned (shrimp cultures and sawmills), which fragment the domestic economy and modify the social order. There are many stories about the apparition of Satan in urban contexts. Many Afro-Esmeraldians believe that wealth cannot be acquired except by making a pact with the Devil (See García 1988).[11]

All the characters of the Semana Santa—Barabbas, Longino, the tropa, the Jews, Pilate, and Jesus—are outsiders. They are mythical beings, from faraway places, who are able to visit the village, like the sirenas, because of the closing of Gloria. With the exception of Jesus, who obviously has a special, positive status within this outsiderness, the other characters are fundamentally negative. They all bear some responsibility for the suffering of Jesus during his Passion and crucifixion. After the Semana Santa of 1990, a Selva Alegreño man in his early forties confided in me that:

These festivities of Semana Santa are nice. They are very animated. Everything that is done comes directly from the Bible. I like Semana Santa because it gives the opportunity to see that those who say that black people are the worst of all are lying! Because one can see in the ceremonies, and also in the Bible, that all of the atrocities that were done to Jesus were not perpetrated by blacks. We black people, we were not there! This is a story of demons that occurred a long time ago among white people. The Jews, who are white, were the worst of all. But the Romans also participated. This story in the Bible about the death of Christ is a story of demons.

If Satan, as the ruler of Hell, is syntagmatically related to the various demons and visiones whom one might encounter while traveling in the forest, he is then related to the worst of all, the Judíos, who have put Jesus to death. This association made by Afro-Esmeraldians between Semana Santa characters and demonic forces, makes sense when considered within the liminal time of the celebrations: Satan has virtually no opposition from Thursday through Sunday, and the forces he controls are free to roam and become visible. I argue that the Judíos, above and beyond representing the people who killed the Christ, are also a metonym—as the most brutal and demonic of all humans—for urban, white, and white-mestizo elites. Whites and white-mestizos are, from the perspective of Selva Alegre, urban Others with social, economic, and political power.

Michael Taussig (1980) has shown how, in South America, dominant discourses have constructed the Other—especially the black Other—as a master of black magic, a victim of old traditions that maintain him in a state of savagery, close to the forces of nature among which he lives, and with special connections to dark, that is, demonic, powers. The Afro-Esmeraldian Semana Santa, and most particularly its representations of Judíos, inverts the hegemonic discourse of otherness in which blacks are associated with the Devil. Afro-Esmeraldians identify evil forces with the white people who killed Christ (and rule the cities). The Devil is mostly active in places where they themselves have little control, and which are far from the village. Quiroga wrote the following about the use of the Devil in counterhegemonic discourses of otherness:

Although indigenous and black people have to some extent accepted, and in a few cases profited from the dominant discourse that attributes to them the power of healing by making a pact with the Devil, they also question and invert these associations. Through narratives about Satan people recognize the entropic aspects that accompany the expansion of the white man's economic and political system. In these narratives, the metonymic associations linking God, order, whiteness, cities and civilization are rejected. (Quiroga 1994: 152)

The Afro-Esmeraldian Semana Santa and its expression of black resistance to the racial/spatial order celebrates, oppositionally, a local point of view and metonymic associations linking God, order, blackness, village, and traditions. In effect, the representations of demonic Jewishness contrast strikingly with the respectable "presence" of blackness. The nondisguised population of the village provides a good illustration of the respectable and orderly quality that blackness has on the ceremonial scene. Unlike the actors directly engaged in the reenactment performances, the audience respects the prohibitions against running, noise, quick gestures, etc. In church and during processions, their body movements express restraint. They pray and sing religiously, while the tropa patrols tumultuously and the Judíos run around screaming. To counter the negative presence of the Jews, the villagers invoke the domain of the divino—despite its closure— with the magic words of Padre Nuestros. Their dignified behavior, respectful of traditions, is juxtaposed with the exuberance of the Judíos and the tropa. Except for Christ's trial, when Pilate asks the audience whom he should set free, Barabbas or Jesus, and the audience responds "Barabbas!" and demands the crucifixion of Christ, the villagers do not participate in the performances of reenactment. Their disciplined involvement in the prayers, songs, and processions occurs on a plane other than that of the reenactment of Christ's Passion. When asked about the responses of "Crucify him!" by the village population during Christ's trial, various women told me that *A este momento, nosotros hacemos como si eramos los mismos Judíos*, "At that particular moment, we act as if we were the Jews." This brief and unique participation in one of the reenactment performances is made as surrogate Jews, not as blacks.

The presence of the Santos Varones on the scene of the performances also denotes the respectability of blackness and respect for traditions. Their behavior follows the Semana Santa prohibitions; they are calm and sober. They organize the various ceremonies efficiently and cautiously manipulate the sacred images of Christ and the Three Marías. With the exception of the Santo Varón, who (calmly) impersonates Pilate[12] during the reenactment of the trial in front of the church, their presence is on the same plane as the audience. Their participation in the performances of reenactment is limited to reading sacred texts. They sometimes ask the audience to pray or sing. They are the celebrations' specialists. Their prestige in the community comes from their age: they are seen as knowledgeable about the Bible and the Semana Santa traditions. Indeed, Afro-

Esmeraldian Semana Santa celebrates the metonymic associations linking God, order, blackness, village, and traditions.

A distinction must be made between Jesus and the other actors involved in the reenactment plays. Barabbas, Longino, the tropa, and the Jews all break the prohibitions against running, screaming loudly, making quick movements, and so on. Jesus, in contrast, acts with humility. Unlike Barabbas, who during the procession of Good Friday dances and sometimes behaves erratically, Jesus moves slowly, he does not dance, and his behavior is predictable; he endures pains, falls with the cross on his shoulder, etcetera. This behavioral opposition is, in many ways, the expression of a more profound dichotomy between the divino and the demonic. Disrespect for traditional prohibitions mark Barabbas, Longino, the tropa and the Judíos as demonic beings, who do not respect the rules. This separation of Jesus, who was Jewish, from the rest of the Judíos has been made by the Roman Catholic Church since the beginning of its history; its more or less official anti-semitism never included Jesus.

The demonic quality of Barabbas, Longino, the Romans and the Jews is also apparent in their disguises, which significantly include leaves. In Selva Alegre's Semana Santa, just as it is the case in the Afro-Esmeraldian Festival of the Kings, leaves appear to point to either undomesticated animality or to a demonic quality, as well as to suggest a faraway geographic origin. The leaves of the Monte del Calvario, which serve as background for the crucifixion, also evoke demons (non-*divino* forces) and animality. I suggest that the more leaves a particular character has, the more distant his geographic origin and the less ''human'' or more demonic he is. The greatest contrast in this regard is provided by Jesus and the Jews. While Jesus is absolutely deprived of leaves—his crown of leaves stands for a crown of thorns—the Jews are entirely covered with them.

Thus, Jesus—the physical manifestation of God—is metonymically linked to the Selva Alegreños by his demeanor, in contradistinction to the Jews and their symbolic representation of whites.

Isidoro Moreno (this volume; and 1997) has shown how, by the end of the sixteenth century, black Sevillians organized in brotherhoods to celebrate Semana Santa and other religious festivities insulted whites who were opposed to their participation in the Holy Week processions by calling them ''Jews.'' Moreno writes:

The qualificative of *judío*, that is to say ''recently converted,'' was perhaps the most demeaning one that could be addressed to people who considered themselves members of the most important [white] brotherhoods, and who publicly displayed with pride their old Christian and aristocratic heritage, and the purity of their blood. It is for that very reason that it was used by black men and women to return the offensive insults they were receiving from Spaniards during Holy Week. . . . In the short play *Los negros*, the owner of Dominga [a slave woman] ridicules her because of the color of her skin, saying that she looks like ''the tunic of solitude,'' to which she responds ''at least we are not the Jews who led Christ to his Passion.'' (Moreno 1997: 85)

Afro-Esmeraldian Semana Santa is, to use the definition given by Frank Manning, a "celebration," because it involves both "play"—"proclivity to transform and transcend the structural arrangements, behavioral requisite, and normative principles that prevail in ordinary situations" (Manning 1983: 20)— and "ritual"—which aims to replicate and reinforce hierarchies of ordinary reality (Manning 1983: 20–27). Afro-Esmeraldian Holy Week's playful qualities are at work in challenging and reversing the Ecuadorian racial/spatial order. At the local level, however, the celebrations also validate the ordinary hierarchy and specialization of gender roles. In traditional Afro-Esmeraldian contexts, women are mostly responsible for the domestic space (the house, meals, children, help on parcels, etc.) while men, who usually control the finances of the household, are more geographically as well as sexually mobile (see Whitten 1974; Rahier 1994). Although women are very much involved in the Holy Week celebrations, their role in the organization of the celebrations and in the reenactment performances is nonetheless a subaltern one. They sing and pray in the church, they accompany the various processions along with children and men, they make noise behind the Monte del Calvario, they dress Jesus and the Pícaro on Good Friday. In contrast, all the actors involved in the reenactment performances are men. In 1990, a seventy-five-year-old woman—particularly interested in Semana Santa—accompanied the Santos Varones in every step of the celebration, helping as much as she could. After the reopening of Gloria on Sunday afternoon, I asked the Santos Varones if she could be considered as being one of them; they all responded negatively: *No puede ser! Una mujer no puede ser Santo Varón, pués!*, "It's impossible! A woman cannot be a Santo Varón!" Their response illustrates the dominant perspective of the patriarchal community. Women, seen by men as inferior, are also said to share a sort of essence that gives them a particular spiritual and supernatural quality. They are sometimes associated with Satan in specific narratives about visiones: the tunda, the sirenas, the brujas, the *tacona* are all female. However, as Quiroga wrote, "the Devil [is] a polysemic and paradoxical figure [which] is associated with femininity in different ways. In some narratives femininity is related to the virginal domestic economy and its resistance to the penetration of the external male capitalist system" (Quiroga 1994: 146). Accordingly, women are seen as possessing the power to resist the Devil: *el diablo con la mujer no quiere fiesta*, "the Devil does not want to party with women." "The Devil [. . .] never makes pacts with women and frequently women help men get rid of the Devil after they have made pacts" (Quiroga 1994: 147). In fact, the various stories told about the anti-Satan power of women question "male authority, wealth accumulation, and power which are based on the greater articulation with the capitalist sector. Capitalist development in the area has meant new opportunities for some men who have accumulated money and power. Most women, by contrast, have been deprived of a livelihood and a source of income as a result of the ecological changes and the biases brought by the recent political-economic transformations" (Quiroga 1994: 147). Perhaps, the nonparticipation of women as disguised actors in the reenactment performances should be interpreted in light of these narratives about women and the Devil. The maleness of Satan and his world demands that only men impersonate the demons who are visiting the village.

CONCLUSIONS

The various aspects of the Afro-Esmeraldian Semana Santa in the village of Selva Alegre become intelligible when situated within national, provincial, and local contexts. At the national and provincial levels blacks are seen by whites, white-mestizos, and white-mulattos as occupying the lowest position in the racial/spatial order, a people deprived of culture who live in rural areas close to nature and demonic forces. However, at the local level—black village and black region[13]—the hidden transcript of Afro-Esmeraldian Semana Santa rejects the premises of the dominant discourse by inverting the racial/spatial order, putting it on its head, as it were. In a locally centered perspective, whites and white-mestizos who live in faraway cities are demonized, their relationship to Satan underlined, while blackness and local cultural traditions are oppositionally presented as respectable, with God on their side. Evidently, the racial politics of the hidden transcript of Selva Alegre's Semana Santa is embedded within spatial dimensions. Spatial structures are central to Afro-Esmeraldian Holy Week.

The distinction between "presence" and "representations" allowed the inclusion into the analysis of the immediate contexts of the ceremonies and the spatial dimensions within which they are inscribed. That distinction permitted as well the consideration of the various performative planes of the celebrations: the performances of the disguised actors versus the presence of the audience. The space/time liminality of plays, rituals, and celebrations is too often thought of—in a simplistic way—as existing only in its opposition to the "normal" time of daily life. As this chapter suggests, liminality may consist of a multiplicity of levels within which specific performances and presence(s) take place.

NOTES

Many thanks to Peter Sutherland and Daniel Weir for suggesting changes after reading an earlier version of this chapter.

1. Fieldwork was conducted in Selva Alegre during the Semana Santa celebrations of 1989, 1990, and 1991.

2. See the film *The Longest Hatred: The History of Anti-Semitism*, part 1 ("From the Cross to the Swastika"), Films for the Humanities & Sciences, Corporation for Public Broadcasting, n.d.

3. Demographic estimations about the racial and ethnic composition of the Ecuadorian population vary quite a lot. National censuses do not inquire properly about racial and ethnic identity. Here is the estimation I work with: of 10 million Ecuadorians, around 5 percent are Afro-Ecuadorians, around 40 percent are indigenous people, around 50 percent are mestizos and white-mestizos, and around 5 percent are whites. The term

"white-mestizo" is very much in use in Ecuadorian society and among social scientists. The people called "mestizos" tend to have darker skin than the white-mestizos and usually present physical features that clearly indicate indigenous ancestry. Most of the white-mestizos are included in the local middle classes and in the national elite of entrepreneurs.

4. In canoes on the river. There are no roads that reach Selva Alegre; see Figure 2.1.

5. See videos of the Centro Cultural Afro-Ecadoriano, in Quito.

6. All translations are mine unless indicated otherwise. The text of the *Siete Palabras* has been hand copied from a missionary.

7. In the Festival of the Kings, which takes place from January 6 through January 8, the white cucuruchos can have their heads covered either with a white cloth or, when no cloth is available, with a piece of cardboard.

8. The village of Selva Alegre has a small generator that is mainly used during festive days (Christmas, saints' days, Semana Santa, etc.). Every household head contributes financially to the purchase of fuel.

9. The Combonians are an Italian religious order.

10. The other black region of Ecuador, in the northern Andes.

11. See the *Cuadernos Afro-Ecuadrianos*, published by the Grupo Afro-Ecuatoriano during the 1980s.

12. According to the New Testament, Pilate did not want to crucify Jesus; the Jewish people—under the influence of their priests—did.

13. All the villages on the banks of the Santiago River have an exclusively black population.

3

Re-/Presenting Black Female Identity in Brazil: "Filhas d'Oxum" in Bahia Carnival

Carole Boyce Davies

Popular representations of black women in Brazilian Carnival are of hypersexuality, nakedness, and a certain exoticism linked to sex-tourism. These representations simultaneously make "Carnival in Brazil" synonymous with Rio's carnival of tourism. Thus two distortions are reproduced, both of which encode race and gender in very specific ways. These stereotyped representations of women and of carnival, marketed internationally, run counter to the complexity of black women's actual participation in Rio Carnival itself as well as that of the rest of Brazil and of Salvador-Bahia in particular, where this study is located.

Of particular relevance to this paper is the way these distortions erase African-oriented Carnival. Thus the construction of a hyper-tourist-driven Rio Carnival, similarly fails to delineate sufficiently the *escolas de samba* and *blocos-Afro* of Rio de Janeiro itself. Myrian Sepúlveda dos Santos in her paper in this collection, "Samba Schools: The Logic of Orgy and Blackness in Rio de Janeiro," delineates some of the inner structures of the Rio samba schools. These, I am asserting, often use the carnival occasion to make political statements in theme, music, and costuming about the condition of Afro-Brazilians—particularly their racial, social, and economic locations within the larger Brazilian state. Robert Stam (1988, 1989) challenges Roberto DaMatta's reading of a flattened Carnival in which race, gender and a host of identities are of little consequence in the context of Carnival (1991). Rather, Stam asserts that there are various carnivals and that racial politics are often squarely and deliberately located in Brazilian Carnival.

The actual source from which much of (Afro)Brazilian culture emanates, the northeast, is perhaps the most exploited culturally in the context of Rio-tourist

Carnival constructions as it is simultaneously erased. The largely black north-eastern region of Brazil, and principally Bahia, continues to generate cultural practices and forms that then influence the rest of Brazilian artistic life, particularly at the performative level. An interesting discussion of Afro-Bahia Carnival in this context is Christopher Dunn's "Afro-Bahian Carnival: A Stage for Protest" (1992), which describes well some of the history of *blocos-afro*, particularly Ilê Aiyê (founded in 1974) and Olodum (1979). Black working class in orientation, these blocos-afro were "not the occasion for ritual inversion of social roles for these participants," Dunn asserts, "but rather an opportunity for young Afro-Brazilians to affirm their racial and ethnic identities" (12).

In history and orientation, the blocos-afro offer re-interpretations of pan-Africanist politics in order to challenge racist exclusions of Afro-Brazilians from Brazilian economic and social structures. They simultaneously establish another set of identifications with particular African diaspora locations selected for their histories of resistance to domination. Thus, Haiti with its history is particularly evocative, as are Cuba, South Africa, the United States, and a number of other selected African-diaspora locations. On the carnival fabric of Ilê Aiyê for 1994, for example is the caption "Black America, The African Dream" (*America Negra O Sonho Africano*) with imprinted photographs of Malcolm X, Fannie Lou Hamer, Marcus Garvey, Martin Luther King, Jr., as well as Vôvô, one of the founders and present leader of the group, and Mae Hilda, its spiritual mother. An African map occupies the center of the design and above it is an African mask with the name Ilê Aiyê. Thus in terms of music, lyrics of songs, the use of textiles, dance, the ritual of Carnival itself, blocos Afro in Bahia and other aspects of Bahia Carnival, re-/present African history in the Americas, make specific political connections, and educate as they entertain.

Antonio Risério's *Carnaval Ijexa* (1981) uses the word *reafricanização* ("reafricanization") to describe, from the 1970s on, an entire process of deliberate re-africanization of Afro-Brazilian culture. Still, this word "reafricanization" to many activist Brazilians suggests that Afro-Brazilians had lost some sort of static African culture. Many would like to see instead an understanding of a dynamic set of reinterpretations of African culture in Afro-Brazilian history, particularly when forms like *candomble*[1] consistently infuse Afro-Brazilian culture and indirectly much of the larger Brazilian society. Still, I find Risério's book a helpful presentation of the range of contemporary Afro-Brazilian carnival forms and their various connections and contexts. Absent from Risério's book is any information on the question of gender in Carnival. His primary interest as his title suggests is the Yoruba (Ijexá)-derived Carnival forms which he sees as Afro-Bahian carnival.

This paper addresses some of these issues as it explores questions of gender and the performative, memory, ritual, cultural re-invention in the context of festival traditions in African diaspora culture. It is linked, in a way, to an earlier paper, "Black Bodies, Carnivalized Bodies" (1994), in which I examined the multilayered representation of women at the level of body and space. This specific study is based on an *afoxé* (traditional Carnival group), Filhas d'Oxum in Bahia Carnival. Filhas d'Oxum is a new, 1990s-style, all-female afoxé that has as a specific intent the re-/presentation of black female identity in Brazilian culture. The execution of their carnival presentation challenges the popular stereotypic, exotic representations of women by putting in its place a carnival of beauty and joy in femininity that emanates from the orisha (goddess in some understandings) Oxum (Oshun) as she is interpreted in Afro-Brazilian (Yoruba) orisha tradition. I will therefore examine the larger context of the afoxé in carnival in Bahia and then talk about the re-/presentation of women in Carnival via this particular group and then conclude by describing my own research process and the meaning of the performative aspects of this group as it relates to the claiming of public ritual space for Afro-Brazilian cultures and people.

AFO/ṢE: MAKING IT HAPPEN

Afo/ṣe in Yoruba literally means "I command it and it happens." It refers to that which is said that can achieve actuality. It is the power of the word; it refers then to the power that is used in certain forms of speech that causes something to happen. In other words, it is the spoken force of *ashé*—the power to be.[2] I define ashé as moving "across two large discursive fields: that of spirituality and that of creativity. With its meaning and associations of what it is to be human in the world, questions of existence, the power to be, the dynamic force in all things."

In *Carnaval Ijexá. Notas Sobre Afoxés e Blocos de Novo Carnaval Afro-baiano*, Risério (1981) cites Olabiyi Yai, a Yoruba scholar of oral literature similarly on this point. Yai conjectures on the assignment of the name that the early Afrocarnival groups perhaps exchanged magical incantations between them and that gradually the word "afoxé" passed into popular usage as a definition of Afrocarnival groups in Brazil (12). Thus, while afo/ṣe in Yoruba means the spoken power in ashé, in Afro-Brazilian culture a very particular transformation has taken place—linguistic and cultural—which expresses well the process of Afro-diaspora transformation (Boyce Davies 1996). In this particular case, afoxé has literally moved out of the specific linguistic history of its Yoruba origins, principally the level of the incantatory (word) into the area of the performative (body). And, in the contemporary period, there exists another level of meaning in Yoruba language contributed by Afro-Brazilians, which allows afoxé to become the general descriptor of traditional Afro-Brazilian carnival. Relationally, afoxé thus now occupies a position in terms of Carnival history, roughly equivalent to "oldtime carnival" or "traditional masquerade," in the Caribbean, for example.

Afoxé in Bahia, Brazil, is the name given to a particular type of carnival band that occupies an intermediate space between the popular blocos-Afro and ritual candomblé. The *Dicionario de Cultos Afro-Brasileiros* (1977) defines afoxé as "*Rancho negro que sai durante o Carnaval, na Bahia. E festa semi-religiosa, realizada como uma obrigação por elementos de certos candomblés''* (40). [Black group of revelers which parades during Bahia Carnival. A semireligious festival realized as an obligation in certain Candomblé entities] (my translation). According to Daniel Crowley in *Bahian Carnival* (1984), an afoxé is "the unique *grêmio* of Salvador, traditionally recruited from Candomblé houses with costumes derived from India, Africa or Brazilian history, accompanied by chants, a drum *bateria* playing distinctive slow rhythms and *alegoria* floats representing African or Asian subjects" (20). He goes on to identify, in 1983, twenty-three afoxés with Filhos de Gandhi, founded in 1949, being one of the oldest of this group. This proliferation, in his view, seemed to signify a rebirth of earlier afoxés such as Filhos de Oba, Lordes Africanos, Congos da Africa. Other precursors of the contemporary afoxés include: Reis do Congo, Embaixada Africana and Pandegos da Africa (Gudolle Cacciatore 1977); Pierre Verger's *Retratos da Bahia 1946 a 1952* (1990) shows photos of *Filhos de Oba* (Plate 121) and Filhos de Congo (Plates 117–120), and *Embaixada Mexicana* (Plate 116), which resembles Trinidad's traditional Robber Mas in costume.

It is impossible, however, to discuss afoxé in Bahia without some extended consideration of perhaps its most important exponent—Filhos de Gandhi (Sons of Gandhi). The group itself has produced its own text, *Filhos de Gandhi. A História de um afoxé* (Felix 1987), which is based on oral histories, memories, and conversations with some of its principal participants and some early photographs.

In one of the few available studies, "O afoxé Filhos de Gandhi pede paz" (The Afoxé Filhos de Gandhi Asks for Peace), Antonio Morales (1988) expresses what many Afro-Brazilian activists and scholars have identified—a pattern of resistance that includes the various sisterhoods and brotherhoods (such as Irmandade da Boa Morte and Filhos de Gandhi), Candomblés and Quilombos.

Filhos de Gandhi was formed by a group of stevedores as a direct response to the assassination of Mahatma Gandhi in 1948. According to Morales they were described as follows: "*Um grupo de pessoas de estiva, categoria profissional predominantemente negra, muito ligado ao candomblé decidíu levar a público a sua religião, certamente como forma de afirmação étnica*" (269) [A group of stevedores, linked to candomblé, decided to make public their religion as a form of ethnic affirmation]. For them, Gandhi because of his association with peace, his use of white, carried the energy of Oxalá of the Afro-Brazilian Yoruba orixá cosmology who is also identified as the principle of peace. Thus the group in its origin made a variety of statements of resistance: First, since candomblé was persecuted tremendously during that time and not allowed to make public representations, their adoption of the energy of Gandhi allowed them a public presence that confronted the racist authority that was denying their existence; second, it was an affirmation of life and Afro-Brazilian presence; third, it effected an intersection of two major diaspora, Indian and African, in the representation of Gandhi as the spiritual figure who carried the group's name; fourth, it allowed a group of working-class men public space. It is important that these men were stevedores, as this gave them access to receiving information from outside the country and to utilizing their links with the exterior, international community for the benefit of the internal, local Afro-Brazilian community.

The link between afoxé and candomblé was therefore significantly rearticulated in the existence of the early Filhos de Gandhi. Interviews with the founders of the group identify this connection deliberately. Humberto Ferreira in interview with Morales (1988) says the following: *"O candomblé era uma religião perseguida pelas autoridades e nós quando fundamos o Gandhi, tentamos demonstrar que saímos pacificamente. Por isso resolveu-se adotar o nome de Gandhi que era o precursor da paz no mundo"* (269). [Candomblé was a religion persecuted by the authorities and when we founded Gandhi, we were trying to demonstrate that we were parading peacefully. For this we resolved to adopt the name of Gandhi who was a precursor of peace in the world] (my translation).

The fact that the Catholic church which consistently seeks to deny and suppress Afro-Brazilian spirituality called them a *bloco de feticeiros* (a group of wizards) or *Candomblezeiros* (Candomble worshippers) makes the point. And true, the group marched (and continue to march) the streets chanting various ritual Yoruba songs and chants under the slogan of peace and dressed in the color of peace associated with Oxalá (see Figure 3.1). Crowley (1984) identifies the link between afoxés and candomblé houses in the way in which "the theme song of Filhos attempts to integrate Gandhi into the cult hierarchy in 'Salutation to Oxalá,' the Orixa of African divinity who represents God the Father" (24). Significantly as well, a number of *paes de santos* (Candomble leaders) consistently participate/d in *Filhos de Gandhi* from its origin and a specific link with one of the oldest houses *ile axé apo afonja* has been identified.

Today the group continues to be oriented to peace so much so that in some views it maintains a very conservative presence as distinct from the overt racial politics of the *blocos-Afro*. But Filhos de Gandhi is the largest of the groups, and they constitute a stream of white flowing for miles down the streets of Bahia when they parade for Carnival. They continue to make powerful public appearances at important ritual and public events like the *lavagem de Bonfim*, (the ritual washing of the steps of the Church at Bonfim) and the popular *Festa de Yemanja* (celebration of the Orixa Yemanja) in Rio Vermelho and a variety of other festive and popular events—particularly Carnival, where full numbers are represented.

The group remains exclusively male. Thus the question of gender in afoxé becomes important. While some of the afoxés tend to incorporate both men and women, Filhos de Gandhi is principally a brotherhood.[3] Women affiliated to the men of the group had at one point formed a female parallel called Filhas de Gandhi (Daughters of Gandhi) which "chose as subject the local ritual of washing the steps of Bonfim Pilgrimage which takes place in early February in a Salvador suburb with no reference at all to India or Gandhi beyond their name"

Figure 3.1. Filho de Gandhi member in costume.

(Crowley 1984). This is the first gendered reference to an all women's identification of an afoxé. It is important to assert here, as well, that the masculinist
orientation of afoxé as represented in Filhos de Gandhi tended to relocate women
to the periphery which they are not in candomblé ritual. Since Filhas de Gandhi
arose as a group affiliated to them, they were therefore seen by some in the
community as principally the women of members of Filhos de Gandhi.

Some of this tendency has carried over in some ways to Filhas d'Oxum (Daughters of Oxum) which some see as a new version of Filhos de Gandhi. This is aided by the fact that the primary organizer of Filhas d'Oxum, Rosangela Guimares, is the wife of the current leader of the Filhos de Gandhi. My research reveals, however, that while there are close links in terms of history, origin, and the expectation of support from the men; there are clear differences in the nature of the groups, which I will delineate later. My first encounter with Rosangela was in the headquarters of Filhos de Gandhi.[4] She made a point of telling me that the group had acquired its own house, which was being renovated, and that she hoped to have office space included—with modern equipment—in order to manage the group's interests. Thus, separate space was the first and most significant aspect of the group's negotiation of identity. One of the primary interests she indicated was caring for the security of women during carnival. Filhas d'Oxum, she indicated, was open to all women of whatever racial identification or designation since ''all women suffer and often do not have the space they need to become the best they can be.'' And, I observed later, in the context of Carnival, that it is with security, that the support of the men is expected. She added though that the group wanted to amplify the condition of black people in Brazil. She wanted to see beauty, joy, life, which is the true energy of Oxum, triumph over adversity.

Thus, in politics and orientation, while there were initial assistance from the brothers, Rosangela was clear about not being identified as a female component of Gandhi and was very articulate about the possibilities of women in society and their right to realize their dreams. Clearly with its name and its identification with the Afro-Brazilian orixá of Yoruba derivation, Oxum, a specifically female orientation, linked to beauty, fertility, female power, wealth, and bounty, this group makes a more direct and public connection than Filhos de Gandhi could have, by naming itself in 1990s context with the name Filhas d'Oxum (see Badejo 1996). For one thing, it reinscribed the importance of the orisha tradition in a public way and removes itself at the level of the *performance of its name* from the male Gandhi. Further, by claiming itself as an all-woman afoxé, it makes a statement of women counterorganizing in contexts of male exclusivity.[5]

TRANSFORMING THE REPRESENTATION OF WOMEN IN BRAZILIAN CARNIVAL

As I have argued, the popular constructions of Afro-Brazilian women by the dominant society, especially in the context of tourism and Rio Carnival, locate a specific construction of women as the most visible. Thus in the context of nakedness, sex and hyperexoticism, a specific type of woman is held aloft and the majority reduced to a mass of undifferentiated dancers. The distinctions that Carnival in Salvador da Bahia presents along the order of a reconstituted African identity become significant when the question of female identity is accounted for as is done in the case of Filhas d'Oxum. For one thing, Bahia Carnival is not as much for spectators as it is a participatory event. In this instance, women reclaim the space of ritual for political statements that critique dominant discourse of gender, race, sexuality.

Bahia carnival and festival traditions are rich with resonance and iconography, directly traceable to African, particularly ancient Benin (Nago-Yoruba and Angolan) forms. Blocos-Afro such as Ilê Aiyê (birthplace/roots) and Olodum (the overarching orisha) in their names, patterns, rituals, musical rhythms, carnival themes, relationship to community, activism maintain this political, historical, and aesthetic relationship with Africa. For example, each of the blocos-Afro begin their Carnival parading with a ritual offering to Exu-Elegbara, the orisha of the crossing, of openings, of pathways, of chance (luck or ill fate). A series of other offerings are designed to open the pathway and protect the passage through the Carnival. Ilê Aiyê's in particular has as its spiritual mother—Mae Hilda—who is a *mãe de santo* in her own right and functions as a kind of spiritual guide and organizing presence for the important decisions the group makes. Both Ilê Aiyê and Olodum have created an active community presence, in terms of education, art, music, dance, working with homeless children, and creating employment.

Afoxés like Filhos de Ghandi and Filhas d'Oxum, provide an even closer integration of the questions of spirituality with community activism. Generally involved in community work, afoxés tend to have more direct links with practices of candomblé in terms of rituals, intent, music. According to Daniel Crowley (1984), while the afoxés and blocos-Afro are "directly concerned with Africa and its presence in Brazil," the afoxés often have a closer relationship with Candomblé houses. Some afoxé members he continues "actually participate in Carnival as the fulfillment of a religious vow," and therefore sometimes in fulfilling some obligation of service to the community.

The intersection of spirit work/community work in which the healing of the community is prominent replays some of the traditional meanings of ritual. *Filhas d'Oxum*'s self-image is not only as a Carnival group, but an organization of community women, with a mission to feed the community and provide a sense of well-being as far as women desiring things of beauty as well as women's representation is concerned. For example, it has an active community program of feeding the community one day a week and is otherwise involved in issues of poverty in the surrounding neighborhood. Rosangela Guimares, its leader, I discovered, often uses her own money to provide food if funds are not available.

The honoring of Oxum, the goddess of fresh waters, is its central purpose. But this honoring, given the representations of Oxum, the elements she is assigned in this cosmology, is related to a larger set of meanings about female identity and power. Deidre Badejo develops some of these ideas in her book *Òsun seegesi* as far as the community relationship is concerned in the Òsun festival in Òsogbo in Western Nigeria. As such, in presentation, *Filhas d'Oxum* becomes almost a mobile version of the same logic of the *terreiro* (the sacred community space in which Candomblé is practiced and lived) and from another angle is a mini-Oxum festival within the Carnival. This climaxes in the Filhas final dispatch, which occurs the Thursday after Carnival when the group meets in Piata (a beach community about ten miles from the city of Bahia) and then parades through the streets to Lake Abaete, a lake of white sand and warm water, which was traditionally a place of washerwomen in Bahia and which has a number of ritual associations with the orisha Oxum. The dispatch includes offerings of flowers, food specific to Oxum, and ritual bathing of large numbers of the community who come for blessings, purification, witnessing. Possession is common among members of the afoxé as well as the witnessing community during this dispatch (see Figures 3.2, 3.3, 3.4).

A series of transformations of the representation of black women in Brazil is affected. The first and most obvious is that women are not represented in terms of hypersexuality and nudity, but in a certain joy in the reclamation of female power. The claiming of public space in the context of Carnival to perform female identity under the full range of representations that Osun represents is another feature of this transformative process. The colors with which Osun is associated in Afro-Brazilian orisha tradition—gold—communicates brilliance, wealth, and a certain kind of self-assurance and confidence in the possibilities of black elegance and beauty. So this is a performance that, while it is in the eyes of the public a performance *of* women, it is a performance *for* women.

Pierre Verger in his "The Orishas of Bahia" (1993) identifies some of the various versions of Oxum that appear in Bahia. These range from Oxum Ijumú queen of all Oxums, who has a close connection with *ajés* (witches), Oxum Oshogbo, who is famous for helping women bear children, Oxum Ayalá, the big mother, Oxum Apará, the youngest of all with a warlike nature; Oxum Abalú the oldest, Oxum Abotô, the most feminine and elegant; Yeyé Karé and Yeyé Ipondá, who are both warlike in conduct. Thus rather than a singular representation of a female identity, multiple versions of womanhood are operative. The generational aspects are also accounted for in this range of representations. In re-presenting Oxum in carnival in this way, then, a variety of female identities are offered rather than one flat, exoticized, or otherwise reduced version of what it is to be a woman (see Figure 3.5).

DESFILANDO, COMING OUT TO PLAY IN THE CARNIVAL

After doing some preliminary research for my larger project on "Women, Creativity and Power in Afro-Brazilian contexts,"[6] the existence of an all-female Carnival group brought together in one place the three salient aspects (women, creativity, power) of my project. I resolved that if it were possible, I would try to do a study of them. A series of conversations with Afro-Brazilian research contacts led to one of them accompanying me over to the building of Filhos de Gandhi in order to introduce me to Rosangela Guimares. Most had identified her as the group's dynamic leader who had a series of clearly articulated posi-

Figure 3.2. The offering of flowers and perfume to Oxum at Lake Abaete.

Figure 3.3. *Lavagem*: Washing the heads of participants and the community at Lake Abaete.

Figure 3.4. A Filhas d'Oxum member overpowered at the Lake Abaete Despatch ceremony.

tions on the issue of women and their roles and possibilities in Afro-Brazilian context. This initial inquiry produced a rather extended conversation with Rosangela Guimares, who welcomed me instantly once she understood my project. Among other things, I told Rosangela that I was generally interested in learning

Figure 3.5. Young girl participants in Filhas d'Oxum.

about the representation of women in Carnival in Brazil as well as in the larger
social structures. Second, coming originally from Trinidad, I told her that I
wanted an opportunity to study some of the Brazilian forms comparatively. We
arranged succeeding appointments.

My next step was to consult Afro-Brazilian friends (artists, sociologists, activists) and indicate what I was planning to do, but more so to inquire if there were particular questions that they would like me to ask. From these discussions and my own interests, we formulated a number of questions that would guide my inquiry. These were as follows:

1. Why the name Filhas d'Oxum?
2. When did the group begin?
3. What are its objectives?
4. What requirements are there for participation in Filhas d'Oxum?
5. What kind of women can participate? Is it for black women only?
6. Are white women welcome participants?
7. Are persons in this group singly those who carry the Oxum energy, or are other orisha also indicated?
8. What type of relationships does the group have with the ritual aspects of candomblé?
9. Is there any conflict in using an entity like Oxum as a Carnival figure?
10. What is the significance in having a bloco/afoxé for black women?
11. What is the exact relationship Filhas has with Filhos de Gandhi?
12. What do you think is the most important problem that black women have to address in Brazil?
13. What is the source of power for black women?

   It is important that these questions were not going to be posed in their entirety, but that I would raise them sequentially as possible in formal interview contexts or that they would be revealed as the research process continued. Upon learning that I had several questions, Rosangela agreed to a formal interview. However, several crises occurred at the appointed time for each interview. For one thing, the Filhas were in the process of moving into their own house during this period and wanted to complete it before the Carnival arrived. Some of the times we had arranged to meet I found Rosangela in the building itself helping the men to work on the floors, just returning from a visit to the shoemaker consigned to make the sandals for the group; organizing the cutting of fabric for various aspects of the costume. Clearly, these times were all inappropriate for interviewing a busy woman, and instead I often offered to help, to which she would instead respond with casual conversation and a rest break over a beer or some other refreshing drink.
   A few direct answers were given, though: The group started in 1991 and Oxum was selected because of her maternal orientation as the mother of all waters. Rosangela apologized each time for the inconvenience and instead one day asked me to participate in the Carnival as a guest of the group, indicating that this would answer all the questions I had. Knowing that Carnival is to be experienced if it is to have meaning, I was ecstatic at this invitation for a variety of reasons. For one thing, it signaled a different type of relationship of trust and

removed the time frame and formal interview orientation that was initially in place and instead made me the participant I wanted to be in the entire process rather than a spectator. As well, my Trinidadian Carnival inclinations were satisfied.

For the next few weeks I made several visits to the house for all sorts of reasons. Whenever I was in Pelourinho, I would drop by. On several occasions I went directly there to help. One evening, for example, my task was assisting in the cutting of numerous pieces of different types of gold fabric. All of this was cooperative work, with some women sewing, others cutting, friendly conversation, singing popular carnival songs. A carnival headquarters is a busy place and this was no different. But in the midst of that they continued the Wednesday community feeding as an obligation, sometimes with some difficulty while keeping the carnival preparations in place.

Some of my own observations in process was that they use Oxum as the principal energy of the group, but there is an actual referencing and praise of a variety of Orixa, predominantly female. On the walls are drawings of representations of Iansa and Yemanja. The feeding of the neighborhood children and adults on Wednesdays, often bread and soup, a year-long commitment is as integral a part of the meaning of the relationship with Oxum as it is a politics of community organization.

A variety of offerings were located in different locations in the house, behind doors, for example. An altar with a variety of Christian elements but also money, a written request in a bowl of honey, a lit candle is prominently located. All the women, especially Rosangela, worked in the kitchen preparing food and serving. So there is an ongoing interaction with two sets of communities— visible and invisible—the ancestors and the living community.

In the end, I paraded with them for Carnival. The group came out in the night each time and danced the street accompanied by piped music from the Filhos de Gandhi *trio electrico* (a huge tractor trailer that carries all the sound equipment and some members of the group, singers, etc.) and a core of male percussionists who provide music for the group. The music for the afoxé tends to be more percussive in orientation than the drum core of the blocos-Afro. While the last day of the parade is a dispatch that meets at Piata and then parades a few miles to Lake Abaete, where there is another ritual offering, a community washing ritual that I have already identified, the opening of Carnival is an offering at the crossroads. (See Figure 3.6.)

In terms of costuming, because of the colors of Oxum, gold and yellow predominates. There are a variety of other color groupings that coordinate. For example an adolescent and little-girl section wore mostly white and silver. An Iansa section wore red and gold. One group of women wore all white. The predominant versions of different costumes were gold. While the blocos-Afro tend to use very specific fabric they have designed from year to year, the afoxé Filhas d'Oxum used color and texture to re-present a traditional entity in multiple ways in contemporary times. Each year are effected a number of var-

Figure 3.6. Offering at the crossroads in the center of Pelourinho.

iations, but what remains constant is the predominance of gold. While Filhos de Gandhi is associated with white and a bit of blue, wearing the same costume year to year, Filhas d'Oxum maintains a gold association and even further, a set of variations not permitted in the very specific Gandhi uniform.

By the end of the dispatch and in the days following, it was clear that my various preliminary questions were answered in various ways or at least I was able to provide my own interpretations for them.

CLAIMING A PUBLIC SPACE FOR RITUAL

The house that is headquarters to Filhas d'Oxum is a basic two-story structure in Pelourinho, consisting of two front rooms, a balcony, a kitchen and dining area, and a back patio. Behind the steps of the entryway is constructed a font to Osun with some offerings. In an open area upstairs is a reception area that serves as a place for feeding, as it is directly in front of the kitchen. It is also the space from which the carnival activity emanates. When I met Rosangela at the headquarters of Filhos de Gandhi she came across as full of ideas but with a clear recognition that she was in an assistant role there. In the Filhas d'Oxum house she was in charge of operations—organizing the house itself, supervising the feeding of the community, supervising construction work, herself working as seamstress, cook, construction helper—making sure the people stayed on point. Always gracious, she offered food and gestures of friendship each time I visited.

So while in some of the community's eyes this is still a subgroup of Filhos de Gandhi, the relationship in my view is more one of origins and some practical sharing for the protection of women in Carnival and the larger structures one needs to mount a Carnival band. Without research one is unable to delineate the complex set of articulations that were being posited. A mother of five children—ranging from three to eighteen years old—a wife as well, a former teacher who researches well her carnival representations, Rosangela Guimares is also a community cultural worker in the full sense, bridging in ways, unlike Filhos de Gandhi that space between service and commercial organization.

The house, then, is a location from which all emanates; it is here that ritual elements are prepared and rituals take place before making a public appearance. As in Candomblé ritual, there is a complex negotiation between the inner and outer space. The night of the first coming out for Carnival, for example, a core of participants, each dressed to portray an orisha, spent time in the house preparing themselves for the external presence. Once they came out publicly, the group made its way with firecrackers popping as is done at certain points in Candomblé rituals (often signaling the presence of the Orixá) up the streets to the center of Pelourinho. There, in a circle at the crossroads, offerings were made for the safe comportment of the group, protection from danger, and an entreaty to the energies and especially *exu* to provide safe passage. That having been done, the Carnival display began, moving slowly toward Castro Alves Square and then further into the center of the city, striking iridescent yellow and gold.

The Carnival presentation then became a ritual space with the same play between inside and outside, a negotiation of public and private space, thresholds. A definable beginning in the public sense is the offering at the crossroads and a similarly definable closing on the Thursday after Carnival is significant as well, for it is outside Carnival space into the ''Lenten period,'' but within a definite other time sequence that does not accommodate itself to the Christian calendar.

The high point of the dispatch is the offering of flowers and food in bowls at the lakeside in Abaete, a traditional location for Osun and historically a place where other similar offerings have been made. Rosangela herself almost becomes transformed and embodied with the energy of the force of orisha and enters the water as streams of people come in lines to have water poured on their heads. Possession is common in this event from participants in the group as from the public until Rosangela herself, overcome, on the occasion when I participated in the event, was led away by her assistants. An amazingly powerful ritual moment, the idea of community work and spirit work was bridged in this process.

Clearly, the re-/presentation of women in the context of Carnival was one that sought to draw on traditional energy and power as identified in the female aspects of the Afro-Brazilian Yoruba cosmology and to relocate it in the carnival context. Carnival, then, is not about display and dance and body only—but the actual reclaiming of a certain ritual space, the mobility of traditional orisha practice and the identification of a particular link with the community as identified in the feeding and washing. The private/public negotiations, the carnival display itself that educates, and the healing as identified in the water are also significant aspects of this representation of the body of the culture of Afro-Brazilians. Moreover, there is a movement from circumscribed space (Filhos de Ghandi headquarters) to their house and further from the house of Filhas d'Oxum to the streets; from the streets to the lake. A series of public gestures in terms of the ritual and the meaning of Oxum in orisha tradition, Candomblé, Afro-Brazilian culture, African identity, and its reinterpretations are effected. And in particular the ongoing re-/presentation of female identity in these contexts consists in performing a range of black female identities.

NOTES

Many thanks to Milson Manuel dos Santos of Bahia, Brazil, for assistance in executing this project.

1. Refers to the set of practices of African religion in Brazil, particularly those of Yoruba derivation. See Abdias do Nascimento, *Brazil, Mixture or Massacre?*

2. Femi Euba in conversation with author in Quito, Ecuador, at International Congress of Americanists in the context of the presentation of a related paper on ashé: ''Spirit Work/Community Work: Ashé and Quilombismo in Contemporary Afro-Brazilian Contexts'' provided this interpretation of the meaning of afoxé.

3. Named after Mahatma Gandhi by longshoremen, Filhos de Gandhi started the project of breaking through the contempt under which Candomblé was held by deliberating working some of the iconography publicly under the cover of the ''passive resistance and peace of Mahatma. See Morales 1988.

4. Interview conducted January 18, 1995.

5. A more popular version of this in U.S. context could be the Million Man March

of 1996, in Washington, D.C., which deliberately excluded women, and the Million Woman March of 1997 in Philadelphia, ''the city of brotherly love.'' Jonelle Davies repeatedly pointed out this connection to me. I thank her for this contribution.

6. As part of my Fulbright professorship in 1995.

4

Samba Schools: The Logic of Orgy and Blackness in Rio de Janeiro

Myrian Sepúlveda dos Santos

THE PARADE: SEX, GLORY, AND FUN

In the first decades of this century, the black and poor people of Rio de Janeiro took to the streets and had a good time during carnival. Men and women marched down the streets to the sound of percussion instruments and danced to the syncopated rhythm of drums in highly joyful and sensual movements. These popular manifestations defied the rules of everyday life, displaying prohibited religious rituals and challenging the institutional order. There were no costumes, elaborate masks, or well-organized parades. It was instead an unrestrained and all-embracing festivity that continued, uninterrupted, for three days and three nights.

At present, the samba-school parade is an impressive and dazzling feast for the eyes and ears. It consists of highly decorated floats and a huge concentration of elaborately costumed people singing, dancing, and marching in synchronized movements. For tourists, the array of beautiful women exposing their naked bodies high atop tall floats is an appealing feature. The sensual dance of the mulatto women, who swing their hips and stretch out their arms in extremely erotic gestures and movements, is an intriguing sight for tourists and Brazilians alike. The men are not to be left out; they too perform a sensual dance, as they juggle their tambourines and gyrate to the rhythm of drums.

According to the press, fifty million dollars and more than fifty thousand people are involved in the production of the parade. Ninety thousand people watch it, seated in luxurious boxes or on ordered concrete bleachers. To complete the scene, there are lights and television cameras along the route. Helicopters fly over the mile-long parade to ensure that all of the festivities are caught on camera. The large number of billboards with messages warning against HIV infection suggests that people, particularly tourists, see the festivities as an opportunity for casual sex. The samba schools have become legal. They perform a disciplined spectacle. With powerful commercial interests and nothing to fear from the authorities, the samba schools have grown into massive institutions despite their increasing links with illegal organizations and, most recently, the drug cartels.

What does this massive festivity have to do with blackness? In spite of all the evidence to the contrary, the carnival parade is not just about sex, glory, and fun. Rather than a homogeneous festivity, it is, in fact, an event that involves a number of separate samba schools. Each school has its own participants, history, and identity. Carnival is Rio's major celebration; it has strong ties to black culture and has existed since colonial days, despite sweltering weather, heavy storms, national calamities, epidemic diseases, and world wars.

Over the last three decades, studies of carnival have been less interested in descriptive history than in attempts to interpret carnival manifestations as part of a complex contemporary Brazilian society (Leopoldi 1978; Goldwasser 1989; Castro 1994). These studies either show the creative side of carnival practices and the suspension of ordinary conventions (Da Matta 1973, 1980, 1981a, 1981b) or denounce the racial exploitation (Rodrigues 1984), the bureaucratization and commodification of the parade, as well as the confirmation of Brazilian social hierarchy (Queiroz 1992). In this paper my objective is to show that the samba-school parade in Rio de Janeiro has maintained many features linked to black culture that expand the perceptions of the participants' bodies and feelings and increase the scope of their freedom. Going against the grain, I am not interested in just showing the appropriation of ethnic themes by large sectors of the population and their immediate transformation into commodities and national symbols. On the contrary, I intend to show the structures and values that have survived, that have been rewritten and modernized and yet remain identifiably black.

By "black culture" I refer to neither a fixed essence nor a contingent construction to be reinvented. Although challenging an essentialist perspective characterized by the exclusive search for African origins, I argue that despite changing cultural aspects, cultural intermixing and struggles for power, the black population from the poor areas of Rio de Janeiro is responsible for the recreations of the rhythm of the drums and for one of the most sensual and liberating dances within the samba-school parade.

The samba schools consist of big floats and many subdivisions called *alas* (sections, literally "wings"). Each has fifty to two hundred participants, all of whom wear similar costumes and perform variations on a predetermined theme. In the following pages, I focus my analysis on four subdivisions of the samba-school parade: the *comissão de frente* (front line), the couple *mestre-sala* and *porta-bandeira* (master of ceremonies and standard-bearer), *baianas* (women dressed in the typical style of black women from the northeastern state of Bahia) and *batería* (drum section). They can be clearly differentiated from those made up of actors, actresses, soccer players, politicians, fashion models, and upper- and middle-class people. Their importance is recognized not only by the old members of the samba schools but also by the parade judges and the audience. Since the samba schools were first organized, there have been a series of ne- gotiations and struggles for prestige, money, and power. Despite all sorts of influence within the schools, the heart and soul of the parade is still maintained by these special sections that consist—except for the most recent front lines— of people who are mainly black and poor.

This essay is part of a larger research project I am conducting on the samba- school parade in the city of Rio de Janeiro. It relies on data gathered from historical documents and interviews conducted with the help of a group of stu- dents who have worked with me on this project for the last four years.[1]

COMISSÃO DE FRENTE: MEDIATIONS BETWEEN DIFFERENT SOCIAL WORLDS

The first thing spectators see when a samba school begins its parade is its welcoming committee, called *comissão de frente* (front line). It consists of ten to fifteen identically dressed and linearly aligned participants who perform syn- chronized movements. Its main purpose is to introduce the school's theme, as a preview of the coming spectacle. But if comissões de frente today include people wearing dazzlingly colorful costumes, until a few years ago they con- sisted exclusively of very well-dressed black men in suits and ties. The smaller samba schools have the more traditional front lines (see Figures 4.1 and 4.2).

These elegant black men were musicians, community leaders, and directors of the samba schools, and as they opened the parade they mediated between two different worlds. They projected an image of respectability for black people without changing their own style. They urged their fellow members to don new tailored clothing instead of slippers and unbuttoned shirts. One of them, Paulo da Portela, once stated that poor, black men had to keep their necks and feet busy (Silva & Santos 1980). But if their outfits included some elements denoting respectability in the larger Brazilian society, they kept other features from their own world that could not fail to be recognized: in the beginning they wore white linen suits, white shirts, colorful ties, straw hats, and white shoes. To understand better the mediations operated by these black men between two different worlds, it is important to remember that until the 1920s there was scarcely any dialogue between them: the music called samba was restricted to the black and poor populations. Only in the late 1920s, as radio became a popular communications media, were new songs broadcast to an ever-growing public. This was the time when an entire generation of Brazilian popular singers and songwriters was established, including such names as Ary Barroso, Lamartine Babo, and Carmen Miranda. *Sambista* and other popular musicians gathered in the bohemian and

Figure 4.1. Comissão de frente (front line) showing well-dressed leaders of samba schools in 1966 (Agência JB).

Figure 4.2. Costume paraders in 1997 (Marco Antonio Conalcaniti/Agência O Globo).

working-class downtown districts, such as the famous *Praça Onze*. The sambistas, who were mostly poor, black musicians, had to sell the authorship of their sambas to famous radio singers, because they were not yet accepted as being respectable enough to be songwriters. Only in the beginning of the 1930s did sambistas achieve a degree of public recognition and social mobility. This was (as it still is) hard to come by in Brazilian society, and I believe that the samba schools prove to have provided the privileged space in which the diffusion of the new musical style could happen.

If in the first decades of this century, popular carnival festivities were brutally repressed in the streets of Rio de Janeiro, as samba schools became increasingly organized the black and poor population conquered the right to march down the streets without persecution. According to Master Fuleiro, an eighty-five-year old black man who founded the Império Serrano Samba School, the police considered the tambourines weapons. Master Fuleiro was interviewed by our research team in January 1996, one year before his death; this is what he recalled:

I myself was trod upon by the soldiers of the cavalry. They would come and rip our tambourines with their knives because we were not allowed to use them. The police really meant business. . . . That was the law. They said tambourines were weapons. As to real weapons, the good *bambas* [toughs] wouldn't go anywhere without them. They carried razor blades on their bracelets, on their legs. . . . The police were really stupid to think the tambourines were weapons. . . . You never heard of anyone hitting someone with a tambourine, because tambourines cost money and nobody would want to break one.

The struggle for the right to occupy the streets during carnival has been a struggle for the public recognition of the existence and respectability of black culture. The right to walk down the streets during carnival and even to circulate freely in Rio during the rest of the year remains to be won by the poor, mainly black people who still suffer discrimination and are the target of severe repression whenever they venture beyond their neighborhoods. But if today blacks are not completely safe to roam the streets, in the late 1920s, as Master Fuleiro told us, it was even worse and more dangerous.

The conquest of the right to be visible during carnival can be explained in part by the major political changes that occurred in the country in 1930.[2] The well-dressed men in the comissões de frente were key elements in the negotiations with the new populist government of dictator Getúlio Vargas. To give a better idea of the strength of the links between samba-school members and the Vargas government, I would like to quote from the testimony of old samba-school members who were interviewed by my research team. There was a period when all plots of samba parades had to be based on national motifs and the themes of the songs were regulated, but even then most sambistas considered governmental involvement to be positive. They insisted that the most beautiful *sambas-enredos* (the theme samba of a parade, which develops the plot) were those of the Vargas period. Pedro Ernesto, the mayor of Rio de Janeiro appointed by Vargas in the 1930s, is to this day seen by members and directors of the samba schools as the greatest friend and protector they ever had. Doña Zica, an old member of Mangueiria, one of the most traditional samba schools, and the widow of the great Cartola, considered one of the best sambistas ever, had this to say about Pedro Ernesto:

Pedro Ernesto used to come here pretty often. He was a Mangueirense: he did a lot of things for our school. He was the first one to build housing for the school. He gave us a public school too. He wasn't allowed to name the school after himself because he was still alive, so he chose another name. When he died, the Mangueira community attended his funeral, singing to a funeral beat. . . . He made the samba school a place for work. At first, people didn't like it, they used to say that samba schools were for bums. After him, things changed.

The leaders of carnival groups were formerly of two kinds: those who had buying power and financed the carnival street parades within their communities and those who were recognized for their brave and romantic style. The latter were the malandros, who rejected most principles established by conventional society. For them work was necessary not as a major value to be accepted, but as a way to escape from poverty and succeed in society by society's standards (Cândido 1970; Da Matta 1980; Matos 1982). As parades became organized, both types of leaders were replaced by men who relied on the support of the government and the press. These new leaders of the samba schools had the ability to negotiate with politicians. To this day, links with samba schools are highly valued by politicians.

The samba-school parade has provided a space for negotiations between different socioeconomic groups. Musicians want to sell their music; black and poor people want to have their culture recognized, along with the right to march down the streets; the school directors want money and prestige; the middle class wants entertainment; industries want to sell products; and politicians want to legitimize their leaderships. In addition, outlaw organizations such as *jogo do bicho* (a kind of numbers racket) and drug trafficking achieve popular support and a legal façade as they finance part of the samba-school spectacle (Santos 1997).

The black and poor populations were not entirely positive about the numerous regulations that were imposed on their parade since the very beginning; these regulations, however, had positive results. Samba is recognized for its beauty and occupies a special place among the other varieties of popular, urban music and dance in Brazil. At least once a year, black and poor people are the center of attention in Rio. On this occasion, rather than being poor, underprivileged, downtrodden victims of discrimination, they are the masters of samba, performing for foreign audiences and members of the Brazilian elite, thus inverting established relationships. They become the major attraction of a huge spectacle.

Although black cultural features have been consecrated by the whole society, they are not publicly recognized as black and have not led the black population to achieve full rights as citizens. In the 1930s, national heroes became popular elements associated with the ideal notion of the democratic mixture of three races: Indian, black, and white (Mota 1994). Along with Brazilian miscegenation, there is a racist "whitening" of language in Brazil. In that regard, the popular use of more than 200 different color categories constitutes a problem: the white or lighter-skinned individuals always keep their identities linked to privileges. The major consequence of this whitening of language has been the reproduction of strong racial discrimination, hierarchies and inequalities within Brazilian society (Fernandes 1964; Skidmore 1974; Hasenbalg 1979; Hasenbalg and Silva 1992). In turn, racial discrimination has made use of names evoking blackness for music, food, religious practices, and habits difficult. The changing makeup of the comissões de frente (the replacement of the old leaders in their elegant outfits by costumed people) is indicative of new developments in the struggle for power. The front lines no longer represent those who command the schools, nor are black leaders really represented in them. As a matter of fact, the leadership of the schools has become invisible. Instead of old school members proudly showing off their tailcoats, the new choreography is marked by the shadow of the masked revelers in the style of the Venetian carnival. Black men (women were never allowed to parade among them) and the old leaders are losing their place.

MESTRE-SALA AND PORTA-BANDEIRA: MEDIATIONS BETWEEN DIFFERENT SOCIAL TIMES

In the parade, the comissão de frente is usually followed by a black couple elaborately costumed: the *mestre-sala* (master of ceremonies) and the *porta-bandeira* (standard bearer). They perform a special pas-de-deux in royal eighteenth-century attire. The costumes always include large wigs, fans, luxurious clothes and rhinestone-encrusted shoes. The couple dance with elegance, dignity, and restraint, waving to the public and presenting the flag to important spectators. The manners of the old Brazilian nobility are displayed in their posture, actions, and movements. The mestre-sala dances around the porta-bandeira, trying at the same time to be courteous and to protect the banner. Even though to many spectators this man and this woman go unnoticed, for they are only two among thousands, they play two of the most important roles in the parade. The performance is centered on two persons, and it may add ten points (out of a total of 100) to their school's scoring for the evening's competition, whereas the other items judged, such as drums or harmony, involve large groups of people or the school as a whole. The pressure on this couple is so great that it has been reported that when a famous porta-bandeira fell during a parade, she actually considered suicide. Fortunately, the judges did not see her fall, and her school won the championship that year (Castro 1994; see Figure 4.3).

Figure 4.3. *Porta-bandeira* (flag bearer) and *mestre-sala* (master of ceremony) in the royal eighteenth-century attire. At the center, a costumed child who is part of the ceremony. Samba school parade of 1961. (Agência O Globo)

As I have documented, mestre-sala and porta-bandeira are usually black men and women, and this is one of the strongest traditions within the samba schools. Most members of the samba schools still defend the idea that this couple has to be gifted and that the secrets of the profession are only inherited from an ancestor. However, black people have had strong links with the street and popular carnival in the Bakhtinian sense. From the 1600s to the beginning of this century, revelers in costume cavorted in the streets sloshing water on one another in a street festivity called *entrudo*. These practices, which were brought to Brazil by the Portuguese colonization, became very popular and involved the whole society (Eneida n. d.; Riotur 1991; Queiroz 1992). Yet there were other practices as well. According to police records, since 1604 people have used masks to commit robbery, murder, and other crimes. By the end of the nineteenth century, entrudo was seen as dirty and uncivilized, and the laws against it became more rigorous. The disorganization and lack of control of street festivities led the

emerging bourgeoisie to criticize them. They were interested in the modernization of the city, which had to be turned into a safe place free from tropical
diseases, urban poverty, and violence. It was necessary to guarantee the development of the growing trade (Needell 1987; Benchimol 1992; Sevcenko 1983).
A set of rules and police measures were implemented to control the spontaneity
of the manifestations as well as their location. Carnival became a celebration
confined to clubs and theaters. Only organized street groups such as the *grandes
sociedades* (great societies) and *ranchos* obtained authorization to parade in the
streets. Ropes were used to separate the group members from onlookers. The
street carnival that was allowed consisted of selected groups that had the ability
to entertain larger audiences, which became restricted to those who could afford
to pay for the right to watch.

While this transition in carnival suited the bourgeoisie, the poorer population,
usually black, did not adopt any ordered structure in the first decades of this
century. As they came to the downtown area during carnival and celebrated in
the streets, drinking, dancing and fighting, they were severely repressed. In the
beginning of the century, about half of Rio's population was black. Despite a
general belief that associates carnival and samba with the Yoruba people, it
must be emphasized that the majority of Rio's black population descended from
the Bantu people, who for generations were a major presence in the city.
''Semba'' is the Angolan word for ''navel,'' and this term, slightly modified,
became the designation of a variety of sensual forms of song and dance with
African origins. For many, Rio de Janeiro was considered the Old Portuguese
Bantuland (Needell 1987:49). Yorubas came to Rio from the State of Bahia,
became great musicians, and did have a great influence in the creation of samba.
They lived mainly close to the downtown area. But, during carnival, people
from everywhere mingled; those who lived in the suburbs formed street groups
and marched toward the center area of the city. People from the suburbs held a
sort of religious ritual, in which they danced in a way very similar to that of
sambistas, called *jongo*. To this day, it is possible to find jongo in Rio's neighborhoods such as Serrinha and Santa Teresa.

But the point of this historical information is to highlight that all those groups,
which later gave rise to the samba schools, were fiercely persecuted by the police
because of their completely liberating, disorganized and often violent street festivities. How should one understand, for instance, the large space in the Avenue
occupied by the controlled and slow movements of the black royal couple, which
are in sharp contrast with the compact crowd that follows in the other sections?

It is interesting to highlight at least four issues here: First, one may assume
that the rich costumes that always refer to a royal attire represent the inversion
of poverty and everyday existence; indeed, they posit a different reality in which
everyday problems are suspended. The luxury of the clothes, the jewelry, and
the theatrical presentation amuse performers and spectators. However, this formal, elegant eighteenth-century dance contrasts sharply with the erotic movements, rhythms and sounds of participants in the parade. Mikhail Bakhtin (1968)

sees in carnival the counterworld, which is so well described by Maryse Condé in this volume as life turned inside out, free and familiar contact among individuals, profanation of the sacred and the pleasures associated with the flesh. It is useful, however, to consider that different sorts of carnivalization may happen simultaneously; even though the use of masquerades and costumes may be found in many different places and cultures throughout the centuries, their use is contextually bound. In the samba-school parade, as the ''noble'' couple inverts the social order they ''renounce'' the world of pleasure, freedom, and spontaneity. Their masks bring rules, distance, and controlled manners, that is, order among disorder, reason amidst madness. One may say that there is an inconsistency in this performance that is due to its association both with man's nature, as perceived by Bakhtin, and with its location in time and space. Peter Berger stresses this point about the comic (he calls it incongruent) as well as the way it may become a sign of transcendence (1997: 205–215).

Second, it must be noticed that there is no space for innovation associated with the performance of this couple. The dance and costumes are always the same despite the different themes that are carried by the parade. The couple serves as a sort of mediation between different historical times. The attire of the mestre-sala and the porta-bandeira is reminiscent of a time when Brazilian society was strongly hierarchical. Still, many features of this past are present to this day in Brazilian life. If in carnival one mocks what is hard to bear in real life, this couple has been reenacting for decades the representations of power in Brazil. Their continuous performance suggest that some historical features are not temporary at all, but rather have remained alive. They represent sameness in the midst of change.

Third, they represent a quest for identity. Many of the old sambistas interviewed by our research group tell a story about the origins of the samba schools that can also be found in some books about Brazilian carnival:

Before the creation of samba schools, there were violent struggles between carnival groups that ended only when one of them succeeded in capturing the banner of the other group. The winning group taunted the other groups until the next carnival, when the fight started again. *Malandros* were then the great toughs. They did not fear anything, not even police repression. They exerted a sort of charm over women and were praised for their freedom, music and swaggering walk. Straw hats, large silk shirts, and wooden clogs, things they wore, served as protection against common weapons such as razors and pocket knives. These men also dressed as *baianas* using the large skirts to hide knives.

Whether a romantic memory or not, it appears that for many popular carnival in Brazil is still a time for bravery; a place to display values, strength and courage, as well as the means for defending territory. Each samba school is related to one neighborhood and the ultimate aim of their presentation is to conquer the championship in an annual context. It is amply known that memories of slavery were both banished and forgotten, and we do not have many oral traditions about it. But the banners have a distinguished place within the memories of violence throughout time. Some researchers believe that the banners are associated with the sticks carried by slaves in festivities and funerals (Riotur 1991). These sticks with brightly colored cloths tied to them were a means of identifying their former African tribes. In the 1930s, when samba schools were organized, their participants immediately chose their own flags, colors, and rhythms as symbols through which they could be identified, in order to be associated with the reenactment of a past that cannot be recalled. Although no single fixed origin may be established, there is a space of performativeness that reminds us that from the past to the present day carnival festivities have involved a struggle for power. There is a search for identity and a hidden violence within the performance of the pas-de-deux, although the couple needs to be elegantly disguised as representatives of power.

Finally, it should be remarked that the samba-school sections with mostly black participants, such as front lines, baianas, and drum section, are either all male or all female. Boyce Davies' article in this volume, about the representation of black women in Brazilian carnival, also deals with Afro carnival groups that remain either all male or all female, exclusively. The only traditional segment of the samba schools in which we see a black man and a black woman together is the one just described; but then it is interesting to observe that they are using costumes of white people and that there is no trace at all in their performances of the hypersexuality associated with samba schools. Where is the famous sexuality of Brazilian mulatto women?

BAIANAS AND DRUMS: ORGY AND BLACKNESS

The baianas section consists of a group of a hundred or more black and mulatto women wearing long, multilayered skirts, loose blouses, turbans, and a profusion of colorful necklaces and bracelets. Their dance is characterized by spinning, in fast, whirling movements. If a school does not include a large baianas section, it loses points in the scoring. The prestige of these women is not associated with beautiful naked bodies. They are known as great cooks, and until recently they were responsible for the important task of organizing the preparation of costumes and adornments. But their main importance is not related to these abilities. These fat old ladies, called "aunts," are extremely respected and are among the main upholders of the festivity. They elicit a sort of reverence from the audience. They are the ones who bless the event, and who often are leaders in Afro-Brazilian religions such as Candomblé and Umbanda. In the past, old black women known as "aunts" organized famous parties and Afro-Brazilian religious centers, which were crucially important for the strengthening of black identity. To this day, it is as if the baianas concentrated the whole energy of the festivity; they make possible the religious rituals of possession in which men and women can just feel the sound of the drums, liberating their movements, feelings and emotions (see Figure 4.4).

Just as strong as the section of baianas is the percussion section of *bateria*. It is made up of approximately three to four hundred men in ordered rows. They start the parade, stop in the middle of the parade and, finally, bring up the rear. They are all percussionists; no wind instruments are allowed. The smaller instruments, such as tambourines, tambours, rattles, agogôs, and cuícas, are located in the front rows. These are played with very quick hand motions. The larger drums come in the back rows. The bass drums, emitting the deepest sounds, are placed at either end of the last two rows. One must be strong and be in good physical shape in order to beat the drums fiercely throughout the entire parade. It is a tough task for tough guys (see Figure 4.5).

The band is composed almost exclusively of men, who are entirely absorbed in the sounds of the drums. Although it is not unusual to see their hands bleeding, they do not seem to feel any pain. The rhythm drums set the pace of the parade, one responding to the other. There is a sort of conversation with the beats that provides strong vibrations. The drums have been at the heart of the parade since the beginning of the samba schools and, along with the other percussion sounds, they set the pulse of the entire event. The beating of drums is the sound that unites the components of the school. People report that the sounds of the drums come from nature and make their bodies feel alive. There is a strong feeling that emerges with the beat of the drums, elicited by the desire for pleasure, the joy of being alive. When the drum section goes by, the crowd spontaneously stands up to acknowledge the overwhelming strength of the beat.

I have described well-dressed men, a couple in ancien régime costume, fat old women clad in dresses that completely cover their bodies, and men who are entirely concentrated in the task of beating their drums. Again, where is the famous hypersexuality of Brazilian black women? In Rio's carnival, sex is ever present. Carnival is the time when nude bodies may be displayed; prostitutes feel free to sell their bodies to whomever is willing to pay for pleasure; masks and costumes liberate sex between strangers in forbidden places and ways; homosexuality is celebrated and sexual transactions cross all lines. Although nudity is present throughout the parade, it is absent from the sections where blacks have the most emphatic presence. As a matter of fact, if one browses the magazines and tourist folders about Rio's carnival, he or she will find many more photos of nude white women than of nude black women. Is sexuality placed somewhere outside black performances?

We know that the carnival tradition, far from being a specific aspect of Brazilian culture, dates back to Egyptian, Greek, and Roman cultures, where festivities celebrated laughter and sexual freedom, thus suspending the rigid norms of everyday life. According to Bakhtin (1968), who provided one of the most insightful interpretations of popular carnival, the merrymaking represents a sort of ritual in which the world of daily life is turned upside down. These festivities

Figure 4.4. Baiana: costumed woman in the traditional outfit of state of Bahia's black women, showing deep involvement in her performance during the 1997 samba school parade (Paulo N. Colella/Agência JB).

Figure 4.5. *Baterista* (drum player) completely concentrated in drum beating during the 1997 samba school parade (André Arruda/Agência JB).

represent a form of communication where disguised participants are suddenly alike. They share common places and values, including the desire for justice, equality, and expressive freedom for all human beings. The rules are known by everyone; night is day; sacred is profane; madness and desires are allowed without censure. The liminal character of the festivity includes the suspension of sexual constraints and sexual differentiation. As I have pointed out, however, it is not possible to fix what is sacred and what is profane without considering the social group involved. What is sacred to one social group can be profane to another and vice versa. By the same token, the contents of madness and sexuality change from one place to another.

One of the major languages that is present in samba schools is the celebration of sexual pleasure. This is undoubtedly one important feature of carnival. I argue, however, that the features that characterize sexual freedom in samba schools and which have been responsible for mesmerizing a large public since the 1930s do not represent an inversion of forbidden feelings for black communities; nor do they constitute a discourse based on the inversion of social rules. It so happens that what is part of the ordinary life of black communities often constitutes a complete transgression of the sociocultural rules of the white middle class. I mean, in particular, the free and close contact among individuals.

In a previous work (1996), I argued that it was very important for the samba schools to achieve the right to perform in public in the main avenues of the city. I named the carnival of the black and poor communities "carnival without masks," because instead of a liminal space in which social codes were broken, the samba schools looked for the public space to affirm their social codes. In the past, there were very few costumes in the parades. Baianas dressed as in their everyday life. Carnival was the time when drummers could leave the backyards and show their existence and values to the entire society without being persecuted. They did not need to hide anymore. It happens that these festivities were in the past, as they are to the present, highly sensual, although there is no name to designate "sensuality" in Afro-Brazilian speech. The sensuality that one could observe then was very different from the surrealistic practices through exaggeration or profanation of today's carnival. The profanation had to do with the social and political rules of exclusion rather than with social restrictions to sexual intercourse.

Thus, one of the main features of the samba schools is a sensuality that is associated with the old black festivities, which have maintained collective and community links as their major values. It is the feeling of a single moment that repeats itself infinitely with the beat of the drums, bringing the whole crowd together. There is a sensual orgy here that is collective and deals with the energy of the whole, of the many bodies that touch each other. This energy is deprived of individualistic perceptions of bodies and minds. This sensuality or energy I am talking about is, therefore, completely different from the sexuality based on a duality of bodies and minds, in which orgasm comes with the pleasure resulting from the control and enjoyment of the other body.

In samba schools there is a sort of sensuality that contains the complex set of symbolic representations that is recurrent in black communities. It is well known that it is difficult to talk about blackness in Brazil because of the massive miscegenation and multiple definitions of race Brazilians are committed to. In an official survey developed by IBGE (Brazilian Institute of Geography and Statistics), Brazilians defined themselves in more than 200 colors. The point I have made takes all these facts into consideration. In samba schools we find not only many layers of meaning, but also an intermixing of different symbolic manifestations. I would like to emphasize, therefore, that I am not saying that there is a sort of ''black sensuality'' that can be related to a specific race or fixed culture. Rather, I have pointed out the presence of some sensual features that have been observed along with the development of Brazilian communities in which blacks and Afro-Brazilian symbolic manifestations have predominated since colonial days. As one observes these manifestations, one cannot but recall Paul Gilroy's studies on the recurrent features of black music throughout the postslavery Black Atlantic (1993).

One of my interviewees was a famous leader of Mangueira. Dona Neuma, a very clearheaded and articulate old woman, who has an astonishing power over political authorities and the media, described to me the community life of Mangueira. To her, the major enemy of samba schools was not drug trafficking, but the new evangelical sects that were taking over her neighborhood. Newly converted people, she complained, locked their doors and abandoned samba. Indeed, as we talked I observed that there were a large number of visitors walking in and out of her house. As she invited me to the table, I had the impression that she was expecting more visitors. But according to her, I could always find big pots of food in her house, and I could always show up without previous notice. This was a tradition, she said, that came along with her old friends and members of the samba schools. She was not saying that there was a strong friendship among neighbors or families: she was talking about the feeling of someone who belonged to a large community whose limits were not given by nuclear families or professional links. A woman did not need to ask another to look after her children, said Dona Neuma, because they all knew they had to take care of the children who played in the streets. She could not bear closed doors. It is not a matter of solidarity in the sense of minding the interests of others, but a different perception in which the happiness, sadness, and problems of others are considered one's own. There have been different theories about cultural domination and control over black communities. If they are to be taken literally, then Dona Neuma must be mad to keep her door open in one of Rio's most ''dangerous'' neighborhoods.

Thus, I would like to emphasize once more that there is a sensuality in the singing and dancing of samba that is neither expressed by naked female bodies nor related to the masquerade, per se. The samba-school sections that have been preserved by black communities do not include naked women. As a matter of fact, the polarity between male and female is not even present there. The sections are often made up of fully dressed men or women. Rather than showing inverted and repressed feelings during carnival, black and poor communities take to the streets to celebrate the festivities for which they have been persecuted for centuries. To sum up, my point consists in saying that the orgy in the samba schools is mainly due to the creation of a people able to celebrate their own festivity, honoring their own values and gods.

It is not my intention to set up the samba schools as singular phenomena completely separate from other cultural values and moods of Brazilian society. Samba received influences from European music and, I would say without being an expert, even from Catholic chants and hymns. One of the most important festivities in the colonial period, whereby black and popular musicians presented their songs to each other, was the famous Catholic celebration called Festa da Penha. Besides, as a port, Rio received people, customs, and sounds from everywhere in its bohemian areas. It is also important to remark that, from the 1930s to this day, the parade has gone through several transformations, and along with them many manifestations of those black and poor neighborhoods were increasingly intermixed with codes brought by the expanding audience and multiple patronage. Along with these changes were the masquerade, the luxurious clothes and floats, and the hypersexuality of black women, whose sinuous belly movements assumed a highly erotic meaning and raised them to the status of stars in shows for tourists. It is always worth recalling, however, that even today the mulatto women and their swinging movements are not exotic at all in any neighborhood *pagode* (a samba party with singing and dancing). The naked female body has different meanings: at least one for those who associate it with a complete subversive pleasure and another for those who hallow it.

I would like to underscore the point that there is not just one universal sexual language. There are several of them, which can always be read differently. In Brazilian society, some authors have pointed many different sexual languages (Parker 1991), and I would say that some of them are shared by whites and blacks, as well as rich and poor people. First, there remain traces of the old rural and patriarchal societies. These societies strictly separated women from men, nobles from commoners, and planters from slaves. Whereas sexual interdictions were very restrictive in relation to the white women of the *casas grandes* (big houses) of the plantation owners, they were loose when applied to sexual intercourse between white men and black women.[3] In this context, sexual morality and sexual interdictions have multiple standards. This chauvinistic and middle-class morality is still visible in Rio, coexisting with many other machoist traditions. Whereas the Catholic Church envisions sex as a mere means for reproduction, the evangelical sects strictly prohibit carnival manifestations, which are viewed as the work of the devil. In Afro-Brazilian religions, homosexuals are less repressed than in Roman Catholicism, but even in them there are several restrictions to homosexual practices, specially to lesbianism. Women are not found among those who have power or money in the samba schools, although some women hold immense religious prestige. We know that total freedom, sexual or not, does not exist, since any way of defining human existence imposes restrictions on it. The process of urbanization and modernization, rather than diminish control over sexuality, brought a new set of values and ideas (Parker 1991). The hygienic and medical discourses on sexuality emerged in association with the new habits imported from European industrial societies, thereby establishing new patterns of normality for sexual behavior. Michel Foucault (1978) has correctly argued that scientific treatment of sexuality created a rigid set of moral values in the regulation of individual sexual behavior. Public institutions and the media have promoted a systematic sex education that has, on one hand, dispelled many taboos within the patriarchal systems and, on the other, claimed equal rights for any sexual gender. But even this attitude invests sexuality with an aura of self-determination and responsibility that is utopian and implies new constraints.

These discourses on sexuality have different meanings, which coexist with one another in different ways and according to different social groups and historical conjunctures. The transgression of these discourses are also multiple and differentiated. I mean that despite all sorts of constraints that are present in samba schools relating to political and economic negotiations (Augras 1993; Chinelli & da Silva 1993; Santos 1997), there is a sense of freedom for the participants. For three days, the parades encourage a large part of the population to live under rules that do not prohibit sexuality and that allow orgy within the frames of collective energy as an option. One major hallmark of Rio's carnival is the quite visible presence of transvestites and homosexuals. The denial of the sexual polarity between male and female is celebrated in balls, in street parades, and by individual revelers. It involves people of different skin color, cultures, and social groups. The other hallmark is certainly the profusion of nude bodies. Mostly women, but also men, transvestites and homosexuals exhibit their almost completely nude bodies and celebrate both casual sex and the commercialization of sexuality. It is evident that what might be a part of contemporary Brazilian sex life is still celebrated as a carnival prank or as an obscene celebration of the flesh. Yet it is clear to me that even considering carnival as an escape from social restrictions, it is undeniable that it carries those brief interruptions of time that keep the hope of freedom alive. The challenge, however, is to grasp the meaning of these transgressions in each social setting.

It must be pointed out that the forms of merrymaking we observe in balls, street manifestations, and samba schools during carnival are not the same; even in a single samba school parade there are different versions of merrymaking. The samba schools have an organizational form that allows them to better preserve links to their original communities and to incorporate sectors of the larger society. This dual organization has been described by Roberts DaMatta in his famous book about carnival, rogues and heroes (1980). Anyone who can afford the school's costume can buy it and join the parade. But there are special sections, such as those I have been investigating, that are mainly reserved for the members of old and mostly black communities. This sort of double organization has allowed older leaderships to retain some of their privileges and social codes in spite of both the power of politicians over them and the increasing openness of the parade to a large public. The spectacle the samba schools offer, therefore, is not an homogeneous one. It should be read in a way that reflects its complexity. The most traditional sections are all male or all female. Cross-dressing and transvestitism are strictly forbidden in those most traditional sections, as is nudity. Again, the issue of "incongruence" comes up. These restrictions are a paradox, if we consider not only that carnival is the place of inversions, gender included, but also that originally the baianas were actually tough men in drag. Yet they are meaningful if we consider that samba schools are associated with the manifestations of old black communities with an African heritage. There, the beating of the drums and the sweaty bodies touching one another superseded nude bodies and gender classifications in the liberation of emotions and feelings suppressed from everyday lives.

In short, those who go to the samba-school parade looking for sex see what they want to see and are blind to what appears to them as lacking meaning. Whereas the mulatto women dancing can be seen as highly erotic by the tourist, blond female tourists probably cast the same spell on Brazilian colored people. Samba schools raise the possibility of creating a desired world altogether different from the existing one. As different cultural realities meet, there are exchanges of features in unpredictable and multiple ways. Yet if Rio's parade occupies a highly distinctive place among carnival festivities, it is because black and poor communities have reinvented the festivity as a collective orgy. People are together in this festival, in their bodies and beyond them, for bodies and souls are not separated from each other. It is this religious feeling of togetherness, wholeness, and belonging to something bigger than oneself that has imposed itself on other carnival manifestations. The rituals hold strong community links, which in some way reach a wider public and explode in joy. The experience of getting close to one another, which even in a Latin American society is increasingly menacing, is always breathtaking. The contact with other bodies and souls, as well as the lack of dissociation one feels between an individual body and the collective body, exert a deep spell on the modern human beings who live within individual frames. Carnival, therefore, has not lost its power of turning the world upside down, although the laughable universe of the burlesque is always unpredictable and does not obey any pattern.

NOTES

I first presented a version of this paper in the 49th International Congress of Americanists (Quito, Ecuador, July 1997). I would like first to thank Jean Rahier and all the participants in the symposium "Representations of Blackness in the Context of Festivity" for the great debates we had there. I would like to thank my students Flávia T. Guerra, Flávio O. Freitas, Renata M. Rosa, Roberto B. Nascimento, Patrícia T. Lima, José Carlos V. Cruz and Rolf R. Souza for their work with the samba schools. I would like also to thank the colleagues with whom I talked about this theme and who gave me wise comments. I am indebted to Paulo Henriques Britto for his generous and supportive advice on the English text. Finally, and very particularly, I thank Daryle Williams for his generous and detailed comments on the last version of this paper.

1. This project has been financially supported by the Universidade do Estado do Rio de Janeiro (UERJ) and the Conselho Nacional de Desenvolvimento Científico e Tecnológico (CNPq).

2. In the first decades of this century, Brazil's economy was based on coffee exporting. Those who held power were closely associated with the European elite. Although a republican system had been adopted, a large part of the population did not take part in political elections. Women and illiterate people were not allowed to vote, and there was a strict control over the votes of the rural population, since balloting was not yet secret (Carvalho 1987). With the onset of the Great Depression in 1929, the Brazilian economy plunged into a deep crisis. The major effects of this crisis were, on the one hand, the emergence of a process of import-substitution industrialization, which included new demands for consumer goods from emerging urban sectors, and, on the other hand, a political movement with a strong nationalistic content which resulted in Getúlio Vargas' coup in 1930. On the rise of populism in the Vargas government see, among others Octavio Ianni (1968), Francisco Weffort (1978), Michael Conniff (1981), and Angela María de Castro Gomes (1994).

3. Gilberto Freyre's book *Casa Grande e Senzala* (1983 [1933]), translated into English as *The Masters and the Slaves* in 1956, is notably the book that best shows the complexity of cultural and social interrelationships in colonial Brazil. Yet it must be observed that as Freyre's analyses focused on the reciprocity between master and slaves, it emphasized the Brazilian mixture of races as a positive phenomenon, overlooking the violence and inequalities of the Brazilian racial order.

5

On the Apparent Carnivalization of Literature from the French Caribbean

Maryse Condé

In the *Problems of Dostoevsky's Poetics*, Mikhail Bakhtin asserts that "the novelistic genre has three fundamental roots: the epic, the rhetorical and the carnivalistic" (1993b: 125). He adds that the problem of carnivalization of literature, that is, the transposition of carnival into the language of literature, is one of the most important facing the researcher. Although, he reminds us, carnival is not a literary phenomenon, it permeates all aspects of human creativity. It gives rise to diverse variants and nuances depending upon the time in history, the ethnic groups and the individual festivity. It is essential to remember the ambivalent nature of carnival images. They eradicate the traditional binary oppositions and unite between themselves, for instance, birth and death, blessing and curse, praise and abuse, youth and old age, stupidity and wisdom. Thus, the fundamental carnivalistic act is the mock crowning and decrowning of the carnival king under which lies, as Bakhtin puts it, "the very core of the carnival sense of the world—the pathos of shifts and changes, of death and renewal" (1993b: 125).

Carnivalized literature aims at a shift of authorities and truths of world orders and contains a whole new outlook on the world.

There is no need to recall here the role played by carnival in the popular festivities of the Caribbean islands. Its importance apparently dates back to the very beginnings of time. On the plantations carnival broke the rigors of bondage and the universe of incarceration. It was a time when anything was allowed, when, as the saying goes, "the gaze of white folk no longer burns the eyes of niggers." The slave could look his master in the eyes, ask for money, and jeer at him. At the beginning of this century the white elite in St. Pierre in Martinique fashioned a Puritan facade, except during carnival. In *Le discours antillais* (1981) Edouard Glissant describes for us the burlesque weddings during carnival when the roles are reversed and the men take the place of pregnant women. Today, Vaval (an effigy representing carnival) is set alight on Ash Wednesday amidst a frenzied crowd of every race and social class dressed symbolically in black and white. The fire has the power both to cleanse and destroy the world. This torching is the ludic symbol of the death of the white Creole (the *béké*), the well-to-do and the end of tyranny. In literary works from the Caribbean representations of carnival are common. In *The Dragon Can't Dance*, by Earl Lovelace, the carnival even represents a powerful metaphor for the functioning and dysfunctioning of society.

In this paper we have focused our attention on two contemporary Martinican authors who, at first sight, appear to meet the criteria of the carnivalization of literature as defined by Bakhtin: life turned inside out, free and familiar contact among individuals, new modes of interrelationships between individuals, carnivalistic misalliances and, above all, profanation. The two writers are Raphaël Confiant and Patrick Chamoiseau. From the prolific work of Raphaël Confiant (an average of four novels a year) we have chosen *Le Nègre et l'amiral*, the first of his texts written directly in French—still not translated into English, surprisingly enough, despite the excessive attention given the author by the media.

Le Nègre et l'amiral is the story of a comical war, a direct confrontation between two mismatched champions: the *Nègre* Rigobert, a penniless ragamuffin, and the powerful Admiral, symbol of France under Vichy. They are surrounded by a multitude of not very commendable characters nicknamed Lapin Echaudé (Hot Rabbit), Siméon Tête Coton (Cotton-headed Siméon), Marcellin Gueule de Raie (Skate-Mouth Marcellin), and Barbe Sale (Dirty Beard). Raphaël Confiant deliberately places the accent on buffoonery and derision to tell us the story of a very dark period in the history of Martinique: the period during the Second World War, when there were two faces to France, the France of the Resistance and the other; the ravages of Vichy on the tropical island and the resistance of the common folk fiercely opposed to Hitler and consequently any form of collaboration. "*Itlé, nou ké pété bonda aw!*" (1988: 109) ("We'll kick Hitler's ass!") sing the demonstrators, absurdly powerless and naive, as they file through the streets. Never a hint of grandeur. Never a hint of heroism. No consideration for truth. The many historical characters waver between buffoonery and pathos: Josephine Baker, Claude McKay, Hitler, André Breton, Claude Lévi-Strauss, and especially General Charles de Gaulle oddly summoned to the rescue of the Martinicans to smash the yoke of the white Creoles. In the center there is Rigobert, the pitiful picaresque hero, the defender, one does not really understand why, of the Gaullist resistance. His exploits are laughable. He attacks a supplies convoy and, chased by the only German in sight, he takes refuge at the top of a tree. The turpitude of the local authorities in perfect collusion with the powers of the state are portrayed in a mode of grating humor.

The grotesque lurks under the surface. The grotesque is never far away, and when a mistress of disreputable color bursts in on the funeral of a white Creole, the occasion turns into bacchanalia. Order and hierarchy are constantly undermined. Decency too. In order to realize the scandalous effect of such a text we need to recall the unremitting faith of the Caribbean reader in Aimé Césaire's definition of committed literature in his *Cahier d'un retour au pays natal*: "My mouth shall be the mouth of those calamities that have no mouth, my voice the freedom of those who break down in the solitary confinement of despair" (1971: 61).

For the Caribbean reader literature is a solemn ground singing the illustration and denunciation of collective oppression. Because of his repeated handling of irony, V. S. Naipaul has made an ambiguous place for himself in the galaxy of great writers. Thus the Martinican critic Roger Toumson has no qualms listing the founding texts of Caribbean literature using a highly significant bibliomythical vocabulary, from Jacques Roumain to Césaire. Founding what? Identity. A collective awareness. But from the very opening of *Le Nègre et l'amiral* the desire to provoke seems to run through the text. Rigobert masturbates in front of photos of famous actresses. Each of his erections is given a lengthy and voluptuous description. Alcide, one of the main characters, has a never-ending erection, despite the unremitting attention lavished on him by the prostitutes. Nothing less than the intervention by the police shrinks it to a reasonable size: "When the brigadier Sonson Bilou hammered three times on the door shouting: 'Open up in the name of the Law! The Law, man!' Alcide immediately went limp. At the beat of an eyelash, the whores knelt down around the bed to watch the incredible deflation and detumescence of his male member" (1988:46).

There is nothing surprising about this in carnivalesque literature. Carnival, in fact, highlights the pleasures associated with the flesh and its desires. It glorifies and sanctifies in an ironic fashion the parts of the human body (the sex and the belly) as well as every form of excretion that were once considered shameful. But such a phenomenon is new in the literature from Martinique. Generally speaking, we are not used to hearing about sex in literature from the French-speaking Caribbean. We could even say it was prudish and squeamish. Patrick Chamoiseau in *Solibo magnifique* complains: "the Universal, ah, the Universal . . . Period: no lament about love. No song of the *koké*. *Négritude* was castrated. And *Antillanité* has no libido" (1988: 29).

French-speaking Caribbean literature has always preferred a noble discourse and the daylight jousting between oppressor and oppressed to the nocturnal revels between a man and a woman. But Confiant, with the bluntness of a schoolboy tackling the apparently taboo, has no hesitation WRITING the unpronounceable: *kokoune, koké* and *grinns*. He seems to be placing his language at the service of carnivalesque authentication in the constant quest for obscenity. This is manifest from the outset in a later novel, *La vierge du grand retour*, where he does not recoil from using carnivalesque blasphemy while rewriting the sacred texts. From the very first pages the reader is warned that this farcical Crusade is also engaged against the Creator. After having abused in a single breath his mother (his physical Creator) and God (his spiritual Creator), Rigobert declares: "I believe in God, I know he exists, but I condemn him. I say he's a first class whore and has proved himself to be far too wicked towards niggers" (1988: 54).

Yet we would be wrong to expect for all that an apology of traditional beliefs. Catholicism and *kimbwa* are irrespectively disrespected. Popular beliefs are ridiculed and travestied. In fact, one of the mechanisms of this apparent carnivalization is the baroque juxtaposition of practices rendered surrealistic by way of exaggeration. If we compare this text with *Solibo magnifique* (1988), the second novel by Patrick Chamoiseau, who won the Prix Goncourt a few years later for *Texaco*, despite the difference in temperament of the two authors, the characteristics remain very much the same. Like Confiant, Chamoiseau deals with a tragic subject: the death of a storyteller and thereby symbolically the death of oral tradition in a society in complete disarray. Solibo dies at the height of carnival (is this a coincidence?), strangled from within by the words of the tale he is telling: "One evening during Carnival in Fort-de-France, between Fat Sunday and Ash Wednesday, Solibo the Storyteller died from a suffocation of words shouting: 'Patat sa!' . . . His audience, thinking it a call and response, answered: 'Patat si!' " (1988: 25).

This passage takes on another dimension, derisive and obscene, for those who know that the word *patat* means the female genitalia in Creole. *Patat*, like the annunciatory three knocks at the start of a performance, announces the emergence of a burlesque cavalcade. Henceforth there follows a parody of a police investigation conducted by the brigadier Bouafesse. A series of terrified witnesses turn up one after the other, some even soiling themselves, others passing on from this life to the next through the ill-treatment of the gendarmes. Throughout the tale, apart from Solibo's, there are no less than three deaths (Charlot, Doudou-Ménar, and Congo). Chamoiseau voluptuously elaborates on police brutality, which is likened to carnivalesque rape of the flesh: "O how we love these acmes of blood, this ever flourishing, ever ready violence without a why or wherefore" (1988: 86). The police knock over the bearers carrying the bloodied stretchers. The patients in a coma toss and turn. The wounded fall into a coma. Such descriptions are perhaps a pretext for the novelist to recall the ravages of the French police state. But above all they are a pretext to portray a gallery of characters with parodic and suggestive names: Sucette, Bête Longue, Ti-Cal, Zaboca, and Nono-Bec-en-Or. Colonized countries attach great importance to names. In Césaire's *La tragédie du roi Christophe* Christophe recalls "his pain at not knowing what name he goes by" (1970: 37) and dreams of cloaking his subjects' names of infamy with names of glory. In Chamoiseau as in Confiant, the intention is different. The name has another function. It is intended as a living authentication of carnivalization. These laughable heroes, who inhabit a universe where disorder forms the very fabric of the world, are above all driven by Eros. For next to Thanatos, Eros is omnipresent. Bouafesse is a great womanizer who in the very middle of the police station is paid torrid respects by Doudou-Ménar. We learn that the late Solibo himself haunted places of prostitution. The animals espouse the madness of humans and the interaction between the two universes is a true indication of a world turned upside down. Chamoiseau not only mixes pornography with Roman Catholicism. He too knocks the sacred aura of Catholicism and *kimbwa*. His derision attacks anything that can be considered sacred, anything that can be considered a norm established by society, that is, propriety and aesthetics.

However, the main element of carnivalization in both these authors' texts remains their usage of language—the verbal extravagance and outrageousness. In 1989 both authors cosigned with the linguist Jean Bernabé *L'Eloge de la créolité*, which has since become the credo of a new literary school. In this manifesto they christened Creole their first language: "Creole, the first language for us Caribbeans, Guyanese and Mascarins, is the initial means of communication of our innermost selves, our collective unconscious, of our common genius, and it remains the river of our alluvial Creoleness" (1989: 43).

In the two islands of Guadeloupe and Martinique, Creole has had a singular adventure. Long considered as a jargon, as a pidgin, then as a picturesque deformation of French, Creole came to be valued by the nationalists as the language of resistance born surreptitiously in the plantation and allowing the slaves to communicate among themselves by excluding the master. In this way it established itself in its own right. Conflicting voices like that of Marie-Josée Cérol in her *Introduction au créole guadeloupéen* could be heard. Cérol writes of a lasting fidelity of the slaves to the African languages, which leads us to regard Creole as the language of unity and compromise between the protagonists in question (slaves from different origins and masters) rather than the core of resistance. Nevertheless, for most researchers, Creole remains a force deliberately stifled by the colonizer, to paraphrase the words of the sociologist Dany Bebel-Gisler. In a somewhat simplistic binary opposition, since it does not take into account the complex faculty of hybridity of the language, French is baptized the language of colonization and Creole the mother tongue. In a peremptory appeal published in the journal *Antilia*, Confiant the Creolophone, orders "every Antillean writer to stop deserting the mother tongue." For the two Martinican writers, Chamoiseau and Confiant, the textual presence of Creole alone guarantees the authenticity of Antillean writing. Thus, according to them, their writing in a language supposedly rooted in Creole facilitates the expression of an Antillean identity travestied through history. Once Jean Bernabé had claimed without much proof that the core of the Creole language was structured on the basis of sexual vocabulary and recalled the multitude of Creole words referring to sex (*kal*—penis, *koukoun*— vagina, *bonda*—buttocks, and *koké*—make love) Confiant had no trouble echoing him, declaring that certain Creole words are untranslatable into a civilized language, that is, French. He pointed out—which appears to us a moot point—that only Creole manages to name the sexual organs and their related practices. As early as the 1900s the novelist Effe Geache, whose pornographic novel *Une Nuit d'orgie à St Pierre* Confiant later prefaced in a significant manner (1992), had made wide use of the resources of Creole expressions to spice up his tale.

In his article "Jouissances carnavalesques: représentations de la sexualité" published in *Penser la Créolité* (1995: 140), the critic Thomas Spear wonders whether the Creole vocabulary does not foster racist stereotypes with regard to Caribbean sexuality. This critic begins to broach the real issues. We can go further and raise other points. We may very well ask ourselves whether, apart from the labored politicoliterary justifications, making use of Creole does not simply boil down to an attempt at exoticizing texts also destined for a French reading public. Let us never forget that the French-speaking Antillean writer, whatever he might say, also writes for the French market which buys and pays tribute to his books. (Confiant won the Prix Novembre and Chamoiseau, the Goncourt, as we mentioned.) Doesn't this extravagance, this tumultuous representation of Antillean sexuality with the added spice of Creole satisfy a need—that of the Other? He is the one transported to an exotic locale. It is through his eyes that Antillean sexuality becomes mouth-watering, burlesque, almost folksy. In my opinion we would be wrong to consider the writing in these texts as the transgression of colonial taboos or the edification of a universe refusing norms and routine. On the contrary they flatter the taste for the diverse, for the different exhibited in French culture. The Tharaud brothers, Paul Morand, and Victor Segalen are there to prove it. These texts do not signify either the breakthrough into literature of a disparaged and marginalized language. Precisely because these writers, hastily baptized the writers of Créolité, still remain readable, resorting to French, sometimes even of the most polished sort. They therefore maintain a minimum of transparency. It is important to recall that Raphaël Confiant stopped writing in Creole in 1988 and from that date on won the favors of the general public who had ignored him up till then. At the time he stated in a French weekly, *Le Nouvel Observateur*: "I had suppressed my desire to write in French for far too long. I had become the victim of a voluntary mutilation."

Now is the time to ask a more fundamental question: what is the true significance of the presence of Creole in the works of these writers? None of the characters in the novels in question here, neither Solibo nor Rigobert, expresses himself in Creole. They waver between two languages. And I repeat it is this interpenetration of French and Creole that allows the two novelists to address themselves to a non-Creolophone public and arouse them to a carnivalesque climax.

If we make an in-depth study of the very beautiful, very literary language of *Solibo magnifique*, for example, we discover a specialized jargon of medicine and sport, imitative techniques, an abundance of neologisms, rare words in the style of Césaire and baroque sequences of images bordering on surrealism. Added to this are parodic references to other texts—by Glissant, Confiant, and St. John-Perse. The linguist Marie-Christine Hazaël-Massieux justifiably writes in the journal *Antilia*: "Chamoiseau writes neither in standard French nor in

Creole nor even in Antillean French, let alone spoken French. He writes in a language which claims to be all that at once and in spite of everything, is his very own.''

We have a problem regarding Chamoiseau and Confiant as markers of words and defenders of Creole oraliture when their texts are a scholarly marquetry of languages and registers and turn out to be genuine palimpsests. Critics have compared these two writers to François Rabelais and the Italian C. E. Gadda. They have been talked about as (politico) linguistic revolutionaries, decolonizers of Antillean literature, and initiators of a new and authentic literary tradition. They themselves have claimed all of the above, and that is the bone of contention: before them and except for them, every writer from the Antilles, including Césaire, has supposedly produced texts lugubriously written in the language of colonization, stamped with the seal of mimicry, mirroring a deep alienation.

For us, understandably, there is nothing of the sort.

Confiant's and Chamoiseau's work on the language, superb without a doubt, is a product of their own creativity, of their personal inventiveness, which uses everything available, from the resources of Creole to those of French and other European languages. Their language is certainly not valid as a model for other creators. What can any writer do but tinker an idiom to the best of his/her ability?

Furthermore, what is behind the apparent carnivalization of this literature? What is behind the riot of words, the exaggeration of images, their total gratuitousness, even though they remain generally appealing, and a raving imagination that could be said to run wild? In an article in the journal *L'Infini*, Milan Kundera went into raptures over the fantastic nature of these texts. In the French Caribbean we are sadly living through the post-Maastricht era. Guadeloupe and Martinique have abandoned their hopes for independence. The writer is no longer the prophet who foretells of a silver lining. The writer no longer predicts, like Césaire in *Cahier d'un retour au pays natal*, black folk

> unexpectedly standing
> standing in the hold
> standing in the cabins
> standing on deck
> standing in the wind. (1971: 149)

On the contrary. They are seen crowding the roads of exile and massing in the dismal suburbs of foreign metropolises. Deep down the writer is conscious that the intellectuals have failed their mission. So what is left?

The pyrotechnics of the text.

II

SOCIAL ARENAS

6

Kwanzaa and the U.S. Ethnic Mosaic

Ariana Hernandez-Reguant

Each year, during the December holiday season, millions of African Americans celebrate a relatively new holiday. Although it was designed at the height of the Black Power movement, Kwanzaa has only recently become a familiar scene in the end-of-the-year season. The mainstream media—newspapers, TV, and radio—have popularized Kwanzaa among the American public in the 1990s and turned it into a symbol of multiculturalism away from its black nationalist origins. Kwanzaa's mass representation has changed from a revolutionary symbol to an affirmation of middle-class values and American citizenship. In a multicultural America, where inequalities based on race and class are obscured under the neutral term of ethnicity, and where struggles for representation and access to resources are increasingly fought on the basis of ethnic allegiance, it is through the display of ethnic identity that African Americans as a cultural group seemingly acquire access to citizenship. The partial shift in the meaning of blackness from a racial to an ethnic signifier reflects not only a broader societal trend but also the possibility of upward mobility through symbolic ethnic allegiances.

The concept of the American nation as a mosaic of diverse cultural groups has been reflected in the annual presidential Kwanzaa greeting. Since 1995, the president of the United States has given a very similar speech:

The hearts of millions of men and women across America and around the world rejoice as together we enter into the spirit of this uplifting holiday (. . .) [that] teach[es] us that when we come together to strengthen our families and communities and honor the lessons of the past, we can face the future with joy and optimism. . . .

Today, we have a renewed sense of hope in America, a hope based on the idea that
our great diversity can unite—not divide—our society. As we rejoice in the rich cultural
heritage of the African-American community during Kwanzaa, let us work together to
ensure that the meaning and energy of this inspiring festival will remain with us throughout the coming year, bringing courage, renewal, and even greater hope for the future.

Hillary joins me in sending best wishes for a wonderful holiday and every happiness
in the year ahead. (Clinton 1996)

The use of the first-person plural throughout the text indicates the inclusion
of both the speaker and African-American Kwanzaa concelebrants in the same
American nation. The speech, also, is generic enough that the same could have
been given about Christmas and Hanukkah, if only the words "African American" and "Kwanzaa" were changed. This is because these holidays have been
made to a great extent equivalent to each other in a model of American society
as a mosaic made up of different but yet complementary ethnic groups, in which
democracy and access to resources are based on the individual's membership in
an ethnic group. What holds these ethnic groups together in one nation is their
unity of values in the "great diversity" of cultures, according to the speech.
That is, it is a common set of moral values that defines citizenship, rather than
race or place of birth. These are the values of individualism and a work ethic
that are said to lead to upward mobility and the fulfillment of the American
Dream. And these are precisely the values celebrated during Kwanzaa and that
make this holiday not a black nationalist ritual of resistance, but a symbol of
blackness framed within a model of multicultural middle-class harmony.
"Blackness" has become a sign for ethnicity in its shift from a symbol of fatal
racial exclusion to one of possible cultural inclusion. The process whereby ethnicity and its associated concept, culture, have become organizing principles of
contemporary American society (Gans 1979) has been extended in dominant
discourses to also include black Americans, a nonimmigrant group previously
categorized as a race with late access to full citizenship. This process has involved the U.S. state apparatuses as well as segments of the black urban community, brought together in an effort to deracialize and thereby make more
accessible a notion of American cultural citizenship—no longer defined through
the naturalizing term of race, but through an idiom of ethnicity, morality, and
cultural consumption. Kwanzaa's presence along with Christmas and Hanukkah
in newspapers, shop windows, billboards, and mall decorations reflects the rise
of multiculturalism as an organizing principle in American society.

The ritual of Kwanzaa as much as its public representations characterizes the
imagined community of potential concelebrants, both from within as well as
from without. Changes in representations reflect Kwanzaa's dynamic relationship with a larger American society extremely concerned with the integration
of newcomers and the workings of democracy. Throughout the twentieth century, the nature of citizenship and the distribution of social resources have been
subjects of debate largely determined by one position defending the "assimi-

lation'' of immigrants into the ''melting pot''—recently reflected in English-only policies in certain states—and another position proposing ''identity politics'' and the need to respect cultural diversity in a society described as a ''cultural mosaic.'' This debate is not entirely a new affair, and it acquired prominence twice before in this century. Policies on the Americanization of immigrants during the 1920s responded to the idea that the United States was a melting pot into which all new immigrants could blend by learning English, civics, and American history. The policy, however, had the effect of perpetuating the segregation of nonimmigrant, non-European groups like blacks and American Indians. Even then, however, there was an opposing view of the United States as a mosaic of distinct cultural groups. According to Joel Kahn (1995), 1920s travel books, novels, and articles on New York presented the city as a mosaic of ethnic neighborhoods that included Negro Harlem. There, the writers of the Harlem Renaissance sought to construct for themselves an ethnic past that was located elsewhere. Like Marcus Garvey, some of them advocated a return to Africa, albeit in a different way. Africa was not a political project of national liberation for American blacks, but an aesthetic inspiration and a source of cultural identity for the urban present (Ogren 1989). As opposed to Garvey's racial transnationalism with political links throughout the African diaspora, Africa, and the Caribbean, the cultural nationalism of the Harlem Renaissance intellectuals was expressed in the context of a metropolis, New York City, that was receiving a constant migratory influx from Europe.

Both at that time and later in the century, views on citizenship and immigration among white intellectuals and within the American government coexisted with a debate among black intellectuals on racial versus cultural nationalism. This was the case again in the 1970s, in the context of a new wave of non-European immigrants, the flight of central city residents to the suburbs—which were thought to prove the melting pot theory by attracting a racially and culturally diverse population (Waters 1990)—and the post–Civil Rights movement desegregation policies, which had resulted in greater access to resources and the political process for African-Americans. In 1972, the federal government budgeted $14 million for the Ethnic Heritage Studies Program, which financed the 1980 publication of the *Harvard Encyclopedia of American Ethnic Groups*. This encyclopedia recast both blacks and whites as ethnic groups, together with 96 others (70 percent of them of European descent). According to this encyclopedia, in sum, everybody in America belonged to one ethnic group or another. The classificatory category of race was thus substituted for a seemingly value-neutral category—ethnicity (Smith 1982)—which would then become the preferred mode of classifying American citizens. Also in 1980, the Census modified its forms because of pressure by white ''ethnic'' groups that needed a means to identify their American-born constituency (Waters 1990). Whereas previously the Census had asked people to classify themselves according to race—as Whites, Negroes, Amerindians, Orientals, or other non-Whites (Smith 1982)–in 1980, U.S. residents were asked to specify their *ancestry*. Ancestry was defined as "the nationality group, the lineage, or the country in which the person or the person's parents were born before their arrival in the United States." Examples of valid answers included: "Afro-American, English, Honduran, Irish, Italian, Jamaican, Korean, Lebanese, Mexican, Nigerian and Polish," and the respondent could offer as many as three (Waters 1990).

As in the 1920s, in the late 1960s and early 1970s, the role of immigration, race, and citizenship in the representation of the American nation was, once again, an issue that was not only in the domain of state institutions but also of civic groups. Among black intellectuals, revolutionary nationalism faded into a movement for cultural awareness. It was in this context that Kwanzaa was first celebrated in Los Angeles in 1966 at the height of the Black Power movement. An offshoot of the Civil Rights movement, and in association with the trend to reclaim African-inspired fashions and aesthetics, Kwanzaa was the brainchild of Maulana Ron Karenga, a black nationalist leader who broke off with the Black Panther Party to form a cultural nationalist organization. Karenga rejected Stokely Carmichael's revolutionary politics and Marxist ideology and proposed cultural and historical awareness as a condition for the liberation of black people in America. His ideological disagreement with Carmichael was a reflection of a similar split taking place within the ranks of the international Pan-Africanist movement, between the Marxist-Leninist and the Cultural Nationalist (*Négritude*) wings of the movement. Karenga was himself influenced by Tanzanian president and Pan-African leader Julius Nyerere, who was a proponent of an indigenous socialism based on African traditions. Nyerere's influence translated into an interest in Swahili language and aesthetics on the part of both Pan-Africanists and Black Power followers (Walters 1993). Swahili's use as a lingua franca among diverse central and eastern African countries and its "nontribal" character made it attractive to Black Power groups in the United States. In response to the trend towards seeking linguistic and cultural roots on the African continent, Karenga himself took a Swahili name that means "the keeper of the tradition" and developed his *Kawaida* theory or seven moral principles—the *Nguzo Saba*—as well as a holiday—*Kwanzaa*—to celebrate these principles, using terminology borrowed from the Swahili language. The 1976 publication of Alex Haley's bestseller, *Roots*, contributed to the widespread movement among black Americans to reconstruct their ethnic past. Symbols of Africa became ubiquitous through American cities: "pictures of Africa were engraved on maps, on clothes, on leather amulets . . . African clothes were worn, African hairstyles were adopted" (Walters 1993: 364). Aesthetics, as well as music, constituted a public display of identity and pride (Gilroy 1987; Van Deburg 1992).

It was not, however, until the late 1980s that this trend culminated in the ethnicization of *blackness* and the parallel popularization of Kwanzaa, when, as a reaction against the Republican push for ideological conformity, the debate on multiculturalism picked up again with more force than ever in schools and campuses throughout the country. While not abandoning the discourse of race to denounce inequalities, moderate black leaders such as Jesse Jackson have supported the multicultural movement and used an idiom of ethnicity to strive for their constituents' symbolic inclusion in the U.S. nation. Adoption of the term "African American," as popularized by Reverend Jackson in 1988, clearly reveals this process of black ethnicization. Paul Gilroy (1987) has showed that the structure of the state determines the shape of political struggles. However, this causal relationship is not entirely unidirectional, if only because the state is a complex conglomerate of loosely coordinated institutions and actors that do not necessarily follow a master plan. As mass culture, considered by Stuart Hall (1977) as "a contested terrain" structured between different interest groups including state institutions, rather than a conscious production of the ruling class, I would argue that the same holds for powerful ideological constructs such as ethnicity that produce primordial attachments. The process of black ethnogenesis is therefore not only an initiative of moderate segments of the black community, or a strategy devised by the U.S. state apparatus, but a complex construct of mutual accommodation between various interest groups.

Like the "invented traditions" documented by Eric Hobsbawm et al. (1983), Kwanzaa seeks to instill moral values and a group identity by claiming a continuity with an ancestral past, in this case located in preslavery Africa. Although initially Kwanzaa promoted an identity based on cultural uniqueness and social difference, it was only popularized when it came to convey in addition its social equivalence to other groups that are categorized as "ethnic." Participation in this identity does not require a change of lifestyle, but an annual expression of symbolic allegiance to the group. This is similar to the relationship, documented by Henry Gans (1979) of some Jewish immigrant groups with Hanukkah, which, without upsetting daily routines, manages to imprint Jewish identity on children through an annual celebration. In these types of holidays, tradition is recreated through symbols while daily lives continue to be pragmatic responses to the demands of work, family, and hierarchical social structures in general (Gans 1979).

As a symbol and celebration of ethnicity, the holiday as well as the public representations of Kwanzaa situate African Americans on the same level as other "hyphenated" Americans by stressing a valuable past located elsewhere, as expressed by Kwanzaa's inventor: "Thus, like Chinese, Japanese, Mexicans, and/or Puerto Ricans who change residence but never lose their home or the living link this implies, so it is vital that African Americans never lose their name or deny their African origins regardless of their life and history in America" (Karenga 1988: 81).

A NEW TRADITION FOR A NEW ETHNICITY

Kwanzaa takes place between December 26 and January 1, conveniently coinciding with Christmas, Hanukkah, the New Year, and school vacations, when families and friends everywhere are most likely to assemble in celebration. The dates were chosen to coincide with the holiday season in order to provide African Americans with a culturally and economically specific choice. As Kwanzaa takes place after ''the end of the high-priced hustle and bustle of Christmas buying and selling'' (Karenga 1988: 32), African Americans may choose to observe the new ritual instead of, or in addition to, the Christian holiday.

As envisioned by Karenga (1988), each of the seven days of Kwanzaa is dedicated to one of seven moral principles:

December 26th—Umoja Day (Unity)

December 27th—Kujichagulia Day (Self-Determination)

December 28th—Ujima Day (Collective Work and Responsibility)

December 29th—Ujamaa Day (Cooperative Economics)

December 30th—Nia Day (Purpose)

December 31st—Kuumba Day (Creativity) (Karamu Feast Evening)

January 1st—Imani Day (Faith)

The seven Nguzo Saba principles or moral values are, according to Karenga (1977), inspired by different value systems in Africa. They constitute ''the moral minimum set of African values that African Americans need in order to rebuild and strengthen family, community and culture and become self-conscious social forces in the struggle to control their destiny and daily life'' (Karenga 1988: 29). These values were defined by Karenga in 1988 as: Unity (Umoja) ''in the family, community, nation, and world African community'' (Karenga 1988: 47); Self-Determination (Kujichagulia), understood not as political independence, but as control over the politics of representation so as not to be ''defined, named, created for and spoken for by others'' (Karenga 1988: 42); Collective Work and Responsibility (Ujima), geared toward community-building and collective problem resolution (Karenga 1988: 56); Cooperative Economics (Ujamaa) or the building of business and the control of the community finances (Karenga 1988: 61); Purpose (Nia) and Creativity (Kuumba) as the determination to build a community and ''restore our people to their traditional greatness'' (Karenga 1988: 64); and Faith (Imani) or the belief ''with all our heart in our Creator, our people, our teachers, our leaders, and the righteousness and victory of our struggle'' (Karenga 1988: 64).

By 1988, these principles had undergone a subtle transformation from the version put forth eleven years earlier. In 1977, Karenga had emphasized the political aspects of Kwanzaa, its capacity for empowerment and political mobilization. By 1988, however, he had placed more emphasis on the cultural aspects, stressing instead the need to struggle in order to ''rescue and reconstruct our history and culture'' (1988: 43). An instance of this transformation concerns the principle of Imani or Faith. In 1977, Karenga's manifesto omitted any reference to any God, except to reject religion as ''spookism.''[1] At that time, Karenga proposed ''a humanistic faith, an earth-oriented, earth-based, people-centered faith in the tradition of the best African philosophies and values'' (Karenga 1977). Now, in contrast, the expression of faith is to be directed toward a supreme being—the Creator—followed by belief in people, teachers, leaders (Karenga 1988). Another principle that changed considerably between the 1977 manifesto and the 1988 book is that of Ujamaa or Cooperative Economics. In the more radical political version of 1977, Ujamaa was understood as a form of ''African socialism or communalism, a socio-economic system in which people come before profit and there is an egalitarian distribution of wealth, a planned economy and collective control of the means to satisfy human needs'' (Karenga 1977). After the Civil Rights movement and the following decade of Republicanism, black nationalist discourses downplayed Marxist politics and class confrontation in order to appeal to a black professional and entrepreneurial middle class. By 1988, accordingly, Ujamaa meant charity and voluntary individual sharing of wealth and is often invoked as a mandate to support black business, rather than as socialism and cooperativism. The author of a popular book on Kwanzaa wrote on this principle that: ''The spirit of our ancestors lives on in the large number of black-owned businesses. . . . In my hometown, there are several McDonald's, including one that is owned by an industrious African-American couple. . . . I enjoy taking a break anytime at their restaurant because I know what they had to go through to establish themselves as business owners'' (Medearis 1995: 84).

This and many such books published from 1990 on, inspired by Karenga manifestoes, convey the Nguzo Saba values in consistency with those of individualism self-reliance, leadership, work ethics, and entrepreneurship. ''Self-help is the best help,'' ''the best therapy in the world is work,'' ''start small, work hard, allow your dreams to grow'' (Harris 1995: 85), and ''scratch a black person and you're sure to find an entrepreneur'' (Copage 1991) are quotes that often precede moral tales of survival inspired by glorious heroes such as Kwame Nkrumah, Steven Biko, and Frederick Douglass and victorious events such as the U.S. Civil Rights movement and the struggle for Emancipation.[2] Although Karenga (1988: 42) claimed that the Nguzo Saba principles conveyed a communitarian view of personhood that is opposed to European individualism, they have in fact come to support middle-class aspirations of upward mobility through work without questioning social stratification and inequalities.

While the Kwanzaa principles are open to interpretation, the ritual instruments and practices have been described in great detail by Karenga (1988: 75–78). Inspired as much by traditional East African harvest ceremonies as by comparable rituals celebrated by other groups in America, the objects used in the ritual ''are both traditional and modern items and reflect both traditional and modern concepts which evolved out of the life and struggle of African American people'' (Karenga 1988: 75). A *mkeka* or straw mat, symbolizing the foundation of everything else, is placed on a table under the kinara or candleholder that symbolizes the ancestors. The kinara holds seven candles (mishumma saba) representing the seven Nguzo Saba principles. The central candle should be black, with three red candles on one side and three green candles on the other side, representing both the colors of the African flag and the Garvey movement.[3] Also placed on the mat is a *kikombe* or unity cup, which holds daily libations for the ancestors; several kinds of fruit (*mazao*) representing the crops as rewards of collective labor; a few ears of corn (*mihindi*) representing the children in the household, and the gifts (*zawaidi*) to be exchanged.[4] Each day one candle is lit, honoring the Nguzo Saba principle of the day. This is followed by libations of wine or grape juice as heroes and heroines from the past are invoked. As this takes place, people call for unity and struggle by saying Harambee and closing their right fists. A family dinner may follow the ritual. On the sixth day of Kwanzaa, which is also New Year's Eve, the dinner feast of the week or Karamu, consists of a potluck for family and guests. At this time, people often dress in African clothing, and the house is decorated in African-inspired motifs. Speeches, performances, and stories are told as the year comes to an end.[5]

In 1996, Kwanzaa was celebrated throughout Washington, D.C., at schools, libraries, museums, community organizations, churches, and homes.[6] Next to black nationalist organizations and Afrocentric groups, mainstream institutions like the Smithsonian Museums, the World Bank, and the Library of Congress sponsored celebratory events and performances. All city newspapers, including the *Washington Post*, the *Washington Times*, the *Washington Afro-American*, and the *City Paper*, echoed the celebrations and published calendars of Kwanzaa events, thus popularizing the holiday among city residents. Every day, performances that stressed the African heritage of African Americans took place at different locations in the city. Weekend dinner parties were organized in people's homes with the occasion and provided the opportunity for gatherings and feasts with friends and family. On December 27, 1996, around 80 people, mostly women, gathered at the Imani Temple, a former Catholic church, now nondenominational and afrocentric, located in Capitol Hill, to celebrate Kujigachulia Day. The evening opened with a skit written and performed by congregation members. The church flyer summarized it as follows:

Today's play is about the Hawkins family. In the first scene Aunt Helen Hawkins and her family arrive at the airport. With her is her great-nephew, Trae Alexander Hawkins II, his wife . . . and their son, Trae Alexander Hawkins III . . . They have come to greet Aunt Helen's Aunt Okereta Marchelea Olatando, from West Africa.

In the second scene the family is preparing to have dinner . . . Marissa and Clarisse are preparing dinner. Trae, Jr., plays on his computer, while Tiffany talks on the phone. Aunt Okereta is napping, and Uncle Jerome and Trae, Sr., are watching basketball. Aunt Helen sits quietly reading.

In the final scene the family arrives at Imani Temple on Capitol Hill to introduce Aunt Okereta to the African-American celebration of Kwanzaa and to partake in the Karamu (feast).

This picture of sub/urban middle-class life—to which I will return later—was followed by the Kwanzaa ritual. Since this was a first-time experience not only for me, but also for many of those present, the ceremony leader explained every procedure, every item used, and every value invoked. A man read the seven "black principles of Kwanzaa" after a short introduction to the important role that both Jesus and Africa should have in people's lives. The Kwanzaa table was then set as two boys played drums. The priests and the elders were called to perform libations as a congregation member from Ghana chanted in his native Twi language. One by one, seven people were called from among the attendants to light the candles. After one member lit a candle, the ceremony director asked: "Did she light the right candle?" "Nooo," responded the congregation. She then explained: "We light one red and one black, and one on one side, and one on the other side." The person who did it wrong walked back to the altar, blew out the wrong candle, and then lit the right one. The ceremony had the feel of a school rehearsal. Kwanzaa is a recent acquisition in this church. In contrast, across the Anacostia River, Union Temple Baptist Church, an afrocentric Baptist church with a history of grassroots activism, has celebrated Kwanzaa since the mid-1970s. There, a few congregation members from all economic strata wore African robes and seemed familiar with the Kwanzaa ritual, which was performed without educational explanations as a troop of drummers played African rythms between the aisles. Black churches have had a pivotal role in the popularization of Kwanzaa. As it occurred with Mother's Day earlier in the century (Schmidt 1995), Kwanzaa's philosophical consistency with Christianity and its symbolisk of identity was welcomed by progressive black Christian churches and their constituencies.

Kwanzaa's emphasis on cultural performance has resulted in its celebration by museums and theaters. On the Mall, on Nia Day (December 30), crowds of mostly black people of all ages clamored to get one of the free seats at a Kwanzaa dance performance at the Smithsonian Baird Auditorium. Dance shows, theater plays, poetry readings, and concerts, together with commercial advertisements of holiday gifts, Kwanzaa Expos, and a broad array of press articles and informational pieces on the appropriate dishes and the right gifts mark the Kwanzaa season throughout the United States. While Kwanzaa is still celebrated especially in black nationalist circles, many black people of all ages and backgrounds participate in celebrations in one way or another. Kwanzaa is not only a home holiday, but an occasion for organizing cultural events that has acquired visibility through its mass-media representation and its use by commercial interests with the goal of penetrating the market niche of the black middle class in a strikingly similar way to those that surrounded the popularization of Christmas and Mother's Day in the nineteenth and early twentieth centuries (Schmidt 1995).

While the first Kwanzaa was celebrated only by Karenga and his colleagues, thirty years later it was celebrated by millions worldwide (*U.S. News & World Report* 1996). However, if Kwanzaa operates as an identity marker, what is most relevant is not the numbers of actual participants, but who and how many people feel that they could rightfully participate in the celebration if they so chose. A survey that I conducted in 1997 among African Americans associated with the University of Chicago showed that all respondents were able to identify Kwanzaa as a specific African-American holiday, despite the fact that 55 percent of them had never celebrated it.[7] The widespread popularity of Kwanzaa is particularly salient among some segments of the black middle class, who are "more open-minded about the adoption of aspects of an explicit African cultural identity" (Walters 1993). These include not only the celebration of Kwanzaa, but also the use of the *kente* cloth as a symbol of a diasporic identity (Adjaye 1997), the acquisition of African art (Walters 1993), the use of West African clothes on occasion, and the enrollment of the children in private Afrocentric schools.

MASS-MEDIA REPRESENTATIONS OF BLACKNESS

Kwanzaa has become popular only in recent years as schools, community organizations and, most importantly, the mass media—printed press, TV, and radio—have supported the celebration as an expression of neighborhood diversity and harmonious coexistence between "ethnic" groups.[8] The mass media frequently play an important role in the creation of national communities and social identities (Abu-Lughod 1989; Abu-Lughod 1993; Anderson 1991). It is largely through the media, for example, that immigrant populations learn about their distant homeland and build social identities in their new country (Hall 1992; Merelman 1995). In the case of African-American identity building, the media have not created the imagined community as Benedict Anderson (1991) would have it, but have contributed to its reconceptualization as an ethnicity, displacing a racial emphasis on much of its cultural discourse. This is in no way a total shift. As Stuart Hall (1996) has pointed out in relation to the British case, the struggle over politics of representation on the part of black people may assume new forms, but this is not to say that previous forms disappear. In this case, an allusion to blackness as an ethnicity is suggestive of blacks' participation in the American multicultural pie consisting of all immigrant groups. This in no way means the disappearance of a racist discourse and of racial politics, but their recontextualization in relation to class. This point has been made by Richard Handler and Eric Gable (1997) in their analysis of public history at Colonial Williamsburg, where from 1986 on the African-American presence has been reformulated as that of "another" immigrant group also participant in the making of the American nation.

Kwanzaa, in the context of multiculturalism, thus takes shape as a public celebration of blackness in a society that grants access to political process and distributes social resources according to the ethnic identity of various groups. Control over representation, as described by the Nguzo Saba principle of Kujichagulia or Self-Determination, has become the most visible arena of political struggle, as it is the case for British blacks (Hall 1996). Because of a coincidence of interests of a number of players, such as state institutions, the mass media, businesses, and the black middle class itself, blackness is reformulated in some cases as embodying middle-class traits.

Stories about Kwanzaa in the printed press—both in white-owned and black-owned newspapers—have changed considerably between 1971, the first time that any major newspaper reported on the celebration, and 1996, reflecting government discourses and public opinion regarding race and citizenship. These media images have contributed to Kwanzaa's popularity and acceptance not only among blacks, but also among the general population. During the 1980s, when the discourse of the political Right spoke of "reverse discrimination, traditional values, and anti-immigration" (Gray 1995: 17), it posited images of middle-and upper-class blacks as proof of racial equality. Examples included characters on situation comedies like *The Cosby Show, Living Single, Martin*, and *The Fresh Prince of Bel Air*—people of "moral character, individual responsibility and personal determination to succeed" (Gray 1995: 19). At the same time, as television shows projected a positive image of the black middle class, newscasts spoke of an urban underclass which was "socially isolated and culturally deprived," inhabiting crime-ridden inner cities and lacking civic responsibility and respect for traditional values (Merelman 1995: 200–224; Page 1997). The solution to their increasing poverty and marginalization, it was suggested, lies in moral and cultural regulation—namely, independence from state-provided welfare, revitalization of the private sector, a return to the traditional family structure, and emphasis on individual responsibility.

At the end of the 1980s, media coverage of cultural issues, involving stories of black self-concepts, identity, and culture increased significantly (Merelman 1995: 210–213). The new emphasis on black cultural identity was reflected again in television shows such as *Roc, A Different World*, and *Frank's Place* and was due in part to the emergence of the FOX network, which, because of economic imperatives, was more responsive to black audiences and their consumption patterns (Gray 1995). As Abu-Lughod (1993) pointed out for Egyptian TV, this phenomenon may also be related to the increasing numbers of black urban middle-class professionals working in the mass-media industry and therefore catering to their own. In addition, the changes in labor and immigration patterns, the legacy of the civil rights movement and affirmative action policies, the industry's needs to expand and capture new markets, and the dissemination of a discourse on multiculturalism after which to model American citizenship, allowed for a middle-class representation of blackness to emerge in the late 1980s in which both conservative and liberal interests converged. Kwanzaa, as a symbol of blackness for the most part absent from the mainstream media during the 1980s, became a familiar scene by the end of the decade. Not surprisingly, its image had evolved from a black nationalist ritual of resistance to a middle-class holiday sanctioned by the Clinton administration becoming, to borrow Helan Page's (1997) terms, "positive and embraceable," images of middle-class blacks came to represent blackness in a nonthreatening way by stressing cultural values rather than political resistance. In media discourse, middle-class blacks were seen less and less as a racial group victimized by discrimination and more as equal players in the politics of culture and ethnicity, while poor inner-city blacks, mostly young, continued to be chastized as socially disruptive (Rose 1994).

A review of major U.S. newspapers revealed that the first article ever dedicated to Kwanzaa appeared in 1971 in the *New York Times*.[9] Until 1987, only the *Washington Post*, the *New York Times*, and black-owned newspapers like the *Chicago Defender* ever reported on Kwanzaa celebrations, mostly covering local events at black nationalist schools, community groups, and churches (Campbell 1972; Carroll 1987; Coble 1988; Cummings 1973; Hunter 1971; Morgan 1978; Reif 1974; Sargent 1982; Stevens 1979; Terrell 1972).[10] Kwanzaa was not portrayed as widely popular outside a few relatively small community organizations. In 1973, the *Times* reported that Kwanzaa was "unfamiliar to the old people but [an observance] that has grown in popularity among younger black Americans" (Cummings 1973). In the District of Columbia, only around 17,000 people celebrated Kwanzaa in 1977 (Camp 1977), and two years later "workshop and community events celebrating Kwanzaa are virtually nonexistent" outside the District, according to the *Post* (Stevens 1979). By 1982, however, Kwanzaa was said to be "significant" to a substantial segment of Washington's black population (Sargent 1982).

Until 1978, when Washington, D.C. Mayor Marion Barry, a former Black Power leader at Howard University, contributed to Kwanzaa's popularity with fund-raising parties and by mailing Kwanzaa, rather than Christmas, cards (Morgan 1978), Kwanzaa was identified as African inspired to counteract the commercialism of Christmas (Campbell 1972; Hunter 1971; Terrell 1972; Sargent 1982; Stevens 1979). For many, Kwanzaa was to substitute for Christmas altogether:

On the door, instead of Christmas wreaths and red-cheeked Santas, is a red and black card depicting a stern African warrior and the seven principles of Kwanzaa. Saturday: instead of spending the day at crowded malls doing last minute Christmas shopping Koko Farrow and her daughter . . . were in the woods . . . gathering holly, pine, and spruce cuttings to place on a straw mat on their living room table, next to red and black candles, fruit and dried corn. Yesterday, instead of opening Christmas presents, the Farrows were with their family and friends at a quiet dinner, reflecting on the year's triumphs and problems. . . . Today, not yesterday, is when the excitement occurs. Today is the first day of Kwanzaa. (Camp 1977)

Throughout the 1980s, views of Kwanzaa as an alternative to Christmas began to coexist with an acceptance of the celebration as a holiday that not only was compatible with but also complementary to other American holidays. A *Washington Post* editorial highlighted Kwanzaa's social benefits:

Any ritual that honors a value or ethical system holds benefit not only for a particular community but also for the nation as a whole. Properly understood, Kwanzaa can provide important identity and tradition for blacks and human understanding more broadly. . . .

Celebrating Afro-American culture can promote understanding of other cultures as well. And it makes no difference that there is no ceremony in Africa called Kwanzaa. Like Christianity, some ideas have humble and confused beginnings. (Gilliam 1984)

By 1986, Kwanzaa was described in the press as a widely followed cultural celebration comparable to Christmas, with its seasonal performances and ad-hoc holiday dishes and fashions. That year, the *Washington Post* printed an article on Kwanzaa on the front page of its Metro section, next to an article on Hanukkah (Marcus 1984). Such placement suggested the elevation of both Kwanzaa and Hanukkah to a higher status to be shared with Christmas as major cultural celebrations. Kwanzaa was later equated to other "ethnic" holidays like Three-Kings-Day, the Chinese New Year, Muslim Day,[11] and the Korean Chusok fest (Slesin 1993). In the following years, articles dedicated to Kwanzaa increased dramatically in both number and length in all major newspapers as well as in black-owned periodicals.[12] Kwanzaa features started to appear earlier in the season, often in weekend, style, home and food sections, and included suggestions for cooking recipes and holiday gifts. As press interest in the holiday grew, Kwanzaa evolved from being a local event or a political position to a widespread cultural celebration of black "heritage" (Carroll 1987; Copage 1990; Harrison 1989; Hill 1991, 1994; Softky 1995).

In the early 1990s as multiculturalism became an important pedagogical concept, schools and museums wholeheartedly embraced Kwanzaa as well as the teaching and display of black history and culture (Handler & Gable 1997; Tousignant 1993). By 1995, most Smithsonian Museums, the Library of Congress, the World Bank, shopping malls, schools and universities had their own Kwanzaa celebrations, often observed alongside Hanukkah and Christmas (Berger 1991; Boyle 1993; Chira 1992; Kaufman 1992; Lawson 1995; McLarin 1993; Wright 1995).[13] At that point, Kwanzaa's popularity positioned the holiday on a negotiating position with other holidays from which to build bridges and therefore legitimated black ethnicity among other ethnic groups.[14]

The depiction of Kwanzaa as an integral part of multicultural America culminates with its use in commercial advertising and its participation in the market politics of big and small corporations alike competing for the niche open by middle classes eager to purchase and display their ethnicity as a symbol of their citizenship. The rapid expansion of the black middle class on the heels of the Civil Rights movement opened a new market niche that has resulted in their higher profile as potential consumers and target of sales strategies (Rogers 1992; Williams 1995a). [15] The Afrocentric aesthetic is a mass trend that moves millions of dollars, to the point that in 1992 Kwanzaa alone became a financial affair worth attention in the *Wall Street Journal*, which noted its growing commercial importance. Kwanzaa has become an opportunity for black businesses, seizing on the Kwanzaa principle of ujamaa, or cooperative economics, to cater to an "ethnic" market by promoting "buying black" as an expression of ethnic solidarity (Brown 1995; Reid 1991). Annual Kwanzaa Expos in New York, Philadelphia and Washington, D.C., attract tens of thousands of visitors spending millions of dollars (Marriott 1991; Martin 1993). Although it started as a small fair in Harlem in 1981, the organizing foundation managed to turn the expo into a big affair, attracting corporate sponsors such as Chase Bank, Revlon, General Motors, and Kraft Foods. At these expos, Kwanzaa cards and kits and afrocentric items including Kente cloths, Kwanzaa T-shirts, plates, napkins, towels and bags, black Huggy bears, CDs, books, sweet potato ice creams, aerobic videos, Africa-shaped clocks, and African monopoly games are displayed and sold by both small business (250 of them in 1996) and by big companies.

Black nationalist groups such as the Chicago-based Black United Front have campaigned against this crass commercialization and to preserve Kwanzaa's "purity." However, as Leigh Eric Schmidt (1995) has argued for other holidays such as Christmas, Valentine's Day and Mother's Day, it is precisely this commercialization that has turned these celebrations into quintessential American holidays. All of them, in addition, are occasions for gift giving and special decorations, which opens the door to their marketization, making consumerism a common form to all American celebrations (Schmidt 1995). Similarly, Kwanzaa's media exposure and popularity has been accompanied by its marketization and its use by companies targeting the black middle class.

CUISINE AND CLASS IN THE MULTICULTURAL CITY

On the sixth night of the Kwanzaa week, which falls on New Year's Eve, Karenga (1977) prescribed "a magnificent feast of various foods prepared by all attending." The Karamu is a potluck that fosters community bonding and usually takes place at a home, church, school or community center decorated with African motifs and the colors of the Garveyite flag—black, red, and green. The ritual dinner includes libation statements and cultural expressions such as songs, poems, and skits by those participating (Karenga 1977). Karenga wrote nothing on the specific foods to be consumed on the occasion,[16] and it was not until the early 1990s that periodicals began discussing menus and dishes for the holiday (Hill 1991, 1994; Carrino 1993; Harris 1995a; Levitt 1994; Softky 1995; Sullivan 1991; Sweets 1996). In recent years, with Kwanzaa's popularization as an American ethnic holiday, there has been a proliferation of Kwanzaa gift books that either include recipes or are exclusively dedicated to cuisine.

This recent association between Kwanzaa and a normative cooking, as well as the parallel revival of soul food, reflects indeed a process of ethnic identity building in association with the increased media visibility of the black middle class in the context of a multicultural model of society. Pierre Van den Bergue (1984), and more recently Percy Hintzen (this book) have shown that food, as much as language and religion, is often used by groups as a marker of their ethnic identity, particularly in the context of the multicultural cities of Europe and North America. By stressing through food as much as through ritual the links with a larger African diaspora and a distant homeland, Kwanzaa becomes all the more American.

Authors agree that appropriate Kwanzaa dishes are those cooked in the style of (1) Creole and soul food of the southern United States, like Creole shrimp, sweet potato spoon custard, soul food dip, and Kwanzaa fried chicken; and (2) foods from Africa, the Caribbean, and South America, like Liberian pineapple nut bread, West African potato foo foo, Moroccan honey chicken, and Trinidad collalo stew (Copage 1990, 1991; Harris 1995b; Hill 1991; Jones 1993; McLester 1985; Medearis 1995). Kwanzaa cookbooks and articles offer an annual culinary journey through the Americas and Africa that links African Americans to their African past as well as to their American present, and situates them within a diasporic community of Africans, in a similar way as that described by Arjun Appadurai (1988) in India. These books, which include dishes from regions away from the urban centers where those books are marketed, convey a community notion that extends throughout the national territory. However, in the African-American case, Kwanzaa recipes convey not only a notion of identity that spreads across a territory larger than that of the United States but also the presence of a past that is at the core of the construction of ethnicity, rather than that of nation, as in India.

The Kwanzaa menu represents both the physical and the cultural "survival" of African Americans through ingredients like okra, black-eyed peas, and peanuts that traveled with the slaves between Africa and America and constitute silent witnesses to the "African Holocaust." The materiality of these foods and their presence at the Karamu table demonstrates the existence of a resilient culture with a pre-American past, similar to other immigrant groups. Kwanzaa food situates people in a deeper time and larger space frame that transcends the moment of the United States to include an African past and a diasporic experience stretching across five continents. The goal of ethnicity building is furthered by the fact that Kwanzaa food is to be shared communally. Thus, in cookbooks, recipes are seldom organized into menus, but rather presented as dishes that can "easily be adapted to feed as many guests as your house or hall can hold" (Medearis 1995: 2) or else "packed away and taken elsewhere for a larger communal supper" (Harris 1995b: 75).

The epitomized "luxurious" and "lavish" feast described in Kwanzaa cookbooks (Copage 1991; Harris 1995b) is not feasible for every member of the group. Those who can afford it, the middle-and upper-classes are the target consumers of cookbooks, food, and gifts. It is middle-class urban professional families like the *Plymouths* and the *Browns* of mid-town Manhattan and Capitol Hill that are depicted in newspapers and magazines holding Karamus (Harris 1991; Hill 1991, 1994; Nguyen 1996). Those who can are also urged to spend their "cash among the folk" and "seek out specialty merchants who sell African fabric for use as table cloths" (Harris 1995: 126); who can afford and are supposed to appreciate dishes such as *Avocado Mousse with Shrimp Sauce* and

Endives with Pears and Roquefort, "a winter salad that's absolutely elegant"
and very appropriate for "business networking" (Harris 1995b: 96). These are
also consumers concerned with dieting and healthy eating, and thus recipes are
adapted to U.S. tastes, availability, and current medical concerns (Hughes-
Crowley 1990).

The diversification of consumption patterns that buying power entails includes
an interest in cuisine that taps into the aspirations of travel and leisure that are
characteristic of the middle classes, according to Appadurai (1988) and Mintz
(1996). In India, Appadurai (1988) connects the popularization of cookbooks
with both the rise of an urban professional middle class and with the state efforts
to culturally unify the nation. Similarly, in the United States both the rise and
increased visibility of a black middle class as a result of the Civil Rights movement and affirmative action policies, as well as the multicultural movement of
the late 1980s onward have produced the creation of a specific African-American
cuisine. The Kwanzaa culinary boom needs, in consequence, to be framed within
a larger movement that has revived soul food, as evidenced both through the
publication of numerous cookbooks and through the opening of specialized restaurants (see Mintz 1996).[17] Van den Bergue (1984: 393–395) argues that it is
precisely in the context of the multicultural city that ethnic cuisine, like ethnicity,
becomes self-conscious. While soul food restaurants were traditionally located
in African-American neighborhoods, into which most whites hesitate to venture,
new fancy restaurants dedicated to "nouveau soul" are located in major urban
centers such as Chicago, New York, Atlanta, and Los Angeles. These nouveau
soul restaurants attempt to attract a professional clientele in search of an ethnic
experience (Asimov 1994; Hamm 1996; Rose 1997; Williams 1995a, 1995b).[18]
Often pricey, their menus include dishes that although inspired in traditional
southern cooking, incorporate new ingredients as well as health concerns:

Something has happened to soul food of late. The dishes are often fancier, and sometimes
healthier than the meals prepared by grandmas in sweltering Southern kitchens or by
cooks uptown at Sylvia's or downtown at the Pink Tea Cup. Call it nouvelle soul. . . .
   Nowhere is soul food more haute, or the scene hotter, than at Café Beulah . . . [where]
well-heeled neighborhood residents and luminaries like Naomi Campbell, Quincy Jones
. . . and Toni Morrison (she has actually invested in the restaurant), sup on black-eyed
pea and arugula salad with honey mustard dressing and sauteed chicken livers with
peppered turnip greens and barbecue mustard sauce. (Williams 1995a)

In this way, grandma's food, based on the slave diet of the southern United
States, is upgraded to a nouvelle African-American cuisine.[19] While this type of
soul food is not everyday fare for most urban blacks, but an experience of pride
in tradition to be savored any time outside the home, Kwanzaa food is festive
food. Its consumption is ritualized, and it includes a broader array of dishes that
extends to African and Caribbean menus usually unavailable at soul food restaurants. Although part of the same phenomenon, the goal of Kwanzaa food

goes beyond that of soul food. It is to periodically remind urban professionals, that is, those who have departed from their rural past, of their "heritage" before and beyond their American experience. The 1994 opening of a new Manhattan restaurant called Kwanzaa, catering to New York black professionals, epitomized this association between Kwanzaa and the black middle class (Asimov 1994). The limited success of soul food, and of Kwanzaa food, for that matter, on bridging across U.S. ethnic boundaries, reminds us that the ethnogenesis process that takes place in the multicultural city continues to coexist with racial and class barriers that are not easily crossed.

AN AMERICAN, A NEGRO, TWO WARRING IDEALS IN ONE DARK BODY?[20]

When the Reverend Jesse Jackson announced in 1988 during his electoral campaign that "just as you have Chinese Americans who have a sense of roots in China . . . every ethnic group in this country has a reference to some historical culture base" (quoted by Smith 1992), he was stressing that the term "African American" not only denotes an origin, but also a present. By affirming the reconciliation of both the African and the American ideals, it constitutes an affirmation of American citizenship and the illusion of equality with all other hyphenated Americans, if only in the cultural domain (Hernandez-Reguant 1995). The use and success of this new term indicated a favorable climate of black public opinion as well as the opening of a political arena in which electoral contests are played against a background of ethnic particularisms that sum up to the whole of American citizenship. Ethnic identities are contextual and fluid and develop in a dialogue with other such groups as well as with the larger society and structures of government, as Gilroy (1987), Hintzen and Gina Ulysse (both in this book), among others, have shown. The popularization of Kwanzaa has been a part of this trend to claim an African heritage among black Americans (Walters 1993: 84) whereby African-inspired fashions, performance, and aesthetics have become symbols of an American ethnicity among many others. This symbolic journey from race to ethnicity is the opposite of that experienced by black British citizens in recent times who, as recent immigrants from different areas of the world and speaking different languages, have however been categorized as a single racial group (Gilroy 1987). In the United States, the opposite classificatory shift has been a response to a wider social and political debate over the role of immigration in the American nation, and, in consequence, over the nature of citizenship and democracy. The ethnic hyphen, however, still marks a distance from nonhyphenated Americans (Williams 1989), despite the claims of the *Harvard Encyclopedia of American Ethnic Groups*. In this case, furthermore, the representation of African-American ethnicity excludes groups such as inner-city dwellers, who remain racialized and with little hope of upward mobility, as Tricia Rose (1994) has documented. This is not to say that working-class and inner-city African Americans do not partake in Kwanzaa celebrations, but that by and large, they are excluded from Kwanzaa's public representations.

In the multicultural landscape, race is to nature as ethnicity is to culture. The concept of ethnicity seeks to displace that of "nature" and substitute it with "culture." An emphasis on culture as value free helps to present an appearance of social equality between all cultural groups. While class and race are associated with social stratification and inequality, ethnicity and culture are presented as neutral concepts, at most associated with social "differentiation." Ethnicity and culture, as a consequence, do not stand as obstacles to achieving the American dream, so long as the cultures that make up the American mosaic aspire to "bourgeois norms of social acceptance, legal protection and relative material comfort" (Brown 1995: 207). In other words, as long as the members of ethnic cultures adhere to the ethics of work, family, and upward mobility—upon which American identity is based—they will be accepted by the larger society. However, ethnicity is not entirely separated from the naturalizing tendencies of race. In the ethnic discourse, culture is still transmitted through biological ties, which constitute the source of culture's resilience even in the eventuality of collective memory loss or even physical isolation. Common ancestry is expressed in the present through cultural beliefs and practices. Inversely, tradition is legitimated biologically as rooted in genealogical links, and is considered a "cultural anchor," and the source of "cultural authority" and authenticity (Karenga 1988). That people who belong to the ethnic group can recover and reconstruct their "lost historical memory and cultural history," even if cultural continuity breaks down, is the guiding motive behind the celebration of Kwanzaa and the Nguzo Saba value system (Karenga 1988: 44). Culture, as an attribute of ethnicity, is therefore resilient, and its solid and long past ensures its projection into the future. This is represented in the Nguzo Saba principle of Nia or purpose, which is conferred "in light of our historical and cultural identity" and propels people into the action of restoring their "collective cultural memory" (Karenga 1988). This is the annual goal of Kwanzaa: renewing historical memory through a ritual that promotes group bonding and a shared commitment to values that are rooted in this (im)memorial past. This past is not narrated as a succession of causal events leading up to the present, but rather as a distant moral state of nature situated in Africa (Hernandez-Reguant 1995), which is the ultimate source of a common identity to all people of African descent: "We as an African people share in the great human legacy that Africa has given to the world . . . the fathers and mothers of human civilization . . . it is this identity which gives us an overriding cultural purpose and suggests a direction" (Karenga 1988: 64).

Since Marcus Garvey and the Harlem Renaissance, African-American intellectuals have sought to integrate Africa in the African-American imagination in different ways—from an exotic past that inspires a different present in the artistic sphere, to a political option in nationalist discourse. The search for a past located elsewhere occurs in a context in which other groups of society legitimate themselves and their presence in the United States in terms of such past and the diasporic journey that links them to the present. This is however a strategy for representation as well as for access to resources. Identities need to be performed, that is, publicly enacted and represented in order to achieve social sanction. For this reason, struggles over public images of self and their mass dissemination are a part of any performance of identity. As Rose (1994) points out, cultural representations of blackness have usually been ''bifocal,'' that is, have targeted a double audience, one black, another one white. Furthermore, self-definition occurs in the context of a dialogue and/or competition and/or opposition with other groups, as both Hintzen and Ulysse show in this volume. The formation of ethnic groups, specifically, is often an initiative of the middle classes with an interest in acquiring full citizenship and greater political and economic power within the larger society. The story of Aunt Okereta illustrated how Kwanzaa, from its *quasi* revolutionary origins, has become a symbol of middle-class respectability in the context of the multicultural city. As a reflection of the reconceptualization of blackness as an ethnic signifier, only superficially away from racial determinism, Kwanzaa representations depict black middle-class aspirations of upward mobility, greater political participation and social visibility, and their immigrantlike origins. But Kwanzaa is also a symbol of a generation, born in or before the 1960s, that is struggling for that middle-class respectability in urban America. While *Hip Hop* and other youth cultures denounce police brutality and lack of opportunities for social mobility (Gilroy 1987; Rose 1994), Kwanzaa transmits hope and the possibility of success through Nia and Imani. And while Tipper Gore engages in a crusade against *gangsta* rap as a product of anti-American barbarism, Bill and Hillary Clinton welcome the celebration of Kwanzaa as a product of American civilization. Insurmountable differences stand between the two, for they are rooted in class and abysmal economic disparities.

However well intended, the widespread celebration of Kwanzaa at museums, companies, schools, college campuses, churches, and community organizations and its media representation throughout American cities does not signal the unconditional welcome of all black people into the multicultural American mainstream. Rather, it recognizes those who share middle-class values of work, family, civic mindedness, aspirations of upward mobility and a unique ''cultural heritage,'' while still marginalizing alternative voices and images that question the dominant ethic.

NOTES

I want, very specially, to thank Jean Rahier for his repeated encouragement and his invitation to participate in a panel on ''Representations of Blackness in the Context of Festivity'' that took place during the 49th International Congress of Americanists, in Quito, Ecuador, in July, 1997. I want to express my gratitude to the panel participants as well as to the following individuals for their valuable comments and assistance during the numerous drafts of this paper: Raj Balasubramanian, Lisa Buck, Kamari Clarke,

Renate Fernandez, Dana Holland, Anthony Marcus, Daniel Noveck, Stuart Rockefeller, Sharon Stowers, and Daniel Suslak. The Department of Anthropology at the University of Chicago provided me with logistical and administrative support for a survey I conducted on Kwanzaa practices on campus. The Anacostia Museum, in Washington, D.C., assisted me in planning my attendance to numerous Kwanzaa events. I also want to thank Eve Ferguson, Wilbert Burguess, Reverend Willie Wilson and the many other brothers and sisters who kindly shared their Kwanzaa 1996 with me in Washington, D.C.

1. Spookism is "the intense emotional commitment to non-human centered principles and practices which place humans at the mercy of invisible and omnipotent forces" (Karenga 1977).

2. Examples include Stokeley Carmichael, Huey P. Newton, Booker T. Washington, Frederick Douglass, Clara Brown, Aesop, Amenhotep, Steven Biko, Carter G. Woodson, and anthropologist Jonetta B. Cole.

3. These colors were chosen by Marcus Garvey in 1920 to represent the Black Liberation Movement in America. Black is said to represent the color of the race, red represents the blood shed in the struggle, and green represents the land.

4. Gifts are not mandatory. Rather, they are supposed to be given as rewards for good deeds done by the children. They should include at least one book and a "heritage symbol," such as a flag or a poster (Karenga 1977, 1988).

5. In addition, people may hold ritual Kwanzaa dinners in any given night of the sequence to celebrate the principle of the day, some times after fasting during the day. Karenga stated, however, that fasting was not a part of the Kwanzaa principles (Karenga 1977: 15). Nevertheless some people do. In Chicago, the Karamu is usually held on the very last night of Kwanzaa, that is, on New Year's Day (Conrad Warrill, personal communication, Chicago, July 1997). Many people, however, may prefer to celebrate New Year's Eve in other ways and hold the Karamu on either the Friday or Saturday of the Kwanzaa week.

6. Fieldwork for this project was conducted during the months of December 1996 and January 1997, in Washington, D.C.

7. The survey was conducted by mail among African-American registered students, faculty, and administrative staff at the University of Chicago during the month of June 1997. It was facilitated by the University of Chicago Office of Minority Affairs. This is obviously a very skewed sample of the population mostly because of its high educational levels. Eighty-one percent of the 65 respondents were graduate students, faculty holding Ph.D.s or administrators with baccalaureate and master's degrees; the rest were college students. Nobody younger than eighteen participated in the survey, and ages ranged between eighteen and seventy-five. Those most likely to celebrate Kwanzaa were between twenty-five and forty years of age (50 percent), and between 40 and 45 (62.5 percent), that is, people born between 1953 and 1973. Females were also most likely to celebrate Kwanzaa than males, as were married individuals with children. All respondents identified Kwanzaa as an African-American celebration of cultural identity except for two people (3 percent), who expressed their opinion for banning the holiday altogether. Two respondents (3 percent) added that they would like Kwanzaa to be celebrated in only one day rather than seven.

8. In fact, in the University of Chicago campus survey, 44 percent of respondents said that they first learned about Kwanzaa through the mass media. The rest answered as follows: 13 percent through friends, 9 percent through family, 20 percent in school or college, 6.5 percent through community organizations, and 2 percent at church.

9. In the *New York Times Index*, Kwanza (with one "a") first appears both as a classificatory category and as the subject of an actual article in 1971. The *New York Times* spelled Kwanzaa with only one "a" through 1985.

10. In analyzing these newspapers, we should be mindful of the fact that while the *Times* tends to be oriented toward a national and international audience, the *Post* is more locally oriented, despite including extensive coverage of government issues. Washington, D.C.'s population was around 70 percent black. In addition, during this time, D.C. had Marion Barry first (around 1972) as a head of the D.C. School Board (at the time the only elected body in the city) and then as an elected mayor from 1978 on. Barry had previously been a local leader of SNCC during the Black Power years. This may explain why the *Post* continued to report on black issues during the late 1970s and into the Reagan era, while the *Times* did not.

Black-owned newspapers like the *Chicago Defender* and the Baltimore and Washington *Afro-American* were often owned by conservative families, and their orientation seldom is radical nationalist—while they reported widely on the African-American community, they do not necessarily dedicate much space to black nationalist issues. The *Chicago Defender*, in particular, dedicates wide coverage to "high society" events. Data on these newspapers is also hard to obtain, since they lack annual indexes and are often not complete in microfilm version. I have examined the *Chicago Defender*'s microfilm collection at the University of Chicago Regenstein Library. Up until the mid-1980s, Kwanzaa was rarely mentioned. Beginning in 1972, Kwanzaa events were mentioned in calendars for the holiday season, and only occasionally would there be a feature article on the celebration. The *Amsterdam News*, of New York City, is an exception.

11. "Muslim's Day has no basis in Islamic theology or culture. Rather, explained Mohammed T. Mehdi, secretary-general of the National Council on Islamic Affairs, it is an attempt to gain acceptance for American Muslims, while giving their children an Islamic alternative to Christian Christmas, Jewish Hanukah, and African American Kwanzaa." The day is supposedly celebrated on the third Friday of December, and in 1994, "though the day still is largely unknown, two New York banking giants—Chase Manhattan and Citibank—have included references to it in office holiday displays" (*Washington Post*, December 10, 1994, B7). This event points at the fact that Kwanzaa is considered by many non African-Americans as a well-established American holiday.

12. In the *Chicago Defender* there are scattered articles on Kwanzaa until the mid-eighties. In 1986, the paper dedicates an editorial to Kwanzaa at the end of December, and from then on, every year the paper has published several feature articles on the positive aspects of the holiday (six articles in 1989, seven in 1990, six in 1991, twelve in 1992, fifteen in 1993, eleven in 1994 and 1995, and ten in 1996). Many papers throughout the country have carried annual stories on Kwanzaa since the late 1980s. These include the *Boston Globe*, the *Chicago Sun-Times*, the *Detroit News*, *Florida Today*, the *Los Angeles Times*, the *San Francisco Chronicle*, *St. Louis Post-Dispatch*, the *Times Picayune* in New Orleans, *USA Today*, the *Village Voice*, and the *Wall Street Journal*. Magazines include *Black Enterprise* (1991, 1993), the *Chronicle of Higher Education* (1994), *Cooking Light* (1994), *Ebony* (1995), *Ebony Man* (1995), *The Economist* (1994), *Essence* (1989–1996), *Glamour* (1991), *House Beautiful* (1996), *Newsweek* (1995), *Time* magazine (1991), and *U.S. News and World Report* (1996), among others.

13. Both the Anacostia Museum and the Museum of African Art had been organizing them since the late 1970s.

14. "Kente Claus" was a figurine designed as "a cross-cultural breakthrough" and "an icon of cultural pride and political correctness" (Marriott 1996).

15. *Essence* (December 1995), for instance, recommended miscellaneous items as Kwanzaa gifts, ranging from $25 to $90. At $75 in 1993, a Kwanzaa set included seven candles, a candle holder, a unity cup, a flag, and a booklet (Gaines 1993).

16. In addition to Christmas and Hanukkah cards, Hallmark introduced a line of Kwanzaa cards in 1992 (Groom 1993).

17. Black Nationalist organizations have repeatedly denounced this phenomenon as one corrupting the initial purpose of Kwanzaa.

18. Softky (1995), who participated in Kwanzaas during the 1960s with Karenga himself, recalled people eating soul food. The current usage of not eating pork is attributed to the fact that many of the first Karamu concelebrants were Muslim. Alcohol was proscribed as well.

Although isolated articles and books suggested specific dishes to be cooked during Kwanzaa as early as the mid-1980s (Mason-Draften 1986; McClester 1985), the Kwanzaa culinary boom did not take place until the early 1990s. The *New York Times* (1986, 1990, 1995), the *Washington Post* (1991, 1994, 1995), and the *Chicago Tribune* (1991) have published recipes for Kwanzaa. As for black publications, the *Chicago Defender* (1994, 1995), the oldest black-owned newspaper in the country, has also published them, as well as *Ebony* (1995) and *Essence* (1994, 1996). To these have been added many other papers throughout the country, as well as magazines such as *House Beautiful* (1996), *Vegetarian Times* (1993), *Food & Wine* (1995), and *Cooking Light* (1994).

19. The interest in soul food peaked at two moments, 1970 and 1993–95, when most soul food cookbooks were also published. The first of these moments coincides with the height of the Black Power movement, and the second with the rise of multiculturalism in the United States. The earliest soul food cookbooks, before 1962, were directed mostly to "Negro maids" and were mostly published by churches, small black presses, and independent authors. The latest ones, in the 1990s, are often coffeetable books, and are published by commercial presses like Simon & Schuster and HarperCollins. Kwanzaa cookbooks are included during the second peak: they were published in 1991, 1994, and 1995, as part of the soul food revival.

20. From W. E. B Du Bois (1989: 45)

7

Identity, Arena, and Performance: Being West Indian in the San Francisco Bay Area

Percy C. Hintzen

INTRODUCTION: WEST INDIANS AS A "MODEL MINORITY"

The San Francisco Bay Area is a ten-country region that stretches over 160 miles from north to south and 40 to 50 miles from east to west at its widest point. It surrounds the San Francisco Bay, an expanse of water that empties into the Pacific Ocean. The 1990 United States Census places the region's population at 6,253,311. The area contains some of the richest counties in the United States, with housing prices ranked among the highest in the nation. It is also the location of numerous research universities, colleges, and research institutions including Standford University, the University of California, Berkeley, and the University of California, San Francisco. It is one of the most ethnically diverse regions in the United States and a prime location for immigrants, particularly from Asia and Latin America.

In 1990, there were 9,019 persons living in the Bay Area who listed themselves as West Indian (excluding Hispanics) in their first or second response to the "ancestry" question on the 1990 U.S. Census. This compares with a total West Indian–born population of 727,191 in the United States and 842,101 persons listed as having West Indian ancestry. Many of these 1,569,292 persons are clustered in New York City and, increasingly, in Miami. New York City alone, it is estimated, contains around half a million "West Indians."[1]

With other immigrant communities, West Indians have come to be considered in popular understandings as a "model minority" exhibiting the ideals of success applicable to the white mainstream population of the United States. The term pertains to the notion of meritocratic success. It applies, particularly, to

American racial discourse. Different groups are understood, accordingly, to get what they earn and deserve (see Fong 1989; Yong-Jin 1994; Petersen 1966; Steinberg 1981 for discussion of the model minority and its origins). As such, West Indians are seen to have overcome obstacles of poverty and migratory disruption to achieve, on merit alone, middle- and upper-middle-class socio-economic status. Scholars like Thomas Sowell have used this putative success of West Indians to refute arguments that African-American poverty is the result of pervasive effects of racial discrimination:

The West Indian success pattern likewise undermines the explanatory power of current white discrimination as a cause of current black poverty . . . color alone, or racism alone, is not a sufficient explanation of income disparities within the black population or between black and white populations. Even educational disparities do not account for the West Indian higher socioeconomic status, for in New York metropolitan area they have no educational advantage, in terms of years in school, over native blacks. (Sowell 1978: 43)

One explanation for West Indian success provided earlier by sociologists Nathan Glazer and Daniel Patrick Moynihan refers to the unique cultural baggage that these migrants bring with them. West Indian culture, it is argued, extols the virtues of hard work, savings, and investment: ''The West Indians' most striking difference from the Southern Negroes was their application to business, education, buying homes, and in general advancing themselves. . . . They average high in intelligence and efficiency, there is practically no illiteracy among them, and many have a sound English common school education. They are characteristically sober-minded and have something of a genius for business, differing almost totally, in these from the average rural Negro of the South'' (Glazer and Moynihan 1963: 35). This view has been supported by pointing to the supposed overrepresentation of West Indians among the successful black population of the United States. Thomas Sowell makes reference to this in his argument: ''West Indians have long been greatly overrepresented among prominent Negroes in the United States. From Marcus Garvey, James Weldon Johnson, and Claude McKay in an earlier era to Stokeley Carmichael, Shirley Chisholm, Malcolm X, Kenneth Clark, James Farmer, Roy Innes, W. Arthur Lewis, Harry Belafonte, Sidney Poitier, and Godfrey Cambridge in more recent times'' (Sowell 1978: 41).

The arguments for West Indian success are much more important for the part they play in the ideological terrain of race relations than for what they say about the reality of the West Indian immigrant presence. Such arguments also are important for the construction of West Indian identity in the United States. Scholars such as Philip Kasinitz (1988), Kristin Butcher (1994), Reynolds Farley and Walter Allen (1987), who have studied West Indian migration over the last ten years are coming to different and more nuanced conclusions about the supposed success of West Indian migrants. Butcher (1994) found little difference in employment rates, marriage rates, average weeks of work, and average wages between native-born African Americans and West Indian male immigrants. Moreover, she found African Americans who had moved across state boundaries to be even more economically successful than immigrant blacks. Farley and Allen (1987) concluded that when location of residence, family type, and education are controlled, the observed income gap between the African American and West Indian becomes quite small and that African Americans actually earn more than their West Indian counterparts. Francis Dodoo (1991) found the returns to education to be lower for West Indian migrants when compared to African Americans.

Evidence to the contrary notwithstanding, the myth of the model minority continues to persist in popular understandings of the West Indian migrant. This myth receives constant reinforcement both from within and outside the group, sustained by invariable predispositions to identify, as examples of West Indian success, those migrants and their descendants who have risen to positions of national prominence.

The overwhelming majority of West Indians are located in New York City. They are employed, overwhelmingly, in the service sector. For this majority, there is a disjuncture between their own socioeconomic reality and the model minority myth. Low income and occupational status hardly qualify as examples of a ''model minority.'' Within this majority, the contradiction between socioeconomic reality and popular understanding is resolved through a respecification of its own West Indian identity and the emphasizing of other bases of identity formation. Studies have shown children of low-skilled West Indian immigrant workers to be particularly predisposed towards a racialized identity as African American (Waters 1990). While first-generation immigrants overwhelmingly differentiate themselves from African Americans, this proves to be the case for their children. Even though acknowledging their West Indian background, the overwhelming majority of the latter understand themselves to be, in a major sense, African American and see little advantage to a West Indian identity (Waters 1990).

This does not mean that a West Indian identity is unimportant. For the West Indian lower class, however, the meaning of ''West Indianness'' seems to diverge significantly from popular conceptualizations of West Indian success. Impressionistic evidence suggests that West Indian identity is important instrumentally—as a basis of access to service sector jobs or to resources and services set aside exclusively for immigrants.[2] West Indians dependent upon the service sectors in New York tend to live in geographic communities particularly centered in Brooklyn, but also in Queens and the Bronx. There are, in addition, areas of commerce and retail in Brooklyn, where most West Indian–owned businesses are located (not necessarily exclusively). These businesses cater to West Indian tastes in food, clothing, music, and so on. The areas of West Indian commerce have become public sites for the display of West Indianness. They provide locations where West Indians demonstrate their presence and make claims for a space in the city and in the United States at large. In other words, there are identifiable "West Indian" communities in New York. West Indians use the physical location of such communities for the symbolic display of their identity. However, neither the sites, symbols, nor rituals of West Indianness in New York lend themselves to self-representations as a model minority. There is nothing particularly "affluent" about the West Indian physical communities in New York. They are located in the working-class neighborhoods of Brooklyn, the Bronx, and Queens. Socioeconomic reality preempts displays of success and affluence.

Thus, West Indian identity is contextualized within the ethnicized reality of New York. West Indians have become transformed into one of the city's myriad ethnic communities with, probably, no more or less significance attached to their identity as West Indians than that attached to the identity of members of any of New York's other ethnic communities. They participate in the symbolic discourse of ethnicity in New York in ways identical to other ethnically identified groups. They exist in the contextualized ethnic space of New York City. As such the rituals of kinship, country, friendship, and associational ties are probably much more significant in self-representation and in understandings of "who one is" than "West Indianness" per se. There may be little interest vested in being West Indian apart from the claiming of ethnic space in an ethnicized location and claims to privileged access to service sector jobs.

This may not be the case when self-representations of socioeconomic status are embedded in West Indian identity. In their self-representations, black middle-class West Indians may have a vested interest in symbolic separation from the black/white dichotomy in the discourse of race in the United States. Such separation can be realized through subjective performance and symbolic display of West Indian identity that incorporate self-representations of model minority status. The imperative for such identific display relates to the discourse of demarcation embedded in the American/immigrant dichotomy. Demarcation becomes the basis of escape from the stigma of being "African American" and of insulation from white racial prejudice. Identific self-representations as West Indian become much more necessary within the context of significantly greater interaction with the white population as socioeconomic equals.

Ariana Hernandez-Reguant, in her paper on Kwanzaa prepared for this book, suggests a similar pattern of class-based ethnicization among the African-American middle class. In this sense, the self-representations of middle-class African Americans contained in the images of Kwanzaa appear to mirror self-representations of their West Indian middle-class counterparts. Like West Indians, these representations are employed to signal their distance from the black/white dichotomy of a racialized America. The rituals of Kwanzaa and the symbolic self-representations conveyed in its images lend themselves profoundly to the values associated with white American middle-class morality. They are the values, argues Hernandez-Reguant, which explain the generalized acceptance of Kwanzaa by mainstream society and the position it has attained alongside other ethnic celebrations. Hernandez-Reguant goes out of her way to emphasize the ethnic, rather than racial, character of Kwanzaa. Its rituals and symbols pertain to ethnicized images of difference rather than racialized ones. Kwanzaa is but one form of ritualistic representation providing the symbolic bases for African-American inclusion into the ethnic mosaic of America alongside other ethnic communities including those of the European Diaspora.

Data presented by Mary Waters (1990) strongly support the claim that middle-class West Indians are much more predisposed to uncategorical embraces of West Indian identity. Unlike their urban working-class counterparts, the majority of suburban and college bound teens she interviewed represented themselves as West Indian. Through the reification of their immigrant status, they were able to claim and maintain a distinct demarcation between themselves and African Americans. Thus, self-representation as model minority West Indian appears related to socioeconomic status, interaction with whites, and residence in non-segregated neighborhood. It represents, also, the "ethnicization" of West Indian identity.

A study of West Indians in Los Angeles conducted by Joyce Justus (1976) provides additional evidence of the association between self representations as West Indian, on the one hand, and class factors including residential and oc-cupational patterns. In Los Angeles, an overwhelming majority of the recent migrants are professional or technical workers. The blue collar workers among these migrants are employed, predominantly in semi skilled occupations (Justus 1976: 131). There is no residential concentration of West Indians in spatially or geographically defined communities. Justus found a "collective consciousness of West Indianness" among these migrants "which finds expression in a mul-tiplicity of Caribbean organizations" (Justus 1976:132). She found, also, class exclusiveness with lower-class West Indians being "often rebuffed in their at-tempts to make social contacts and associate themselves with the middle class." She identified among the migrants many of the traits associated with model minority status. She identified, also, distinctive efforts to distinguish themselves from African Americans (Justus 1976: 142–143).

Cursory evidence from an unsystematic survey of West Indians in the San Francisco Bay Area conducted in 1991 (Noguera-Devers 1991) suggests that the socioeconomic profile of the West Indian population is quite similar to that of Los Angeles. Despite difficulties of reliability posed by the "snowballing" reputational method of selecting respondents for the survey (it excluded potential respondents not normally associated with other West Indians), the study does provide some picture of the composition of the community. Of those inter-viewed, 49 percent held professional or technical jobs, 11 percent held clerical jobs, and 25 percent held jobs located in the service sector. The two latter categories were compounded by a heavy representation of students in the sam-ple, totaling 36.4 percent. Many of these students were employed in the service and clerical sectors. These figures suggest that, in the aggregate, the occupational status of West Indians in the San Francisco Bay was higher than that of both whites and African Americans. This was reflected in the educational attainment of the West Indians interviewed. Ninety-four percent had graduated from high school and 85.1 percent had some college experience. These figures indicate higher levels of educational attainment than both African Americans and whites in the Bay Area. Median family income for the West Indians interviewed was $22,188, which exceeded that for African-American families ($16,025) but was less than that for white families ($26,376) (Noguera-Devers 1991: 10–12). The income of West Indians was, obviously, skewed downward by the large amount of low-earning students among the respondents.

This project has benefited from the presence of myself, as principal investigator, as an active member of the West Indian community in the San Francisco Bay Area since 1979. It has benefited, also, from my own participation in the West Indian community of New York particularly between the periods 1973–79, supplemented by extended and frequent visits to New York since then. The impressions developed from such participation have informed systematic efforts at data collection in the San Francisco Bay Area and, to a lesser extent, in New York beginning in 1989 when the project was first conceived. Data were gathered particularly through participant observation, systematic collection of oral histories in the San Francisco Bay Area, and in-depth informal interviews with members of the West Indian communities in both New York and the San Francisco Bay Area.

IMAGES OF IMMIGRANTS IN CALIFORNIA

On July 1, 1996, in the state of California there were around 8 million foreign-born residents in a total population of 32.4 million. This amounted to 33 percent of all foreign-born residents residing in the United States and 25 percent of California residents in 1996. Because of their numbers, migrants and their families have a high degree of visibility. At the same time, the images and understandings of immigrants held by the population of mainstream Californians are not uniform. These images and understandings relate to cognitive constructs containing notions of worth, desirability, and merit that apply differentially to migrants based on their particular countries and regions of origin. There is the pervasive image of the ''illegal'' that attaches primarily to Mexican and, to a lesser degree, Latino immigrants, particularly those from Central America. These constructed images are fed by constant articulations and rearticulations of Mexican/Latino illegality in the popular media and by politicians. They are reified by pictures and stories of masses of ''illegals'' crossing the United States border with Mexico. Mexicans and Latinos are represented as threats to national integrity and as making illicit and illegal claims upon state resources. Typically emphasized in these representations are the costs to the ''taxpayer'' of providing services to illegals and their children. Mexicans and Latinos are seen in popular representations to be taking jobs away from legal residents. During the eighties and nineties, these historically constructed representations fueled escalating, extreme anti-immigrant sentiment. It culminated in the passage of California Proposition 187 in 1992, which was aimed at prohibiting access by illegal immigrants to state provided services, including education and health care.

Undocumented California migrants and their documented counterparts from Mexico and Central America tend to be clustered in the labor-intensive sectors of the economy, particularly in agriculture, in the textile and garment industries, in construction, and in the service sector, especially the "care" services. Thus, in their socioeconomic and occupational status they tend to resemble West Indian migrants on the East Coast. Since the historically constructed images of the "undesirable" migrant receive reification in California almost exclusively in the form of the Chicano/Latino, a space is created for alternative representations of West Indian migrants.

Understandings of Asian and Pacific Rim migrants (excluding Latin America) emerge out of the cognitive constructs of the "model minority." These constructs receive confirmation in images of economic and educational success. Such images are fed by the visibility of highly educated and wealthy migrants from East Asia (particularly Korea, Hong Kong, and Taiwan) and more recently from South Asia. These migrants took advantage of the 1965 Immigration and Nationality Act to move to the United States. The act reversed the practice of de facto exclusion of Asians from the United States prior to 1965. In its wake, there was an increase by 1041.5 percent in immigration from that continent between 1965 and 1980 (U.S. Immigration and Naturalization Service, 1984: Table 2).

One may logically argue that the historical construction of difference in California made available to West Indian migrants three possible identific "locations" in their efforts at self-representation and identity construction (i) the racialized space of the African American, (ii) the space occupied by the "undesirable" grouping of Mexican and Latino immigrants; and (iii) the identific space of the "model minority" occupied by the "Asian immigrant." A number of factors combined to locate West Indians within the cognitive space occupied by the latter.

First, there was the preexisting generalized representation of West Indians as a "model minority." This, perhaps more than anything else, explains the pervasiveness of the image of success of West Indians in "white consciousness" despite the occupational parallels between Latino migrants on the West Coast and the majority of West Indians in New York City.

Second is the reality of high socioeconomic status among West Indian migrants to California. This has to do with the "pull factors" of West Indian migration to the West Coast that mitigate against the unskilled and low skilled while favoring the qualified and educated. The overwhelming presence of Mexican, Latino, and Pacific Rim migrants in the labor-intensive and service sectors of the California economy has had the effect of shutting out the unskilled and low-skilled West Indian. At the same time, those in the West Indian middle class are particularly suited to exploit opportunities for the skilled and educated in the Californian economy. They can do so by activating their racial identity to provide themselves with access to "Affirmative Action" opportunities available to the African-American population. They have been able, also, to exploit the significant political strength of the African-American community in Los Angeles and in the San Francisco Bay Area. The quite formidable influence of black politicians was developed out of massive political mobilization during the civil rights era of the sixties and seventies. Black leaders were able to garner the support of progressive whites and, particularly, of members of the Chicano/ Latino communities. Political organization and support propelled African-American politicians to mayorships in Los Angeles, Oakland, Berkeley, and San Francisco. It propelled an African-American state representative from San Francisco to the third most powerful position in the state as speaker of the House of Assembly. And it allowed a black mayor of Los Angeles to mount a credible challenge for the governorship of the state by winning the Democratic nomination in 1982. (See Fisher 1992; Horne 1995; Dymally 1972; Sorenshein 1993).

Black political clout in California came with tremendous access to public and private sector resources that allowed the opening up of opportunities for African Americans throughout the state, and particularly in its urban areas. The black West Indian middle class was able to insert itself into this "racial space" created by African-American political power. This is reflected in the growth of the West Indian population in Los Angeles from around 500 before 1950 to around 50,000 by the early nineties. Much of this growth occurred after the mid-sixties (Justus 1976: 131).

WEST INDIAN MIGRANTS TO THE BAY AREA

Images of Bacchus Versus the Model Minority

Subjective performance of West Indian identity in the San Francisco Bay Area is compounded by considerable geographic dispersion and the absence of a central geographic space where symbols of identity can be displayed and identific rituals performed. Members of the community have had to make a conscious effort at self-representation by organizing and participating in identific rituals and by constructing and reconstructing the symbols of West Indian identity. Such rituals and displays occur in numerous "decentralized locations." They are necessarily different and diffuse.

Nonetheless, all efforts at self-representation employ popularized symbols and images of West Indian cultural forms that constitute the cognitive schemata of "West Indianness" shared universally by Americans, and particularly white Americans. As semiotic indices, these symbols and images are universally recognizable. They may be considered the "boundary markers" of West Indianness. As such they act to demarcate the character and nature of the West Indian community. Their representations in music, dance, "spicy food," and a Carnaval spirit indicate a cavalier, fun-loving, bacchanalian, accommodating character.

These identific "boundary markers" combine in subjective performance with a second complex of ritual and performance. These serve as socioeconomic indicators of merit and worth in self-representations as model minority. There is very little relationship between the two. Indeed, they provide contradictory representations of the nature and character of the West Indian. Rituals of demarcation employ the symbols of bacchanalia. Rituals of the model minority employ symbols of achievement, purposefulness, hard work, and family values.

The two sets of symbols and symbolic rituals are integrally connected in the construction of West Indian identity. At the same time, they serve fundamentally different functions. Subjective performances employing boundary defining symbols of demarcation are the critical ingredients in the production and reproduction of the West Indian community. In the ideological terrain of race relations, they serve the function of distinguishing West Indians from the community of African Americans.

Symbolic separation from the black/white dichotomy in the discourse of race is complicated, however, by the strategic importance of a "black" identity for the upward mobility of West Indians and for access to economic and educational opportunities. The dilemma is resolved by confining subjective performances and self-representations as model minority to private and semiprivate spaces and locations from which African Americans are largely excluded. Thus, rituals of self-representation as model minority tend to be performed in exclusive space free from the gaze of the African-American community and away from the arenas where ones "blackness" counts.

The private or semiprivate dispersed locations of West Indian identific ritual performances mitigate against the construction of West Indians as a political community. Nonpoliticization allows West Indians to activate their racial identity as blacks and to publicly identify with the causes of the black community as a basis for developing and sustaining *political* and strategic links. Self-representations as blacks are reserved for instrumental purposes or in the strategic arena of politics. In other words, for West Indians there is a certain ambiguity in their relations with African Americans that is absent in the group's relations with members of other racial, ethnic, and immigrant communities.

SYMBOLS, RITUALS, AND SUBJECTIVE PERFORMANCE: BOUNDARY-DEFINING RITUALS

At the most general level, West Indian identity is symbolized by music, food, and, dance. Reggae, calypso, soca, and zouk are the universal musical forms and steel band the musical instrument that serve as semiotic indicators of the region and its diaspora. In the San Francisco Bay Area they signify the West Indian presence and character.

West Indian musical forms enjoy considerable popularity among broad segments of the population of the San Francisco Bay Area. Reggae, in particular, is played as a matter of course on a few of the more youth-oriented popular radio stations. West Indian music has slots allocated on public and some commercial radio stations. There are several West Indian bands in the area. They are hired by night clubs and to play at private and corporate parties and gatherings. Outside West Indian locations, white Americans seem to provide the bulk of the audience and clientele for these local bands. This is particularly true for the steel bands, most of which comprise predominantly or exclusively white musicians. Performances by local bands are complemented by a constant stream of internationally famous West Indian musical groups playing at large venues and attracting huge audiences. There is an annual Reggae Festival held in San Francisco that is attended, mostly, by young white audiences. The popularity of West Indian musical forms in the San Francisco Bay Area has much to do with white desire for the exotic. It has contributed to the creation of a legitimized space for Caribbean culture.

White embrace of West Indian cultural forms signals an ethnicized construction of the West Indian community outside the black/white dichotomy of American racial discourse. It is this black/white dichotomy that gives rise to *generalized* attitudes of aversion held by whites toward African Americans. It acts to sustain and reinforce among whites a ritualized distance from the self-representations of the African-American community.[3] Thus white embrace of West Indian cultural forms helps to locate West Indians outside the boundaries of American race relations where the rules of aversion that govern black/white relations are meliorated or suspended.

White embrace of West Indians is not an embrace of equals. It is, rather, the embrace of the exotic. Thus, in their boundary-defining rituals of demarcation, the West Indian community is forced into exoticized performances and symbolic displays emphasizing its exotic character. This becomes quite evident in the symbolic use of food as a signifier of identity.

Clubs and Restaurants

Ethnic restaurants serve as locations for the publicization of identity. They are particularly central to the process of exoticization. This is no less the case for West Indian restaurants in the San Francisco Bay Area. Over the past twenty years, a number of these restaurants have opened and closed in San Francisco, Oakland, and Berkeley. Their dishes and menus constitute powerful symbolic manifestations of exoticized images cognitively linked to popular universal understandings of the West Indies. Typical dishes are West Indian staples such as curried goat, peas and rice, rotis, Jamaican patties, plantains, and stewed fish. Beverages include ginger beer, sorrel, and mauby. The dishes and beverages are not allowed to "stand on their own" in symbolic communication despite their "natural" and obvious association with the West Indies. Rather, the restaurants use their menus to highlight the exotic character of their offerings. Descriptions of the dishes employ generalized popular exoticized images of the West Indies. Sometimes, the dishes themselves are given new and exotic names. One Berkeley West Indian restaurant, tellingly named Caribbean Spice, provides a typical example of this pattern and tendency. In its menu selection, standard West Indian dishes have been given new names evocative of the popular and exotic images of West Indies held by white society. Included are dishes with names like ''Reggae Chicken and Sexy Rice,'' ''Hotter than Hell Pepper Pot,'' ''Lambada Fried Fish,'' and ''Crazy Goat,'' raising visions of dance, sex, heat, and wild abandon. Beverages are served in glass jars, contributing to an image of primitive naturalness. Such primitivism is reflected in the ''jungle'' decor of the restaurant. Notwithstanding efforts to highlight the exotic, everything is done to signal accommodation and accessibility directed, particularly, at the white clientele. For example, a concocted drink called ''ginpin'' (a combination of ginger beer and pineapple) was highlighted in the beverage selections of Caribbean Spice. The owner explained that the pineapple was added to decrease the harshness of the ginger in efforts to cater to ''white'' tastes. This predisposition toward accommodation and accessibility is typical. West Indian patrons are routinely told that spices and peppers are reduced in the preparation of the dishes to make them more palatable to the white clientele. The images of dance, sex, heat, normlessness (i.e., craziness), nature, and welcoming accommodation are evocations of the popularized images of the West Indies that prevail in the consciousness of inhabitants of the northern industrialized world. These images occupy the semiotic center in the publicization of the West Indian presence and the reification of its character and predispositions.

Food, music, and dance combine in a semiotic cacophony in all of the semi-public locations of West Indian identific performance. But the restaurants are much more than sites for the publicization of what is exotic and different about West Indians. Together with West Indian clubs (in 1997 there were only two clubs identified as West Indian), they serve as semipublic arenas where West Indians in the San Francisco Bay Area engage in ritualized self-representations and identific performances of their identity. They are where most in the West Indian community socialize publicly on a continuous basis. In this regard, they serve as surrogates for spatial ethnic communities.

The two clubs and some of the restaurants go out of their way to present themselves as cultural centers. One of the clubs offered dance and exercise classes (to the accompaniment of West Indian, Brazilian, and African music) during the day. Both clubs and some of the restaurants interspersed their evening activities with cultural entertainment and with the occasional fashion show. Most hosted performances by various West Indian and Brazilian Carnaval costume bands taking part in the annual San Francisco Carnaval held in May. One of the restaurants serves as the location of the Mas Camp for one of these bands. As such, it is the place where costumes are made and displayed, activities organized, and the masquerade band headquartered.

Thus, publicized West Indian spaces employ universalized and exotic symbols as boundary-defining mechanisms. Within these spaces, the West Indian community in the Bay Area attempts to define itself through informal rules of access that underscore its difference from the African-American community. These rules are characterized by the exclusion of African Americans, and by inclusiveness, tolerance, and accommodation of whites, Africans, Asians, Chicano/Latinos, and Pacific Islanders.

The two West Indian clubs and the West Indian restaurants in the Bay Area are locations not merely for performing West Indian identity, but for positioning West Indians among the group of third-world immigrants. Typically, reggae music is played more than any other music at these clubs and restaurants. This is because of the universal popularity of this musical form and its ability to attract white, Chicano, Latino, Asian, and Pacific Island audiences. The clubs intersperse African and Latin music with their standard fare of West Indian music. This practice has acted to attract a diverse group of patrons. The exception to this diversity are members of the African-American community.

None of the clubs plays any African-American music despite the popularity of rap among West Indian youths, and rhythm and blues and jazz among the older generation. The owners of one of the clubs explained the absence of African-American music to be the result of its potential to attract "the wrong crowd." They explained that the club was African American before they took it over and detailed a number of problems with drugs and violence associated with its former clientele.[4] There is a generalized expectation of exclusion of African Americans from West Indian semipublic arenas of performance. Such an expectation was underscored when, in the late eighties, African-American youths attracted to reggae began to attend the Caribbee, one of the two West Indian clubs. The latter is located in Oakland—a city with a large population of African Americans. Many complaints were raised by the West Indian clientele about the presence of the African-American youths. Soon, the older West Indians began to stay away altogether, claiming that the club had gone "downhill." They chose, instead, to patronize the second of the West Indian clubs located in a white upscale peninsula community across the Bay. Thus, the demands of ethnic demarcation are accompanied by a pervasive use of separation from and exclusion of members of the African-American community when West Indian identity is being publicly thematized.

Thus, in their publicized performance of identity, West Indians signify their distinctiveness through symbolic use of "exotic" boundary-defining images. In the process they reinforce their sense of difference from African Americans. At the same time, particular emphasis is placed on accommodation and inclusiveness of other racial and ethnic groups.

The San Francisco Carnaval

The semiotics of unity with immigrant "third-world" populations prevail. The most publicized display of West Indian identity, exhibiting the most comprehensive manifestations of symbols of the exotic and of difference, occurs at San Francisco Carnaval held annually on the Sunday of the Memorial Day weekend. Significantly, Carnaval is not perceived as an exclusively West Indian event, but one that is shared among various exoticized communities, with Brazilians and Caribbeans occupying pride of place. Even though confined to the Chicano district of San Francisco, there is not much evidence of Chicano participation. Rather it is the exotic Latino that is on display. In other words, the San Francisco Carnaval provides the opportunity for the West Indian community to demonstrate publicly its boundary-defining exotic character, its immigrant status, and its accommodation of multiculturalism. It is a performance directed at a predominantly white audience.

The arena provided by the San Francisco Carnaval is ideal for the performance and display of West Indian identity. A New York–born Panamanian-Jamaican and a Panamanian were among the first organizers of the event. Soon, the West Indian community began carving out its own "space" in the event with the help of a Trinidadian with ties to the San Francisco Arts Council. The San Francisco Carnaval began in 1978 as an impromptu festival in the Chicano/ Mission District of San Francisco. It soon developed from a neighborhood festival into a parade from the Mission District to downtown City Hall. It has grown since then to an event attended by over six hundred thousand spectators from throughout the Bay Area and beyond. There are between fifty-five and seventy parade contingents, with over 10,000 participants. Since 1985, the street parade has been confined exclusively to the Mission District. A two-day "celebration of food and music" has been added. Hundreds of pavilions and booths are set up at a location at the end of the parade route. Concessionaires sell food, art, and handicrafts from throughout the world. A number of musical bands, many imported from the Caribbean and Latin America, serve up a fare of musical performances on several open air stages. These performances are accompanied by an audience of thousands, many dancing to the music. On the day of the parade, orchestras and disk jockeys with amplified musical systems accompany the various costumed bands through the streets. When the actual parade is over, the orchestras and bands set themselves up at numerous locations among the pavilions and food stalls.

Carnaval provides the perfect arena for demonstrating the association between West Indians and other migrant communities, particularly Latin Americans and Africans. English-speaking West Indians are joined by those from the French, Dutch, and Spanish-speaking Caribbean. Ethnic accommodation and the polyglot character of West Indian identity is signaled by the inclusion of Native American and Chicano performances. This underscores the open accommodating "spirit" of West Indians. The emphasis of the Carnaval on dance, music, food, and elaborate costume bands, some featuring scantily clad women and men, highlights the image of an exotic Caribbean.

At the same time, the San Francisco Carnaval is definitively not "American" and, particularly for West Indians, not "African American." The symbolic representations of African-American community in music, dance, food, and performance are visibly absent in the arena of the San Francisco Carnaval.

American participation, primarily through costume bands of elementary schools and school marching bands, is confined to schools with large migrant or Chicano populations or to predominantly white elementary schools.

African Americans who participate do so through contact and identification with the West Indian community. There is one West Indian costume band organized and led by an African-American woman. Through years of association with the West Indian community, the organizer of this band has become, in effect, West Indian. Her association began with a friendship that developed between herself and a West Indian neighbor. It escalated into almost total involvement in the affairs of the community to the point where her African-American identity virtually disappeared. This, as we shall see, is typical of the terms of access of African Americans into the West Indian community. They have, in effect, to become identified as West Indian.

There is little, therefore, to attract members of the African-American community to the San Francisco Carnaval, and their presence is noticeably absent among the predominantly white group of nonparticipants who flock to view the parade and to attend the food and music festival. This is hardly surprising since, to a large extent, the San Francisco Carnaval provides the most public arena for the symbolic display of difference between West Indians and African Americans.

Open House Events

Acting as complements to the more public sites of West Indian self-representation are "open house" events where invitation is through word of mouth or some form of public announcement. Such events include public dances and large parties. They can be "potluck" affairs or guests may be asked to pay an entrance fee or to make a monetary contributions. These affairs are almost exclusively West Indian. They seem to be inner directed as rituals of reification and self-reinforcement through which the West Indian community reproduces itself. The focus is almost exclusively upon music, food, and dancing. Occasionally they include cultural presentations sometimes in the form of displays of Carnaval costumes or of West Indian dance. Events such as these provide an arena for the most exclusive display of West Indian identity. This is where the West Indian community constitutes and reconstitutes itself.

RITUALS OF MODEL MINORITY

The publicized performance and display of West Indian identity serve to define the boundaries and character of the West Indian community and to maintain and reinforce notions of distinctive difference between West Indians and African Americans. The private ritualized performance of West Indian identity, while incorporating the exotic symbols evident in the public sphere, are organized around symbolic self-representations of model minority status. In the subjective performance of identity, emphasis is placed upon abundance, success, hard work, and family values. Model minority status, with the implication it carries for meritocratic achievement and white middle-class morality, does not lend itself easily to exocitized displays. Thus, the themes of difference are ritualized in less exoticized ways.

Clubs and Associations

Clubs and associations, because of their exclusive membership, are located in the interstices between the public and the private. They are semiprivate entities with public visibility. The latter makes them ideal vehicles for the public thematization of socioeconomic status. Their exclusive character allows considerable control over terms and conditions of entry. Thus, exoticized symbolic displays are less important given the exclusiveness of their ethnic composition. Perhaps the most important of these associations and clubs in the San Francisco Bay Area are the Jamaican Association and various soccer and cricket clubs. There are, as well, a Trinidad and Tobago Association and a Guyanese Association. There was an attempt in 1993 to form an African, Caribbean, and American Network International as an overarching cultural and social organization and Chamber of Commerce for the West Indian community with some African participation. On the agenda of this organization was an effort to establish a West Indian Town along the lines of Chinatowns in American cities.

The Jamaican Association has been in existence for over fifteen years. Membership is open to all West Indians in the Bay Area even though Jamaicans predominate. The critical core membership of the association comprises a group of highly successful professionals. In its meetings, there is strict adherence to rules and regulations. The association's events are highly formal affairs usually aimed at fundraising and, as such, fairly costly. It is an ideal forum for the demonstration of West Indian success.

Cricket matches provide another venue for West Indians where the themes of difference, inclusion, and accommodation are central to the ritualized performances of identity. The playing of the game of cricket on an American playground is, in itself, a symbol of refined difference. This becomes particularly evident when juxtaposed with the typical games played by Americans on playgrounds with their characteristic fast pace, physicality, and aggressiveness. Cricket teams are generally mixed with a predominance of players from one or another of the cricket-playing countries of the British Commonwealth. There are two West Indian teams in the San Francisco Bay Area. In addition to their West Indian players, these teams have players from India, New Zealand, and Australia. Many of the players on the teams have high-income jobs, and quite a few are university graduates. Everywhere, there are demonstrations of symbols of success: in the cars driven by team members and their families, in the clothes that are worn, in the expensive lawn chairs and umbrellas, in the jewelry, in the toys brought to entertain the children.

The ritual of the cricket match serves as a demonstration of the inclusiveness of the West Indian community and its willingness to accommodate non–West Indians. Accommodation is not open, however, to all and sundry, only to members of groups seen as possessing desirable characteristics by mainstream America. The event of the match thus serves as a focal point for identification with British, Australian, New Zealand, and South Asian migrants who are either white or are identified particularly with success.

The family plays a central role in self-representations as model minority. Through an emphasis on the "family," West Indians seek to project a morality and ethic that are different from popular (white) conceptions of African-American family life. These conceptions derive from beliefs that the African-American family is chaotic and unstructured. Images of the ideal family are pervasive in West Indian self-representations. They are very much on display at cricket matches. West Indians bring their families and friends to the games, which take on a picnic atmosphere. The event continues way beyond the end of the actual game itself at the home of one or another of the team members. The location of the home provides an arena for the further display of the stable and intact family unit.

Notwithstanding their function in the thematization of model minority status, cricket matches are decidely West Indian events. Exoticized symbols of West Indian identity are incorporated into self-representations at cricket games. Food that is stereotypically West Indian is prepared for the team by the families of the players. There are usually one or more boom boxes playing West Indian music. West Indian beer (usually Jamaican Red Stripe or Guinness Stout—a favorite among West Indian males) and rum are the alcoholic beverages of choice.

University Groups

Given self-representations as a model minority, it is not surprising that much of the ritualized performances and symbolic representations of the West Indian community in the Bay Area are centered upon education and particularly higher education. Bay Area universities provide ideal arenas for ritualized displays of worth and merit. Self-representations as West Indian act to preserve and maintain the boundary between West Indian and African-American students. Thus, West Indian students at Stanford University and the University of California, Berkeley, have organized themselves, on a somewhat occasional basis over the years, into informal, and semi-formal West Indian student groups. At Stanford, the gatherings tend to be less formal, with students meeting in each other's apartments or homes, where West Indian food is served. These gatherings are attended, most of the time, by West Indian professors, who occasionally host them. At the University of California, Berkeley, the tendency among West Indian students has been toward a much more formal organization. Students meet to hear seminar presentations by their counterparts and by faculty on West Indian topics. They invite, also, West Indian faculty from Stanford and Berkeley to informal events as a basis of "networking." For the most part, West Indian students at these two institutions shun African-American student organizations and do not participate at all in African-American-oriented campus events.

The communication of a West Indian identity in an academic arena locates the student within the boundaries of the model minority. This is particularly important at Bay Area universities given the collective understanding of West Indians as successful and high achievers. Through their self-representations as West Indians, these students are able to insulate themselves from the racist stereotypical image of African Americans as unintellectual and as undeserving of a place in higher education. Many retain, assume, reassume, and/or emphasize their distinctive West Indian accents in the academic arena. They emphasize their West Indian background in class discussions and in discussions with professors. These rituals of identity serve to locate them within the space of the educational achievers and to separate them from the taint of educational underachievement and affirmative action preference attached to African-American students. It is not surprising, therefore, that students of West Indian parentage or backgrounds who formerly identified as African American quickly embrace a West Indian identity once enrolled in Bay Area universities.

House Parties

Most ritualized performances of West Indian identity in the San Francisco Bay Area occur at private gatherings in the home. Such gatherings serve as the primary means of communicating model minority status. While the universalized stereotypical symbols of the West Indies evoke the "Carnaval spirit," the opposite is true of identific performance when model minority status is being displayed and performed. Here the themes of order, formality, family, organization, success, preparation, and hard work are very much in evidence and on display. As such, rituals of self-representation as model minority are confined largely to the homes of those who have achieved visible success. West Indians of low socioeconomic status are noticeably excluded from these events and can feel quite uncomfortable should they attend. Their presence conflicts with collective self-representations as model minority. The tastes and style on display in the private arena of the home help to maintain and preserve the class exclusivity of subjective performance. Formality, rituals of introductions, elaborate and abundant displays of food and beverages, and material displays of success confine such events to the successful. They act to exclude those who are less successful from the circle of reciprocal displays of West Indian success.

The ethnic composition of the guests at these events can vary considerably. Invited non–West Indian co-workers, neighbors, and friends of both the hosts and guests provide an outside audience to these ritual displays and performances. The presence of these guests underscores the openness and accommodating nature of the West Indian character. Thus, private house gatherings provide arenas for self-confirmation of West Indian success among the West Indian community and for the display of model minority status to a non–West Indian audience.

The home is an ideal site for the display of education, occupation, achievement, and income (through display of material possessions). It offers the host an opportunity to display the material trappings of success. Ritual displays serve, as well, as boundary-defining symbols of West Indian identity. Thus, the food is "West Indian." Rum is the alcoholic beverage that is most visibly displayed despite an abundance of alternatives. There is emphasis on abundance in the displays of food and beverages.

The rituals of these gatherings are designed, particularly, to highlight success and achievement. Guests are usually introduced to each other with information provided about their respective jobs and education. The casual and informal (almost offhand) nature of such introductions masks their symbolic significance in the West Indians' self-representation as successful. However, benign, this pattern of introduction is pervasive and institutionalized.

Celebrations and rites of passage provide occasions for hosting ritualistic displays of success. Birthdays, anniversaries, christenings, graduations, and baby showers are ideal opportunities for public acknowledgment of the accomplishments of both hosts and guests. Speeches laud the successful achievements of both hosts and guests. Less formal gatherings are held in celebration of public holidays such as Christmas, New Year, Thanksgiving, Labor Day, Memorial Day, Super Bowl Sunday, and so on. These occasions, by their very nature, provide only limited opportunity for the formal accounting of the successes of hosts and guests.

Everywhere, there is the collective display and celebration of the family. Spouses, parents and, when appropriate, children participate and engage in symbolic celebration of the family at both the private and less private, formal and less formal events. Except at the more formalized evening gatherings, children are ever present, accompanying their parents. Sometimes the children engage themselves in activities separate and distinct from the adults. Sometimes, they join in the latter's activities, particularly during periods of dancing or when formalized presentations and announcements are being made. Birthdays of children and of elderly adults are occasions for celebration, as are graduations and christenings.

West Indian private (as opposed to open house) parties have an almost uniform organizational format. They are held in the evenings. They usually begin with a semicocktail gathering after which a buffet-style meal is served. This is followed, usually, by speeches and ceremony. They end after an extensive period of dancing in a space designated for that purpose. Small clusters gather in other rooms of the house chatting and consuming beverages. Thus, these gatherings have a formal structure that is evident even in the "less formal" affairs such as barbecues, picnics, and other outdoor events.

There is a certain degree of status (usually occupational) segregation in the clusterings at these events. As the gatherings become larger, the tendency for such segregation increases. It is much more pronounced at the more public events such as at large parties, dances, nightclubs, and even Carnaval. Thus, exclusivity serves, as well, as signifier of class position within the West Indian community itself.

AMBIGUITY AND CONFLICT IN IDENTITY CONSTRUCTION

There are a number of pulls on persons of West Indian descent in their effort to carve out an identific space for themselves in the milieu of American society. The choices that they make are not necessarily clear-cut and obvious. This is particularly true given the conflicting pulls of West Indian versus African-American identity. At times and under certain circumstances West Indians can and do reject their West Indianness for identification as African Americans. At other times, they find themselves caught between the identific pulls of both communities.

Soccer

These conflicts are particularly strong for younger and less-successful West Indian males who can display considerable ambiguity in their forms of self-representation. In the San Francisco Bay Area, soccer matches provide perfect arenas for the display of ambiguous identity. Unlike cricket, there is less ritualized formality in the playing of soccer games. The game's physicality and fast pace closely resembles that of the typically "American" games of baseball, basketball, and football. So is its exclusively male composition when played by the West Indian youths. There is little emphasis on family participation. Spectators are usually exclusively male. Thus, soccer appears to provide a bridge between West Indian and American identities. It is ideally suited to young and less-successful West Indian males without the wherewithal to engage in the subjective performance of model minority status. West Indian youth are not isolated from the growing universal attraction of African-American popular culture, particularly music and dress. This makes them much less resistant to identification with African-American culture. Their own reality of low socioeconomic status is rendered incongruous with self-representations as a model minority. Such incongruity reinforces a tendency to embrace many aspects of African-American identity.

Soccer provides an ideal bridge between African-American and West Indian identity given its physicality, pace, and tempo and its recent and growing popularity among American youth. It is not entirely out of place in the American milieu and enjoys considerable popularity in Northern California. At the same time, the game continues to retain its sense of "foreignness," reflecting an ambiguity that is quite consistent with the self-representations of West Indian youths.

Despite its character as a bridge, the game of soccer retains its role as an arena for self-representation as West Indian with all that that entails. There are a number of West Indian soccer teams in the Bay area. The composition of the teams place emphasis on their "third-world" character with Latin Americans and Africans participating with West Indians on the "West Indian" teams. Some teams have a few English players as well. Every year, there is a "Caricom Tournament"[5] an event where teams representing the various islands of the region play against each other. It is an all-day family affair conducted under a picnic atmosphere accompanied by West Indian music and with West Indian food on display.

At the same time, however, self-representations of West Indian identity through the game of soccer are largely devoid of subjective performances of model minority status. Successful West Indians tend not to attend soccer matches. As a result, displays of achievement at the game tend to be minimal. The failure to attract the educated and occupational elite may be due to the game's ambiguity and the parallels in its symbolic structure and location to stereotypical and racist images of the African American. The game is played very aggressively, with constant bickering and verbal skirmishes between team members and among the teams themselves. The West Indian teams are located in Oakland, a city that is strongly identified with the African-American community. Many of their games are played in that city. The contrasts between soccer and cricket are telling. Cricket is formal, nonphysical, leisured, noncontentious, and definitively foreign. It provides an ideal opportunity for the display of family unity. Cricket games are played, exclusively, in the affluent suburbs. There is no cricket team based in Oakland. Thus, the cricket match provides an arena for combining symbols of difference with those of model minority status in West Indian self-representations. Soccer, on the other hand, provides a site for assertions of West Indian identity devoid of images of success. It provides the youth with the symbolic means of embracing what is American, and particularly, what is African American, without having to forgo assertions of their West Indian identity.

Military and Marriage

The competing pulls of identity are particularly evident among West Indians who have served in the United States military. Over the years, a small but significant number of West Indian migrants, primarily males, have been stationed at one of the many military bases in and around the San Francisco Bay Area. Some joined the military during the Vietnam War for the opportunity it provided to obtain legal resident status and eventually citizenship. Others saw in the military a secure and guaranteed job with desirable benefits and opportunities. A number of these West Indian military veterans have settled in the San Francisco Bay Area. Some have been quite active in the affairs of the West Indian community.

The military offers very few opportunities for self-representation as West

Indian. There are few benefits to be derived from assertions of one's West Indianness. As a result, many West Indian enlistees choose to embrace African-American culture and identity. This is precisely the point being made by one of the West Indian veterans living in San Francisco: "So I was in the military in-depth in American society. As a matter of fact, it was to the point where I had sort of almost escaped being a West Indian, I was so embedded in American culture, black American culture, which I really—had a chance to learn about and be around and just absorb" (interview with West Indian veteran).

For many, this immersion in the reality of the African-American world and the embrace of an African-American identity are reflected in patterns of dating and in the selection of marriage partners. Many of the veterans who settled in the Bay Area married African-American women while in the service. Once out of the service the path back to the West Indian community for these veterans proved quite problematic. These veterans possessed much of the characteristics of a model minority. Most had used their veterans' benefits to buy their own homes. Most used their skills and military service to get access to skilled occupations and/or to higher education. Given their income, occupational status, and their home ownership, they came to match the ideal of West Indian achievement. At the same time, however, self-representation as West Indian was complicated by their continuing ties, through their spouses, to the African-American community. In their attempts to manage these conflicting pulls, a small group of veterans formed an informal clique within the West Indian community. The creation of the clique appeared to be an attempt at resolution of the conflict. The African-American wives developed, for the most part, a particularly strong bond among themselves, participating with each other in self-representations of their African-American identity. At the same time, the West Indian males remained free to develop and maintain their involvement with the West Indian community and in its rituals of self-representation. Veterans and their African-American spouses typically hosted events that incorporated rituals and symbolic representations of both communities. These included gatherings to view sporting events on television such as the hosting of parties on Super Bowl Sunday, gatherings for birthdays, barbecues, and special holidays such as Christmas and Easter. In other words, they chose to host events on occasions that were celebrated by both sets of identific communities.

For the most part, the African-American wives of the military veterans seemed to get on well with each other. Relations with West Indians were, for many, fraught with tension, forcing some of their husbands to make a choice. Some marriages ended in divorce. In every such case, the West Indian divorcé chose a West Indian as his new partner. In one instance, the veteran made a trip back to the West Indies immediately after separation from his wife, met a woman from his island, got engaged, and was married almost immediately when the divorce became final. Another separated from his American wife to begin a relationship with a West Indian woman, opened a business that catered to West Indians, and became one of the organizers of a West Indian carnival band participating in the San Francisco Carnaval festival. A third made the decision to return to the Caribbean. Most of the veterans who remained married to African Americans eventually disappeared from the arenas of West Indian collective self-representation.

A few of the veterans were able successfully to negotiate their West Indian identity while remaining married to African Americans. This was particularly the case when their American spouses became highly integrated into the West Indian community. Many of these wives severed most of their connections with African Americans. This same pattern was also evident among nonveterans who married Americans.

CONCLUSION

Identity is contextual. It emerges within the social space where hegemonically imposed understandings and their contestations intersect with existing cultural, social, economic, and political realities. It is conditioned by the resources and understandings brought as baggage by those who are collectively identified. It is preordained neither at the collective nor the individual levels. The identific community can and does negotiate a space for itself in the social reality in which it exists. The individual is not at all confined to the collectivized space constructed out of such negotiation.

Persons from the English-speaking Caribbean who live in the San Francisco Bay Area have chosen a West Indian identity because of its popular association with the model minority myth. But the choice is complicated by the need to identify as black to gain access to resources of upward mobility. By asserting their racial identity as black, West Indians in the United States make legal and official claims to resources reserved exclusively for the African-American community. They mobilize to protect and enhance their socioeconomic interests by making common political cause with the African-American community. At the same time, it is the need to establish and maintain an ethnicized difference from African Americans that fuels assertions of a West Indian identity. West Indians in the San Francisco Bay exploit exoticized images of difference to separate themselves from the terms of racial discourse. Difference is asserted and communicated through identific boundary-defining ritual performance and symbolic displays. These signify an accommodating and sensuous West Indian that is desirable and nonthreatening—one that is amenable to white embrace. Rituals and displays of "foreignness" assert the separation of West Indians from the American racial milieu.

As public assertions of West Indianness, symbolic displays and performances are essential to the publicizing of a West Indian space in the ethnic mosaic of the San Francisco Bay Area. At the same time West Indians seek to assert their status as "model minority" in their rituals of self-representations. They do so through symbolic displays of studiousness, intellectualism, success, hard work, material accomplishments, and commitment to family. The contradictions between exoticized images of West Indian difference and mainstream images of success associated with model minority status are managed through the practice of separation. Exoticized images of West Indianness are displayed most evidently in public (or semipublic) sites and arenas. The display of model minority status is reserved for the private spaces of the home or for semiprivate activities open exclusively to the West Indian middle class.

West Indians in the Bay Area are forced to grapple with the conflicting pulls of a racialized black identity versus an ethnicized immigrant identity. They are forced to preserve and maintain the commonality of their ''black'' identity and to develop pragmatic and strategic ties with African Americans to gain access to resources for upward mobility. At the same time, they employ their West Indian identity to distance themselves from the racialized definitions emerging out of the black/white dichotomy in American racial discourse. Under certain conditions, efforts to separate the two can prove problematic. In their assertions of identity some may find themselves forced to make a definitive choice. This has been particularly evident in the cases of veterans married to African-American wives. A pattern of syncretism seems to be emerging among those West Indian youths whose claim to model minority status may be tenuous. Patterns and forms of self-representation among these youths seem to incorporate, successfully, images of both communities.

In being West Indian, the residents of the San Francisco Bay make choices that are conditioned by the contextualized reality of the area. For West Indian communities elsewhere, the choices and realities of identity may be fundamentally different.

NOTES

1. These figures were cited in Mandle 1996: 174. They were obtained from the United States Bureau of Census 1990: 26–28.

2. Such evidence is based on personal observations and a familiarity with the West Indian community of New York on a continuous basis between 1973 and 1979, on a semicontinuous basis as a frequent visitor to New York since 1979, on observing family and friends who reside in New York City, and on discussions with informed observers of the West Indian community.

3. This is notwithstanding the historical reality of American cultural syncretism whereby black forms have permeated white American culture.

4. Interviews with the owners of the club conducted in 1996.

5. The Caribbean Community—or Caricom, as it is known—is the group of English-speaking Caribbean countries that have joined in a formal organization for the purpose of economic integration, coordination of foreign policy, and functional cooperation.

8

Uptown Ladies and Downtown Women: Female Representations of Class and Color in Jamaica

Gina Ulysse

Over the last two decades, female representations of class and color in Jamaica have changed dramatically as a result of both the advent of modern dancehall—a subculture that is associated with the black masses and a significant increase in female income-earning opportunities.[1] Those who have benefited from these new gains and other economic shifts since the labor movements of the 1930s have had an unprecedented degree of social autonomy that has resulted in a modification of the complex local class structure and its various components. In turn, the class structure has become even more refracted through color because of the social mobility of blacks.[2] Historically, in the dominant ideology, lower-, middle-, and upper-class status have been marked respectively by the representation of females as either "lady" or "woman." In recent years, with the changing economic conditions in Jamaica, there has been increasing economic mobility both upward and downward across class lines. Yet social status, particularly for individuals who are upwardly mobile, is ever more rigidly policed.

This essay examines class-based struggles over definitions of blackness, beauty, and femininity within the context of lower-class females' economic independence, which enables them to redefine the gendered identities that have been ascribed to them historically. Focusing on interactions between and within the classes, I argue that through the reappropriation of stereotypes, lower-class female representations of blackness challenge the dominant order.[3] I focus primarily on self-presentation, which is loaded with historical, material, symbolic, and class-based meanings. My research with Afro-Jamaican Informal Commercial Importers (ICIs) examines female representations of blackness at the intersection of class and color in popular arenas such as beauty pageants and the

world of dancehall. The essay combines historical and contemporary ethnographic research material to frame and explain the complex situation of lower-
class females, among whom are ICIs, as they negotiate race, class, color, and
gender in their daily lives.

To a notable extent, my approach has been influenced by Ruth Behar's work
as an ethnographic storyteller (1990, 1993). Similarly, it attempts to construct a
complete social world that is as symbolic as it is political and material. The
interplays between and within genders, the local and the global, the past and
the present create a wider field within which the reader can extract a tale. This
essay has two major parts. In the first, I examine the historical connotations of
the concepts of "lady" and "woman" as oppositional racial and color categories that affect the lives of all females and those of black females in particular.
This dichotomy was reinforced during colonialism through the desexualization
and subsequent idealization of white females and the hypersexualization of African females. It reinforced the racially coded white Madonna/black whore polarity. To unpack the categories of color, I analyze these racialized gendered
identities in a historical context as they are reflected among the colored populations and in beauty pageants. Reconfigurations in the economic class structure
and their subsequent impact on the color order further fragmented the black/
white dichotomy into the current black/brown polarity. In its second part, the
essay documents the boom in informal importing and the concomitant rise and
expansion of dancehall to examine the continuities and discontinuities of this
"lady"/"woman" polarity to better explain its impact on lower-class women,
including ICIs. Dancehall is framed in the context of the racial/spatial order of
uptown/downtown. I conclude with several moments in which class-specific performances of female identities have contested the middle-class standard.

UPTOWN/DOWNTOWN: SPACE/CLASS AND GENDER

Uptown/downtown is a geographical division of central Kingston. The separation is clearly demarcated by two main streets, Half-way-Tree and Crossroads.
Uptown is north of downtown. The northeastern sections of the city include the
suburbs of Beverly Hills, Mona Heights, and Upper St. Andrew. Barbican,
Cherry Gardens, and Stony Hill are several of the more central and northwestern
middle/upper-class pockets within this city. However, throughout these areas it
is not uncommon to find shacks within the valleys surrounding the hills. The
different sections of downtown include Tivoli, Rema in the west, and Telaviv
and Southside to the East. The downtown area is particularly complex because
it is further divided by partisanship between followers of the Jamaica Labour
Party (JLP) and the People's National Party (PNP). As Faye Harrison notes,
these boundaries are somewhat volatile because they are "loci of safety, danger,
neutrality [which] are contingent and subject to recodification" (1997: 460).[4]
Most Kingstonians live their lives in accord with this spatial divide. The middle
and upper classes who work downtown drive to their homes uptown in their

cars with rolled-up tinted windows. They cross the uptown/downtown line only to attend cultural events at the Ward Theatre and the National Gallery of Art, which are both located south of the border. It must be noted that when an event (such as the Pantomime) is attended by individuals across the social structure, the prices of tickets and location of seats often upholds existing social boundaries. Lower-class individuals venture uptown mostly for work as domestic helpers, clerks, or gardeners. At the end of their workday they are often seen walking down the hills to the bus stops where they catch a ride home. Since the lower classes can hardly afford to shop uptown, they frequent markets, arcades, and shops located downtown for their consumer items and seldom venture uptown to socialize. This spatial divide also has its correlation in the concepts of "lady" and "woman"; as the former is associated with uptown and the latter is identified with downtown.

THE "LADY" AND THE "WOMAN"

One of the many regularities in female lives is the performance of gendered identities. "Lady" and "woman" are two such categories; they are based upon historical ideas of gender. Drawing from Judith Butler (1990), I argue the performance of both of these identities constitutes a necessary survival strategy. In the English-speaking Caribbean, although female identities span a continuum, they often reaffirm the dichotomy between "lady" and "woman."[5] This duality, a Victorian product, was part of a taxonomy reinforced by British colonials to facilitate hegemonic rule. This taxonomy manifested itself in the colonies through the production and the reproduction of racial/class/color hierarchies in the form of arrangement of people, identities, labor, and concomitant expectations of behavior. Most importantly, the lady/woman polarity demarcated and regulated the racial/spatial boundaries of the colonial order. Though distinctions between the Creole and the British were especially recognized by travelers, all the white females were ladies and black females were women or girls.[6]

Following "race," one of the other factors that determined the position of the female population in these societies was "class," which was in turn inextricably linked to ideas of labor and leisure. These differed considerably between urban and rural areas where the division of labor, size of the labor force, and its organization determined the type of work and the amount of time devoted to it. One's occupation, social position and, later, property rights depended specifically upon one's blood quantum and how these genetic combinations were imagined to manifest somatically. It was in this context that the correlation between class and color became legally and socially legitimated, yet remaining a fluid boundary.

Among British colonies in the Caribbean, the preoccupation with color gradations was distinct in Jamaica, where the colonial system recognized and categorized the various possible types of interracial mixtures. Accordingly, the offspring of a white man and a black woman is a mulatto; the mulatto and the black produce a "samba," from the mulatto and white comes the quadroon; from the quadroon and white comes the "mustee"; the child of a mustee by a white man is called a "musteffino," while the children of the musteffino are free by law and rank as white persons for all intent and purposes (Henriques, 1953: 46). The colored population often received differential treatment than blacks from the planter/master class because of racial proximity. To continue reaping these benefits, a colored/Creole culture re-created that emulated the manners/customs of the dominant class. According to Roger Abrahams and John Szwed, interpersonal performance was a countervailing force against enslavement (1983: 30). Thus color manifested as class became an important index of a person's worth. In his study of distinction and the judgment of taste, Pierre Bourdieu argues "social identity lies in difference, and difference is asserted by what is closest which represents the greatest threat" (1984: 479).

Among females, difference or distinction was established through representation and the appropriation of European social identities (Beckles 1989; Bush 1990). For example, as Gad Heuman notes, colored females emphasized their affinity with the dominant class as they sought to imitate European fashions, often in an exaggerated form. Brown [women] frequently dressed in the latest and loudest clothes to outdo their white competitors. They also established various educational societies including the Society for the Diffusion of Useful Knowledge and the St. James Institute for Promoting General and Useful Knowledge (1981: 14). As Heuman stresses, these organizations allowed the brown population to differentiate themselves from blacks and to assimilate aspects of European civilization (ibid.). Distinction was practiced in other ways as well as females with ambiguous phenotypes were able to define/redefine their identities to construct themselves as "ladies" as opposed to "women." However, this ability to reconstruct oneself was not without limits, because colonial legislation supported by European racist ideologies and practices ultimately constrained colored/Creole females.

Nonetheless, females who possessed physical characteristics and mannerisms that blurred the boundaries between lady and woman risked never attaining higher social status through marriage or profession or by association unless they "ladyfied" themselves. The recent study by anthropologist Lisa Douglass of Jamaican elite families shows the extent to which race, class, and color still determine the marriage patterns of this group: family members and friends apply extreme pressure on individuals to endogamous (1992). She further reveals that among the elite, a cultural feminization of females that stresses continuity of this "lady" ideal is still widely practiced.

In 1993, I experienced this culture of femininity firsthand while conducting preliminary fieldwork with several ICIs. Miss T, an ICI who is dark-skinned and of lower-class origins, insisted I accompany her to the hairdresser on Sundays. We arrived midmorning and remained until midafternoon. During this time, she got her hair and eyebrows done as well as a manicure and a pedicure. This beauty salon (an informal setup in someone's house) was frequented by

ICIs of various ages from early twenties to fifties. During the beauty regimen, conversation revolved around the importance of grooming and taking care of oneself, the latest dance, DJs or reggae singers, men, and the foolishness of women who depend on them. The younger customers, who often came in the latest styles of clothing, shoes, or nail polish, would turn the conversations toward fashion, or what is the latest fad and where to buy it. Miss T, who always expressed her dissatisfaction with my preference for baggy clothes, frequently chastised me for not wearing my hair out rather than pulled in a bun and for keeping my nails unpolished and short.

Soon, I began to give myself manicures with her encouragement so my hands would "look nice and pretty." Eventually, I started to get my hair done when I accompanied her. One of my biggest complaints was the amount of time this required. At this salon, there was a consensus among the clients that we must make ourselves beautiful at any cost (this price included time as well as money). As Miss T always stressed, "if it is for yourself, nothing is too expensive." Without fail every Sunday was grooming day. This process of beautification has many significations and is central to both individual and group construction of a feminine identity, sexuality, and economic status.

For these individuals, making oneself beautiful implied undergoing this process of getting made up—having the hair processed, getting the nails polished, and so on. This weekly ritual was important to the ICIs for several reasons. It contradicts an existing stereotype of the ICI and her foremother the higgler, as a plain, large, unsophisticated (unfashionable and cosmetically unmade) "woman" who has been historically juxtaposed against the "lady." I explain this in greater detail below. Second, their occupation requires a type of roughness in their demeanor—necessary to survive the daily challenges at the arcade and in the male-dominated business of importing—which in many ways defeminizes them anew by existing middle-class standards. Hence, this process of feminization in the beauty salon reaffirms their femininity, and this interest in keeping up with the latest trends highlights their sophistication. Having a sense of style and fashion is very important in the Caribbean, especially because the performance of gendered identities is based upon and understood in the context of representation.[7]

Others have found that despite some exceptions, generally the black/brown middle and upper classes are particularly invested in maintaining this black/white dichotomy with its specific gender dimensions (Austin-Broos 1987; Henriques 1953, 1957; Wilson 1973). As Douglass notes, Jamaicans expect "any female who is white to be a lady and exhibit a consistent feminine demeanor . . . the fairer the female the greater likelihood that she is indeed a lady" (1992: 247). A lady is, by definition, educated and refined. She should always be a wife. Her status derives from matrimony and the extent to which she is devoted to her husband and family. Other characteristics ascribed to her include the femininity that she exudes: diminutive size and unobtrusive manner, high heels and exquisite grooming, soft voice and careful diction. She does not use vulgar language or even patois. She distinguishes herself from all men and common women through body language. A lady knows her place; when she goes out socially by night her husband escorts her; she avoids public transportation and must never walk (ibid., 246). And according to the *Daily Gleaner* (Jamaica's oldest daily paper), a lady stands and sits with her legs together and when she dances she does not "wine." That is, she avoids the expansively/explicitly sexual hip movements of the dance style associated with ghetto women (ibid., 245). For the middle and upper classes, the quintessential lady is still the queen of England. Runners-up include the latest Miss Jamaica winner, who is seen as the epitome of the uptown girl—espousing middle-and upper-class ideals of beauty, femininity, and values. The extreme importance and high social status ascribed to Jamaican beauty contest winners reinforce the fact that these pageants are critical sites in the reconstruction of female identities.

COLONIALISM AND AFROPHOBIA IN BEAUTY PAGEANTS

Jamaica has been polarized between black and white since colonialism despite the persistent presence of the colored, Chinese, East Indians, and Syrians who populate the island. The prominence of colored as a social category determined by both physical and cultural distinctions only serves to solidify the black/white dichotomy. Moreover, individual colored identity is assessed by both blacks and whites differentially on the basis of degree of African and European assimilation. Hence, analysts have distinguished between "two Jamaicas," one European and the other African (Curtin 1955), and within Jamaica as a whole, the latter has always been a rejected group. As Maxwell Owusu found, among the ruling groups and educated elite and occasionally among segments of the "working class," there is a widespread view that any concession to the persistence or recovery of African historical consciousness implies a choice between a more prestigious and technologically more powerful European civilization and a less prestigious, debased African savagery and barbarism (1996: 7). Because African and European traits pervade all aspects of Jamaican life from religion, language, family pattern, and other aspects of culture, Owusu continues, Jamaica has had to face the problem of "living with Africa" in the Caribbean. This problem is apparent in local definitions of beauty.

Beauty has historically been color-coded in Jamaica. In other words, it has been characterized in relation to color divisions. The eighteenth-century "Set Girls" parades (which were held primarily in Kingston) and the contemporary beauty pageants they forecasted attest to this divide. These parades were annual events held during Christmas, when enslaved and free females, representing the principal social or racial categories of the colonies, were set against each other: there were brown sets and black sets and sets of all the intermediate gradations of color. They sang and they swam along the streets in the most luxurious attitudes, but the colors were never blended in the same set, no blackie ever interloped with the browns; nor did any browns in any case mix with the sables.

They always kept in mind the distinction between black woman and brown lady (Scott, 1852: 251–252). As a nineteenth-century travel account of Jamaica reveals, there was indeed tension between the black and brown populations. John Bigelow writes "while the entente cordiale between whites and colored is strengthening daily, a different state of feeling exists between Negroes or Africans and the browns. The latter shun all connection by marriage with the former and can experience no more unpardonable insult than to be classified with them in any way" (1970: 260). As I discuss below, these social distinctions and tensions were perpetuated in/by national beauty pageants.

The Miss Jamaica contest began in the 1940s. According to Natasha Barnes, it took place in "a racial landscape where femininity was the jealously guarded domain of white females . . . [they are] wrapped in a mantle of respectability and civility that was denied to black people in general and black females in particular" (1994: 474). This contest soon became problematic because of its white bias, which excluded the black majority of the population as well as the Chinese and East Indians. As a result, during the late 1950s, other contests sprang up that were more representative of the diverse population. One of them was the "Ten Types, One People" pageant held in 1955, and sponsored by the *Star*—the evening edition of the *Daily Gleaner*. This pageant selected ten winners and gave them titles that corresponded to a pure or composite picture of the different races, ethnic variations, and colors of the people occupying the island: Miss Apple Blossom (white European), Miss Allspice (part Indian), Miss Ebony (black), Miss Golden Apple (peaches and cream complexion), Miss Jasmine (part Chinese), Miss Mahogany (cocoa-brown complexion), Miss Pomegranate (white Mediterranean), Miss Lotus (pure Chinese), Miss Sandalwood (pure Indian), and Miss Satinwood (coffee and milk complexion) (ibid., 478). The purpose of this pageant, which lasted only five years, was to recognize the many races and ethnic groups who make the Jamaican people. Ironically, it took this "multiracial" approach for blackness to be publicly treated as beautiful, albeit without natural hair.

With national independence in 1962, and the seeming disappearance of whites, the colored/Creole population emerged as a dominating socio-economic and political force. This group appropriated some of the elements of European ideology to establish their position as superior to the black masses. The white/black opposition of the old order transformed into a brown/black dichotomy, with whiteness looming in the shadows. European facial features and skin color continued to reflect the ideal as a signifier of social position and access to various resources. The Miss Jamaica Pageant, which at this time came under the auspices of the government, reflected this process.

Prior to independence, resistance to the old social order had been in the making. From the mid-1920s through 1935, Marcus Garvey's movement sought the economic and social independence of peoples of African descent in the New World from the colonial system and advocated black repatriation to Africa. In fact, Garvey was driven out of Jamaica for stirring racial tensions. In the late

1930s, Rastafari emerged as a radical opposition to the white bias which impoverished and marginalized the black masses locally and throughout the world. Finding their birthplace in "Ethiopia," Rastafarians fashioned an everyday resistance via yet another black Jamaican identity which challenged the racial order. Rastafari beliefs, practices and aesthetics overtly contested the European culture which pervaded the urban centers of the island. As Rastafari became more popular, their members were continually persecuted. The persecution abated eventually and some conditional acceptance came with the international rise of Bob Marley as representative of reggae music and the use of Rastafari and reggae symbols by Jamaican political parties.[8]

Formal opposition to the brown order came from within the brown middle classes as well with the formation of the Council on Afro-Jamaican Affairs (CAJA). Through constitutional means, this organization sought to eradicate socioeconomic injustice in Jamaican society and to educate the black masses to be proud of their African heritage. Fundamental to their approach was the establishment of informal and formal with Africa. In 1964, they organized the first Miss Jamaica Nation Beauty contest to refute the national pageant. The winner was not only dark skinned, but her prize trip was to Malawi, for Malawi's independence celebrations, and then to Ghana, Nigeria, and Kenya as the guest of these governments. The CAJA embraced the African continent primarily to alleviate the "racial separatism" that plagued Jamaica and, as stated in their newsletter to raise the level of social and political consciousness of the Jamaican masses (Owusu 1996).

In spite of these political visibilities, the white bias persisted in the national pagent. In 1967, judges omitted the dark-skinned favorite contestant with her Afro hairdo from the final stages of the competition. However several years later, the Miss Jamaica crown was bestowed upon the Afro hairstyle of two dark-skinned beauties. This was a reflection of the changes brought upon by the Black Power movement brewing in the nation. In 1972, Michael Manley headed a Democratic Socialist government that emphasized gender equality and denounced the Miss Jamaica pageant as a "cattle parade." For two years, the pageant was not held. A year later, the Miss Jamaica Pageant was privatized and the contests resumed. From then on, most winners were once again "Mahogany types—defined as Jamaica cocoa brown, neither full black nor very light-skinned" (Barnes, 1994: 479). Racially mixed females have always been the majority of contestants, as they represent the new hegemonic beauty ideal. This celebration of the brown-skinned feminine beauty as representative of the nation is a departure from what Norman Whitten and Arlene Torres (1992) call *blanqueamiento* (whitening) ideology that is popular in the Caribbean.

Jamaican organizers have stressed that the winners chosen have been those who have the potential to win international pageants. Indeed, to date, Jamaica is the most successful Caribbean country in the beauty industry. The island has won Miss World three times, and contestants usually rank highly in other international competitions. Several of these former contestants have received international contracts with top American and European modeling agencies. At home, these models enjoy supermodel status. They win instant fame and recognition, write-ups in the society pages, appear in music videos, and endorse local products, productions, and services. Marriage with well-established corporate leaders is also a likely outcome. All of this occurs regardless of the extent of their popularity or lack thereof abroad.

Throughout different stages of my fieldwork, I became increasingly aware that conventional beauty—with a European flair—is a highly prized commodity that gives one unlimited access to otherwise scarce opportunities. It is no wonder that young girls cite past and current winners as their female role models or the person they would most like to be. Consequently the local beauty industry has expanded. Numerous modeling agencies were founded to capitalize on this local and global demand for Jamaican beauties.[9] The more established ones include Pulse and Elite, which represent the majority of past and current winners. It must be noted that Elite was created by Spartan, the same company which had purchased the rights to the Miss Jamaica pageant. These agencies are like finishing schools, where young girls are taught proper comportment, table manners, grooming techniques, exercise, diction, and social conversation among other skills. Miguel Models and a couple of agencies started to represent darker-skinned females, thus challenging the European standard of the more institutionalized Pulse and Elite agencies. To date, however, contestants from these agencies have not won any major titles in Jamaica, though they have had some success in pageants held abroad (especially in regional pageants), where they are seen, ironically, as more representative of Jamaica.

Despite their international success, several Miss Jamaica winners have been harassed by the public during the event itself and well after the end of their reign. Since the pageants began, they have only been occasionally controversial. Winners who have caused more uproar have been those of exclusively white parentage (whether European or Middle Eastern—as this group has become honorary whites). Chinese contestants and winners have also stirred some controversy, whereas East Indians have enjoyed popular support. The black-Chinese tensions stem from black perception of this group (who are traditionally part of the merchant class) as belonging to the oppressive mechanism that exploits and marginalizes them.[10] In the Caribbean the relationship between blacks and Indians differs significantly from island to island and from moment to moment. According to Walter Rodney, in Jamaica, similarities in the colonial experience of Indians as indentured laborers is the basis for more solidarity with blacks (1969). Hence, black affiliation with Indians is due in part to the fact that they are to an extent closer to blacks in the local class/color order. Indeed, the identity of pageant winners is a political issue that highlights the social and economic problems of the country. Pageants are about economic status as well as social position. An older female importer, one of the organizers of an ICI beauty contest held in the 1980s, stressed to me that class status ultimately determines the winner. She noted: "I don't believe a poor somebody can enter and win.

You have to be up there. You have to be in a society class because the things you require are expensive and you have to be up there. There are some pretty girls down here (meaning downtown) but they would never win.''

Because of the continued absence of dark-skinned females from national pageants and the significance of racially defined beauty as another marker of class identity, numerous tertiary contests have emerged throughout the island. These include Miss Caribbean Queen, Miss City of Montego Bay, Miss Jamaica Independence to name a few. In the late 1980s, the United Vendors Association (UVA), an organization that represents ICIs, held a beauty contest at its annual awards dinner. As one of the organizers noted, this event was "to recognize and honor the hard work of vendors." Older traders were given a certificate in recognition of their seniority, that is, the number of years they devoted to this occupation. Younger ICIs from different arcades participated in the beauty contest, which according to one of the organizers "was done just like Miss World." Contestants competed in categories that included evening dress, swimwear, and sportswear. Prizes were given, purchased with money collected from vendors in all the participating arcades. After three years, this event was discontinued. The renting of the ballroom of Kingston's Oceana Hotel and other expenses rendered this event too costly for the association.

One of the many purposes of this pageant was to counter the stereotype of the ICI (which I discuss in greater detail later) as an aggressive, loud, black woman. The nature of the work of vendors requires behavior, comportment, and presentation that uptown has deemed unladylike. By crowning a Miss UVA, vendors affirmed their femininity and recognized the beautiful among them. These pageants are local-national contests and do not challenge or rival the more established local-international pageants.[11] They are not as well funded and sponsored and receive little to no media attention. They feed a popular national interest in celebrating beauty and also reaffirm that the definitions of beauty espoused by the primary pageants disregard the black masses.

Undoubtedly, Jamaicans are well aware that correlations between beauty/femininity and whiteness in particular (and brownness by association) still prevail. As a friend once expressed, Miss Jamaica "has to have tall (long) hair, she don't look like we." That is, she cannot look like the majority of the population. The greatest cultural challenge to this standard of beauty and color as personified by the "lady" came from dancehall, which gave birth to alternative spaces/events that both exhibit and celebrate the black female body in downtown culture.

DANCEHALL: EXHIBITION/CELEBRATION OF BLACKNESS DOWNTOWN

The local rise of dancehall coincided with global political-economic restructuring in the late 1970s and early 1980s. The effects of the neoliberalist capitalism as led by the JLP were highly visible throughout the island as the class and color divide became even more entrenched. Across the social structure, unemployment rose especially among the female population, which experienced and responded to this situation in different ways.[12] Many of the black urban lower-class suffering from the impact of structural adjustment programs became self-employed higglers who infiltrated the import/export market.[13] They exported agricultural produce to neighboring islands to earn foreign exchange. There they purchased canned goods, paper products, shoes, and so on for import to retail and wholesale at home. Soon, these lower-class vendors were competing with the established formal import businesses. The rapid growth of their commerce resulted in government attempts to control their informal activities through policy. In 1982, they earned the paradoxical official title of informal commercial importers (ICIs).

Brown middle-and upper-class females felt the harsh realities of the recessions and the inflation that threatened to destabilize their standard of living. Those who could afford to migrate left the island for the United States, Canada, or Europe. Others remained in Jamaica to see their economic status plummet, forcing them to change their consumption patterns and to become part of the "respectable poor."[14] Although numerous males and females abandoned their middle-class professions to become ICIs, perhaps an even greater number maintained their low-paying formal sector jobs and supplemented their incomes with different types of informal activities such as commercial importing.[15]

Accompanying these trends in economic destabilization was an escalation in political and social violence that anticipated the depreciating value of life in Kingston's slums. Concomitantly, illegal commodity trading expanded as *Ganja* (marijuana) traffic grew to uncontrollable proportions. The island became a regional trans-shipment point in the Colombian cocaine trade. With the import of guns and export of drugs came the global rise and recognition of the Jamaican drug posses (this self-imposed label revealing members' penchant for and glamorization of Hollywood Western films).[16] Rex Nettleford notes that although these male groups reject middle-class standards and values, their objectives are still to attain motorcars, homes with swimming pools, and high incomes (1972: 97). Although his claim was made twenty-five years ago, it is still applicable today.

Unsurprisingly, it was in this context that DJ-style reggae music emerged from downtown to displace the popular yet fading roots reggae. As Grant Fared notes, music has always functioned as a space where intense ideological contestations about Jamaican society have been conducted (1998: 58). Though modern dancehall music is quite distinct from its predecessor roots reggae—which was largely based on Rastafari-inspired uplifting spiritual and politically conscious messages that dominated the airwaves for nearly two decades—it is also a music of protest. In the street corners near main electric power lines where dancehall sessions are held, oversized speakers are stacked to blast the monotonous electronic bass and drum rhythms that accompany the oral mastery of performers. These tunes, delivered in the Jamaican language primarily by lower-

class young men, consist of different styles and orientations.[17] The more popular
of these styles is *slackness*, which consists of sexual and "gun" lyrics. Though
it was predominantly entertainment of/for the lower-class dancehall, like any
other subculture, appealed to the younger generations across the social structure.
Nonetheless, music identified with the black masses in Jamaica was seen as
vulgar and reinforced class-based divisions between high and low culture (see
Peter Wade, this volume). Many of the songs were quickly deemed offensive
by the middle-and upper-class "social gatekeepers" as well as by the conservative segments downtown for their disregard of the moral order. They prompted
editorials, radio shows, and television programs that attacked dancehall for its
vulgarity. Ironically, in other ways, dancehall upholds other aspects of the social/
moral order through its celebration of an uncontested compulsory heterosexu-
ality. Its main emphasis has always been on sex, sexual prowess, an extreme
and fatal sense of homophobia, and the freedom to express these within a context
of blackness.

Since economic autonomy has never implied sexual equality (Safa 1986), the
female body became a primary site of exhibition and commentary within dancehall. According to Louis Chude-Sokei, the body of the black woman became a
threatening physical and economic presence (1997: 222). This was partly a response to the new economic empowerment of lower-class females working primarily in informal economies.[18] These individuals are the grandmothers,
mothers, sisters, and girlfriends of the DJs. Simultaneously, in the formal sector,
a significant number of females occupied midmanagement positions. This, combined with their increasing presence at the University of the West Indies (UWI)
and secondary schools, resulted in a discourse on the social marginalization of
lower-class black males.[19] As in U.S. African-American communities, the black
female is stereotyped as the usurper of masculine agency, a female who threatens
to destroy the black family, the race, and the hopes of a once-great black civilization (Pierce and Williams, 1997: 195).

In some ways, dancehall songs were a reaction to this discourse in which the
image of the matriarch has become oppressive. It perpetuates some aspects of
gender inequality while foregrounding new ones. As Carolyn Cooper notes, in
Rastafari's biblical derivation, the female was ambivalently perceived as both
deceitful and vulnerable (1993: 131). Because of this potential for evil, Rastafari
subjugated females to their maternal role and hailed them Mama Africa—in
another mystification of both females and Africa. Thus, the Rastafari specified
the female body be completely concealed with long, flowing African-inspired
garments and their hair covered with head-ties. Over time, in dancehall, the
black female body was less and less concealed. Simultaneously, in the lyrics
this body (which is sometimes reduced to sexual parts) was, according to Chude-
Sokei, admired, celebrated, possessed, controlled, and feared for its power
(1997: 222). In this process of oversexualization, Chude-Sokei rightly argues
that dancehall also demystified the Rastafarian's Africa. Indeed, black lower-

class masculinity was being reasserted in response to the men's feelings of displacement in relation to the perceived power of black females.

According to Stuart Hall, in black diaspora cultures the body has often been used as though it were the only cultural capital we had (1997: 470). In dancehall, the female body became the ultimate cultural capital—a canvas that is adorned with jewelry and bedecked in clothing that reveals body parts, which are typically covered in daily life among good women and especially among uptown ladies. In the early days, dancehall female participants wore locally made taffeta or sequined dresses and high heeled shoes. Soon, imported sequined dresses became the rage at "sessions" (dances). They were first imported from stores on 34th Street or 7th Avenue in New York City by downtown ICIs. By the late-1980s, many of the ICIs began importing hip-hop and punk clothing and accessories. Men sported the popular baggy clothing with sports logos or patches (originals or copies) or locally tailored two-piece suits in bright-colored lace, satin over ruffled shirts, mesh T-shirts or bare chests. Females who previously wore evening dresses began to wear clothing that emphasized different parts of their anatomy. These new imported items were thrown into a mix to create a new dancehall look that included patent leather, spandex, lace tights, torn stockings, studded bustiers, and Doc Martens boots among other items.

Eventually, they began to eagerly display different parts of the body in "skin-out" clothes and batty riders.[20] In these outfits, many of the participants adopt a persona different from their everyday selves, a persona who breaks away from the everyday social order. At the dancehall, females compete with one another to gain respect and also lure the attention of men. The more daring the outfit and the more sexually uninhibited her dance movements, the more likely she is able to keep her man or attract a new relationship and the resulting material resources.

Prior to the evolution of dancehall, the full black female figure was visible uptown primarily in the popular image of the higgler as a stereotype of "woman." The higgler's body has never been portrayed uptown as a symbol of beauty or sexuality. Rather she represented a hard-working rural "woman" who traveled from country to town carrying loads on her head and sat in the market with her open thighs encircling her basket of wares. Historically, she has been caricatured and juxtaposed against the "lady" (Douglass 1992: 241–249). Dancehall not only projected this full black female form into public arenas, but asserted both its desirability and sexuality. Although dancehall participants include various groups of individuals, including emerging and inherited/traditional middle-class participants, most of those who proudly show their bodies are lower-class and primarily between the ages of nineteen and mid-forties. These females are economically independent heads of their households. Many have made a niche for themselves in the thriving informal economies as higglers, ICIs, and seamstresses (Ross 1998).

More recently the urban ICI has become the new focus of the "lady"/

"woman" dichotomy and has displaced the traditional country (rural) higgler as the epitome of "woman." This independent international trader gained prominence as her business brought her into spaces that people of her social standing seldom occupied (airports, planes, hotels, government offices).

This situation is unwelcomed by uptown individuals who hold the ICI in contempt because she ventures into forbidden territory. Although she is tolerated by the dominant classes, it is not without active resentment. Hence, she almost always has to face reactionary limitations. One of these limitations is enforced by local media representation, which often ridicules the ICI as a caricature of a certain type of "woman." The ICI's affinity for dancehall fashions including hair pieces in flaming colors, wigs, and hair extensions further reinforce their lower-class image. These styles are identified with downtown or the ghettos and are not part of the middle-and upper-class aesthetics. Though the ICI is admired by the dominant classes for her economic wit, she is looked upon with disdain as a large, dark-skinned, uneducated woman who wears loud clothes and heavy jewelry and occupies too much space. She is seen as coarse and unsophisticated, an obvious contradiction of uptown standards of beauty and femininity as personified by the white lady and the Jamaica cocoa-brown pageant winner.

Since they burst onto the scene, ICIs have gained a reputation for their aggressive hustling at the arcades, in airports, and abroad. The ICIs' out-of-placeness partly sets them apart from the rural higgler who may be feisty but is known for her pleasant country demeanor and her respect for the spatial order (Katzin 1959; Durant-Gonzalez 1986). Unlike the cocoa-brown beauty queen who has historically played the role of "island ambassadress" on publicity campaigns abroad (Barnes 1994), the ICI is an "unwilling ambassadress" who was chastised in the media for misrepresenting Jamaica. She does not beckon tourists to "come back to Jamaica" and is not eager to please. In fact she'll likely cuss you first, especially if you get in her way. According to this stereotype, the ICI is very suspicious and distrustful of everyone, unscrupulous in the manner in which she circumvents duties and taxes, and untrustworthy because she charges exorbitant prices for her imported goods.

This stereotype is another oversimplification that ignores the fact that ICIs are far from being an homogeneous group. Not only does this occupation transcend class and color, but among the participants within these social orders additional differences persist. At the arcades that are surrounded by speakers blasting the latest dancehall tunes, there are as many ICIs who are dancehall participants as there are religious fanatics who do not participate in dancehall. Some of the latter are not adverse to this subculture, while others are vehemently opposed to it.[21]

SLACKNESS VERSUS X-RATEDNESS

In the last decade, as the economy stagnated and unemployment rose, violence has surged. Informal economies have become the most reliable avenue of employment for the disadvantaged. Illegal commodity trading is even more pervasive, and the yearly murder rate is at its highest ever.[22] Since 1993, global and local pressures have prompted a resurgence in the popularity of reggae music. This revival has foregrounded the more organic roots or kulcha style in dancehall and has even influenced many slackness DJs to be reborn, writing socially conscious and spiritual songs. Dancehall, which has always been dynamic, continues to evolve and "slackness" has become X-ratedness—that is, even more sexually explicit than before. The new forms of dancing and fashion associated with this style reflect this new trajectory. As a result, divisions within dancehall have become more pronounced.

Different participants have denounced this turn to X-ratedness. For example, the dancehall clothes designer Biggy distances himself from this new trajectory; "I don't go fe (for) the real X-rated Dancehall clothes 100%. Because X-rated a no really Dancehall. Dancehall is a more classic thing than X-rated—you have to look sexy still, but the limits that some people carry, it pass Dancehall" (Soas 1993: 6). Biggy is middle-class and lives in New Jersey. His dancehall designs have earned him a transnational reputation, and his clients include international music superstars like Buju Banton and Queen Latifah. Biggy's world is certainly different from that of the East Kingston seamstresses who sew for the local street vendor, the gunman and his girlfriends, or the ICI in East Parade arcade who retails both local and imported outfits. Hence, it is not surprising that "hard core" dancehall followers catering to people downtown are the ones taking the lyrics and fashions several steps further towards X-ratedness.

Recently, in the media, the level of slackness in a performance has also been used to chastise female DJs, many of whom paradoxically call themselves "lady." Their claim for this title is a subversion of this category. The most notorious of the female DJs is Lady Saw. Her raw lyrics, which are comparable to no other, and her hypersexual stage performances have earned her the X-rated label. In the media, she has been set against other female DJs such as Chevelle Franklyn, whose lyrical content and stage persona is sexual within the limits of the moral order. Lady Saw is even a greater contradistinction to roots reggae female singers such as Marcia Griffiths and Rita Marley, among others. This shift to X-ratedness is also visible in the uptown/downtown fashion clashes.[23]

In an uptown/downtown fashion clash, two groups of females compete against each other on a runway in several dress categories that include sportswear, casual wear, swimwear, and evening wear. Like the clashes featuring dancehall sound systems, the audience determines the winner. These clashes were conceived by entertainment producers, mainly to make a profit by bringing the contrasting uptown/downtown fashions and styles on the same stage in a competitive arena. To date there have been four clashes that feature Carlene, the self-proclaimed reigning Dancehall Queen, and her crew competing against models from a reputable uptown modeling agency. The performance of the downtown crew and the uptown models at these clashes reify the "lady"/"woman" dichotomy. In this arena, the stereotype of the black female is (re)appropriated and hypersexualized.

The first uptown/downtown fashion clash was a three-show series held successively in Kingston, Ocho Rios, and Montego Bay. The first part was held downtown at the Oceana Hotel in the summer of 1992. This clash featured well-known models from the Elite modeling agency, including a Miss World runner-up, versus Carlene and company. After the first show, Elite withdrew its models from the event because this venue was deemed inappropriate for a former Miss Jamaica World contestant. Lesser-known models from the same agency honored the contract and completed the series. The other two clashes have featured models from Miguel Models. This uptown agency has described the clash between uptown and downtown styles as conventional versus outrageous, which borders on the ridiculous.

To date, four uptown/downtown fashion clashes have featured Carlene and Miguel models. In 1993, I attended one of these clashes at Cactus nightclub in Portmore. This event was attended by uptown and downtown individuals and received extensive media coverage. Both groups took their turns on stage, modeling different outfits in a striking reification of the "lady" and "woman" dichotomy. As the show drew to a close, downtown outfits covered less and less of the female body while uptown models, who remained mostly modestly covered (exposing the more "acceptable" midriff areas), were more "stoosh" (uppity). They showed more detachment as they held their heads high, pursed their lips, and cast their eyes down at their rivals and the audience. Caribbean performance artist Jean Small defines "stoosh" as a term used to describe an individual or a group who assume the dress, verbal and nonverbal language, and general behaviour of a higher or more acceptable social class.[24] She notes that "stoosh" behavior always has a negative connotation. Stoosh is a class marker that downtown individuals identify primarily with uptown folks or socially mobile individuals. It is a common practice of distancing typically used and recognized by individuals across the social structure (regardless of color) as a means of establishing social limits. Between and within the different classes, stoosh marks boundaries and assures that these are respected. Locally, the transgressions of these boundaries is called *infradig*, from the Latin *infradignatem*, which means below one's dignity. This term is often used by older generations of the middle and upper classes to denounce cross-class fraternization. Percy Hintzen's essay in this book highlights the extent to which maintaining social distance has transcended locality to become common among West Indians abroad.

As the uptown models performed these subtle techniques to distance themselves from the downtown crew, the latter's skin-out clothes got tinier and tinier, and the dancing became more pornographic at this clash in Cactus. Carlene even went to the point of simulating an orgasm, much to the delight, shock, and surprise of members of the audience, and the show ended with Carlene's downtown crew *wining* on their heads while wearing minimal pieces of fishnet, lace, and nylon lingerie. Interestingly, there are some notable continuities between the set girls parades mentioned above and the contemporary uptown/downtown fashion clashes. These nineteenth-century parades, which were held throughout the island, were a pro-forma arena for what Richard Burton aptly calls "competitive display," an event in which Afro-Jamaican female representations of social or racial categories in the colonies were set against each other.

The boundaries of social and racial categories have become discontinuous. The dancehall queen Carlene is phenotypically almost white and has a full body with large hips and a big bottom—a figure that is more often associated with the woman as opposed to the physical characteristics of the lady.[25] She is of middle-class origins—her family is from outside central Kingston. Of her crew members, Pinky is light-skinned and Sandra is darker. Two of the three Miguel models who represented uptown were by comparison darker-skinned than the dancehall models. Nonetheless, in their clothing and demeanor they were definitely associated with uptown. With their svelte bodies, stockings, high heels, and simply cut, conventional outfits, any one of them could walk into any middle-class dance club or restaurant without turning any heads. Similarly, these contemporary set girls of the uptown/downtown fashion clashes demonstrate that the correlation between class and color are more fluid, especially among Afro-Jamaicans (of all color gradations). Black females are actively (re)negotiating popular constructions of their identities in the diaspora (see Boyce Davies in this volume). Indeed there are black ladies and brown women.

STYLE AND THE SOCIAL POLITICS OF MOURNING

Uptown heads were turned in February 1992 when the deaths of two West Kingston dons brought the dancehall fashion phenomenon into uptown living rooms.[26] Jim Brown, a former don of Tivoli Garden—one of West Kingston's most dangerous JLP garrison communities—was killed under suspicious conditions during his son Jah-T's funeral.[27] The positions held by father and son in their community made their respective interments two of the best-attended events to be held downtown in years. These funerals, which were attended by former Prime Minister Edward Seaga, received full media coverage by radio, TV, and newspapers including the *Daily Gleaner.*

The article in the *Daily Gleaner* on Jah-T's funeral devoted a great portion of the text to the appearance of attendants, especially the females. The writer described the various designs of the mourning females' black dresses and heavy gold accessories including Jah-T's girlfriend's tight-fitting dress and the deceased's white satin shirt and black velvet suit. Several weeks later, the *Daily Gleaner* published a two full-page pictorial with a brief text on Jim Brown's funeral. The piece entitled "Mourning as Spectator Sport" was authored by Jamaica's leading fashion commentator and uptown designer, Norma Soas. Her elaboration on the variation of styles and downtown people's fashion sense deserves to be quoted at length:

The women seemed to wear every piece of fashionable item they owned—all at once. Baubles, bangles, beads abounded. This was a "let it all hang out" [literally] affair. No mini was too short, no tights too tight, no chiffon too sheer, no lace too see through. Hot pants were cheek-by-jowl with lace leggings. Feet were shod in everything from Roman sandals to studded boots. Breasts were encased in bustiers and worn with chiffon big-sleeved blouses. Ankles were wrapped in gold chains with longer thicker versions adorning the neck. Over-sized earrings brushed the wearer's shoulders. Uptown people who might think the dress shown here is inappropriate for the occasion do not really understand the ghetto culture which is vibrant in its own right. This is how a large segment of our female population dress when they go to their fetes. The mourners were not dressing for a funeral. They were dressing for an occasion and this was one of the biggest in their community. This therefore was not inappropriate in their eyes. Rather, these styles are de rigeur for any situation for profiling as this undoubtedly was. This is street fashion, a more sophisticated version of which has been seen in Greenwich Village in New York or Carnaby Street in London. (March 15, 1992)

In her descriptions of these female representations, Soas reaffirms the lady/ woman dichotomy. According to this designer, these females publicly asserted their sexuality in clothing that left little to the imagination. Then she proceeded to analyze and critique the appropriateness of wearing dancehall clothing to a funeral. By emphasizing the particular tastes of downtown females, Soas distinguishes them from uptown ladies.

Later, in another article, Soas highlights the Jamaican racial/spatial order and the dimensions of the lady/woman dichotomy. She notes that it was indeed this funeral which opened the eyes of the folks uptown (who rarely go downtown) to the phenomenon of dancehall fashions. She writes, "the middle-class marveled at the homage to bareness. Many envied the self-confidence of the wearers, most of whom gave lie to the saying that you should only wear clothes that flatter the figure" (1993: 7). Uptown ladies must not bare their bodies in the same manner as downtown women, unless of course it is carnival. Moreover, uptown ladies envy this downtown self-confidence in part because those who do not possess svelte bodies refrain from wearing tight clothing which is considered inappropriate: it accentuates their voluptuousness (read womanliness). Ironically, Soas realizes that for attendees these funerals were arenas for obtaining recognition. Soas' article begins with the following statement: "This was not high fashion but fashion excess. This was mourning as spectator sport with the spectators and mourners as the main attraction" (March 15, 1992). Funerals, because they are arenas in which self-presentation matters, like dancehall sessions, are spaces where individuals can "make a [fashion] statement." Furthermore, Jim Brown's notoriety guaranteed extensive media coverage, an opportunity to be seen or gain recognition beyond one's community. Indeed, as the photos in the pictorial indicate, many of the faces were smiling for the camera.

After former Prime Minister Michael Manley's death, an announcement appeared in the *Daily Gleaner* to outline guidelines for the public at the state funeral. This piece included several informative sections, including one on dress. It recommended that for purposes of conformity and correct procedure during the period of mourning men should dress conservatively and women should dress "appropriately correspondingly" (Young, 1997). These articles provide insight into middle/upper-class ideas about self-presentation and the need to maintain distinction therein. The following are brief examples that further highlight this point.

HYGIENE, EXPLETIVES, HAIR

Downtown women's representation has become a problem for the middle and upper classes, who are losing their ability to dictate the standards of decency and respect. As dancehall permeates more aspects of Jamaican life, the issue of appropriate dress in public spaces is being increasingly contested by lower-class females who point to the hypocrisy of the middle class given their self-presentation and behavior during carnival. Nonetheless, it is no longer surprising to hear of hospitals, malls, and police stations posting dress codes.

In 1993, the emergency section of the Bustamante Hospital posted the following sign: "1) Please cover all body parts!!; 2) Please attend to personal hygiene!!; 3) No setters in hair!; and 4) No Dancehall style!" (Cooper 1993). This sign did not go unnoticed. Media responses to it included the article cited here in a popular magazine as well as mention on local radio shows in favor of and against this issue of decency in emergency situations.

In 1994, a series of imported T-shirts that were popular among downtown youth caused an uproar uptown. These oversize shirts in white or black were designed with large block letters that spelled out "fuck you" or "don't ask me 4 shit." They became the subject of debate on talk radio shows for months. Callers offended by these words began to campaign for prohibition of the shirts. Because of an existing law fining verbalization of expletives in public spaces, the T-shirts were ultimately banned to ensure that the public would not be forced to see these imported obscenities.

In April 1996, an unambiguously black woman sporting Nubian[28] knots was hosting a local morning TV program. Within her first hour on the air, the TV station received calls from viewers across the nation demanding the removal of that "bumpy head gal" or "ugly black woman" from their television screens. Several calls explicitly questioned the appropriateness of this hairstyle—which was perceived by some as unkempt and unfinished—in a public medium. This event sparked much controversy in the media for several weeks. That "bumpy head gal," as she became known, is a poet of middle-class status whom many consider the heir apparent to Louise Bennett—the grande dame of Jamaican oral poetry. Again newspapers, radio, and TV concerned with this public expression of afrophobia sought to bring closure to the incident. Within days, numerous black/dancehall/downtown and fewer middle-class females adopted this new hairstyle and wore it proudly everywhere. Young girls were seen wearing this hairstyle with their school uniforms, despite the fact that in some schools in Jamaica dreadlocks are still prohibited.

In August 1997, Island Jamaica Film released the film *Dancehall Queen*, which was coldly received by the middle-and upper-class reviewers who labeled it "vulgar." On the contrary, the film received popular support from the masses who filled the theaters during the entire release of the picture. This movie focuses on the daily trials of Marcia, a lower-class black (dark-skinned) woman from downtown. Marcia, a self-employed pushcart vendor, negotiates the violent realities of street vending (as individuals fight over space) and her challenges as a single mother who ultimately encourages her teenage daughter to accept the sexual advances of her benefactor. Desperate, she turns to the world of dancehall, constructs a more sexualized persona and eventually challenges the stoosh, middle-class, brown reigning queen. In a final confrontation, Marcia claims both the title of dancehall queen and a substantial cash award.

As people waited to get into the Carib theater, the popular interest in this movie became apparent as lines grew longer and young and old males and females came from downtown to see this movie. At particular moments in the film, echoes of "pow! pow! buyaka! buyaka!" bounced off the walls of the theater from audience members expressing their satisfaction.[29] Certain aspects of downtown life were being realistically portrayed on the big screen. Dissatisfaction was also heard among viewers during the final dance competition, as Marcia's performance would fail in the real dancehall world. Nonetheless, shouts of excitement filled the theater because Marcia "beat the system," as an attendant testified. As dancehall DJ Buju Banton sings and as this movie has shown, for downtown folks "opportunity is a scarce commodity in these times." For females already constrained by the limits of informal economies, the body becomes a form of material capital—a vehicle to facilitate a way out of the ghetto.

These examples suggest that indeed there is a tense dialogue going on between black/brown, downtown/uptown, lower/middle classes on issues of representations of blackness and femaleness and definitions of these identities. As Faye Harrison stated in her study of a working-class downtown area, there is "a deep sense of disappointment, alienation and anger which informs agency among the dispossessed" (1997: 460). These feelings, Harrison stresses, are the result of "rising expectations and unfulfilled promises since independence" (ibid.) have created tensions between black and brown people that are played out in numerous visible and invisible sites. These days, a most common saying among the lower class is that it is "black man time now." These words were first echoed during the movement toward independence in the 1960s. They were heard again when P. J. Patterson became the first elected dark-skinned prime minister in 1991. Six years later, his reelection was foregrounded by a renewed public discourse of blackness and the politics of identity in this "plural" society. As a young female notes, "I voted for him because he was of my nation." Among blacks, there is resentment toward the pervasiveness of white/brown and cultural aesthetics that emulate Europe as representative of the nation.[30]

GETTING "MAXIMUM RESPECT!"

Every day Afro-Jamaicans are continuously reminded that their phenotypic characteristics are not valued. The persistence of images that reinforce the lady/woman dichotomy combined with daily challenges to their achieved identities and ascribed position within Jamaican society provide constant reminders that they do/will not attain higher social position regardless of economic status. A number of downtown ICIs have become economically successful and compete with the traditional Chinese and Syrian merchant groups. They buy houses in uptown neighborhoods and send their children to better schools. In many cases, their consumption patterns surpass that of the respectable poor. Unwilling to and/or incapable of adapting their inherited lower-class identities to uptown standards, they are socially marginalized. Because they do not share the same social values, the traditional middle class distances themselves from them. There are multiple levels to this social divide. These include the continuous inbreeding of prejudices and racism among the upper classes and the elite. As a middle-class activist notes, the middle-class lady would never invite a woman to tea for fear she might arrive dressed up in batty riders.

Despite the ongoing discursive tension between uptown and downtown ideals of beauty and femininity, across the economic structure black females often aspire to European ideals in body type and hair styles. Those who seek social mobility and have not been socialized into the culture of ladylike femininity have to and do go through rigorous processes of alteration to be or maintain this feminine ideal. Peter J. Wilson rightly argues that many women of the lower classes who are unable to meet the elite social standards of femininity never become members of the upper class, and many do not care (1973: 234). Lisa Douglass adds that this choice is not without consequences, as the females who do not strive to (and I would add succeed in) attain uptown feminine status are precluded from any long-term social affiliation with the powerful in Jamaica (1992: 246). This reaffirms Butler's assertion that those who fail to perform their gender identity appropriately (according to uptown standards) are regularly punished (1990: 273).

Although I agree with Wilson and Douglass, I think their conclusions can be taken further. I would stress that among females of the lower classes there is an awareness that social class position is inherited. To the middle and upper classes, changes in economic status does not detract from one's position unless one reconstructs her social identity. As a result, many lower-class females consciously reject the middle-and upper-class ideals of beauty and identity and reassert their own notions because the former are not simply unattainable, but also undesirable. For these women, social, economic, and political exclusion is not merely a consequence of failing to assimilate, but an everyday reality. As stated above, social status has always implied a choice between black and brown/white. Although a penchant for Afrocentric views has always coexisted among the traditional or inherited black and brown middle classes, historically, social mobility and social acceptance have required the denial or forgetting of family relations, friendships, and the adoption of and adaptation to a white or European culture (Douglass 1992: Henriques 1957). For those reasons, many lower-class females do not care to gain middle-and upper-class acceptance because they do not perceive the consequences mentioned above as particularly significant to their lives. Furthermore, they are now actively engaged in re-creating different sites of power and redefining the meanings of respect.

Downtown women who display the very body parts their uptown counterparts must cover to maintain their "lady" status often feel more comfortable with their bodies. Black lower-class females are less interested in conforming to uptown standards, especially since personal experiences have taught them that they will never be socially accepted. They do know that one's body type, clothing, comportment, and other socially defined criteria are markers of one's social status. Many of the physically larger ICIs I encountered accept and celebrate their bodies as an extension of their blackness and proudly proclaim their downtown identities. On the other hand, middle-class informal importers regard this title of ICI pejoratively and even consider it insulting.

These days it is not uncommon to encounter women dressed in full dance-hall gear complete with colorful wigs that match the clothing in the middle of the day in uptown supermarkets, the airport, the bank, the mall. As these individuals or *passes* (female posses) stroll down the aisle or the street, their faces register an attitude that dares anyone to comment on or object to their presence or style of self-presentation. They often receive the desired response as trails of whispers follow their every step, prompting them to give you a cut-eye or kiss their teeth as you stare. They walk slowly, languidly, profiling, marking out a territory as they make their presence felt. Like those T-shirts banned several years ago, they are an affront to the dominant classes, especially demure and proper uptown ladies who are now forced to acknowledge them if for no other reason than because they now also possess and manipulate the hegemonic U.S. dollar.

CONCLUSION

The existing gap between the consumption patterns of the different social classes is rapidly decreasing. As more working-class individuals amass capital through their participation in informal economies and by any other means necessary, they now consume the same goods that in the past were symbols of social class status. The feeling of distance that the middle class could buy with the U.S. dollar to assure itself of its status is now under siege.

As more blacks continue to prosper economically, the social class system has become more fragile and the policing of status even more rigid. Lower-class female representations of gendered identities indicate awareness of this rigidity. Jamaican class and color hierarchies are inherently tenuous, predicated upon the asymmetrical interaction between components that are situationally determined whether these be physical, cultural, or material. Consequently, color, class, economic, and social categories are not mutually exclusive. One's social position no longer reflects his/her economic status and one's color is not always indicative of social position, especially among peoples of African descent. The disjuncture between class and color, economic and social power, and their daily subjective manifestations is one of the primary reasons that the representation of difference by socially upward, mobile blacks and browns is becoming more explicit. This distance is often manifested in the acceptance of middle-and upper-class ideals that will set these individuals apart from the masses. This further reinforces the racial hierarchy and shows the extent to which the white bias pervades Jamaican culture. Because of the predominance of this bias, struggles against the hegemonic ideals inevitably entail a range of paradoxes and contradictions. We need only look at dancehall to find a few examples.

In 1991, Buju Banton released a single titled "Love Mi Browning," about his preference for lighter-skinned females. The singer professed: "Mi love me car/Me love me bike/Me love me money and ting/But most of all me love my Browning." This song caused such an uproar that the singer apologized with another tune titled "Love Black Woman." Another DJ, Nardo Ranks, wrote a rebuttal entitled "Dem a Bleach," which narrated the pervasive use of skin-bleaching creams among light-skinned females. Indeed, the desire for the browning beauty ideal is not mere rhetoric. To date, Carlene's reign has lasted over six years. She has superstar status and her local and international public appearances command local media attention. She has traveled to North America, Europe, and Japan as representative of dancehall. It seems that the "competitive display" rule that has governs dancehall since its emergence is hardly applicable to her. She has no "known" rivals. As a local participant notes, "she's always going to be the Dancehall Queen that is until someone who looks just like her rises up to the challenge." Except, of course, in the movies.

NOTES

The material covered in this paper is based on archival and field research conducted in Jamaica in July–December 1993, June 1994, and October 1995–September 1996. This research was funded by an International Predissertation Fellowship from the Social Science Research Council and the American Council of Learned Societies with funds provided by the Ford Foundation and a grant from Inter-American Foundation program for Latin America and the Caribbean. Writing was funded by a Rackham Fellowship from the University of Michigan and the Center for Afro-American and African Studies (CAAS). I am indebted to the ICIs and the people at the UVA for their knowledge and patience. Thanks to Jean Muteba Rahier, the editor of this collection. Respect always to my "passe" Jennifer Bond, Diane Lankein, Melissa Johnson, Opal Linton, Jennifer Scott, and Irmina Ulysse for their insights, comments, and unconditional support. And maximum respect to Evans Young, Rosario Montoya, and Louis Chude-Sokei for reading drafty drafts and for their encouragement. As this paper is part of a larger work, there are many ideas that have not been developed here because of the limitations of space. However, I accept responsibility for the arguments therein.

1. In this paper, I use the word "female" to recognize the locally acknowledged distinctions between lady and woman and the historical meanings embedded in these socially constructed categories.

2. The concept of social class used here is premised on what Diane Austin-Broos (1994) calls an "inheritable identity" that is based on social markers such as family lineage, education, and occupation. Like Ralph Trouillot, I understand color as a social construction that refers to more referents than phenotype including the depth of skintone, hair color, hair texture, and facial features. Color categories never operate alone. They are inextricably linked to the various markers of social class noted above in addition to income, customary behavior, and other characteristics. As Trouillot stresses, combinations of these social traits can move a person from one category to a more or less proximate one" (1990: 112–113). Hence class and color are far from definitive. Because Jamaica is racially heterogeneous and social, political, and economic changes of the past have had an impact on the population, the upper strata of the class structure are no longer as color specific. Nonetheless, the vast majority of the blacks are lower class, browns are middle class, and whites are the elite. Because of the limitations of space, I employ these simplified class categories, recognizing that there are further subdivisions.

3. Elsewhere I show how this challenge to the dominant order has lead to its increasing rigidity.

4. Although these boundaries are volatile because of tension between the two parties and their followers, the tension between certain apparatuses of the state and downtown has become increasingly aggressive. For example, in August 1997, the police launched an attack on gunmen in which shots were fired from a helicopter raining bullets on Tivoli Gardens. The many facts and truths of this case still remain unexplained. This troubling incident and others before highlight the fact that certain downtown areas are under siege.

5. Elsewhere, I construct a schemata that includes the distinctions and similarities among "gal" and its variations, good and bad woman (Austin-Broos 1987) and rebel woman among others.

6. Barbara Bush (1981).

7. Representation is loaded with meanings that highlight the recent impact of transnational cultural flows on local consumption and manipulation of imported items as well as the value and status ascribed to these goods (see Freeman 1997 for a similar point among neohigglers in Barbados).

8. Rastafarians' position in Jamaican society is well documented (see Waters 1985). I also attribute the acceptance and manipulation of Rasta symbols to several factors including the economic power of Reggae which helped revive a failing tourist industry and its role as a vehicle for economic (and to some degree social) mobility for the lower classes.

9. These include Attitude Model Agency, Best of the Best Model Agency, Creme de la Creme Modeling Agency, Jade Marc Models, Sage Models, to name a few.

10. Historically the relationship between blacks and Chinese in Jamaica has been one of antagonism. The Chinese riots of the 1960 and tensions between Chinese merchants and ICIs downtown in the 1970s are just two examples.

11. Richard Wilk makes a similar point regarding the proliferation of beauty contests in Belize (1996).

12. For example, from 1960 to 1978 the number of women employed in the manufacturing sector dropped from 43,865 to 19,400. Male unemployment, during that period, increased from 45,658 to 58,000 (Bolles, 1981: 85).

13. The Structural Adjustment Policies required drastic devaluation of local currency, wage ceilings, and the lifting of price controls on some food items. These reductions affected the lives of lower-class females significantly. As a result many turned to the informal sector as international higglers. Higglering (or market trading) is a traditional occupation of lower-class women that has its roots in slavery. The traditional or local higgler is a black woman who sells rural farm produce in urban markets.

14. M. Owusu (1996) uses this term to distinguish those who maintain or inherit social status despite significant losses in economic power. As I have found many of the respectable poor supplement their incomes with informal economic activities importing.

15. I have found that they engage in this practice seasonally (that is, several times a year, in accordance with retail sales dates in the buying country) to maintain their lifestyle and social status. Faye Harrison notes that in the mid-1980s international migration for work became a common practice among working-class females. They visit their transnational families for extended periods of time and do a little baby-sitting to earn money to send or bring back home. Even middle-class females take jobs as nannies and domestic helpers to tolerate an otherwise embarrassing and humiliating decline in social status (1997: 455).

16. These *posses* were in fact descendants and successors of the Rude Bwais (boys) gangs that emerged out of the poverty-stricken ghettos of downtown Kingston during the 1960s. Young, out of work, exasperated, and anti-authoritarian Afro-Jamaican men embarked on a life of rapes and other crimes to abate their desperation and hunger. In that brutal and fatal fashion, they sought to redistribute the uneven concentration of material resources between uptown and downtown. Their rhetoric emphasized the impact of white/brown oppression of the black majority. Eventually, they were politicized by government parties through a process of political patronage. These youth gangs were rewarded with cash, short-term jobs, and guns. In return, they assured the electoral support of local voters, protected local residents from armed enemy insurgents and enforced the will of the party. This has been attributed to the JLP party's attempt to control its western constituency (Small, 1995: 11). By the mid 1980s, these political armies became systematically entrenched in a transnational traffic of contraband, illegal immigrants, and consumer items, well beyond the scope and control of their original patrons.

17. These styles include *slackness*, roots or Kulcha (culture) among others. Songs comment on various topics on DJing, interpersonal power relations, gun worshipping, and current topical issues.

18. During this period, informal importing became a popular profession. From the late 1970s to early 1980s, the "registered" number of ICIs jumped from several hundred to over ten thousand (McFarlane-Gregory 1993).

19. Errol Miller's (1988) work placed him at the forefront of this movement.

20. A pair of short shorts (known as Daisy Dukes in the United States) that accentuate and reveal the lower parts of the buttocks.

21. For example, Christian females wear their hair natural and do not use cosmetics.

22. In the last decade the murder rate has rapidly risen to nearly 1,000 per annum.

23. These were premised on the sound system clashes, which are musical competitions, where opposing sounds match wits . . . hyping up the crowd, and toasting (ridiculing the other sounds's members) (Andrew Campbell, aka Tuffie, 1997: 203).

24. Interview with Jean Small.

25. Carlene has since trimmed her figure considerably, in part as a result of her international popularity.

26. *Don* is a title of respect that derives from local affinity for the Italian Mafia system. Also bestowed upon the leader of a demarcated geographical area in poor neighborhoods who oversees everything from finding and allocating work for residents, local fund raising through petty crime and/or drug trading, and redistribution of these resources and provision of safety to the community.

27. His body was found burned, by an unexplained fire, in his prison cell the same day as his son's funeral.

28. A popular hairstyle consisting of partitioned single braids that have been tucked in.

29. These mimicked the sounds of gunshots usually voiced with the index and middle finger up in the air performed at the dances.

30. Brian Meeks (1997) describes this current condition as a state of hegemonic dissolution.

9

Representations of Blackness in Colombian Popular Music

Peter Wade

Some years ago, a referee of a book manuscript I submitted to a publisher for evaluation wrote that a major problem with my work was that it assumed that there was such a thing as "black culture" in Colombia. In her (or his) view, the culture of black people in that country was simply a variant of Iberian culture found all over Latin America. This opinion, associated with the perspective that black people in much of Latin America shared a common culture with non-black people of a similar class position, seemed to me short-sighted at the time in that it took for granted widespread popular and official notions about Colombian national identity which held that, while indigenous peoples had evidently distinct cultures, black people were simply ordinary, albeit mainly lower-class, citizens. In Brazil or Cuba, it might be admitted, black culture did exist in clearly African-derived religious practices, but in countries like Colombia blacks spoke Spanish, practiced Catholic religion, and in general had "lost" their African heritage.

Such a view seems all the more out of touch today when Colombia's new 1991 constitution admits that the nation is pluriethnic and multicultural and gives special rights to black communities defined as culturally distinct. Even before this time, however, it was evident to me that black people constructed, in specific contexts, variants of cultural complexes that were identified both by them and others as distinct. It is perhaps in the realm of music and dance that this was, and continues to be, most evident. Such difference was not, however, derived in some simple way from Africanness. Instead, it derived from the way black people used and adapted various musical styles to create cultural forms that could be seen as an expression of their own identities.

Marshal Sahlins (1993) has argued that currents of radical constructionism in contemporary social anthropology sometimes lose track of real historical continuities when they assert that all culture is continually reconstituted and always changing. It is true that all culture is, in some sense, "invented," but this does not mean that it is always created from scratch. Sahlins asserts that "cultural continuity appears as the mode of cultural change" (1993: 19); that is, people's attempts to maintain a cultural continuity, or cultural difference, for themselves, is the very mode of cultural change. He states: "for the [indigenous] people concerned, syncretism is not a contradiction of their culturalism—of the indigenous claims of authenticity and autonomy—but its systematic condition" (1993: 19). For black people in Colombia, the constantly changing forms of musical expression that are characteristic of the many different and varying contexts in which they act do not form a random collection of styles, but are instead the "systematic condition" of blackness as a cultural identity (see Wade 1995a). What was at one point in time "black music" has often derived more from European traditions than African ones and may become identified more as "Colombian" than "black" music over time. As this happens, other styles become signifiers of blackness, perhaps more through the way they are listened and danced to rather than in terms of particular musical features. An emphasis on continuity, from this perspective, does not mean a continuous search for African roots—a contemporary fashion in some currents of Afro-Colombianist anthropology (Friedemann 1993; Friedemann and Arocha 1986)—but for the recreation of black musical and performance styles in new contexts (see Myrian Sepúlveda dos Santos, this volume, for a similar argument in relation to Brazilian carnival).

In this essay, I explore this theme with particular reference to changes that took place in Colombia from about the 1930s through the 1960s and 1970s as styles strongly associated with the country's Caribbean coastal region, styles seen as black and mulatto by many, became the core of Colombia's commercial popular music, displacing the styles identified with the whiter Andean interior, an area that was (and is) the "center" to the coast's "periphery." First, however, I will explore a couple of pre-twentieth-century contexts in order to give a comparative dimension to the analysis.

COLONIAL CABILDOS

Music played by black people has generally occupied an ambiguous and ambivalent place in the minds of non-black Colombians. In the colonial era, for example, slaves were allowed to form *cabildos* (councils or associations) in which they could sing and dance (see Isidoro Moreno, this volume). These associations were constantly subject to control by the colonial authorities, just as the republican states tried to control the activities of the music and dance groups that were the post-colonial counterparts of these cabildos (Wade 1993: 88–90, 278–280; Aretz 1977; Friedemann 1988). On the one hand, then, they were permitted in the interests of providing an authorized space within which music and dance could supposedly be contained; equally they were suppressed when they seemed to be breaking free from the bounds of this control. Music could be seen as an instrument for assimilating slaves. Egberto Bermúdez (1992) described the case of seventeenth-century *villancicos* (carols), songs venerating a Catholic God written specifically for black slaves in the colonies by Spanish composers for the purpose of evangelizing slaves. These composers used African or sometimes Creole words in the lyrics, as well as imitating what seemed to them an "African" accent in their transcription of the words.[1] On the other hand, religious authorities took an important role in controlling what they saw as "inconveniences and sins" that originated in certain dances (the bishop of Cartagena in the 1730s, cited in Perdomo Escobar 1963: 318). These dances were not necessarily "black" dances in a straightforward sense, but since blacks (and Indians) often made up a substantial part of the emerging mixed-blood lower classes and since it was the dancing habits of these classes that caused concern for the authorities, the "inconveniences and sins" in question were often linked to the lower (and "darker") ranks of the socioracial hierarchy.

THE WORLD OF THE BOGAS

The same kind of ambivalence can be seen in a very different context and period: that of the Magdalena River of the nineteenth century. This river was the principal route connecting Bogotá and the interior of the country in general to the Caribbean coast. Steamboats were only gradually introduced after 1823 and well into the nineteenth century transport was generally via a huge raft, *champán*, poled laboriously by black and mulatto boatmen, *bogas*, who originated in the Caribbean coastal region (which I will henceforth refer to as La Costa, the Coast). Travelers tended to be white Colombians or foreigners and, in their diaries and travel writings, often commented on the bogas' behavior. The journey was long (up to six weeks) and tedious; the conditions were sweltering and cramped. The bogas' tool was a long pole with which they impelled the raft by sticking one end in the river bank or bed, lodging the other end against the shoulder and then walking the length of a hard canopy, under which the passengers sat.

According to James Hamilton, a European traveler of the time, the vibration and noise this caused "completely put a stop to reading or writing" (1827: I, 79). Interestingly, he also referred to how the bogas varied "the monotony of their movements by a sort of short jump or dance." Another English traveler noted how the pace of the bogas varied "according to the singing, if such it may be termed, of the 'patron,' or steersman, who . . . ke[pt] making a noise all the while, in which the only articulated sounds [were] 'Yaw, yaw-yee, yaw,' which [were] incessantly repeated in a sort of undertone" (Anon. 1828: I, 211). Charles Stuart Cochrane remarked on how the men broke the monotony "with a variety of cries and ejaculations, whilst they ke[pt] up a pantomime of bodily contortions, stamping, dancing, wriggling, and twisting in a thousand ludicrous postures, unutterable and inimitable" (1825: I, 74). The travelers equivocated between describing the bogas' activities as, on the one hand, "bodily contortions" and "noise" and, on the other hand, "dancing" and "singing." The equivocation was, I think, loaded with meanings defined by notions of a work ethic and bodily propriety. The bogas were clearly working, implying the sense of discipline and ordered, productive effort given to the term by the liberal ideologies of industrializing Euro-America (which were having such an influence on Latin America at the time). In that sense, the boatmen failed to live up to what was required: their work was a "pantomime." Travelers frequently also commented on the bogas' propensity to "show off" (i.e., perform rather than work) and on their indiscipline (see below), even as they recognized the tremendous physical exertion required to impel the raft. On the other hand, if what they were doing was dancing and singing, then it was still "ludicrous" and closer to "wriggling" than the highly controlled bodily movements of dance as defined by the rules of etiquette and decorum that governed not only Euro-American but also Latin American elite and middle-class society (see Quintero Rivera 1996).

The bogas were social inferiors, but they had these white travelers at their mercy for the time being and lost no opportunity to make fun of them. Everyone who had contact with the bogas suffered the barbs of their sarcastic wit. Cochrane felt uncomfortable as they stood round, cracked incomprehensible jokes, and laughed at him as he ate (1825: I, 74–75). Writing his memoirs in the late nineteenth century, José María Cordovez Moure recounts the tale of the Antioqueño bishop, Juan de la Cruz Gómez Plata, who traveled up river to Bogotá in 1850. The pilot ordered silence from the bogas out of respect for the august personage, but the latter was distressed at the snail-like pace of the raft. Informed that this was due to the obligatory silence imposed on the bogas, the bishop authorized them to "say what they will, on condition that we go quickly."

"Given permission to break the silence, the *bogas* impelled the *champán* along with vigor and made up for their enforced verbal abstinence, giving tongue to a torrent of oaths, insolences, swear words and blasphemies against the bishop in such terms that the latter preferred a slower pace to being obliged to listen to that storm of improprieties, enough to make them founder" (Cordovez Moure 1957: 482).[2]

Rafael Gómez Picón, writing much later, said that as the bogas passed the working hours, "they would sing traditional songs . . . or invent impromptu remarks that mockingly alluded to the sufferings of the white passengers, who listened without daring to respond" (1945: 351). Cordovez Moure also observed: "the boga of the Magdalena is superlatively clever and roguish, does not miss any opportunity of mortifying the whites with his scorn and will not shrink even from begging; when he begs he uses this formula: 'White man, give me a *peseta* for a drink' " (1957: 483).

Another thing that annoyed the white travelers was the bogas' predilection for drinking and dancing sprees in the riverside ports along the way, which "they would not leave until the last drop of liquor was drained and their romantic affairs brought to a close" (Cordovez Moure 1957: 482). For the bogas this seems to have been one of the major diversions. Prudencio Vidales, who worked as a boga during his youth and was interviewed at the age of ninety by sociologist Orlando Fals Borda recalled—and it is interesting to compare his prosaic insider's account with the more flamboyant versions of the travelers whose sensational renderings are perhaps worthy of the bogas themselves: "Not everything was bad as a boga. We would also have fun, not only with the manatees [a sort of water mammal sometimes used for bestiality by the bogas], but also with the stories we'd tell and, with the help of rum, we'd go along singing *coplas* and *décimas* [sorts of sung verses]. . . . In the ports where there were fiestas, which were and still are frequent, us *bogas* would stop and dance *bunde, berroche*, and *mapalé* to the sound of the *gaita* or the *caña'e millo* [types of cane flute] with candles in our hands" (Fals Borda 1979: 48A). Hamilton was astounded to see his *bogas*, after thirteen hours poling in the sun, "the gayest of gay in the dance." He added: "In one of these favorite dances, the attitudes and movements are very lascivious" (1827: I, 93–94). Cordovez Moure also noted how on days of fiesta the bogas dressed in brilliant white and, with a challenging attitude, would drink, eat, flirt, and eventually dance the *currulao*:[3] "during [the dance] the negroes without a blush perform before their partners erotic movements, replete with obscene words which, the lewder they are, the more applause they draw" (1957: 484).

In the opinion of nineteenth-century parliamentarian José María Samper, the currulao, full of "shameless lubricity," revealed "all the brutish energy of the black and the zambo of the northern coasts of New Granada [Colombia]" (1980: 93; see also Peñas Galindo 1988: 59). Nevertheless, all the passengers with whom Samper was traveling at the time wanted to observe the scene they came upon in the tiny hamlet of Regidor—except the women "whose eyes were not up to viewing this extravagant dance" (Samper 1980: 93). He described a scene similar in many respects to other descriptions of the same era: a group of musicians—playing a conical drum, a *gaita* or cane flute,[4] a scraper, an iron triangle and a tube rattle—were surrounded by a rotating circle of eight male-female dancing pairs holding aloft candles, themselves surrounded by a circle of spectators who would periodically join the dance, replacing one of the pairs. Shocked by the dancers' movements, "of a voluptuousness, of a shameless lubricity, the description of which I do not wish to, nor should I attempt" (93), he was also surprised by the absence of vocal activity—no lyrics, no words, not even any shouts.

His account is full of different, almost contradictory elements. He confessed himself barely up to the task of narrating the scene: "Difficult, very difficult, would be the description of those coarse, uniform faces, of those figures that seemed, when they moved, like shadows or phantoms from a dream or, when they remained immobile, like the rough and blackened tree-trunks in a forest devoured by flames'' (93). This "romanticism" was augmented by the light of the fire against the "immense cavern" of the surrounding forest. To Samper these bogas seemed steeped in an exotic fantasy world that almost defied description. On the other hand, there was also something prosaically workaday about their dancing: "Enthusiasm is lacking and, instead of any poetry, any art, any gentle emotion, deep, new, surprising, one sees nothing in the scene but the mechanical instinct of the flesh, the power of habit dominating matter, never [does one see] the heart nor the soul of these savages of civilization. Not one of them enjoys dancing, because dance is a necessary occupation like any other. Hence the strange monotony of the spectacle'' (Samper 1980: 93–94).

Oddly, then, there is something mechanical and worklike in the dance, far removed from the gentle enjoyments of "civilized" art. Paradoxically, while the bogas' work seemed like dance, their dance seemed like work. They are lost in romanticism but are also purely mechanical. This perception of confusion was only to be expected from Samper, for whom these were people of "savage features, fruit of the crossing of two or three different races, for whom Christianity is a shapeless mixture of impiety and idolatry, the law an incomprehensible confusion, civilization a thick fog and [for whom] the future, like the past and the present are confounded in the same situation of torpor, indolence and brutality'' (1980: 88). Samper ends his description thus: "Civilization will not reign in this region until the day that the *currulao*, the horrible synthesis of contemporary barbarism, has disappeared'' (1980: 94). Such, apparently, was the power of dance, but the real paradox lies in the fact that the mechanical monotony of which Samper complained in the bogas' music and dancing was precisely the rhythm that industrial laborers were increasingly adopting as they moved to the tune of the "civilized" world. The monotonous, repetitive nature of "instinct" that Samper thought he observed in the dance was both brutish and machinelike, and he used both organic and mechanical imagery to describe it.[5] Outside the influence of "civilization" it was useless, languishing in torpor. In his view, these people needed the influence of (organized) agriculture and commerce. The subtext is that, with these, such energy could be put to good use, providing the material infrastructure for the "gentle emotions" that the gentle folk of civilized (mechanized) society could expect to enjoy.

At work, then, the bogas moved in ways that seemed to travelers' eyes like dance but were more like bodily contortions. At play, their movements were "lascivious" and "obscene." In either case, their dance and song were beyond the pale of "civilized" standards of propriety. Yet the travelers seemed endlessly fascinated by the bogas and, while they looked down on them, were impressed by their endurance and their sexual energy, themselves taken as sure signs of a "primitive" nature. This ambivalence of colonial and neocolonial relations, especially with regard to sexuality, has of course been noted for other situations (e.g., Young 1995).

The bogas were blacks, mulattoes and *zambos* (people of putatively black and Indian descent). The dances that Prudencio Vidales mentions above (bunde, berroche, mapalé) are characteristic of La Costa as a whole, a region that has a very mixed population. In this sense, boga culture—if such a term be allowed for the time being—was not something entirely specific and separable, not a clearly demarcated "black culture." Yet, in the context of the bogas' interactions with the white travelers it is clear that a fairly clear boundary was being established in which "blacks" and "whites" were opposed categories. Music and dance—so linked to notions of propriety (Quintero Rivera 1996)—were also clearly instrumental in establishing that boundary, a moral boundary of radicalized difference that signified notions of civilization and savagery, work and indolence, productive and unproductive mechanicalism. As Gina Ulysse also shows for Jamaica (this volume), styles of dancing, bodily movement, and dress are powerful markers of racialized social standing, although these markers are not by any means necessarily stable ones.

COSTEÑO MUSIC, BLACKNESS, AND NATIONAL IDENTITY

In the twentieth century, music associated with black people and with regions where black populations live has again been viewed in an ambivalent fashion. Very different perspectives have been articulated by different sets of people. We can see the same ambivalence playing between the attractiveness and the threat of people and aesthetic expressions linked to notions of primitiveness, but now this ambivalence becomes increasingly implicated in ideas about national identity. Blackness had been an important element in nineteenth-century discussions about emerging nationality, since it was against the supposed barbarism and laziness of blacks (and Indians) that images of the new nation were being constructed (Wade 1993: ch. 1; Wade 1998; Graham 1990). Now images of blackness, often evoked by music, took on a more central role as that music became a popular commercial form and came to represent "Colombia" as a nation. In the process, however, the explicit nature of blackness was often lessened—"whitened"—and retained as only one meaning among many. The status of this music, which originated in La Costa, as not unequivocally "black" to start with, helped this process. La Costa is a highly mixed region with certain areas where black populations predominate (e.g., the poorer areas of Cartagena, the coastal fringes of the region) and other areas where one sees a mestizo population with evident African, native American, and European heritage. Therefore, although it is often seen—by people from all regions of the country— as rather "black" compared to certain areas of the Andean interior, it is not straightforwardly so. Blackness is much more certainly associated with the Pacific coastal region, where black people have historically mixed much less and where they form a large majority.

In the 1920s and 1930s, small orchestras called "jazz-bands" started to appear in cities of La Costa—especially Cartagena and Barranquilla—and soon after in the cities of the interior such as Cali and Bogotá. These orchestras used an instrumental lineup that was common all over the Americas and the Caribbean,[6] and they played a similarly eclectic and international repertoire of music, including North American foxtrot, Cuban boleros and guarachas, Argentinian tangos, and Mexican rancheras. Guitar-based duos and trios also played some of this repertoire. Such music formed the staple diet of the Colombian radio stations that multiplied after the first one was founded in Barranquilla in 1929. Orchestras in La Costa also began to orchestrate some of the local music that went under the name of *cumbia, porro, gaita,* and *fandango.* Some of this music was being performed by small groups of rural origin (who might nevertheless play in urban contexts) with the basic instruments of drums, cane flute, scraper, and so on. Some of it had been incorporated into the village and town brass bands that had emerged all over the country from the early nineteenth century and which also played European dance music (waltzes, marches, polkas) and newer American styles such as the *habanera,* derived from the Cuban *danzón.* These groups and especially the brass bands formed the context within which many of the leaders of the new orchestras learned their music, although they often also received more formal training.

When orchestrated by the new jazz-bands, porro and cumbia soon found their way into the elite social clubs of La Costa, despite some initial resistance to their plebeian origins and "vulgar" nature; there was also resistance from such reactionary quarters to some of the Cuban music that was also becoming so popular. In orchestrated form, this Costeño music (i.e., music from La Costa) was increasingly acceptable, although it still retained a "hot" quality that made it eminently danceable, with a strong rhythmic structure, retained in part from its roots, and colorful, tight brass arrangements. In addition, the orchestras themselves were often made up mostly of light-skinned men, although there were also occasional black or mulatto artists. From the late 1920s, Costeño music was being recorded outside Colombia[7] and became a staple of Colombia's first record company, Discos Fuentes, which, although it was founded in 1934 (originally as a radio station), did not start to press its own records until the early 1940s. There are many important names behind the spread of this music, but central ones include Lucho Bermúdez, probably the most influential band leader of his time and an international figure; Pacho Galán, also important although he tended to remain in his native Barranquilla; José Barros, better known perhaps as a composer than an artist; Antonio María Peñaloza, again better known as a composer and arranger.

In the context of the rapid commercialization of music as a commodity, Costeño music was winning the day, and it was doing so against the received musical emblem of Colombian national identity: *bambuco.* This music was associated with the Andean region and played on stringed instrument lineups of various sizes (from a lone guitarist or player of the *tiple,* a treble guitar, to a full string ensemble with guitars, mandolins, tiples, etc.). In the late nineteenth century, in the context of the musical nationalism common in all of Latin America at the time, bambuco had been lionized by the country's intellectual, political, and artistic elites, although the *pasillo,* a creolized waltz also found in many other regions of Latin America, was just as popular (Wade 1998; Béhague 1996). *Bambuco* was also the subject of the first recordings by Colombian artists working with the New York record companies in the 1910s and 1920s.[8] As Costeño music grew in popularity, however, bambuco increasingly lost its central place.

The reception of Costeño music in the interior of the country was not always friendly. It was identified with new fashion trends (including other styles such as Cuban *guarachas*), blackness, and loose morals. There was already prejudice in some circles against popular music seen as "vulgar." For example, the Radio Nacional, founded in 1940 as the state radio station, sought to improve the general public with classical music, news, drama, and educational programs. The programs included some popular music, but the station still wanted to maintain highbrow standards. In 1940, a national daily carried an article about the new radio station: "Do you want to listen to all kinds of music? Orchestras, artists, *estudiantinas* are all there [on the Radio Nacional]. Do you want to dance? There are several hours of jazz. Are you an idiot? Look for vulgar and stupid records on another station." The author then lists several popular hits, Mexican and Cuban, as examples of such records and continues: "on this station there are hours of great chamber music conducted by the master Espinosa, *música brillante* [light music], a marvelous string quartet, several hours of jazz-band, traditional music by [Alejandro] Wills [an exponent of bambucos and pasillos]" (*El Tiempo*, March 18 1940, p. 13).

Costeño music is simply ignored here (Lucho Bermúdez did not hit Bogotá until about 1943), but the dismissal of popular Mexican and Cuban hits—boleros, corridos, and rumbas—contrasts with the explicit acceptance of North American "jazz" and, of course, bambucos and pasillos. The main division here was between highbrow and lowbrow music and this extended to include even avowedly popular music, divided into acceptable and vulgar. The Radio Nacional did not program Costeño music at this time: the program of "popular Colombian music" scheduled for Tuesday afternoon on March 2, 1940, included mainly pasillos and bambucos (*El Tiempo*, March 2, 1940, p. 2).

Other writers in the press took a similar line. One piece titled "Christmas and Nationalism" bemoaned the "foreign" influences on Christmas celebrations: "The manger, the Christmas carols, the music, the Christmas gifts and all the traditional motifs have been forgotten. An explosive African-sounding orchestra now threatens festivities from which the feeling and simplicity typical of previous celebrations are absent" (*El Tiempo*, December 17, 1940, p. 5). Here the author is likely to be referring to a variety of musical styles—Cuban, Mexican, perhaps North American too—but foreignness is equated with Africanness, and hence blackness, and is set up as an inclusive emblem in opposition to an unidentified traditional purity implicitly located with the writer in the interior of the country.

A few years later, writers were addressing the phenomenon of *porro*. In a piece entitled "The Sweet Music of *Porro*," the author wrote:

From a purely personal point of view, a concert given by a cow being dragged by the nose, three canaries, a broken can being beaten with a broomstick and an idiot selling alcohol would be more harmonious than the sublime harmonies thrown out or extracted from a musical group in the midst of proclaiming to the world that Santa Marta has a train [the title of a porro], that Cartagena has no mountains, and that "eeeeeepa" and that "eeeeeepa" and that "daaaaale compareeee" [shouts typical in Costeño music] and so forth.[9]

In a porro orchestra there are usually only three types of instrument: the clarinet, the drums and a black man howling. (*El Tiempo*, October 23, 1943)

The dancers, according to him, moved like "a sausage suspended on a string, supposing that the string in question were attached to the tail of a dog chasing a cat," and when the dance had finished "the couples exhausted by the contortions, the shoves, the death-defying leaps and the crazy races they have executed, immediately ask for it to be repeated" (*El Tiempo*, October 23, 1943, p. 5). There are remarkable resonances here with the descriptions of the bogas' "bodily contortions" made by some of the nineteenth-century travelers on the Magdalena River and with Samper's description of the currulao. Also notable is the identification of the music with blackness and with animality. As with accounts of the bogas, the impression created is that of lack of propriety and decorum, excessiveness of bodily movement, noise and emotion. Something similar can be seen in a characterization of the Pacific coastal currulao written by a newspaper columnist—the only reference to music from this region that I found for this period: "it is the most genuine manifestation of Pacific *negrería* [collection of blacks]. Euphoria, madness, human overflowings, sobs and howls are its constitutive elements" (*El Tiempo*, November 4, 1946, p. 5).

Another columnist complained that fashion dictated that "we should dance like blacks" and that the culture best received in Colombia was "that which has the acrid smell of jungle and sex." According to him: "Pairs of blondes must dance with effusive movements of the belly, jerks, contortions, leaps and savage shouts. . . . Meanwhile, the drums beat, the gentlemen of the orchestra screech with a tragic fury, as if they were seasoning a joyful picnic of some "mister" [i.e., a white boss] in a jungle in Oceania (*Sábado*, June 3, 1944, p. 13). In 1947, a controversy was sparked in the letters section of *Semana*, the Bogotá-based national weekly, started by a letter from a Medellín reader who accused Costeño music of being "noisy and strident rhythms, manifestations of the savagery and brutishness of the Costeños and Caribbeans, savage and backward peoples" (*Semana*, November 15, 1947).

In sum, then, Costeño music and the dance styles that went with it were associated by some with blackness, Africanness, sexual license, lack of decorum, and vulgarity. Nevertheless, there remained the inescapable fact that it was successful and that even in the elite social clubs of Bogotá, Medellín, and Cali it was danced to by "pairs of blondes" (in fact it was mostly danced to by male-female couples). Some barriers stayed and the accordion music called *vallenato*, derived from a local Costeño tradition of sung verses and played by small groups of two to four musicians, did not enter the clubs—it was seen as too plebeian. Even so, when this music was played by light-skinned guitarists, such as Guillermo Buitrago and Julio Bovea, instead of black and mulatto accordionists such as Abel Antonio Villa, Luis E. Martínez and Alejo Durán, it was still a major success on radio and in record shops.

Why were these styles of music successful? There are many reasons connected with the increasing integration of the country through communicational infrastructure and the migration of Costeños to the cities of the interior in search of education and work, taking with them their favored music. I think a major reason is that the music, especially the orchestrated big-band sound, was seen as fashionable and modern. Although some decried the submergence of "authentic" Colombian culture (whatever that was supposed to be) by "foreign" music, it was nevertheless true that European, North American, Cuban, and Mexican styles—of music, dance, clothes, urban planning—were associated with modernity and the latest in fashion. The city of Barranquilla on the Caribbean coast had many immigrants from Germany, Italy and the United States, among other places, and they or their children were instrumental in modernizing the city, creating elite urbanizations and—vitally—setting up radio stations and record companies (The founder of Discos Fuentes was a Colombian but had been educated in the United States). Costeño music represented something modern, yet something still rooted in Colombia, albeit only one region. It was, after all, unequivocally Colombian in identity. The music thus mediated between the ideas of tradition and modernity that are so crucial to nationalism which, as many have noted, must look equally to the past (for the roots of a unique identity) as well as the future (for hope and progress).

Also vital is the comment by the columnist quoted above that the latest in fashionable culture smelt of "jungle and sex." Mid-century Colombia was a scene of rapid social change in which conservative religious values were still strong but were coming increasingly into question. In middle-class Medellín and even more so in the small towns surrounding the city, dancing was often not approved of. In 1994, one woman recounted to me that her mother liked to dance, but that her father had agreed to marry her mother only if the latter stopped dancing. Later her father also learned to dance, but he would not permit his daughter to do so. For men there was, predictably, little control in this respect. Young men were taken to brothels by older relatives and apart from sex, brothels were also places for music and dance, such that dance was associated with prostitution to some extent. In many provincial towns around Medellín, the red-light district was the main venue for dancing. Young girls were told that those who died after going out dancing would go to hell in mortal sin.

At the same time, women's economic position was also changing. All over the country, a majority of the migrants to the big cities were women, many of whom became domestic servants. In Medellín, industry employed a large number of young females.[10] Research is scarce on the social life of these women, but one middle-class man in Medellín recounted to me how, in the 1950s, he would go to a trade union center in Medellín to dance with young female workers. It is probable that there was some freedom of movement for these women, who also had their own incomes. Comments collected in interviews with working-class women who lived in Medellín in the 1940s and 1950s indicate that young women could go out dancing in groups, despite restrictive ideas about decency.

In this context, Costeño music and dance could obviously be seen as breaking with parental traditions that restricted women's movements with repressive ideas about modesty and decorum. The Costeño music of the 1940s and 1950s was not very explicitly sexual by today's standards. Much of the music was instrumental, and when there were lyrics they were generally not risqué. By the 1960s and 1970s, sexual double meanings in the lyrics and half-naked female bodies on album covers were much more frequent, but in previous decades, the sexy image of Costeño music was evoked more by the dance styles and the overall symbolism of partying and having fun (the most usual theme of the lyrics), as well as by the origin of the music in a tropical region and by the presence of the occasional black artist. The reputation of Costeño immigrants in the cities of the interior, whether black or not (and they were often middle-class, and thus quite light-skinned, students), as sexually active and promiscuous also added to this image of the music.

The image of Costeño sexuality was thus a more ''modern'' sexuality (despite also being supposedly base, coarse, and ''primitive''). It fitted into new and often ''foreign'' ideas about a woman's place and relations between men and women in which there was (a little) more freedom of movement for women and new definitions of what counted as modest behavior. As in Jamaica (see chapter 8), music associated with blackness was also associated with images of a potent sexuality which could be seen as vulgar and obscene. Ulysse notes that some black women reveled in this imagery and even that some ''Uptown'' women were envious of their self-confidence. In the Colombian case, we can see a wider process in which ideas about the (modern) sexuality of blackness seem to have taken on a wider role in the definition of national identity.

In sum, Costeño music became the national music of Colombia (although Colombian styles have generally failed to compete equally in the national market with foreign styles). Both within and outside the country, porro and cumbia became the most popular and best-selling national styles. The music became ''whitened'' as it was orchestrated and commercialized, yet it did not lose a black image entirely. Rather this became, in a controlled and commoditized form, one of its selling points. Thus, for example, from the 1960s through the 1990s, the album covers of *música tropical* as it is often known (although this designation can also include other styles such as merengue) often depict tropical beach scenes and female bodies. The imagery is tropicality, sex, fun, sea, and sun—yet almost never are black women used as models. Images associated with blackness in the Colombian frame of reference are evoked, but the immediate object of sexual attention is generally a white woman.

The problematic of "black culture" is evident in the preceding narrative. Costeño music was not straightforwardly "black music" in the 1920s and was even less so by the 1960s. Yet it could be made to *mean* blackness in particular contexts. Those meanings were generally ones imposed by non-blacks and usually with a racially discriminatory purpose intimately linked to the representation and constitution of Colombian national identity. It was in relation to ideas about how "Colombia" should be imagined that these meanings were purveyed. Costeño music was linked to traits of blackness, immorality, and vulgarity that were thought by some not to have a legitimate place as representatives of Colombian identity, but that seemed to be linked to notions of modernity that was also valued in thinking about the nation.

Costeños fought back and defended their music, but this did not generally involve a vindication of blackness per se within the nation. For example, Costeños replied to the offensive letter about Costeño music (cited above) that appeared in the magazine *Semana*. One wrote that porro was the "authentic expression of the euphoria of a healthy and optimistic people."[11] In similar terms, a Costeño columnist wrote of porro as "the song of the liberated Costeño man who shows to anyone who observes him a boastful demonstration of dionysian joy in the face of life" (Brugés Carmona 1943; see Wade 1998). These responses clearly reinforced the idea of liberated sexuality and the overall *alegría* (happiness) for which Costeño music was famed. In short, Costeño were defending Costeño culture as a model for national culture, rather than black culture itself, even if for many people "Costeño" implied "black."

VALLENATO AND BLACKNESS IN MEDELLÍN

To see how black culture is signified by music in particular contexts outside the textual evocation of blackness, one must examine specific sets of social interactions and relationships. Here detailed ethnographic research is necessary, and I will turn briefly to Medellín, where, in 1985, I did research among black migrants from the Pacific coastal region to the city (see Wade 1993, 1995a). Immediately we are facing a situation in which "black people" were a much more clearly defined category than in La Costa: Medellín had many light-skinned mulattos, but the immigrants from the Pacific were clearly identifiable by themselves and others as distinct. The music these immigrants listened to was varied, but central components were salsa and *vallenato*. The latter had by then developed from the rather local, rustic, accordion-based, three-or four-man groups and (having also left behind almost entirely the guitar-based versions of Buitrago and Bovea) had become a highly commercialized and nationally popular style, although still associated with the working classes, rural and urban. It was hardly "black music," although it was strongly linked to La Costa and played by Costeño artists. Salsa, of course, was not easily identifiable simply as "black music" although some of its stars were black people, and its associations for many listeners were with Caribbean-born artists (Puerto Ricans, Cubans, and so on). In Medellín salsa was listened to quite widely by non-black working- and middle-class people, and there was a salsa-only radio station in a city in which the black migrants were a tiny proportion of the population.[12]

Yet in particular contexts, these musical styles, and especially vallenato, could be used to define a black cultural space. In certain city center bars where only blacks congregated, vallenato was played at high volume to the exclusion of everything else. In contrast, other bars patronized by non-blacks tended to focus on tangos and Mexican-style *rancheras* and *corridos*, while venues that played only salsa were generally more mixed in clientele. A jukebox packed with val- lenato was thus a sign for and of blackness. It signaled to black people that this was a space where they could feel "at home" and, indeed, such bars drew a mixed clientele of domestic servants, students, policemen, construction workers, plus a few professionals, thus crossing class boundaries. It signaled to non-black people that this was a black space that was not actively closed to them, but which might not suit their tastes. In one bar, the owner (non-black, as were all the owners and staff of these bars) had consciously packed the jukebox with vallenato and salsa, aware that by doing so he was effectively losing one sort of trade but gaining another.

Similarly, in some low-income neighborhoods there were very localized zones where blacks predominated. Here it was common to find that informal *bailad- eros* (dance halls—really just the front room of someone's house) were set up on weekends by local black residents. Again, the music played was mainly vallenato, although salsa figured more prominently than in the city center bars. In a number of neighborhoods, such bailaderos had been the focus of conflict with non-black residents, who objected to the noise and the supposed immoral behavior that these places generated. In some cases, these houses were stoned by groups of non-black youths and the black clientele harassed; in other cases, complaints were lodged with the police. Such neighborhoods generally had other places where people could drink and listen and dance to music (which might even include some vallenato), but these were not the focus of conflict and were generally more consolidated venues with all the trappings of a public establish- ment (e.g. jukebox, custom-made seating, lighting, perhaps a dance floor), rather than the much more ad hoc arrangements made by the small bailaderos (which simply used a home sound system, a refrigerator, and a few rough chairs and tables).

As in the city center bars, vallenato became a sign of blackness in the context of these venues and the "space of blackness" that they helped establish in the city. For blacks and non-blacks alike, the music signaled black culture and thus itself became, in that context, black culture. In one sense, this is a chance event. Some other genre of music could have been involved—although perhaps not *any* genre; after all, both vallenato and salsa evoked strong images of the Caribbean and tropicality, and both involved dance as a central component. In another sense, however, we can see strong continuities with the situations examined above. As usual, blacks in these areas of the city center and low-income neighborhoods were stigmatized by other residents as noisy, disruptive, and immoral. As usual, music and dance were integral parts of the way blacks and non-blacks perceived and interacted with each other. That is, there is a historical continuity in the fact that it was music and dance that were central aspects of racialized identifications and interactions.

RAP AND FOLKLORE IN CALI

Similar dynamics to those outlined above are evident in more recent times. D. Pacini (1993) and L. Waxer (1997) have noted how, from the 1970s in Cartagena and later in many areas of La Costa, *"música africana"* (more usually called *champeta* or *terapia*)—a mixture of Zairean *soukous*, Nigerian highlife, Haitian *konpa, soca*, and reggae—became popular among working-class people in the cities and towns of La Costa, displacing salsa to some extent, although not vallenato (see Wade 1993: 79–80). Especially in Cartagena, these people were mainly black. The adoption by Afro-Colombians of music clearly identifiable as black in terms of a kind of globalized, transnational, diasporic black culture that feeds off many Atlantic currents must be seen in the context of the slow emergence from the late 1960s of black consciousness movements in Colombia, themselves modeled principally on North American black activism (Wade 1995b). This is not to say that working-class blacks in the low-income neighborhoods of Cartagena were using this music in an explicit political project. It is simply to say that, in the wake of the tropicalization of Colombian national identity with porro and cumbia, the place of blackness in the national and transnational frame was changing to some extent and taking a more public place.

This said, however, it is not unusual, as I have shown, that Costeños (among them many blacks) should have adopted a musical style that was not (yet) mainstream in the nation. Costeños were, for obvious reasons, the first to adopt porro and cumbia, which then became nationalized. They were also among the first to take up salsa (alongside the blacks of the Pacific port of Buenaventura), which also became a nationally popular music, becoming increasingly softened and sentimentalized into *salsa romántica* in the process. They were the pioneers of vallenato, which also became nationalized and, in a parallel fashion, sentimentalized into a romantic balladlike style. This does not mean that champeta will become a national trend, but it indicates that Costeños seem to consistently identify with musical styles that set them apart in some sense from the rest of the nation. This idea must be seen in context: many Costeños listen to rock, ballads, merengue, salsa and vallenato just as other Colombians do all over the country. Nevertheless, a move from the Andean interior of the country to La Costa has consistently meant a change in the musical audioscape that surrounds the listening traveler. As one style becomes nationalized, other styles emerge or are adopted that maintain this difference (in a fashion similar to that described by dos Santos [this volume] for black carnival practices in Brazil). These musics have sometimes been non-Colombian. With porro, cumbia, and vallenato, their origin within Colombia made them very susceptible to co-optation as symbols of nationhood by the national (and international) music industry. Foreign musical styles may sustain more easily a sense of musical difference in the national audioscape.

These musical genres have had an important evocative and musical link to blackness (and in the case of champeta that link has been a little more explicit). This does not make them "black music" or "black culture" in a straightforward sense, because blackness is never clear-cut and straightforward in Colombia. The blackness of this music, like black culture in general, can be both quite clear when the structure of particular contexts of mutual identifications define the conditions for such clarity and also rather blurred when non-blacks share the same music and other cultural forms with blacks. But blackness is always there as a possible evocation and identification.

This has again been evident in the impact (from the late 1980s) of rap music on a minority of young, working-class, urban blacks in Cali, most of them migrants or children of migrants from the Pacific Coast region.[13] Rap music— foreign in origin and evidently black—has been adopted and performed by many small groups of blacks, male and female, in the district of Aguablanca, an area that comprises the majority of the poorer neighborhoods of Cali. Some groups, notably Ashanty, integrate the music into a wider project of black consciousness and political protest. Some of the members of Ashanty wear Rasta colors and dreadlocks and adopt an Afrocentric discourse. The lyrics of their songs protest against racism, poverty, and violence. Other groups focus less on blackness and more on class issues of unemployment, violence, pollution, and the neglect by the state of their neighborhoods. However, this music has also been adopted by non-blacks in the low-income neighborhoods of Cali, Medellín and Bogotá. For the non-black groups in Cali, racism is not an issue in their lyrics and, although they use the dress styles associated with black U.S. rappers and hip-hop, their primary interest is in broader social and class-based issues and also in romantic themes.

Even something as apparently unequivocally black as rap thus acquires some ambiguity in the Colombian context. Nevertheless, the overall association of the music—the identifications it evokes and that it itself creates—is with blackness. The vast majority of the performers and listeners are young blacks. Rap gigs that took place in Cali in July and August 1997, although they took place in neighborhoods where non-blacks and blacks lived side by side or in city center locations accessible to all, were attended by an audience that was over 90 percent black and that listened to a series of artists who were again almost all blacks. Interestingly, alongside the proliferation of these small rap groups, I found quite a number of "folkloric" dance groups in these neighborhoods. Such groups practiced a generic sort of black folklore derived from the rural traditions of both Pacific and Caribbean coastal regions: currulao, the typical style of the Pacific region, was practiced along with mapalé, a popular and energetic dance from La Costa. In many cases, the members of the rap groups also performed or had had experience with these dance groups. This had not, in my experience, resulted in Pacific or Costeño motifs being incorporated into the music of the rap groups, but it amplified the network of evocations and identifications of blackness in which these young black rappers moved.

Rap is unlikely in my view to be incorporated into the mainstream of Colombian popular music, although elements of rapping as a performance technique have already made an impact on techno-merengue, which does attract a more mainstream audience. In this sense, rap will probably remain as a potential sign of blackness. There are, however, indications that Pacific coast traditional musical styles may be subject to commercialization, not just through the commodification of "authentic folklore" that already exists, but also through the adaptation of currulao by orchestra lineups typical of salsa and/or merengue. In August 1997, the First Festival of Pacific Music took place in Cali, organized by the cultural management division of the regional government. The entry regulations specifically allowed both traditional lineups, based on drums, marimba, and rattles, and larger orchestras which could work toward the "transformation of the vernacular music of the Pacific [region] in accordance with the new sensibilities and developments of popular music at the national and international levels" (festival brochure). Of the seven prizes given, six were won by nontraditional lineups that had performed "modernized" versions of currulao.

It remains to be seen whether this heralds a commercialization of currualo similar to that which occurred with porro and vallenato.[14] The Pacific coastal region and blackness in general have acquired a new place in the Colombian nation with the new constitution of 1991, which recognizes that the country is multicultural and pluriethnic, opens the way for special land rights claims by "black communities" in the Pacific coastal region, and gives certain opportunities for the consolidation of "black culture" in general (e.g., through ethnoeducation). The Pacific coastal region is also the site of rapidly growing commercial and industrial interests and a prime focus for the state, which is trying to link into the growing Pacific rim trading network. In the last couple of years, it has also been an area of increasing conflict and violence as guerrilla and paramilitary groups battle for supremacy. In this sense, aesthetic forms from the region are ripe both for achieving a greater national profile and for being co-opted into commercialized representations of nationhood (although this is likely to be a process in which different sets of interests come into conflict, as happened with porro).

CONCLUSION

The vibrant expression of blackness that has been a feature of all the contexts described above—the colonial cabildos, the world of the bogas, the commercialization of porro and cumbia, the black migrants in Medellín and the place of rap and Pacific coastal folklore in Cali—is notable for its eclectic nature. Different musical forms can be appropriated and turned into a sign for blackness and difference. That sign is never univocal, and it rarely points only and exclusively to blackness, but that does not mean that something called black culture cannot be identified in particular contexts in time and space when the polyvalence of the sign is suspended and blackness becomes the primary meaning and identification.

There are also important continuities underlying the changing contexts of musical expression. These continuities may have some roots in underlying principles of musical and dance performance that derive ultimately from Africa. In this essay, I have not explored that possibility, not because I think it unlikely, but because to focus on Africanisms may divert our attention away from the flexible way in which black culture is continuously emergent. However, as dos Santos argues for Brazilian carnival contexts (this volume), this is not a matter of opposing black culture as "a fixed essence" to black culture as "a contingent construction" to be reinvented at will. Instead I have concentrated on how continuities are defined by the social relations of hierarchy that structure the context in which changing musical styles exist. Blacks and their music and dance have generally been seen by the non-blacks above them in the social structure as immoral, vulgar, noisy, and indecorous; they have also—by virtue of that— been seen as exciting (especially in the sexual sense) and even liberating. By the same token, blacks have also tried to create certain spaces for themselves, for blackness, in which they define the rules of propriety. Music and dance have been central to that process.

NOTES AND ACKNOWLEDGMENTS

The research on which this article is based spans several distinct projects which have been funded by the Social Science Research Council (USA), the British Academy, the Leverhulme Trust, and the Nuffield Foundation.

1. Bermúdez went on to argue that in terms of musical structure, there are elements of these villancicos in the present-day ritual songs of the Lumbalú funerary association in Palenque de San Basilio, a village situated in the Caribbean coastal region of Colombia that is directly descended from a colonial *palenque* or settlement of runaway slaves (see Friedemann and Patiño Rosselli 1983; Schwegler 1996).

2. Unless otherwise stated, all translations from Spanish-language texts are my own.

3. *Currulao* is the term now used for music and dance styles from the Pacific coastal region. In the nineteenth century, the term was often used (by white observers at least) for dances in the Caribbean coastal region that might today be termed *mapalé* or *cumbia*.

4. The *gaita* is a term usually now used for the vertical cane flute of indigenous origin found in La Costa. Samper used it as a generic term for a cane flute and describes the "very high-pitched" sounds that it emitted, suggesting an instrument more akin to the *caña-de-millo*, a traverse cane flute, although he said it had seven finger-holes, whereas Abadía Morales (1991: 53) states that the caña-de-millo has four, as does Bermúdez (1985: 86).

5. He compared the repeated circles that the dancers made both to the wheel of a machine and the "hot whirlpool of fire or sand" seen in a burning forest or a beach lashed by a hurricane (1985: 93).

6. González Henríquez (1989: 87) mentions the Orquesta de Pacho Lorduy of the 1920s, which had a violin, flute, saxophone, clarinet, bass, drums, piano, and lead vocals. The Emisora Atlántico Jazz Band played its first gig in Barraquilla in 1940 with a lineup consisting of trombone, three saxes, trumpet, double bass, drum kit, and piano (Candela, n.d.). Such orchestras often also included other percussion instruments such as scrapers and maracas (which were native to the coastal region) and conga and bongo drums, derived from Cuban lineups.

7. The Costeño artist Angel Camacho y Cano recorded in New York with Brunswick and Columbia between 1929 and 1930 (Spottswood 1990: 1721). He recorded foxtrots and rumbas and Costeño music with vague labels such as *parranda* or *aire colombiano*, but also cumbia, mapalé, and porro (see Barranquilla paper, *La Prensa*, February 7, 1931).

8. Central figures in the history of *bambuco* include Pedro Morales Pino (1863–1926), whose Lira Colombiana toured Central America and the United States (Restrepo Duque 1991: 121–125); Emilio Murillo (1880–1942), a disciple of Morales Pino who, in 1910 and in 1917, made recordings with Columbia and Victor in New York which oddly enough included pasillos but no bambucos (Spottswood 1990: 2145–2146; see also Restrepo Duque 1991: 110–114); Alejandro Wills (1884–1943); Jorge Añez (1892–1952) who played in Morales Pino's Lira Colombiana, before moving to the United States, where, between 1917 and 1933, he recorded, among other things, bambucos and pasillos with Victor, Columbia, and Brunswick (Restrepo Duque 1991: 1–3; Spottswood 1990: 1637, 1696–1707, 2275–2276).

9. *Epa* is a common interjection in Costeño music, roughly similar to "Oh yeah" in Western pop and rock music. *Dale compadre* (do it, compadre) is another such exhortation.

10. Elizabeth Kuznesof (1989) notes that all over Latin America, female employment expanded rapidly from 1940 to 1970. Colombian censuses from 1951 to 1973 show a 55 percent female participation rate in rural-urban migration and in the Colombian industrial census of 1945, women formed between 40 and 83 percent of the blue-collar workforce of the food, garment, textile, and tobacco industries (Sandroni 1982). Data for 1916–1940 show that female workers in Medellín's industry were mainly single and under 25 years old (Gladden 1988). Kathy Peiss (1984) shows that young white working-class women in New York in the early decades of this century had active social lives, centering around cinemas, dance halls, vaudeville theaters, and amusement parks; a central feature of going out was to associate with men.

11. See *Semana*, November 11, 1947, December 6, 1947, and December 13, 1947, letters section.

12. Lise Waxer's research in Buenaventura, a major port on Colombia's Pacific coast, close to the city of Cali, indicates that salsa (and its precursor of Caribbean sounds from Cuba) were more strongly associated with blackness, since black sailors were central to their introduction to the port (Waxer 1997).

13. In 1997, I carried out research on a rap group in Cali and its links to black political organizations, and this section is based on that investigation.

14. In the late 1960s and early 1970s, Peregoyo y su Combo Vacano, based in the port of Buenaventura, began to play some currulao styles alongside renditions of Cuban music (*guaracha*, *son*, etc.), but this did not have a lasting impact (Waxer 1997).

III

AFRICAN AND NATIVE AMERICAN PERSPECTIVES

In Memory of the Slaves: An African View of the Diaspora in the Americas

Peter Sutherland

One never sets foot to encircle the sea;
One can never know where it ends.
　　　　　　　　　—Vodun incantation to the sea-goddess Hou

Resistance is crucial to diaspora representations of blackness throughout the Americas, as most of the foregoing essays argue. Yet Africa, we have also learned, though often a central referent, is neither necessary nor sufficient to account for every resistant voice. But what of other representations of blackness? This chapter, like the final one by Norman Whitten and Rachel Corr, gives a non diasporic perspective. Shifting attention from the Americas to Africa, my essay describes a resistant discourse of black identity in which the transatlantic moral geography of diaspora "roots" and "branches" is reconstrued in mythic terms of *vodun*, the indigenous religion of the Aja people. In the contemporary west African state of Benin (formerly Dahomey[1]), the African diaspora in the Americas constitutes the primary referent for a populist discourse of modern national identity that seeks to resist the foreign values of the state and Christianity by emphasizing the transatlantic unity of vodun practitioners.

My topic is the recently invented Vodun Festival of the 10th of January, whose fifth performance I attended in January 1997. The festival is staged on the beach at Whydah to celebrate the memory of the African peoples who were shipped from there as slaves via Goreé Island to the "land of the whites" (*yovotomen*) between the 1640s and the 1860s (Manning 1982: 30). Whydah was the main port of the former Danhomè kingdom on what European traders used to call the Slave Coast.

The first performance of the festival in 1992 marked the opening of a triumphal arch called "The Door of No Return" (La Porte de Non-retour) built by UNESCO to mark the Whydah beach as a World Heritage Site. The monument takes its name from two other doors of no return located in historical slaver forts at Elmina Castle, Ghana and Gorée Island, Senegal. Unlike the newly constructed monument on the Whydah beach, where the history of slavery is otherwise unmarked by any surviving structure, the other two doors are situated in European dungeons from which captive Africans were finally led to the ships of the Middle Passage.

I learned of the festival from an African-American medical doctor in Baton Rouge who had attended the event in 1996. He was told by a number of priests in Whydah that the festival was intended to purify the Benin people of the guilt incurred by their historical involvement in the sale of slaves to European merchants. In other words, it was a ritual of atonement. Fieldwork, however, did not bear this interpretation out. The interviews I conducted with several of the festival organizers and the translations I made of the speeches given at the festival indicate a systematic avoidance of the question of African guilt and atonement. I return to this striking discrepancy between African and African-American attitudes at the end of this essay.

My focus is the national political significance of the Whydah festival's transatlantic representation of black identity and vodun unity. During an all-too-short two-week field trip, I learned of the ongoing campaign to make the Festival of the 10th of January a national vodun holiday. In doing so, the creators of the festival seek to gain government recognition for the country's majority religion and to integrate its indigenous cultural traditions in the development of modern national identity in Benin by demonstrating their *international* cultural value.

In particular, I focus on the significance of a pervasive rhetorical doubling articulated by the festival. On the one hand, magically redefining Whydah as the sacred center of African diaspora culture in the Americas, the prayers performed at the festival by Benin's Supreme Chief of Vodun, Daagbo Hounon, reimagine the history of slavery as a "double deportation of African persons and gods across the Atlantic from Whydah."[2] Thus, the history of slavery is remembered with a bittersweet mixture of sadness and pride, because it took not only captive African peoples but also African religion to the Americas. As the king of Allada put it in his speech at the festival: "We are happy because our brothers who left here sadly for the Americas reproduced there our ancestral vodun [religion] from here [i.e., Dahomey]." On the other hand, the juxtaposition of the festival site and the Door of No Return describes an apparently contradictory double symbolism of "return" and "no-return.[3]" While the name of the monument emphasizes the fact that the slaves would never return to Africa, the performative symbolism of the festival evokes just the opposite, encouraging contemporary "brothers" in the Americas to return as both ancestral spirits and as tourists to their roots. (Diaspora sisters were never mentioned). Memories of Whydah's terrible past must therefore be forgotten and only good things remembered. Again the king of Allada: "We must forget, we must completely efface, the bad things which happened before our time. . . . This is the place from which our brothers left by boat for the Americas in chains. It was with sadness that they came here. But now, everyone is happy because they have returned in joy."

My analysis of this rhetorical doubling—of ancestors and brothers, of spirits and bodies, of return and no return, of remembering and forgetting, of sadness and joy—throws new light on the concept of "roots" in diaspora discourse, by showing how Benin's traditionalist faction of vodun practitioners is attempting to refashion its public identity in Africa by reference to its cultural "branches" in the Americas. The web of diaspora roots and branches outlined in this essay fills a gap in the transnational map/history of "roots and routes" that Paul Gilroy's (1993) important conception of the "black Atlantic" describes as forming a "counterculture of modernity." Gilroy critiques the narrow nationalism and "ethnic absolutism" of representations of blackness in the discourse of cultural studies in Britain and the United States. Yet nonetheless Latin America, the Caribbean, and Africa are virtually absent from the examples he cites as forming transatlantic black culture. As other contributors have done for Latin America and the Caribbean, this chapter adds one small part of Africa to the map of black Atlantic culture that Gilroy's imbalanced cartography omits.

THE POLITICS AND POETICS OF REVALORIZATION

To understand what the Whydah festival can teach us about representations of blackness, I ask why and how it evokes the memory of the slaves. To answer these questions, we have to understand the politics and poetics of *revalorization*—the term used in Benin's colonial French to describe the recursive goal of modernizing indigenous traditions as a way of producing an indigenous modernity that preserves them.

First, I describe the political context of revalorization to explain *why* Benin's traditionalist faction of priests and kings, the Council of Kings, has developed the Whydah festival to resist the oppressive neocolonialism of government policy and Christian doctrine. I then examine the poetic text of revalorization presented by the festival. I indicate *how* the performative symbolism of different ritual media reinvent traditional vodun conceptions of ancestor worship and the sea to magically evoke a spatiotemporal network of transatlantic diaspora connections linking Benin with the Americas.

Putting text and context together, I argue that the festival promotes the political interests of the Council of Kings, enhancing the value of indigenous vodun culture in Benin by symbolically defining Whydah as the center and source of African diaspora culture in the Americas. Analysis of the festival's logic of remembering and forgetting reveals a problem unsuspected by its creators: the difference between representations of blackness on opposite sides of the Atlantic.

VODUN AND THE COUNCIL OF KINGS

The Whydah festival is organized by the Council of Kings, a traditionalist faction whose assembly of vodun priests and former kings claims to represent the popular voice of Benin's majority religion, vodun. The annual performance of the festival draws vodun groups from all over the country, uniting them with members of the press, TV crews, and foreign tourists to create a media event of national significance. The ritual publicly dramatizes resistance to the long-standing denigration of Dahomey's traditional vodun culture by the shared foreign values of the state and Christian church. Claiming to speak for the people, the festival clearly promotes the interests of traditional political leaders who were disenfranchized by the creation of the modern secular state of Benin at independence. I have yet to learn to what extent their views represents public opinion throughout the country.[4]

The authority of Benin's traditional leaders was (and still is) based in the world-constituting symbolism of vodun—the term from which the English "voodoo" is derived. In the Fon language of Dahomey, vodun denotes not only individual divine powers but also, by extension, the mythicoritual system of communicating with them that the English word "religion" so inadequately translates. In traditional Fon polity, as in the neighboring Yoruba region, there was no separation between "sacred" and "secular" as in post-Enlightenment Euro-American political thought. Priests and kings were interdependent and their power was reciprocally constituted. M. Adoko, third-ranking vodun priest in Benin, explained this complementarity as follows: "Without the power of vodun the kings would not exist, because the king must be chosen by the priests through 'divination' [*fa*]. But without the patronage of the kings, there would be no vodun. The priests are always under the orders of the king."

My interpretation of the festival is based on video interviews I conducted with three of its principal organizers, all members of the Council of Kings, whose political interests in revalorizing tradition variously involve the creation of relations with the African diaspora in the Americas.

Daagbo Hounon, Supreme Chief of vodun in Benin and tenth member of the Hounon lineage of Whydah, claims the festival as his creation. Daagbo Hounon is a traditional title that means "grandfather controller of the sea." Belonging to the Hula people, who traditionally subsisted as fishermen, the Hounon lineage traces its power to the sea and its genealogy back to 1452,[5] as a mural in the palace reception room in Whydah depicts (see Figure 10.1). According to the lineage origin myth, the first Hounon ancestor emerged from the sea as an enormous fish, then transformed into human form, finally returning to the sea at death. A list of ancestors in the palace describes him as *retourné en mer* ("returned to the sea").

Figure 10.1. Mural inside Hounon palace, Whydah, showing lineage ancestors of Daagbo Hounon.

This Hounon lineage narrative is embedded in the maritime creation myth of the sea goddess, Hou. After the birth of the first Hounon, all the vodun gods emerged from the sea to create the various entities in the natural environment—rivers, flora, fauna, and so on. From this cosmogonic priority, members of the Hounon lineage derive not only their title "controller of the sea" but also their status as chief priests of vodun, and their authority over all the voduns of Dahomey whose combined power the supreme chief embodies in possession once a year.

In the last few years, Daagbo Hounon has been extending his traditional field of authority beyond Dahomey by redefining his role as chief priest of vodun to the African diaspora in the Americas. In 1995, he toured North and South America styling himself as "pope of voodoo" in emulation of the Roman Catholic pontiff, whom Daagbo and several other prominent vodun priests met during the 1993 papal tour of Africa.

My second informant was King Kpotegbe of Allada, titular ruler of the senior of the four former Fon kingdoms of Dahomey (Allada, Danhomè, Whydah, and Ardra [Porto Novo]). In an interview at the Allada palace prior to the festival, the king explained his personal interest in establishing a research center to study Benin's links with the diaspora communities in the Americas. At the festival, the king accompanied Daagbo Hounon as royal patron of the ritual, shaded under a parasol and dressed in full regalia with crown, scepter, and smoking pipe all made of solid gold, each sculpturally embellished with a panther. The panther represents what the king described in colonial French as his *fétiche*, the vodun power of his office. His official name, Kpotegbe, means "the panther gives the orders."

My third informant and host during my stay in Cotonou, Basile Gbedige Adoko, claims to be the third-ranking priest in Dahomey's vodun hierarchy. However, in the current competitive climate "where everyone wants to be chief," according to another source, there is no conventionally recognized religious hierarchy. After working as a businessman for Mercedes-Benz in Senegal, Basile Adoko was instructed to succeed his father as priest of a vodun temple in the Benin capital, Cotonou, where he now runs a thriving practice in countersorcery healing. As founder of the N.G.O. Alafya-Gbedige ("peace-long life"), whose purpose is "to research and revalorize the cultural patrimony of Benin," he has managed to place himself at the nexus of cultural politics in Benin, liaising between the country's three major institutions of power: the traditional Council of Kings, the vodun priesthood and the government. In addition, after representing Benin at the Second International Congress of Afro-American Cultures at Bahia in August 1994, M. Adoko was appointed Minister of Afro-American Culture to the Council of Kings by its current president, the King of Ketu.[6]

VODUN, STATE, AND CHRISTIANITY

The festival challenges the long-standing oppression of vodun and its practitioners by the state and Christianity. To understand the convergent neocolonialism of the latter two, it is necessary briefly to review the past twenty-five years of political history in Benin and more recent Christian missionizing in West Africa during the last decade.

During the cold war, in October 1972, President Mathieu Ahmed Kérékou came to power and introduced a Marxist-Maoist regime in Benin. As part of his socialist economic policy, Kérékou banned vodun in the interests of modernization. Public vodun worship became illegal and went underground.

Ironically, Kérékou's *postcolonial* Marxist view of religion reproduced *colonial* European representations of vodun, especially those of Catholic missionaries who consistently depicted its gods as manifestations of Satan and disparaged its practices as superstitious devil worship.[7]

Seven years ago, in 1990, Kérékou was outvoted and the new liberal-democratic President Soglou reintroduced capitalist economics and reestablished the legality of vodun. In this new political climate, the UNESCO monument and the Whydah festival were inaugurated at the Whydah 1992 festivities that officially proclaimed the importance of including Benin's cultural traditions in the development of modern national identity. Last year, as a result of lobbying by the Council of Kings, the festival of the 10th of January was declared a national vodun holiday by President Soglou.

During Soglou's presidency, West Africa experienced an aggressive assault by American Protestant missionaries—Jehovah's Witnesses, Seventh Day Adventists, the Assemblies of God—whose "gospel of prosperity" morally reinforced the materialism of Soglou's new economic policy. Their message gave a fresh capitalist twist to long-standing European representations of African religions as satanic. Rosalind Hackett (1995: 203) writes that, while older "orthodox" forms of Christianity preached that "poverty promotes humility," Protestant missionaries such as Duncan-Williams of the Full Gospel Business Men's Fellowship International typically claims that "to be poor means to be powerless" and, thus, that "poverty is a ploy of Satan." "You see, Satan knows that if he keeps the saints in hole-ridden shoes, in rented houses, with unpaid bills and hardly enough to eat, then he can effectively stop the spreading of the gospel through books, equipment, international crusades and by satellite, radio, television and other means" (Duncan-Williams 1990: 146).

In this Pentecostalist discourse, dominant American consumerist values link modernity, wealth, success, and power as the material signs of religious salvation, while vodun is equated not only with old-fashioned orthodox Christianity, as in the above quotation, but more generally with underdevelopment and tradition. One streetside advertisement I saw in Cotonou graphically portrayed the racial dimensions of such foreign consumerist values, while promoting them as the obvious choice for modern African men. A tall black man elegantly dressed in a formal dark suit—the very embodiment of wealth, sexuality, and power—stands face to face with a beautiful, white, blond woman seated on a giant packet of Bond cigarettes (no doubt named for Agent 007), her elbow intimately resting on his shoulder. The caption reads in French: *J'ai déjà fait mon choix* ("I've already made my choice"). Against this African image of a modernity associated with the emulation of whiteness, the Whydah festival's championing of vodun traditions clearly distinguishes itself as an indigenous counterdiscourse of modernity based on black solidarity.

In April 1996, Kérékou was reelected to the presidency on the basis of a new political platform. Apparently, he was now espousing capitalist economics and promised a more liberal attitude to vodun—a stance the traditionalists I interviewed regarded with considerable skepticism.

In the days leading up to January 10, 1997, the country and the Council of Kings waited to see if he would declare the vodun festival a national holiday, as Soglou had done the year before. At 10:00 P.M. on January 7, M. Adoko was summoned by telephone to attend an eighteen-man presidential advisory committee comprising government deputies and members of the Council of Kings. The committee met each subsequent morning till the eve of the festival to decide the question of the holiday. On the evening of January 9, at his palace in Whydah, I overheard Daagbo Hounon comment skeptically to a group of fellow priests: "Last year, the festival was declared a national holiday because I paid the presidential advisors. This year, I gave them nothing and see what's happened."

On the morning of January 10, discussion on the state-run radio focused on the crucial political issue of parity in state recognition of Benin's three religions. The following statistics were mentioned in support of the festival: 25 percent of the population are Muslim, 15 percent are Christian, and each of these religions has five state-recognized festivals every year. But, although 60 percent of the population publicly declare themselves to be vodun practitioners, there is not a single state-recognized vodun festival for the majority.

Waiting till noon, Kérékou finally refused to declare the 10th of January festival a national holiday, claiming the need for a constitutional amendment to legalize such an action.[8] According to several priests I spoke to, Kérékou's new advisors were intent on undoing all that Soglou had achieved. When the radio finally announced that there would be no public holiday, I overheard one priest say about Kérékou and his advisors in a threatening tone: "Don't they realize who they are dealing with? We are vodun priests and we will fight them with vodun power!"

THE PERFORMANCE

A recently painted mural (Figure 10.2) outside Daagbo Hounon's palace in Whydah announces the maritime symbolism of the festival, dramatizing the remembered past of slaving on the Whydah beach as a triple encounter: of European buyer, African seller, and potential African captive. A three-masted merchant ship rides at anchor on the horizon. On the beach, an African flagman signals a convenient landing place. In the intervening space, a small cutter (*pirogue* in French) diagonally approaches the shore ferrying two Europeans through the reputedly shark-infested surf.[9] Running from the boat in the opposite direction, a terrified African flees headlong out of frame on the right, staring wide-eyed at the viewer, apparently evading capture. It is not the terrors of the ocean-going slave ships of the Middle Passage that Daagbo Hounon's prayers evoke in the Whydah festival, but the moment of no return associated with this preliminary in-shore transit by pirogue from beach to slave ship.

The festival's timing on January 10 refers to the traditional calendrical date for Dahomey families to worship their ancestors at home. The Whydah festival transforms this traditional domestic rite into a national media event uniting local vodun groups from all over Benin in worshipping the spirits of the long-departed slaves as objects of an updated transnational form of ancestor worship.

My analysis of the festival focuses on the performative symbolism of rhetoric, objects, and actions that Daagbo magically deploys in his public prayers to memorialize the slaves and redefine Whydah as the sacred center and origin place of diaspora culture in the Americas. He does so in three ways: (1) by representing the slaves in ritual terms of vodun ancestor worship; (2) by redefining the ocean of the historical Middle Passage in mythic terms as an agent of revelation for the present; (3) by reimagining the history of slavery in magical terms of a two-way traffic of ancestors, spirits, and brothers across the Atlantic.

Figure 10.2. Street mural outside Hounon palace showing slaving encounter on Whydah Beach.

THE TRANSATLANTIC MYTHOLOGY OF DIASPORA IDENTITY

It can hardly be coincidence that Daagbo Hounon, traditional controller of the sea and self-styled pope of voodoo for the modern world, is creating in the Whydah festival a new maritime mythology that reinvents the transatlantic history of slavery and the diaspora in terms of the vodun cosmogony of the sea goddess Hou. He does so by linking three forms of symbolism I examine in what follows: ancestor worship, a sacred tree stump, and a sculpture called the *dexoten*.

The language of Daagbo's prayers represents the Africans who were sold into slavery as "ancestors" (*togbo*)—"our ancestors who went to the land of the whites" in the Americas. But he also calls them "fathers of vodun" (*vodunon*) and "gods" (*vodun*). In interview, Daagbo explained this distinction between fathers and ancestors in geographical terms as the respective founders of vodun in different parts of the world: on the one hand, the free men who developed the roots of vodun in Africa; on the other, the captives who took this "ancestral vodun" (*vodunhuendo*) to found branches in the Americas.

The magical operations Daagbo performs in the festival dissolve the space-time of separation between diaspora roots and branches in the unifying symbolism of ancestral genealogy. The transhistorical relations of imagined kinship are projected into transatlantic space as diaspora consciousness. Daagbo summons the slaves to return to Whydah *in spirit form* as ancestral vodun gods "to see what good (new) things he has developed in the festival," then calls on their contemporary descendants as "brothers" to return to Whydah in human form to "register their identity" in some form of philanthropy.

In interview, Daagbo Hounon described to me how the vodun powers of nature had given a sign that validated his maritime conception of the festival. Recently, a storm washed away the sand on the beach at Whydah revealing a "stump" (*atin*) that Daagbo identified as the remains of the tree to which the slavers used to tie their pirogues. Through such natural signs, he explained, "vodun shows us what kind of thing vodun is." Daagbo described the tree as a new vodun deity, whose power he intends to establish as the presiding vodun of his reign as supreme chief. As such, the tree stump marks the sacred center of a revalorized vodun for Benin and the diaspora. "The site in Whydah must be respected by the whole country as the root of vodun culture," the place from which diaspora religions in the Americas were derived.

"The sea revealed this tree trunk by the beating of the waves on the beach. After that, [the sea] receded rapidly to show that, when the slaves went into the ships, the root of vodun remains in Whydah. When they had to go by ship, they wanted to leave behind their ancestral vodun for me, Daagbo Hounon. That's what's called vodunhuendo ("ancestral vodun"). If you go to some other country, whatever country, you will see vodunhuendo."

After invoking the vodun gods, the ancestors, and the spirits of the slaves, Daagbo concentrates their collective power in the sacred tree stump. The same tree is also hypostatized in the bas-relief frieze atop the Door of No Return, where it functions as the vanishing point of two converging rows of slaves seen in perspective, with their backs to the viewer, faceless, shackled, moving away from their native land, never to return.

During the festival, the tree stump was not clearly visible, enclosed within a concrete podium on which numerous ritual objects were arranged and surrounded by Daagbo Hounon's entourage and a swelling crowd of worshippers, tourists, journalists, and TV crews. The central ritual object was a sculpture called the *dexoten* (Figure 10.3). Daagbo Hounon used it to evoke the tree stump, the departure of the slaves, and the return of their ancestral spirits. It also enabled him to magically "work on the minds" of their living descendants, "our brothers in the Americas," to return to their African roots across the ocean.

Made from bent galvanized metal sheet, mounted on a circular base, and fixed to a wrought iron handle, the dexoten represents seven African slaves surrounding a larger Central European in a pirogue, in front of which is a pilotless plane.

At the climax of his prayers, Daagbo Hounon invokes the sea goddess Hou as he pours libations on the dexoten, simultaneously explaining what it depicts and what he is doing as follows:

I invoke the vodun Hou. [He points to the dexoten, entoning a traditional incantation.] One never sets foot to encircle the sea. One can never know where it ends. [He pours a libation on the dexoten.] Where I have just poured water, that's where our ancestors were attached in the pirogues. See! The dexoten shows the ancestors who left here as slaves for the Americas by boat [pirogue]. Here they are, leaving. The boat is called *kolofran* [the current term for a motorboat]. And off it speeds, going prrrrrraah! But nowadays, today, they [our brothers in the Americas] are taking the plane to return to Whydah, and there it is [pointing to the plane on the dexoten]!

This anachronistic juxtaposition of ancestral slaves in the boat and contemporary brothers in the plane evokes the unity of diaspora consciousness by collapsing the transatlantic space-time of black identity in a rhetoric of return. What does this two-way traffic of ancestors and brothers mean that magically transcends the dichotomy of return and no return?

Daagbo explained in interview that, as well as summoning the ancestral slaves in spirit form, he is also calling on his "brothers in the Americas" to return in human form as dutiful sons. "According to [African] custom, they should return to their village (Whydah) to build something there that will define them, so that from time to time we can invoke their name." "The Door of No Return has already been constructed by UNESCO in 1992, but there is more to be done." In particular, Daagbo hopes to get contributions to construct a school for the *vodunsi*, the female initiates who until now, according to tradition, have had to forego a modern education in order to pursue their religious vocation. Literacy training (*alphabétisation* in French) is central to the project of revalorizing tradition. With literate initiates, Daagbo hopes to save vodun's disappearing oral traditions from oblivion by writing them down.

Thus, the magic plane on the dexoten represents a redemptive vision of African diaspora tourism to the sacred center of a revalorized ancestral vodun for

Figure 10.3. Daagbo Hounon's prayers at the Whydah Festival, 1997. (Note dexoten at bottom right.)

the Americas that the festival locates at Whydah in the icon of the tree stump revealed by the sea goddess Hou. According to one Yoruba priest who currently lives in London, this redefinition of Whydah by the festival is an attempt by the Benin priesthood to rival the status of Ile-Ife, Nigeria—mythic origin place of

Yoruba kings—as the sacred center of African diaspora religions in the Americas.

TOURISM AND ATONEMENT

The maritime mythology developed by Daagbo Hounon in the festival gives a tendentious representation of diaspora identity in which the magical symbolism of movement across the ocean substitutes utopia for history. Attention to the deportation of slaves from Africa is displaced onto the exportation of vodun culture to the Americas. The history of slave procurement by former Dahomeans[10] is thereby "expurgated," to borrow Joan Dayan's (1996: 7) similar complaint about Gilroy's *The Black Atlantic* (more on this below). And the suffering experienced by the slaves in the Middle Passage, so deeply etched in African-American collective memory, is redeemed by the magical reversal of transatlantic movement: slaves long departed in pirogues come back as ancestors and contemporary brothers from the Americas return by plane as tourists and benefactors.

Ironically, in encouraging the return of diaspora brothers as tourists and advocating the concomitant forgetting of the Middle Passage, the festival organizers seem to be unaware of two controversial issues this raises for many contemporary African Americans, to wit: (1) the need for atonement by Africans for participating in the historical slave trade and (2) the commercialization of the history of slavery by contemporary African tourism operators. Edward Bruner (1996) reports that both these issues have surfaced in Ghana during the last few years as points of contention between Ghanaians and returning African Americans over the representation and marketing of slavery for tourism at the Portuguese-built slave fort, Elmina Castle, in Accra.

This is not the place to consider these complex issues in detail. To understand the festival's apparent lack of reference to atonement for Dahomey's historical involvement in selling slaves, one would first have to determine exactly what that history was before approaching the moral issues. Lack of data is not the only historiographic difficulty; one also has to deal with the ethnocentrism of early European representations of the slave trade and the disagreement of scholars who have subsequently criticized such ethnocentrism, in particular the assumptions made by Melville Herskovits (1938), Karl Polyani (1966), and I. A. Akinjogbin (1967) that Danhomè was a slave-trading state. The contrast between critiques by Dov Ronen and Patrick Manning of such ethnocentric scholarship well illustrates this dilemma.

On the one hand, Ronen (1971: 6) rightly cautions against "projecting European attitudes concerning slaves and trade onto the African side." Ronen suggests that the slaves captured in war by the Danhomè state were not primarily intended to serve as commodities for trade with the Europeans, but as victims for the sacrifices to the ancestors performed by the Danhomè king at his "Annual Customs.'' He also argues that, ''apart from the king, few other Africans were involved in the 'trade' '' (7). He claims that all business with the Europeans at Whydah was conducted on behalf of the king by the Portuguese merchant Francisco de Souza, who was appointed as ''chief of the whites'' (*yovogan*) by the Danhomè king, Guezo (12).

On the other hand, emphasizing that slaves formed only part of ''the commodity exchange mode of production [that] dominated the [Dahomey] economy in [the eighteenth century],'' Manning (1982: 43) argues that slave-trading was *not* restricted to the kings of the Danhomè state, but ''was so pervasive that every level of society was drawn into it.'' Manning gives the following breakdown of ''the interactions of all the sectors of the economy'' during the late eighteenth century.

In a sample of two voyages to Ouidah, roughly ten percent of the slaves exported were sold by the Fon state [Danhomè], twenty to thirty percent were sold by big merchants, thirty to fifty percent were sold by small merchants selling three to ten slaves each, and twenty percent were sold in ones and twos by individuals. The state thus had a surprisingly small share of the export trade. . . . [It] regulated Atlantic commerce and was one of many participants in that commerce, but it did not monopolize it. (ibid.)

It is hard to say which of these two alternatives is morally preferable. Both would seem to provide adequate motivation for the systematic forgetting displayed by the festival.

BLACK ATLANTIC

The Whydah festival modifies Gilroy's notion of a black Atlantic counterculture of modernity by reconstruing the relationship between slavery and black identity from an African standpoint. While echoing Gilroy's evocation of slaves and transatlantic transit, Daagbo's prayers at the festival mention neither memories of the Middle Passage nor references to Africa's complicity in the slave trade. The former, which for Sidney Mintz and Richard Price (1992) was constitutive of African-American subjectivity, never informed the memories of Africans who remained in Dahomey. As for the latter, my short period of fieldwork revealed that the festival is not a ritual of atonement as my friend from Baton Rouge was told. It seems better characterized as a politically motivated celebration of Dahomean cultural diffusion abroad designed to stimulate foreign tourism to Benin and simultaneously garner power for the Council of Kings at home by evoking a sanitized memory of the slaves as benevolent ancestors. Nor does the Whydah festival's evocation of slavery and transit give an African answer to Dayan's (1996: 7) complaint that Gilroy expurgates the continuing history of suffering from the memory of the Middle Passage. ''In Gilroy's attempt to anchor 'black modernism' in a 'continued proximity to the unspeakable terrors of the slave experience,' the slave experience becomes an icon for modernity; and in a strangely magical way, the Middle Passage becomes a meta-phor, anchored somewhere in a vanishing history. In Gilroy's transit there is no historical past . . . that could carry the Middle Passage, slavery, ships, and routes into the present transnational drive of global capital'' (ibid.).

The Whydah festival never challenges the duplicity of modernity's univer-salist goal of emancipation that black experience of slavery, imperialism, and racism so clearly belies (ibid.: 2). It develops a different vision of slavery that seeks to incorporate modernity in African tradition by revalorizing vodun in terms of diaspora consciousness with a view to representing the voice of Benin's majority of vodun practitioners in the national public sphere. At the same time, far from resisting the transnational drive of global capital, the festival enlists vodun magic to attract tourists and tourist dollars, especially from North Amer-ica, by redefining Whydah as the sacred center for African diaspora pilgrimage. Thus, in the land from which the Portuguese brought to Europe the racist con-cept of the ''fetish,'' the figure of the slave is now being fetishized in the commodified reinvention of the slave trade for slave tourism.

This commercial aspect of the festival is expressed in a second mural (which I unfortunately failed to photograph), located in the garden restaurant of a tourist hotel in Whydah, where the director of the Whydah Museum invited me to lunch with the Benin minister of tourism during the festival. A disturbing image of Whydah's slave-trade past is represented on the twenty-foot-long back wall of the restaurant's outdoor bar. Unlike the mobilizing terror of evaded enslave-ment on Whydah beach memorialized in the mural outside Daagbo Hounon's palace, here we have the domesticated slavery of restaurant decor. Symmetri-cally depicted at opposite ends of the bar in heroic style, two larger-than-life standing figures of African men who failed to escape capture lend to this pan-orama of ships, pirogues, and flagmen an inappropriately legitimating classical calm. Shackled by neck and ankles, yet strangely acquiescent in their bondage, these twin restaurant slaves preside as the passive icons of a tourist vision of history purged of all danger, struggle, and threat. Instead of bursting out of the picture frame into public space to demand the viewer's critical reflection as in the streetside mural, the slaves in the restaurant mural recede into the back-ground behind the bar.

Shifted to the margins of the picture, their images become the frame of their own depiction, so preventing the accusing past they signify from erupting into the present by semiotic self-negation. Locked in the liminal space of the frame that separates picture from viewer, these twin signs of slavery are reinscribed in the primal scene of enslavement on the beach as the signs of absent history. Surveying not only the slaving beach but also looking at each other, their sym-metry expresses the self-reflexive silence of complicity. Waiting at anchor off Whydah beach, the slave ships reinforce this historical silence by heralding the future. Instead of recalling the impending terror of the Middle Passage, their images presage the emergent technology of international travel, trade, and tour-ism.

CONCLUSIONS

The Whydah festival well illustrates how the construction of identity depends on local contexts of political struggle. Organized by the traditionalist faction of priests and kings, the festival develops the concept of diaspora consciousness to challenge the Benin government's neocolonial values, which undermine the traditional authority of priests and kings. Its performance calls for state recognition of Benin's majority religion, vodun, in the development of a modern national identity sensitive to indigenous culture. To emphasize the value of traditional popular heritage, the festival projects vodun culture into an expanded transnational context by representing Benin as the home of diaspora brothers and the source of diaspora culture in the Americas. This reconstruction is magically achieved by using the symbolism of ancestor worship and an imagined two-way flow of African persons and gods across the Atlantic, in order to identify Benin with the Americas and so promote "roots tourism."

The festival articulates what James Clifford (1994: 311) has called a "contrapuntal modernity"[11]—but with an important geographical difference. Daagbo Hounon's evocation of a transatlantic African community upsets conventional ideas of diaspora consciousness, reversing the usual spatial relations of diasporic nostalgia between "place of origin" and "place of exile" (Safran 1991). It also reverses the usual political relations of diasporic resistance between "minority" and "majority." Clifford (ibid.) suggests that transnational connections help in the struggle against a hegemonic culture by "break[ing] the binary relation of a minority [diasporic] community to a majority society." The Whydah festival inverts this structure. Its resistant voice represents the indigenous traditions of a disempowered majority that challenges the foreign modernity of a minority ruling elite. And it does so, unusually, from the point of view of the place of origin, for whom its brothers in the place of exile become the distant object of desire.

NOTES

I am grateful to the William James Fund of Louisiana State University for funding both my fieldwork in Benin and my subsequent visit to Quito, Ecuador, to attend the 49th International Congress of Americanists (ICA), where I first presented this paper as part of Jean Rahier's symposium, "Representations of Blackness in the Context of Festivity." For their help during my fieldwork in Benin, I am also indebted to Dr. Jimmie Hines of Baton Rouge, Louisiana, who first told me about the festival; "Big Joe" Nortey of Accra, Ghana, who first guided me to Benin; Basile Adoko and his family, my host and facilitator in Cotonou, Benin; Daagbo Hounon of Whydah and King Kpotegbe of Allada, who allowed me to interview them; and Martine de Souza, Director of the Whydah Museum of History, for her critical reading of this article. I also want to thank Norman Whitten, Carole Boyce Davies, Bamidele Demerson, and Jean Rahier for their comments during and after the symposium, and Edward Brunner for his subsequent responses. I especially enjoyed the continuing discussions that took place after the 49th

ICA in the surf on an idyllic beach in Esmeraldas with three of my symposium colleagues.

1. In this paper, I use the name Dahomey to refer to the southern portion of the contemporary Peoples' Republic of Benin, the spatial extent of whose Fon-speaking culture broadly corresponds to the historical territory of the Danhomè kingdom, which incorporated a number of lesser states under its political sway.

2. I am quoting one of the festival organizers, Basile Gbedige Adoko.

3. I am endebted to Carole Boyce Davies' comment at the conference in Quito that the festival sends a contradictory message to African-Americans by issuing an invitation to return to their ancestral roots at a festival held under the shadow of a Door of No Return.

4. I am grateful to Edward Bruner for drawing this to my attention (personal communication, 1997).

5. At the conference in Quito, Norman Whitten pointed out that this date may correlate with the arrival of the first Portuguese ships in West Africa. In support of this possible linkage of the rise of the Hounon priests of the sea to foreign maritime trade, Bamidele Demerson drew my attention to the similar case of the sea god Olokun of Benin City, Nigeria, whose cult linked prosperity and the sea and whose status was enhanced during the period of foreign trade with the Portuguese (Ben-Amos 1980: 28).

6. At the Quito conference, Bamidele Demerson pointed out that the Council of Kings seems to be creating alliances among traditional rivals in the contemporary political arena of Benin: the Nago-speaking kingdom of Ketu was once an enemy of the Fon state Danhomè.

7. Personal communication with M. Sossou, one of the prominent vodun priests who received the pope.

8. At the time of writing, I learned by telephone that the government has declared the 1998 Whydah festival an official national holiday.

9. Seventeen Mina ferrymen lost their lives to the sharks in 1879 (Coquery 1972: 388).

10. Manning reports that "one third of the slaves [exported] from Africa came from the Bight of Benin" (1982: 286, n. 1). "Most of the slaves were from Dahomey.... Aja peoples enslaved most commonly through wars among themselves"(9, 11).

11. Clifford is referring to Said's positive characterization of the condition of exile in the modern world. 'Most people are principally aware of one culture, one setting, one home; exiles are aware of at least two and this plurality of vision gives rise to an awareness of simultaneous dimensions, an awareness that—to borrow a phrase from music—is contrapuntal' (1984: 171–172).

Imagery of "Blackness" in Indigenous Myth, Discourse, and Ritual

Norman E. Whitten, Jr., and Rachel Corr

Todo deve ser cosa provechosa ("all of these things should be profitable").
—Christopher Columbus 1492–1493 [trans. 1989]: 134, 135

The naming of relationships marks the beginnings of moral sanctions.
—Sir Edmund Leach 1982:107

PERSPECTIVES, ISSUES, AND CONCEPTS

Professional perspectives on "race" and "culture" capture something of the enduring imagery of anthropologists and historians. Most cultural anthropologists treat race as a profoundly cultural construct, something that is socially divisive and discriminatory. In biological anthropology, by contrast, the attempt is to define "race" by genetic criteria. In both endeavors it is common to find that professionals dedicated to the study of culture and biology nonetheless project their quotidian or vulgar concepts of race and culture onto the peoples of the world. Writing about scholarly traditions focused on Latin America, Peter Wade (1997) puts it this way: "The study of blacks and Indians in Latin America has, to a great extent, been divided into, on the one hand, studies of slavery, slavery-related issues and 'race relations' and, on the other, studies of Indians . . . the roots of the split go back to the fifteenth century and have spread right through the colonial period, the republican period of nation-building and into the twentieth century" (Wade 1997: 25). This divide, as Wade calls it, generates a conceptual system of serious scholarship wherein historical and ethnographic treatises on native peoples, *or* black peoples, hermetically seal off the data of the alternative people from analytical salience. Indeed, some scholars debate whether the Seminole of the southern United States, the Miskitu of Honduras and Nicaragua, or the Garifuna of Honduras, Nicaragua, Belize and Guatemala should best be viewed as Indian *or* ''Afro-American.''[1]

Five hundred and fifty years ago, during the early-modern ''reconnaissance'' of Africa, Portuguese slavers (*negreros*), directed from Sagres, Portugal, by Prince Henry the Navigator, began to mark the diverse peoples of Africa as *negros* (blacks), whom they brought to Iberia in the caravels (also called *negreros*, black bringers) to be sold for profit as chattel slaves (Moreno, this volume; Russell-Wood 1995). This cultural practice of glossing all of the people of a continent (previously known by their diversity—Jelof, Biafara, Bran, Berbesí, Mandinga, Baõl, Cazanga, Fula, Zape and so many more) by a monochromatic color term, *negro*, coincided, perhaps ironically, with the beginning of large-scale conversions of diverse Africans to Christianity in the region of the Congo (Russel-Wood 1995; Thornton 1995).

Fifty years later, and five hundred years ago, Cristobal Colón, the first profit-seeking European slaver in the Americas, claimed to have reached the gateway to Asian markets. He had witnessed the expansion in the Portuguese-sponsored African slave trade and learned from it. He marked the beginning of moral sanctions by naming all of the people of the Americas *indios* (Indians) and established European hegemony over all of their lands, thereby creating a system sometimes called ''landed slavery'' (Wynter 1995).

As Western histories continue to celebrate the genius of Prince Henry the Navigator and the discoveries of don Cristóforo—Bearer of Christ and Admiral of the Ocean Sea—the bifurcation of the two continental populations that they and their disciples defined as the ''black'' and the ''indian'' endures. This European-designed cultural polarity of antipodal races provided a simplified, color-coded map for the organization and exploitation of cheap labor. It gave the capitalist world and its scholars two primary races, forever (it sometimes seems) to be separated as distinct cultures, distinct peoples with distinct histories, subject to the polarized learned scrutiny by professionals as cultural worlds that have little or nothing to do with one another.

Thus continue the legacies wherein, in vulgar Western scholarly discourse, African Americans share something of a less-than-authentic ''African'' worldview and ''Indians'' share a somewhat acculturated, but disappearing, preconquest cosmology. Most who study African American cosmologies studiously avoid Native American studies, and those scholars of Native Americana see African Americana as intrusive and perhaps polluting (exceptions to this are noted in this text and in the references, but see especially Forbes 1993).

Naming and the consequent instantiation of ''moral sanctions'' that began in Southwestern Europe over five and a half centuries ago endures with remarkable resiliency in scholarship in the Americas and is especially manifest when one looks at the academic specialties focused on ''Afro-Americans'' *or* on ''Indians.'' This imagery is part of an embedded paradigm that colors and nuances scholarship back to its roots of oppression of Africans and of Native Americans. It is the purpose of this chapter to chip away at the barnacles of binary deception by looking for perspectives on "blackness," or *lo negro*, within indigenous South American symbolic vehicles of expression and ethnic depiction.

Let us return to culture; it is here that the sense of festivity, ritual, mythology, and discourse reside. It is also here that the generative qualities of "race" may be found across the academic divides. Leach's perspective, cited in the second epigraph, emerges from a paradigmatic view of culture. It leads to Clifford Geertz's contribution, as stated in *Local Knowledge* (1983: 1; see also Leach 1976): "cultural phenomena . . . should be treated as significative systems posing expositive questions." Such systems carry meaning and raise questions. They constitute what one needs to know to understand the individual and collective thought of people living a particular way of life.

Significative systems that pose expositive questions are fundamentally tropic (Sapir 1977: 3–32; Crocker 1977: 33–66; Fernandez 1991): they are composed of figures of speech that themselves form and revolve around representations (Combs-Schilling 1989: 27). The representations we seek here are those of *lo negro* as they arise in indigenous contexts of festivity, mythology, and stylized discourse. These are contexts where creativity and reflexivity, as well as tradition and structure, prevail.

Imagery, creativity, and reflexivity . . . constitute a tripartite construct of mental processes. . . . Imagery is the corpus of images—concrete and allusive, stable and changing, patterned and chaotic, mimetic and inventive—developed by individuals from many sources in the course of their interactions. People draw on this corpus to create; creativity is the execution of expression of imagery, the communication of inner imagery to others. Reflexivity is the inward looking process that involves the incorporation, integration, and interpretation of social interactional experiences. (Whitten and Whitten 1993: 7; see also Babcock 1980, 1987)

This chapter deals with texts and images wherein indigenous people reflect on a theme that emerged in western scholarship in the Americas, in the 1500s. Texts and images are drawn from mythology and festivity, from discourses on shamanism, and from public performances of native people of South America.[2]

SUBSTANCE AND PARADIGMS

In this essay we draw from literature on native knowledge systems that are themselves historically embedded within Hispanic settings in Northern South America. The concepts that subsume blackness in Northern South America include those of phenotype (*negro, zambo,* and *mulato* in Spanish), those of self-liberation (*cimarronaje, palenquismo, liberación*) and those of social and political upheaval (*levantamiento, alzamiento, sublevación*). The metonymic and metaphoric relationships among the concepts of phenotype, self-liberation, and social and political upheaval constitute dynamic and transcendent cultural paradigms of ethnic quality, ethnic space, ethnic history, ethnic narrative, and ethnic tension.

Throughout this chapter we deviate substantially from vulgar ethnic categorization and assume that all culture is interethnic, and that all ethnicity is intercultural. As such, the paradigms of the dominant may be embedded and transformed within cultural systems taken historically to be at the antipodes of scientific or humanistic anthropological and historical discourse.

We first discuss qualities of blackness as they are found among the Yekuana of northern Venezuela, in the Watunna myth cycle. We then move to the Emberá and Noanam (Noanamá, Waunamá) of Western Colombia and Panama, here looking at their sacred topography that structures historicity. From these two lowland rain-forest areas (one Amazonian, the other Pacific coastal) we move into the Andes to the Quito Runa of the urbane capital of the Republic of Ecuador to present information expressed during the Yumbada festival associated with Corpus Christi. Because the concept of *esmeraldeños* (black people from the Pacific-coast rain-forest province of Esmeraldas, Ecuador; see Rahier, this volume) emerges in the Yumbada, as well as representations of Upper Amazonian (or *montaña*) people, we draw material from Chachi indigenous peoples of this coastal province, for a glimpse of their view of ''blackness'' in historical and contemporary perspectives.

Remaining in the Andes, we turn to the Salasaca Quichua native people of central Ecuador, as *lo negro* is expressed in the festivals of Caporales and Carnaval that mark the turn of the new indigenous year. Finally, we move back to Amazonia to understand our subject as it is expressed among the Canelos Quichua of Ecuador, as it emerges in their cosmogony of human and spirit origins, with special attention to the Wayalumba supai.[3] A discussion then follows. (Figure 11.1 displays these territories.)

YEKUANA, AMAZONIAN VENEZUELA

In the famous Watunna myth originally recorded in German by Marc de Civrieux and edited and translated from the Spanish into English by David Guss, black people are associated with the black currasow (*pava de monte*), Kurunkumo. In this context black people are dreamed into being by Odosha, evil brother of good creator Wanadi (the son of the sun), as slaves to the evil Spaniards (the Fuñuru), and also as agents of Spanish oppression, the soldiers of the army.

With the Fuñuru came a people called Kurumankomo, the black people. They were servants of the others. Their father was a black man, named Mekuru. He was Kahiuru's servant. They were good, poor people too. The Fuñuru made them work. They didn't give them any money. Lots of them ran off to the jungle and mixed with the Iaranavi [the good Spaniards, with whom the Yekuana had good relations of trade]. That's how

Figure 11.1
Indigenous Territories

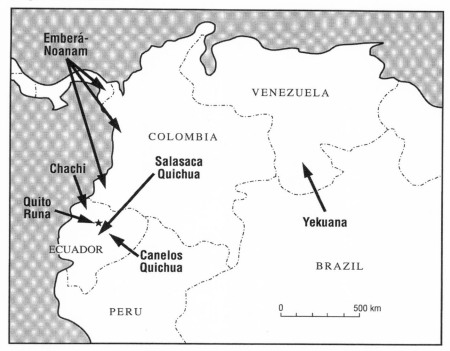

the Murunmatto, the mestizos [mulatos], were born. They have our color. They're our friends. (Civrieux 1980: 156)

This tale telling by the Indigenous Carib-speaking Yekuana resonates well with tales of the only black people to have emerged from this area in historic times. Venezuelan ethnographer and historian Berta Pérez recently found that the elements of alliance between indigenous people, the problematic issues of emergent *mestizaje*, and the asymmetric power relationships unfolding during the colonial era, are expressed in Afro-Venezuelan tales of *la pantera negra* (black panther), a legendary ancestress of *cimarrones* (self-liberated people) who fled slavery in Dutch Guiana (now Suriname), who traversed one of the most difficult and treacherous terrains in the world, and who emerged in the upper Caura River region in the eighteenth century and migrated downriver to near the Orinoco by 1850, where they live today (Pérez 1997, 1998).

Where an indigenous myth cycle ends with the departure of Wanadi to the sky world, the Afro-Venezuelan myth of the legendary black panther woman begins with the ethnogenesis of the endurance of Négritude in Venezuelan Amazonas. Similarly, with regard to the working of gold and *guanín* filigree and other jewelry, Nina S. de Friedemann (1974) found that contemporary legends of the black people of Guélmambí, southwestern Colombia, tell of how they took over the artistic work of native people on the demise of the latter. In Ecuador, historian P. Rafael Savoia traces a migration of self-liberated mixed black-indigenous people from Esmeraldas to Bahía de Caráquez, where they continued the maritime trade for which the indigenous people of the area were famous, after the virtual demise of the Manabí native people of this area due to the European conquest.

NOANAM AND EMBERÁ, PACIFIC LOWLANDS OF PANAMA-COLOMBIA

Themes similar to those in Yekuana myth and cosmology about the forces of evil and good of contemporary life are salient among the stories told by the Noanam and Emberá of the Darién of Panama and in the Pacific Lowlands of Western Colombia. Here we find what Stephanie Kane (1994: 107) calls a scale of sentient beings that includes people or beings called *libres* (free) and *cimarrones*. *Libre* and *Cimarrón* are two key Emberá (and Noanam) categories for the merger of human and spirit power. *Libre* is a term that embodies the historical association of blacks with self-liberation.

Cimarrón, according to Richard and Sally Price (1993: 283), comes from the Spanish language of the Americas, with Arawak language roots (the Arawak, specifically Taíno, were the first people encountered by Columbus in the Bahamas on October 12, 1492). It emerged in the Caribbean and mainland of South America around 1500, first to refer to feral cattle, and then, shortly thereafter, to refer to runaway indigenous and black slaves taking refuge in the *haiti*, or forested hilly region, of the large Caribbean islands (and of the interiors of the Guianas, Venezuela, Central America, and Colombia, which had different names). The Taíno designation for such a refuge zone became the name of the western side of the Island of Hispaniola (named "Española" by Columbus in 1492), Haiti, when the people there successfully revolted against French colonialism in 1804.

The imagery of *cimarronaje* or *cimarronismo* (see Jaramillo Uribe 1963: 42; Zuluaga R. 1988) among the Noanam and Emberá is that of mysterious, free, dangerous, spiritual, but also corporeal beings (their footprints can still be seen) completely familiar with the deep forest, and committed to free life beyond the confines or reaches of "white authority." These cimarrones may be other Emberá or Noanam, or blacks, or a mixture of indigenous and black spirit people, called *zambos*. "As political economic mediators between the Emberá and the outside world," Kane writes, "*black-kampuniá* are located between Emberá and all other *kampuniá* (outsiders who have power to condition everyday life, despite their physical absence). As symbolic mediators between Emberá and the otherworld (outside as unknown), black-*kampuniá* are located between Emberá and devils/animals/*hai*, who may take on *kampuniá* guise. The duality of their roles is conflated in practice, making much social interaction with black *kampuniá* a paradoxical combination of appreciation and fear for Emberá'' (Kane 1994: 107).

Colombian ethnographer Luis Guillermo Vasco (1985); following Déluz (1975: 8), describes six stages of initiation of the Emberá shaman. In the fifth phase, a being called Onasi, described as both *negro y libre* (black and free) occurs. This conjoined force of blackness and freedom becomes part of the route the Emberá shaman travels. After the shaman is liberated from the black libre, he may carve the *bastones de hai (bastón* is Spanish for ''staff'' and *hai [jai]* refers to ''spirit'' in Emberá and Noanam). In one story of the origins of Emberá shamanism Vasco narrates how the first *haibaná* acquired her mystical powers.

The first *haibaná* was a woman who encountered spirits who invited her to their tree house. The woman was like a person drunk, or in trance, but she had drunk no chicha nor had she taken *pildé (ayahuasca* or *yaje—Banisteriopsis caapi* with vegetal additives). She returned several times to the tree house of the spirit world. She eventually took her husband to this spirit dwelling, which was really a Palo Santo. In this house, among other beings and things, there were many *negros* who were neither indigenous nor human. They were *como espíritus,* ''like spirits.'' The *negros* were adorned with crowns of flowers, and they also danced to a different drum beat than that familiar to the Emberá; and when they rested they sat on seats of power like those of the Emberá. The woman gained power from the spirits, including the black peoplelike spirits. After a fight with her husband she went on to teach others shamanism, embodying thereby the feminized spirit power of blackness and freedom in what was to become an indigenous male domain.

The Colombian ethnographers Gerardo Reichel-Dolmatoff (1960) and Arturo Muñoz (1996) both write of a master water spirit, called *pulvichi* in Noanam and Emberá, or *la madre de agua* (water mother-master) in Spanish. In spite of the feminine depiction in Spanish, la madre de agua is conceived of as a ''fierce, Black man, [who may] overturn canoes and drag people into the water, drowning them'' (Muñoz 1996: 48). Reichel-Dolmatoff (1960) describes this being as a monster with a black face who drowns or swallows travelers in their canoes. According to Juan Córdoba (1983: 73), an Afro-Colombian anthropologist from the Chocó, la madre de agua is a being who can be sent by Emberá or Noanam indigenous shamans to cause harm (see also Losonczy 1997).

La madre de agua is prominent in the indigenous narratives about historical societies of cimarrones, among maroons themselves (e.g., Price 1983: 70) and in West African tales (e.g., Nunley 1987), as well as in indigenous cosmology of Amazonia (Whitten 1985, 1988; Whitten and Naranjo et al. 1976; Luna and Amaringo 1991), where it is often known by the Quichua designation *yacumama* (water mother-master). It is often seen as a chthonic force and may represent the power of the hydrosphere against social forces of oppression, as one author has argued elsewhere (Whitten 1988).

The emergence of three ''distinct'' systems of biocultural being—*negro, in-*

dio, blanco—is part of a Noanam creation myth that accounts for the origins of human races, just as in the Yekuana Watunna myth. In this myth we find that a master spirit, Edau, became a protector for free blacks, *libres*, who came to the Chocó as *cimarrones* escaping white-sponsored commercial slavery. It also accounts for the emergence of the three races at the Upper Chocó, at Bahía Solano, as hierarchicalized spirit forces that generate hierarchicalized *"razas"* of the colonial era (Lucena Salmoral 1992:138).

QUITO RUNA, ANDEAN ECUADOR

The Yumbada, which often takes place during the period of Corpus Christi, now renamed Inti Raymi, in Andean Ecuador, offers a striking imagery of the antipodes of *el mestizaje*. El Mestizaje, "the blended one," or "hybrid one," or "cross-bred person," refers here to the Ecuadorian embodiment of mixed peoples that signals an imagined community of lesser national beings for the white elites (Whitten and Quiroga 1998). During the Yumbada the prominent human constructs are those of the white *prioste* (festival sponsor) offering the *fiesta* to the Catholic Church. Prominent stereotypic representations in the festival are the indigenous "Yumbo" from the forested Andean slopes (montaña) and the Black, as *"molecaña"* (sugar-cane grinder) from the low, hot rain forest of coastal Esmeraldas province. Through it all the performers refer to themselves as Quito Runa. "Runa" is the Quichua word for "fully human being." When used in Andean Spanish, it is often a pejorative term for an indigenous person, or even a dog. Frank Salomon describes the black imagery as portrayed by the Quito Runa in this way: "Four *negros de Esmeraldas* or *molecañas*, men disguised as blacks of the north coast, guard the *loa*. Their inky masks glitter with golden eye-brows and scarlet lips. Their clothing is that of the backwoods rough rider; their motif is the violence and raunchy humor attributed to coastal blacks" (Salomon 1981: 166–167).

This heartily masculinized imagery of blackness contrasts totally with that of the alumbrantes, women who, "bearing giant white candles for the church, radiate a feeling of cleanliness, quiet, and modesty" (Salomon 1981: 167). And, as protectors of a beautiful, blond, white-dressed little female *loa*, these images of blackness in Quito Runa ceremony strongly suggest fertility that begets the quality of being Zambo, and thereby being from the Zambo republic of the mid-sixteenth century from whence the molecañas came to Quito (see, e.g., Cabello Balboa 1945; Phelan 1967). One is reminded also, perhaps, of the black spirit-man, evil Odosha, who steals the wife of his brother, good Wanadi, in the tales of the Watunna among the Carib-speaking Yekuana of Venezuela; or of the free, dangerous, libidinal cimarrón of the Emberá and Noanam of Colombia. This particular *negro* festival character of urban Quito seems to be the epitome of what the Chachi of Esmeraldas call Juyungo (e.g., Ortiz 1943).

Milton Altschuler (n.d.) describes the evocation of *lo negro* as a human-spirit quality of shamanic blackness in an unpublished manuscript developed from his doctoral dissertation. During a Chachi shamanic curing the healer "speaks" power words: *moreno . . . indio . . . bravo . . . enfermidad . . . brujo* (dark one . . . indian . . . fierce . . . sickness). He also chants in Spanish, the foreign language of domination: "This man is sick, I know, I know, cure, cure, *negro*." He explains that the use of terms such as *negro* and *moreno* during the mixed-language incantations is necessary because of the knowledge of black people of powerful, killing magic, and the "fierce indians" who left their mystical and dangerous powers behind in the pottery and stone artifacts that are common in this region (Altschuler n.d.; see also Barrett 1925: 353–381).

Milton Altschuler's revised doctoral thesis manuscript and the book by Eulalia A. Carrasco (1983) make it clear that while the blacks of Esmeraldas and the Chachi share the same universe, their origins are entirely different, their moralities are entirely different, and all of the contrasts between the Chachi and black people coalesce in the dangerous fusion of the "*razas*," in the persona of the Zambo, the fount of both danger and freedom. We return to this theme in our conclusions.

SALASACA QUICHUA, ANDEAN ECUADOR

In Salasaca, festivals transform the figure of the black from one epoch to the next. The same polar meanings of blackness in Yekuana mythology—of oppressed slaves and the fierce soldiers—emerge in two different Salasacan festivals: the soldier image of Caporales, celebrated in February, and the slave image of pre-Lenten Carnaval (Guevara 1969–1970; Scheller 1972). The fiesta of Caporales is associated with the Catholic feast days of Los Reyes (the Kings, Magi) and the baby Jesus. In this representation the blacks represent soldiers who guard the treasures brought by kings for the baby Jesus. This period fuses images of different black peoples from both Spanish Catholic imagery and from Salasacan historical experience.

During Caporales each actor who portrays a black person enacts a stereotype of a man of color from the coast who is passing through Salasaca. This portrayal is often that of a soldier in the army of Eloy Alfaro Delgado during the time of the great Liberal Revolution of the late-nineteenth century—the *alfarada*, as it is sometimes called, of 1894–1895—that caused a national social transformation. Or, a petroleum worker moving through this indigenous parish to the eastern oil fields of Amazonia during the recent epoch of economic transformation.

Each *negro*, as the dancers are called, is paired with a *doña*, "woman of esteem," who is a strong young man dressed as a Salasacan woman. The *negros*, dressed in soldiers' uniforms and carrying a machete, dance with the doñas while moving their swords up and down, up and down, in their scabbards. The movement suggests combat and sexual prowess. Exegetically, for the Salasaca, the blacks represent military and sexual potency. Young men who have performed as *negros* in this festival report that as they dance they shout, *hoyaaá! como*

zambo! como yana! como negro! (like black!). They claim to be from Esmeraldas, where black people live, or from Manabí, where blacks fought in the
Liberal revolution. Some say that they are on their way to the Oriente (Amazonian) provinces to seek their fortunes in the petroleum camps. They say that
they are taking a stroll (*el pasito*) through the parish of Salasaca, and they
comment on the beauty and desirability of the women there. Some actors grab
sexually and roughly at single women, who fiercely resist their advances.

The black soldier image itself has polar meanings within the festival of Caporales. It can stand for a liberator or for an oppressor. The Salasacan actors
smear cooking oil and soot from blackened iron kettles on their faces, carry
swords and wear soldiers' uniforms. According to one exegete, the ritualized
behavior of those mimicking *"negros"* may enact that of the soldiers once sent
by the Spanish (and white) *hacendados* to harass indigenous women. The portrayal is homologous to the Yekuana mythic "agent of Spanish oppression."
The *"negros"* are also portrayed by the Salasacans as the coastal black soldiers
sent to protect president Eloy Alfaro, considered in Salasaca, as elsewhere in
Ecuador, to be a liberator of black people and of indigenous people. This protector role of the ex-president is analogous to that of the protector role of the
Esmeraldeño *molecañas* (each of whom carries a machete on his hip) in the
Quito Runa Yumbada, where they protect the lovely young, female, white *loa*.

According to oral history, Salasacans collaborated with the black coastal soldiers to disguise President Eloy Alfaro as an indigenous woman so that he could
safely travel northward through the sierra to arrive in Quito, where he was
assassinated. In Salasaca people share a consciousness of the common struggle
of Afro-Ecuadorians and indigenous people against oppression. As one Salasacan said:

The dark people [*morenos*] were also part of him. Part of Eloy Alfaro [they were on his
side]. They left slavery. Also, they were treated as children. [The *hacendado*] treated
dark people [*morenos*], blacks, badly. Because of this Caporal [festival] is just like what
happened with the black and the black is dressed with clothes [associated with the imagery of blackness]. The dark people have always walked together with the indigenous
people. This was the time of the good president [Eloy Alfaro]. The festival of Caporales
is thus a time to give thanks. Because he is part of the indigenes of the dark ones. The
indigenous people and the dark people are one.

The protector role of the festival *negro* soldiers extends into the afterlife as well.
Just as the Salasacans and black soldiers accompanied Eloy Alfaro safely
through the highlands, the *negro* soldier from the festival of Caporales accom-
panies the soul of the sponsor through or around purgatory. Salasacans locate
purgatory at a sacred crossroads near the border of the parish. People say that
there is a four-handled deep kettle (*paila*) under the ground at this location, and
that "devils," "demons," or "spirits" (*diabloguna, diablo*, Spanish; *guna*, Quichua plural) put the souls of deceased Salasacans in the cauldron to boil. This

image is present in some sixteenth-century European representations of Hell (see, for example, Taussig's [1987: 210] discussion of the anonymous painting, *Inferno*, ca. 1550).

To guard the soul of the sponsor during this dangerous festival journey, the *negros* use their swords to frighten the "devils," who otherwise could trap his soul in the kettle. Once the soul has passed the dangerous crossroads and its hellish purgatory, as represented by the spirit kettle, it may travel safely to the afterlife. Some Salasacans say that they have actually experienced the vision of souls, purgatory, and the black guardians. These exegetes are the *wanushca-causari*, the "resurrected-dead" (dead returned to life). They report that they passed briefly into the afterlife either following a brief "death" or, in times past, when taking *ayahuasca* (soul-vine, a hallucinogen composed of *Banister-iopsis caapi* and vegetative additives [Whitten 1976, 1985; Luna and Amaringo 1991]). There they saw the soul of the sponsor of the Caporal in the middle of a group of *negros* and *doñas* who were protecting it, and they saw the *negros* use their swords to frighten the diabolic spirits and hold them back.

This image, which blends indigenous representations with European colonial concepts of hell and purgatory, corresponds to the historical depiction of the indigenous salvation of Eloy Alfaro. The "devils" during Alfaro's time were the high-ranking bureaucrats and wealthy politicians who wanted to ensnare the good president, just as the diabolic spirits of the crossroads seek to trap the soul of the Caporal sponsor in their spirit kettle.

The contra-image of *lo negro*, represented as an embodiment of enslavement by whites, and conterminous with oppression of indigenous people, is also enacted in a Salasacan ritual drama during Carnaval. A Salasacan man and boy paint their faces black to portray, respectively, the *tayta negro* (black father) or *yaya negro* (also black father) and the *"ashinegrito"* (roughly, black lover boy). The *tayta negro* sells the black youth to the Salasacan sponsor of the festival. Some people say that the *alcalde* (mayor) examines the youth for physical strength, sometimes checking his teeth as one would a bovine or horse, and sometimes asking him to show how he works with a machete. His feet are also checked to be sure that they are not crooked. After the alcalde agrees to "buy" the youth, the *ashinegrito* throws capsicum red pepper onto the cooking fire, causing the women to run out of the *yanuna wasi* (dark, blackened, smoke-filled cooking house) so that the *ashinegrito* is able to escape with plenty of cooked meat.

Throughout highland Ecuador the image of *lo negro* in the context of indigenous festivity and indigenous artistic portrayal fuses images of different black personages across many centuries. One of the best known and most publicized of these is the Mama Negra (Black Mother) festival held in the city of Latacunga in November. Among other events celebrated is the liberation of black slave miners in Cotopaxi by indigenous people from that province. Other images of blackness in Ecuadorian Andean festivity include the Black King of the three Magi coming from "Abyssinia" to view the Christ Child and to guard his treasures, sixteenth-century Spanish imagery of Moors, black troops from the wars of liberation in the nineteenth century, and more. Still other images relate to indigenous historicity with regard to black slavery in the Andes and coast and to soldiers and runaways during colonial and republican times. Movements and migrations of black and indigenous people into ethnically defined spaces motivated by economic situations such as the nineteenth-century gold rush and Amazon rubber boom, and the twentieth-century petroleum boom that brought Afro-Ecuadorians from the coast, through the sierra, and into indigenous Amazonian territories, are also portrayed. Analogous booms were those of cacao and banana that brought indigenous people from the Sierra and Oriente to the coastal provinces. Any and all epochs and movements may be fused or separated in indigenous festival images of "blackness."

CANELOS QUICHUA, AMAZONIAN ECUADOR

In the myth segment of Sicuanga Runa, the toucan liberator person in Canelos Quichua tales, Sicuanga frees two beautiful women, Widuj Warmi (black woman, from *Genipa americana*) and Manduru Warmi (red woman, from *Bixa orellana*) from a cage of spiny bamboo. They were enclosed in this snare by foreign monkey person, Machin Runa. This story of indigenous liberation is very different from a Canelos Quichua tale of origin of blackness as both a spirit force and as a mystical forest person.

Blackness emerges as follows (Whitten 1985: 84–87). Wayalumba Supai lives in a natural entanglement of spiny ferns deep in the Amazonian rain forest. He emerges from this entanglement with a different kind of drum, which he beats to attract children to him. Wayalumba is self-liberated. By his drumming and by his dancing he emerges as another force, called *zambu*, or *negro*. The Quichua word *yana*, black, as in *yana runa*, black person, or *yana supai*, black spirit, is not used in these tellings. Wayalumba is black; the spirit (*supai* in Quichua) is of the various epochs of cultural time and dimensions of cultural space. He may come forth in beginning times-places, times of revolution of Eloy Alfaro, times of the grandparents, or present times.

His imagery is of the forest—spiritual, dangerous, and libidinous—but he resides near indigenous settlements. He is very similar to the conceptualization of the cimarrón in Emberá-Noanam and Chachi cosmology. He is part of the indigenous biosphere, but he is not of the same original sources. Like the *negros* of the Yekuana, the Kurumankomo of their Watunna myth, the Wayalumba Supai is part of a creation that involves the Spanish conquest. He is not "Sacha Runa" (Whitten 1976); nor is he "Yumbo" or "Auca." Wayalumba is of the forest; yet he is intricately connected to the history and legacies of the Spanish Conquest, of the people of today, and to the emergence, within history and destiny, of blackness.

As we reach an end to this preliminary sojourn among the color signifiers of conquest as encountered in indigenous portrayals of blackness, we find that the indigenous connections between peoples beg for more complex signifiers. The colonial signifiers of conquest map poorly, if at all, onto South American humanity in its diversity. Within systems of indigenous representation we find an embedded paradigm of conquest and capitalist signifiers to be manifest in myth, discourse, festivity and ritual, but the indigenous webs of signification within which *lo negro* is suspended dynamically, remain, as they must given Western polarized scholarship, problematic. What is clear is that among the indigenous peoples of northern South America, historicity engages with spiritual forces to conflate images from mythic times with past colonial and postcolonial encounters and mixtures of black and indigenous people.

In Pastaza province of Amazonian Ecuador the demonic figure of Wayalumba supai transforms to a quotidian comparison with modern-day esmeraldeños (Whitten 1985), as indigenous people discuss their oft-time competitors in gainful employment situations. Also, from time to time, imagery of a *negro supai* (black spirit) emerges. This spirit is portrayed with a pipe of tobacco in his mouth and a large machete on his hip. Once again, we are reminded in all of this of the dramatic festival performances of the Salasaca Quichua as they merge and separate images of slavery, black soldiers, and modern-day petroleum workers; the way the Emberá place archetypical black imagery in their cosmological framework as a shamanic messenger; and how the Yekuana origin myth cycles include blackness in multiple dimensions in their historicities.

DISCUSSION AND CONTEXTUALIZATION

The West European concept of "raza" emerged from obscure roots in Spanish (and in Italian, French, Portuguese, and English) around 1500. At this time the idea of distinct imagined systems of biocultural "beings"—*blanco, negro, indio* empowered a vast system of colonial values of white supremacy and black and Indian subservience. In Latin American colonial, republican, and nation-state ideologies this system of ethnic polarities has been and is said to be mediated by *mestizaje*, even to the point of bringing into being a *raza cósmica* through the biological and cultural transformation of *negros* into *mulatos* and *indios* into *mestizos* (Carballo 1989: 13–16; Vasconcelos 1989: 31–52, 93–99).

Key markers in a paradigm of dominance, and sometimes hegemony, that have been of fundamental importance in the Western Hemisphere from about 1500 are represented in Figure 11.2.

Here, according to some dominant conceptualizations, white genes mingling with Indian genes produced a "half-breed" (*casta*, "breed") race of *mestizos*. White genes "mixed" with those of black Africans to produce *mulatos*, people analogous to the cross between a horse and a donkey to produce a mule (Forbes 1993: 131–220). Both of these mixtures were governed by the racist construct of hybridity wherein the higher status in racialist rank (the white, *blanco*) gave superior genetic stock to the lower (Indian, *indio*, and black, *negro*) to serve thereby as a civilizing cultural factor (Forbes 1993). Black and Indian mixes

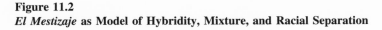

Figure 11.2
***El Mestizaje* as Model of Hybridity, Mixture, and Racial Separation**

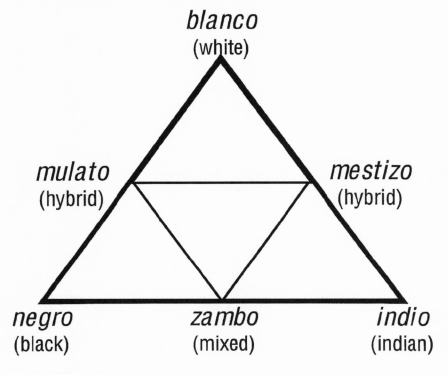

produced the *zambo*, or "black indian," a cultural status that permeates colonial accounts of dangerous people. The danger emerges because of the absence of genetic mediation of whiteness and, consequently, a blend of savagery in a conjoining of ethnic antipodes.

Obviously, given such a set of symbols brought into being in the Americas more than 500 years ago, cultural stereotypes and ethnic formations came to reflect, accept, and reject one another during the entire "modern" epoch of the West. The set of symbols that forms images of segregated humanity and its embedded polarizations is paradigmatic. By this paradigm, evocation of one symbol, or one facet of one symbol, implies the others in shifting but discernible patterns of signification.

At the antipodes of class-status relationships emanating from the wealthy and fair of skin color to the poor, are those people generally represented in northern South America in various walks of life as *negro*, on the one side, and *indio*, on the other. Literature on concepts of "indianness" within black historical narrative, ritual, and mythology is fairly well known to many specialists in Afro-Americana. However, information on the reciprocal embeddedness of the concept of *"lo negro"* in indigenous lore and ceremonial practice, is most obscure. The reason for such obscurity may be that specialists in indigenous cultures of South America do not carry with them the same sort of imagery as do the peoples who are subject to their studies. This is not altogether so, of course, or we would not have been able to come to grips with Yekuana, Noanam, Emberá, Chachi, Quito Runa, Salasaca Quichua, or Canelos Quichua concepts about blackness in their cosmologies and cosmogonies.

The professional imagery of anthropology is, all too often, part of a deeply embedded and remarkably persistent cultural paradigm with its roots in fifteenth- and sixteenth-century early modernist thought, wherein human commodities came to be known and expressed as racial categories. In the Americas the most important of these categories became those of *negro*, for chattel slavery of African Americans, and *indio*, for the landed slavery of indigenous Americans. Given this polarity inadequate attention has been given to understanding the interethnic, intercultural character of such an embedded paradigm within indigenous local knowledge systems. Unfortunately, in other words, our specialties seem to "buy into" the paradigm itself to create our professional divides.

When we turn our attention to such systems, even with the sketchiest of data, as presented here, we come face to face with our own history and understand in a more complex manner the intercultural historicity of the original people of South America, whose legacies and destinies intertwine with the cultural qualities of blackness and whiteness. A search for such history, which Natalie Zemon Davis (n.d.) calls braided traditions, takes us far from the *mestizaje* of vulgar political discourse that characterizes the self-styled hybridity of prominent literary and scientific ideologues (e.g., Canclini 1995; for a severe critique of Canclini see Rosaldo 1995).

This chapter and the research it reflects aims to cast initial comparative light on black imagery in indigenous cultures of northern South America. And it tries to do so in such a manner as to sharpen our scholarly reflexivity vis-à-vis a cherished set of Western images about our constructions of ancient cultural antipodes.

ON RACE, CULTURE, AND CAPITALISM

To continue this discussion, concepts of "race" are profoundly cultural. They came to reflect, in the sixteenth century, underlying postulates of West European hegemony. Indigenous peoples, originally unbeknownst to them, acquired the stigmatic label *indio* and the contra-concept of *negro* as the hypostatized antipodal analog of their dual positioning by *blancos* (or Spaniards) at the bottom of both class and ethnic hierarchies. These terms were applied initially by Cristobal Colón as part of the Admiral's claim to have reached India by sailing west in the Atlantic and on into the Caribbean, which he took to be "Japan" (Cipango, the Island of Cuba), the gateway to profitable Asian markets. He tried to open the portals of wealth through the acquisition of gold, pearls, and spices.

He initiated slavery in the Americas and tried to show wealthy and powerful Europeans how "indians" could be easily outwitted for the wealth of their land, and how their bodies could be turned into substantial profit.

Those people—native inhabitants of the "Precolumbian Americas"—could not escape the stigmatic and pejorative systems of signification bound to the hegemonic paradigm that constructed them as *indios*. Indeed, the Spanish organized its colonies by sharply dividing the "Republic of Spaniards" from the "Republic of Indians." And, while *negros* abounded, as slave and as free, they existed in a liminal state, in the absence of any republic except one that they themselves constructed. Examples of the latter would be the República de Zambos of sixteenth-century Ecuador (Cabello Balboa 1945; Phelan 1967) and the various Repúblicas de Cimarrones in Venezuela and in Colombia (Guss and Waxer 1994; Friedemann and Cross 1979), that of the Zambos (Miskitu) of Nicaragua and Honduras, that of the Garifuna who moved from St. Vincent Island in the Lesser Antilles to Central America, and so many more (see Price 1979; Whitten and Torres 1998a, 1998b; Torres and Whitten 1998).

As the formal division between Spaniards and "Indians" was being developed in the Spanish colonies throughout South and Central America, the traffic in black slaves increased exponentially, and the movements toward self-liberation (marronage, *cimarronaje, palenquismo*) accelerated (see, e.g., Price 1979; Guss and Waxer 1994). While blackness had no formal construct other than in the laws of slavery or the realities of *cimarronaje*, the quality of being black, whether *ladino* or *bozal* (free or slave; see Moreno, this volume), became fused in its separation to the qualities of whiteness and "indianness."

The cultural construction in the Americas of a colonial tripartite "racial" system mediated by ideological mestizaje is paradigmatic: reference to any one key signifier (*blanco, indio, negro*) of the hegemonic ideology automatically evokes key markers of the other two contrastive categories (e.g., Córdoba 1983: 80–95; Whitten and Torres 1998a, 1998b). Furthermore, each pair of reference points signifies a middle point, where "racial mixture" begets powerful intermediate categories: *mestizo, mulato*, and especially *zambo*. The first two of these reflect the European concept of hybridity, while the latter defies hybridity.

The *zambo* category is important because, in racist theories of hybridity, mestizaje is taken to mean the "mixing" of the "civilized features" from the "white" with those of the savage or barbarian "indian" or "black." The *zambo* category is a "mix" of non-European, noncivilized traits, and its characteristics beget inherently dangerous, powerful people, given to disorder and disruption. The quality of *zambo* had no place in the Euro-American colonial hybridity theories that mixed civilized with savage to create a pliable "mestizo race" of New World–born Creoles (*criollos*). Yet, historically, it is one of the most powerful categories for self-ascription for those who resisted colonial rule, founded *palenques* (fortified free villages), and raided (and even traded with) the plantations, towns, and settlements that dotted the profit-making colonies.

In this historically founded paradigmatic system of racialized cultural representations, indigenous people came to place those classed as *negro* (also *mulato* and *zambo*) in specific niches of history, identity, and topography within specific regions and in specific time frames. Concepts drawing on such history, identity, and topography are enacted in ritual, narrated in myth, and subjected to endless systems of discourse about the cosmos, including here nature, humanity, animality, and the numinous and ambiguous.

To the best of our knowledge, comparative studies of such racial topography focusing on concepts of blackness in indigenous cultures of northern South America have not been undertaken. It is the purpose of this essay, then, to draw attention to some initial tracings in what remains a vast moral topography of entwined cultural awareness that ethnographers of "South American Indians" seem more often than not to ignore, and of which so many specialists in Afro-American diaspora studies seem unaware. We hope to increase interest in indigenous and African American hermeneutics through this brief demonstration, to expand thereby the horizons of serious ethnography and serious reading of the recorded historical texts.

ALTERNATIVE CONTEXTUALIZATIONS

We have presented materials on indigenous views of *lo negro* and our analysis to this point has stressed the legacy of racism in such views. But there is much more to be said, of which we now wish to contribute some seeds for thought. Throughout our discussion of indigenous concepts, issues of inner power, shamanic power, spiritual power, cosmic power, and ethnic power emerge. Writing of systems of power in Africa, William Arens and Ivan Karp (1989) offer insights that fit nicely into systems of local knowledge in the Americas: "Transformation is the key to understanding concepts of power in African societies. A central cultural theme . . . is that the powers agents have allow them to transform the world. Transformative capacity is a key element in people's understanding of power" (Arens and Karp 1989: xx).

One cannot read texts from the Yekuana, Emberá, Noanam, Chachi, Quito Runa, Salasaca Quichua, Canelos Quichua, or from the Saramaka, Garífuna, Miskitu, or black esmeraldeños, without coming away with this same sense of transformative capacity tied to people's understanding of power. Concepts of force that can be used for good or for evil seem to be generally embedded in cosmologies of people, especially in contexts where paradigmatic hegemony is manifest. Powerful forces, seen as spiritual bordering on the quotidian, affect bodies and souls, as in illness, impoverishment, and exploitation. Such powers can be tapped, in turn, to heal the body, to soothe the mind, and to resist dominance. Indigenous reflexive awareness of forces and powers as cultural phenomena is what we are presenting. Such awareness needs no boundaries, and cultural diversity is a generative feature. This takes us back to our early assertion that all culture is interethnic and that all ethnicity is intercultural.

We noted above, in several places, that the two polar ethnic paradigms of *negro* and *indio*, in western modernist mentality, are offset by a nonhybridized concept of ethnic merger, the phenomenon of the *zambo* in colonial and contemporary discourse. The analog to *zambo* within indigenous cultures of Ecuador seems to be found in the concept of *yumbo* (see Whitten, Whitten, and Chango 1997). In metasymbolic terms the image of the Zambo and that of the Yumbo may, during times of crisis, represent bodies of human beings with shamanic powers who come from the lowlands—''below'' the pinnacle of bureaucratic control—to challenge that control system. The greater force is found in the unity of the Yumbo and the Zambo, a unity of diverse personages that rejects whiteness and *mestizaje* to form a union in the Americas devoid of racialist or racist classification. Here cultural diversity is crucial, but boundaries become transformed into braided legacies and intertwined destinies.

Although this issue must await another presentation, we can attest to the presence of trepidation, in the past (e.g., Salomon 1983), and in the present, of those above in class hierarchies in northern South America, of unities of indigenousness and blackness. The unification of the West European hypostatized ethnic antipodes, the African American and the Indigenous American, surging from bottom to top of class hierarchies implies the unification of spiritual and cosmological attributes, transformed to phenotypic attributes and their associated cultural characteristics. Out of early European colonialism, and enduring through republican and modern epochs, the associated social and political power of the nonhybridized unity of antipodal *razas* challenged and challenges the dominant societal model of the *blanco*, with its attendant mestizo and mulato categories as biological and cultural transformations within a *blanqueamiento* mobility system created during colonial rule (see, e.g., Whitten and Torres 1998a).

Confining ourselves to Ecuador, with which we are the most familiar, it is certainly the case that the indigenous Uprising of 1990 (Whitten 1996), the March for Land and Life of 1992 (Whitten, Whitten and Chango 1997), and the most recent (1997) Columbus Day March to Quito from Ecuador's four cardinal points (north, south, east, and west) stressed the fusion of powers of people of diversity against the materialist forces represented by hybridizing and whitening. Figure 11.2, presented above, stems from hegemony and domination. Figure 11.3, below, presents a crude sketch of how such surges appear as a diagram of counterhegemony and counterdomination.

CONVERSATIONS

At the 49th International Congress of Americanists in Quito, Ecuador, in July 1997, it was gratifying to find more than sixty-five people crowding into a relatively small room at 8:00 A.M. Saturday to listen to this presentation and to comment meaningfully on it. Present, among others, were Venezuelan ethnographer and social analyst Nelly Árvelo de Jiménez, who worked for many years with the Yekuana; several scholars from Colombia and Europe, with intimate, firsthand, extended experience based on years of field research with the Noanam

Figure 11.3
An Ecuadorian Model of Counterhegemony

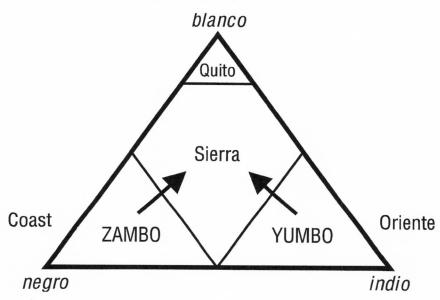

and Emberá; specialists in Afro-Latin American cultures in many nations; many Ecuadorianists with experience throughout the Republic; Africanists, specialists in U.S. cultures, and at least one colonial historian from Spain.

The leader of the symposium, Jean Rahier, presented a very provocative paper on the image of the Jew in black esmeraldeño Semana Santa. This, together with one by Isidoro Moreno on religious black brotherhoods from fourteenth-to eighteenth-century Spain and another by Peter Sutherland on recent festival (and tourist) representations of American Vodun in the ancient slave port of Whydah (now Benin, once Dahomey) dovetailed nicely with our presentation. It became quite clear that the African diaspora is one of many intertwined traditions that continue to span Africa, Europe, and the Americas. And it became most apparent that representations of power in the African diaspora are not confined to people with a particular skin color or other physical features. Blackness has to do with spirituality, with forces, with the known and unknown, with history and historicity, with cultural transformation and endurance. The collection of presentations made in Quito underscored all of these features, and much more. This book presents a coherent statement about multifaceted reflexivity with its own transformative powers.

Members of the symposium commented favorably on the dimensions of *lo negro* that we presented from our reading of literature and from our own ethnographies. One repeated comment was that the myths, stories, discourses, and festivities that reveal something of *lo negro* in indigenous discourse are changing. Each scholar with experience among the Yekuana, or Emberá, or Chachi attested to the fact that cultural phenomena are dynamic. They change and shift, new emphases enter, transformations occur. We certainly agree. We also asserted, however, that the racialist reference points of *indio, negro,* and *blanco,* mediated by a false projection from *blanco* as *mestizaje*-embedded *blanqueamiento* of racist hybridity, nonetheless endure and those who discussed these matters agreed with us.

We all concluded on the note that when dealing with African American imagery anywhere in the Americas, we certainly must read, reflect, and think about indigenous American imagery on the same or similar subjects. And conversely, those seeking to understand indigenous cosmology must not ignore that which is well embedded in the various systems of Négritude. There are many voices out there in the cultural worlds of Hispanic domination; the counterhegemonic social movements that we learn about now and then are but the most dramatic of enduring realities of interethnic, intercultural reflexive historicity and struggle. To listen more carefully to the multiple modes of alternative conceptualizations on power, hegemony, resistance, and defiance is essential to a necessary transformation of serious ethnography and serious history. On this chord we conclude this moment of our brief, but ongoing, conversation.

NOTES

The authors share primary interests and experiences in Ecuador and for this reason deal with that nation when generalizing. Corr has undertaken extensive ethnography in Andean Salasaca, and Whitten has undertaken extensive ethnography among the Amazonian Canelos Quichua and Achuar Jivaroans, as well as with Afro-Ecuadorians and Afro-Colombians. We are collaborating on a project that spans Andes, coast, and Amazonia.

Part of the research contributing to this essay was funded by two Arnold Beckman Institute Grants through the Research Board of the University of Illinois at Urbana-Champaign (1994–1995 and 1996–1997). Funds contributing to research in Ecuador that turned up materials presented here came from a Research Grant to Corr by the Center for Latin American and Caribbean Studies of the UIUC. We gratefully acknowledge earlier assistance and related collaboration that led to facets of this essay provided by Diego Quiroga, Isabel Pérez, and Arlene Torres. We thank Jean Rahier for inviting us to the symposium at the 49th International Congress of Americanists in Quito, Ecuador (July 1997), where an earlier and shortened version of this essay (eight pages) was originally presented, in Spanish, by Whitten, and for his encouragement and critical perspectives on the subject of this ongoing research and this particular contribution. Arlene Torres, and Dorothea Scott Whitten read various drafts and commented significantly on what became our final submission.

1. (See, e.g., Bateman 1990). The name "Seminole" derives from "Cimarrón" (see Sturtevant 1971). The Miskitu got their name through their alliance with the British, from whom they obtained muskets which they used against the Spanish (see, e.g., Helms 1977;

Hale 1994). "Musket" became transformed from the weapons to the weapon bearers as "mosquitoes" (like "musketeers") and thence Miskitu. The Garífuna have been called the "Black Carib," because they came into historical being on St. Vincent Island in the Lesser Antilles through interbreeding between native people, known as "Island Carib" and black cimarrones and perhaps slaves. Garífuna (plural Garinagu), which these people call themselves, derives from "Kalinago," the name by which Columbus came to know the "Carib" of Eastern Venezuela and Guyana. The Admiral dubbed all Carib speakers, and other native peoples who resisted his profitable advances, "Cannibals" (from whence comes the name "Caribbean") against whom "just wars" could be fought and the vanquished enslaved (see, e.g., González 1988; Whitehead 1988; Hulme and Whitehead 1992). Thanks to Columbus, the word "cannibal" replaced "anthropophagy" in English.

2. We seek here to tease out dimensions of a dominant Euro-American racist paradigm as this emerges in various transformations from a few select indigenous cultures of Amazonia, northwest coast, and Andes of South America. We have no intention of cataloging such materials. The paradigm that emerges is *mutatis mutandis* comparable to others characteristic in North America (see, e.g., Willis 1966; Blu 1980; Deagan and MacMahon 1995). We are looking at broad analogical representations; we are not trying to make specific comparisons. Such mass comparisons might also be made between South American and North American contexts that conjoin ceremonial or festive representation of blackness and indigenous historicity.

For but one illustration, one could reflect on the Emberá concept of the black *kampuniá* imagery or the Yekuana and Salasaca soldier imagery or the libidinal black imagery of the Quito Runa and Salasaca Quichua vis à vis the Pueblo (Hopi, Zuñi, Tewa, and others) Chákwaina Kachina images. This major spirit being, portrayed in masked costume and figurines ("dolls") represents a black *wuya* (Hopi), "chief" or "clan leader," a warrior-spirit image from the past that appears at an annual ceremonial period of fertility and healing. Various representations of this black figure from Pueblo history have been carried from community to community by leaders of different indigenous clans, with whom Chákwaina, his mother's brother, his children and other clan members, are identified. According to Frederick J. Dockstader (1985:11), the Chákwaina image "represents Estebán, the Negro [black, hispanicized, *ladino* explorer] or Moor guide, who led Fray Marcos de Niza to Cibola in 1539 and was killed at Hawkiuh [a Zuñi community], for his arrogant behavior and molestation of Indian women. The appearance of this Kachina and the fact that Chákwaina is known in all the pueblos as a horrible ogre, support the legend" (see also Wright 1977; Washburn 1980).

Given our methods, we would ask how the Kachina "Chákwaina" manifestations in costume and carving, and stories about "Estebán" (Estebánico, Estevánico) emerge in indigenous pueblo discourse, mythology, ceremony and festivity, and what analogies might be drawn with the Pueblo peoples' grasp of dominant western paradigms and how their own contestations are configured (for more information on this expedition, led by the guide "Estebán" see, e.g., Núñez Cabeza de Vaca 1963).

3. Quichua is a variant of Quechua, language of the Imperial Inca. It is pronounced "Queéchwa." Quechua languages are spoken by more than 12 million people in Colombia, Ecuador, Peru, Bolivia, Chile, and Argentina. It is the largest native language system in the Americas and extends from the Andes eastward into Amazonia and southward into the Southern Cone.

Bibliography

Abadia Morales, G. (1991). *Instrumentos musicales: Folklore colombiano*. Bogotá: Banco Popular.

Abrahams, R., and J. F. Szwed. (1983). *After Africa*. New Haven, CT: Yale University Press.

Abu-Lughod, L. (1989). "Bédouins, Cassettes and Technologies of Public Culture." *Middle East Report* (July–August): 7–11.

Abu-Lughod, L. (1993). "Finding a Place for Islam: Egyptian Television Serials and the National Interest." *Public Culture* 5: 493–513.

Adjaye, J. K. (1997). The Discourse of Kente Cloth: From Haute Couture to Mass Culture. In *Language, Rhythm and Sound*, J. K. Adjaye and A. R. Andrews, eds. Pittsburgh, PA: University of Pittsburgh Press.

Agnew, J. (1989). The Devaluation of Place in Social Science. In *The Power of Place*, J. Agnew and J. Duncan, eds. Boston; Unwin Hyman.

Akinjogbin, I. A. (1967). *Dahomey and Its Neighbours, 1708–1818*. Cambridge; Cambridge University Press.

Altschuler, M. (N.d.). "River People of Ecuador: A Study of Cayapa Law, Politics, and Indian-Negro Adaptation." Esmeraldas, Colombia: N.p.

Anderson, B. (1991). *Imagined Communities*. London; Verso.

Anon. (1828). *Recollections of a Service of Three Years During the War of Extermination in the Republics of Venezuela and Columbia*. London; Hunt and Clarke.

Anon. (1988). Interview of Raphael Confiant. *Le Nouvel Observateur* (Paris), 62.

Appadurai, A. (1988). "How to Make a National Cuisine: Cookbooks in Contemporary India." *Comparative Studies in Society and History* 30(1): 3–24.

Archivo Palacio Arzobispal de Sevilla. *Legajo 94 de la Seccion Hermandades*.

Arens, W., and I. Karp, eds. (1989). *Creativity and Power*. Washington, DC: Smithsonian Press.

Arteaga, J. (1992). Alfaro y los negros. In *El negro en la historia: Raíces africanas en la nacionalidad ecuatoria*, P. R. Savoia, ed. Quito: Centro Cultural Afroecuatoriano, 75–80.

Artez, I. (1977). Música y danza en America Latina continental (excepto Brazil). In *Africa en America Latina*, M. Moreno Fraginals, ed. Mexico and Paris: Siglo XXI and UNESCO.

Asimov, E. (1994). 25 and Under. *The New York Times*, A26, C24.

Augras, M. (1993). "A Ordem na Desordem." *Revista Brasileira de Ciências Sociais* 21: 90–103.

Austin-Broos, D. J. (1987). "Pentecostals and Rastafarians: Cultural, Political, and Gender Relations of Two Religious Movements." *Social and Economic Studies* 36(4): 1–39.

Austin-Broos, D. J. (1994). "Race/Class: Jamaica's Discourse of Heritable Identity." *New West Indian Guide* 68(3–4): 213–233.

Babcock, B. (1980). "Reflexivity: Definition and Discriminations." *Introduction to Semiotica* 30(1/2): 1–14.

Babcock, B. (1987). Reflexivity. *Encyclopedia of Religion*. New York: Macmillan, 234–38.

Badejo, D. (1996). *Osun Seegesi. The Elegant Deity of Wealth, Power and Femininity*. London: Africa World Press.

Bakhtin, M. (1993a). *Rabelais and His World*. Cambridge, MA: MIT Press.

Bakhtin, M. (1993b). *Problems of Dostoevsky's Poetics*. Minneapolis; University of Minnesota Press.

Barnes, N. (1994). "Representing the Nation: Gender, Culture, and the State in the Anglophone Caribbean." *Massachusetts Review* 35: 471–492.

Barrero, J. (1979a). "Costumbres, Ritualismos y Creencias en Torno a los Muertos en el Campo de San Lorenzo." *Apertura* 2: 25–49.

Barrero, J. (1979b). "Creencias y Costumbres." *Apertura* 3: 26–41.

Barrett, S. (1925). *The Cayapa Indians of Ecuador*. 2 Vols. New York: Museum of the American Indian, Heye Foundation.

Bateman, R. (1990). "Africans and Indians: A Comparative Study of Black Carib and Black Seminole." *Ethnohistory* 37(1): 1–24.

Beckles, H. M. (1989). *Natural Rebels: A Social History of Enslaved Black Women in Barbados*. London: Zed Books.

Béhague, G. (1996). Music since c. 1920. In *Latin America Since 1930: Ideas, Culture and Society*, L. Bethnell, ed. Cambridge: Cambridge University Press, 10: 307–363.

Behar, R. (1990). "Rage and Redemption: Reading the Life Story of a Mexican Marketing Woman." *Feminist Studies* 16(2): 223–258.

Behar, R. (1993). *Translated Woman*. Boston: Beacon Press.

Ben-Amos, P. (1980). *The Art of Benin*. New York: Thames and Hudson

Benchimol, J. L. (1992). *Pereira Passos: Um Haussmann Tropical: A renovação urbana da ciudade do Rio de Janeiro no início do século XX*. Rio de Janeiro: Secretaria Municipal de Cultura, Turismo e Esportes.

Berger, J. (1991). At Public School 139, A Hanuk-Chris-Kwanz-Etc. Pageant. *The New York Times*, D3, B.

Berger, P. L. (1997). *Redeeming Laughter: The Comic Dimension of Human Experience*. New York and Berlin: Walter de Gruyter.

Bermudez, E. (1985). *Los instrumentos musicales de Colombia.* Bogotá; Universidad Nacional de Colombia.

Bermudez, E. (1992). Cantos rituales de Palenque de San Basilio: Aproximación a su estructura musical. Bogotá: VI Congress of Anthropology in Colombia.

Bernabé, J., P. Chamoiseau, and Raphael Confiant. (1989). *Eloge de la créolité.* Paris; Gallimard.

Bigelow, J. (1970 [1851]). *Jamaica in 1850.* New York and London: G. P. Putman.

Blu, K. (1980). *The Lumbee Problem: The Making of an American Indian People.* New York: Cambridge University Press.

Bolles, L. (1981). Households' Economic Strategies in Kingston, Jamaica. In *Women, Men and the International Division of Labor,* J. C. Nash and M. P. Fernandez-Kelly, eds. Albany: State University of New York Press.

Bourdieu, P. (1984). *Distinction: A Social Critique of the Judgement of Taste.* Cambridge, MA: Harvard University Press.

Boyce Davies, C. (1994). "Black Bodies, Carnivalized Bodies." *Border/Lines* 34/35: 53–57.

Boyce Davies, C. (1996). "Transformational Discourses, Afro-Diaspora Culture and the Literary Imagination." *Macalester International* 3 (Spring): 199–224.

Boyce Davies, C. (December 1997). *Beyond Unicentricity: Transcultural Black Intellectual Presences.* 50th Anniversary of the Creation of *Présence Africaine,* Paris, unpublished manuscript.

Boyle, A. (1993). Schools Are Forgoing Holiday Celebrations. *The New York Times,* D5, 13CN 10:5.

Brady, A. A. (1995). *Kwanzaa Karamu: Cooking and Crafts for a Kwanzaa Feast.* Minneapolis: Carolrhoda Books.

Brandon, G. (1993). *Santería: From Africa to the New World.* Bloomington and Indianapolis: Indiana University Press.

Brown, A. (1979). *Color, Class and Politics in Jamaica.* New Brunswick, NJ: Transactions Books.

Brown, W. (1995). Wounded Attachments: Late Modern Oppositional Political Formations. In *The Identity in Question,* J. Rajchman, ed. New York; Routledge.

Brugés Carmona, A. (1943). Noción del porro. *El Tiempo* (Bogotá), sec. 2, p. 2.

Bruner, E. (1996). "Tourism in Ghana: The Representation of Slavery and the Return of the Black Diaspora." *American Anthropologist* 98 (2): 290–304.

Bunch, L. G. (1990). A Past Not Necessarily Prologue: The Afro-American in Los Angeles. In *20th Century Los Angeles,* N. M. Klein and M. J. Schiesl, eds. Claremont, CA: Regina Books.

Burton, R. (1997). *Afro-Creole: Power, Opposition and Play in the Caribbean.* Ithaca, NY: Cornell University Press.

Bush, B. (1981). "White Ladies, Colored Favorites and Black Wenches: Some Considerations on Sex, Race and Class Factors in Social Relations in White Creole Society in the British Caribbean." *Slavery and Abolition* 2 (2): 245–262.

Bush, B. (1990). *Slave Women in Caribbean Society, 1650–1838.* Bloomington: Indiana University Press.

Butcher, K. F. (1994). "Black Immigrants in the United States: A Comparison with Native Blacks and Other Immigrants." *Industrial and Labor Relations Review* 47: 265–285.

Butler, J. (1990). *Gender Trouble: Feminism and the Subversion of Identity*. New York and London: Routledge.

Cabello Balboa, M. (1945 [1582]). *Obras*. Vol. 1. Quito: Editorial Ecuatoriana.

Camp, P. (1977). Kwanzaa. A Different Kind of Celebration. *The Washington Post*, D26, B1a.

Campbell, A. (aka Tuffie). (1997). Reggae Sound Systems. In *Reggae, Rasta and Revolution: Jamaican Music from Ska to Dub*, C. Potash, ed. New York: Schirmer Books.

Campbell, B. (1972). Harlem Pupils Get Early Start on Kwanza. *The New York Times*, D20, A47: 2.

Canclini, N. G. (1995). *Hybrid Cultures: Strategies for Entering and Leaving Modernity*. Minneapolis; University of Minnesota Press.

Candela, M. (N.d). "Orquesta Emisora Atlántico Jazz Band." Barranquilla, Colombia: N.p.

Cândido, A. (1970). "Dialética da Malandragem." *Revista Estudos Brasileiros* 8: 8–21.

Carballo, A. L. (1989). *Prólogo. José Vasconcelos: Edición Justina Sarabia*. Madrid: Ediciones Cultura Hispánica.

Carrasco, E. A. (1983). *El Pueblo Chachi*. Quito: Abya-Yala.

Carrino, W. (1993). Kwanzaa. *Times Picayune*, D30, F1:1.

Carroll, P. (1987). Celebrating an African Companion to Christmas. *The Washington Post*, D24, DC1c.

Carvalho, J. M. d. (1987). *Os Bestializados*. São Paul: Cia. das Letras.

Castro, M. L. V. d. (1994). *Carnaval carioca: Dos bastidores ao desfile*. Rio de Janeiro: Funarte.

Celestino, O. (1992). "Les Confréries Religieuses à Lima." *Archives des Sciences Sociales des Religions* 80: 167–191.

Cérol, M.-J. (1991) *Introduction au créole guadeloupéen*. Pointe-à-Pitre: Editions Jasor.

Césaire, A. (1970). *La tragédie du roi Christophe*. Paris: Présence Africaine.

Césaire, A. (1971). *Cahier d'un retour au pays natal*. Paris: Présence Africaine.

Chamoiseau, P. (1988). *Solibo magnifique*. Paris: Gallimard.

Chamoiseau, P. (1993). *Texaco*. Paris: Gallimard.

Chinelli, F., and L. A. M. da Silva. (1993). "O vazio da ordem: relações políticas e organizacionais entre as escolas de samba e o jogo do bicho." *Revista do Rio de Janeiro* 1 (1): 42–52.

Ching, B., and G. W. Creed, eds. (1997). *Knowing Your Place: Rural Identity and Cultural Hierarchy*. New York: Routledge.

Chira, S. (1992). A Museum That Children Can Conquer. *The New York Times*, N27, C1:1.

Civrieux, M. de. (1976). Los Caribes y la conquista de la Guayana Española. *Montalbán* 5: 875–1021.

Civrieux, M. de. (1980 [1970]). *Watunna: An Orinoco Creation Cycle*. Ed. and trans. by D. M. Guss. San Francisco: North Point Press.

Clifford, J. (1994). "Diasporas." *Cultural Anthropology* 9 (3): 302–338.

Clinton, W. J. (1996). "Message on the Observance of Kwanzaa." *Weekly Compilation of Presidential Documents* 32 (50): 2489.

Coble, K. P. (1988). RAP Inc. Celebrates Holiday of Principles. *The Washington Post*, D29, DC3b.

Cochrane, C. S. (1825). *Journal of a Residence and Travels in Columbia, 1823–1824*. London: H. Colburn.

Columbus, C. (1989 [1492–1493]). The *Diario* of Christopher Columbus's First Voyage to America, 1492–1493. Abstracted by Fray Bartolomé de las Casas. Transcribed and Translated into English, with Notes and a Concordance of the Spanish by O. Dunn and J. E. Kelley, Jr. Norman: University of Oklahoma Press.

Combs-Schilling, M. E. (1989). *Sacred Performances: Islam, Sexuality, and Sacrifice*. New York; Columbia University Press.

CONADE (1980). El Estrato popular urbano en Esmeraldas. *Informe de Investigación*. Quito: CONADE.

Confiant, R. (1988). *Le Nègre et l'amiral*. Paris: Grasset.

Confiant, R. (1996). *La vierge du grand retour*. Paris: Grasset.

Conniff, M. (1981). *Urban Politics in Brazil. The Rise of Populism, 1925–1945*. Pittsburgh: Pittsburgh University Press.

Cooper, C. (1993a). Las Lick. *Lifestyle Magazine* (July/August).

Cooper, C. (1993b). *Noises in the Blood: Orality, Gender and the Vulgar Body of Jamaican Popular Culture*. London: Macmillan.

Copage, E. V. (1990). Out of Africa. *The New York Times Magazine*, D23:27.

Copage, E. V. (1991). *Kwanzaa: An African-American Celebration of Culture and Cooking*. New York; Quill.

Coquery, C. (1972). ''Le blocus de Whydah (1876–1877) et la rivalité Franco-Anglais au Dahomey.'' *Cahiers D'Etudes Africaines* 2 (7): 373–419.

Córdoba, J. T. I. (1983). *Etnicidad y estructura social en el Chocó*. Medellín: Editorial Lealon.

Cordovez Moure, J. M. (1957 [1893]). *Reminiscencias de Santa Fe y Bogotá*. Madrid: Aguilar.

Crocker, C. (1977). The Social Functions of Rhetorical Forms. In *The Social Use of Metaphor: Essays on the Anthropology of Rhetoric*, J. D. Sapir and J. C. Crocker, eds. Philadelphia: University of Pennsylvania Press, 33–66.

Crowley, D. (1984). *Bahian Carnival*. Los Angeles: Museum of Cultural History, UCLA.

Cummings, J. (1973). City Blacks Begin Fete of Kwanzaa. *The New York Times*, D27, A41:3.

Curtin, P. (1955). *The Two Jamaicas: The Role of Ideas in a Tropical Colony, 1830–1865*. Cambridge, MA: Harvard University Press.

DaMatta, R. (1973). O carnaval como rito de passagem. *Ensaios de Antropologia Estrutural*. Petrópolis: Vozes.

DaMatta, R. (1980). *Carnavais, Malandros e Heróis*. Rio de Janeiro: Zahar.

DaMatta, R. (1981a). *Relativizando: Uma introdução à antropologia social*. Petrópolis: Vozes.

DaMatta, R. (1981b). *Universo do Carnaval: Imagens e reflexões*. Rio de Janeiro: Ed. Pinakotheke.

DaMatta, R. (1991). *Carnivals, Rogues, and Heroes: An Interpretation of the Brazilian Dilemma*. London and Notre Dame: University of Notre Dame Press.

Davis, N. Z. (in press). Braided Traditions.

Davis Thompson, H. (1989). *Let's Celebrate Kwanzaa. An Activity Book for Young Readers*. New York: Gumbs & Thomas.

Dayan, J. (1996). ''Paul Gilroy's Slaves, Ships, and Routes: The Middle Passage as Metaphor.'' *Research in African Literature* 27: 7–14.

de Cires, J. M., and P. E. Garcia. (1997). El tablero de ajedrez sevillano: Bautizos y matrimonios de enclavos. In *La Antigua hermandad de los negros Sevilla. Etni-*

cidad, poder y sociedad en 600 años de historia, I. Moreno, ed. Seville: Universidad de Sevilla-Consejería de Cultura de la Junta Andalucía.

de León y Manjón, P. (1909). *Historial de Fiestas y Donativos*. Sevilla, Spain: Producción de Guadolquivír.

Deagan, K., and D. MacMahon. (1995). *Fort Mose: Colonial America's Black Fortress of Freedom*. Gainesville: University Press of Florida/Florida Museum of Natural History.

Déluz, A. (1975). "L'initiation d'un chamane embera." *Bulletin de la Societé des Americanistes* 39: 5–11.

do Nascimento, A. (1989). *Brazil: Mixture of Massacre. Essays in the Genocide of a Black People*. Dover, MA: The Majority Press.

Dockstader, F. J. (1985). *The Kachina and the White Man: The Influences of White Culture on the Hopi Kachina Cult*. Revised and enlarged. Albuquerque: University of New Mexico Press.

Dodoo, F. N.-A. (1991). "Earnings Differences among Blacks in America." *Social Science Research* 20: 93–108.

Douglass, L. (1992). *The Power of Sentiment: Love, Hierarchy and the Jamaican Family Elite*. Boulder, CO: Westview Press.

Drewal, M. T. (1992). *Yoruba Ritual: Performers, Play, Agency*. Bloomington: Indiana University Press.

Du Bois, W. E. B. (1989 [1903]). *The Souls of Black Folks*. New York: Bantam Books.

Duncan, J., and D. Ley, eds. (1993). *Place-Culture-Representation*. New York: Routledge.

Duncan-Willams, N. (1990). *You Are Destined to Succeed!* Accra: Action Faith Publications.

Dunn, C. (1992). "Afro-Brazilian Carnival: A Stage for Protest." *Afro-Hispanic Review* 11 (1–3): 11–21.

Durant-Gonzalez, V. (1985). Higglering: Rural Women and the Internal Market System in Jamaica. In *Rural Development in the Caribbean*, P. I. Gomes, ed. New York: St. Martin's Press.

Dymally, M. M. (1972). The Rise of Black Political Leadership in California. In *What Black Politicians Are Saying*, N. J. Wright, ed. New York: Hawthorn Books, 32–43.

Eneida. (N.d.). *História do Carnaval Carioca*. Rio de Janeiro: Record.

Essence. (1995). Stocking Suffers. *Essence* 26.

Fals Borda, O. (1979). *Historia doble de la costa*. Bogotá: Carlos Valencia Editores.

Fared, G. (1998). Wailin' Soul: Reggae's Debt to Black American Music. In *Soul: Black Power, Politics and Pleasure*, M. Guillory and R. C. Green, eds. New York: New York University Press.

Farfan Ramos, F. (1914). *Archivo de Cofradias*. Sevilla: Betica.

Farley, R., and W. Allen. (1987). *The Color Line and the Quality of Life in America*. New York: Russell Sage Foundation.

Feld, S., and K. Basso, eds. (1996). *Senses of Place*. Santa Fe, NM: School of American Research Press.

Felix, A. (1987). *Filhos de Gandhi. A Historia de um afoxé*. Salvador: Bahia, Grafica Central Ltda.

Fernandes, F. (1964). *A integração do negro na sociedade de classes*. São Paulo: Dominus.

Fernandez, J. W. (1991). *Beyond Metaphor: The Play of Tropes in Culture*. Stanford, CA: Stanford University Press.

Fisher, S. (1992). *From Margin to Mainstream: The Social Progress of Black Americans.* Lanham, MD: Rowman and Littlefield.

Fong, C. V. (1989). Tracing the Origins of a Model Minority. A Study of the Depictions of Chinese Americans in Popular Magazines. Department of Sociology, University of Oregon.

Forbes, J. (1993). *Africans and Native Americans: The Origins of Race and the Evolution of Red-Black Peoples.* Urbana: University of Illinois Press.

Foucault, M. (1978). *The History of Sexuality.* New York: Random House.

Fra Molinero, B. (1995). *La imagen de los negros en el teatro del siglo de oro.* Madrid: Siglo XXI.

Franco, A. (1979). *La esclavitud en Sevilla y su tierra fines de la Edad Media.* Sevilla: Diputacion Provincial.

Franco, A. (1985). "La esclavitud en Andalucía al término de la Edad Media." *Cuadernos de Investigación Medieval* 3.

Freeman, C. (1997). Reinventing Higglering Across Transnational Zones: Barbadian Women Juggle Triple Shift. In *Daughters of Caliban: Caribbean Women in the 20th Century*, C. Lopez Springfield, ed. Bloomington: Indiana University Press.

Freyre, G. (1983). *Casa grande e Senzala: Formação da família Brasileira sob o regime da economia patriarcal.* Rio de Janeiro: Livraria José Olympio Editora.

Friedemann, N. d. (1988). "Cabildos negros: refugios de Africanía en Colombia." *Montalban* (20): 121–134.

Friedemann, N. d. (1993). *La saga del negro: presencia africana en Colombia.* Bogotá: Instituto de Genética Humana, Pontificia Universidad Javeriana.

Friedemann, N. d., and J. Arocha. (1986). *De Sol a sol: genesis, transformación y presencia de los negros en Colombia.* Bogotá: Planeta.

Friedemann, N. d., and C. Patiño Rosselli. (1983). *Lengua y sociedad en el Palenque de San Basilio.* Bogotá: Instituto Caro y Cuervo.

Friedemann, N. S. d., (1974). *Minería, descendencia y orfebría artesanal: Litoral Pacífico (colombiano).* Bogotá: Universidad Nacional, Facultad de Ciencias Humanas.

Friedemann, N. S. d., and R. Cross. (1979). *Ma Ngombe: Guerreros y ganaderos en Palenque.* Bogotá: Carlos Valencia Editores.

Gaines, P. (1993). Kwanzaa Takes Root in Holiday Season. African Celebration Becomes Force in US Popular Culture. *The Washington Post*, D28, B1.

Gans, H. J. (1979). Symbolic Ethnicity. In *Ethnicity*, J. Hutchinson and A. D. Smith, eds. New York: Oxford University Press.

García J. (1988). *Cuentos y Décimas Afro-Esmeraldeñas.* Quito: Ediciones Abya-Yala.

Geache, E. (1992). *Une Nuit d'orgie à St Pierre.* Paris: Arléa.

Geertz, C. (1983). *Local Knowledge: Further Essays in Interpretive Anthropology.* New York: Basic Books.

Gestoso, J. (1917). *Curiosidades antiguas de Sevilla.* Sevilla: N.p.

Giddens, A. (1985). Time, Space and Regionalisation. In *Social Relations and Spatial Structures*, Derek Gregory and John Urry, eds. New York: St. Martin's Press.

Gilliam, D. (1984). Spirit Still Stands. *The Washington Post*, D31, B3d.

Gilroy, P. (1987). *"There Ain't No Black in the Union Jack." The Cultural Politics of Race and Nation.* Chicago: University of Chicago Press.

Gilroy, P. (1993). *The Black Atlantic: Modernity and Double Consciousness.* Cambridge, MA: Harvard University Press.

Gilroy, P. (1995). Roots and Routes: Black Identity as an Outernational Project. In *Racial and Ethnic Identity. Psychological Development and Creative Expression*, H. W. Harris, H. Blue, and E. Griffith, eds. New York: Routledge.

Gladden, K. (1988). "Women in Industrial Development: The Case of Medellín, Colombia." *Journal of Popular Culture* 22 (1): 51–62.

Glazer, N., and D. P. Moynihan. (1963). *Beyond the Melting Pot*. Cambridge, MA: M.I.T. Press.

Glissant, E. (1981). *Le Discours Antillais*. Paris: Seuil.

Glissant, E. (1990). *Poétiques de la relation*. Paris: Gallimard.

Goldwasser, M. J. (1989). *O Palácio do Samba, estudo antropológico da Escola de Samba Estação Primeira de Mangueira*. Rio de Janeiro: IUPERJ.

Gomes, Angela María de Castro. (1994). *A Invenção do Trabalhismo*. Rio de Janeiro: Relume-Dumará.

Gomez Picón, R. (1945). *Magdalena, rio de Colombia*. Bogotá: Editorial Santafe.

González, N. L. (1988). *Sojourners of the Caribbean: Ethnogenesis and Ethnohistory of the Garifuna*. Urbana: University of Illinois Press.

Gonzalez Henriquez, A. (1989). "La rumba costena en los anos 20." *Revista Dinars* 228: 86–91.

Graham, R., ed. (1990). *The Idea of Race in Latin America, 1870–1940*. Austin: University of Texas Press.

Gray, H. (1995). *Watching Race: Television and the Struggle for "Blackness."* Minneapolis: University of Minnesota Press.

Gregory, D. (1989). Areal Differentiation and Post-Modern Human Geography. In *Horizons in Human Geography*, D. Gregory and W. Rex, eds. Totowa, NJ: Barnes & Noble.

Gregory, D. (1993). Buys in the Hood. *Essence* 24.

Gregory, D., and J. Urry, eds. (1985). *Social Relations and Spatial Structures*. New York: St. Martin's Press.

Gregory, D., and W. Rex, eds. (1989). *Horizons in Human Geography*. Totowa, NJ: Barnes & Noble.

Groom, R. (1993). It's in the Cards. *The Washington Post*, D8, C1.

Guevara, D. (1969–1970). "La fiesta de Caporal y los Reyes Magos en Salasaca, Ecuador." *Folklore Americano* 16: 94–133.

Guss, D. M. (1993). "The Selling of San Juan: The Performance of History in an Afro-Venezuelan Community." *American Ethnologist* 20: 451–473.

Guss, D. M., and L. Waxer. (1994). Afro-Venezuelans. In *The Encyclopedia of World Cultures*. Boston: G. K. Hall & Co. 7: 24–29.

Hackett, R. (1995). The Gospel of Prosperity in West Africa. In *Religion and the Transformations of Capitalism*, R. Roberts, ed. London and New York: Routledge, 199–214.

Hale, C. R. (1994). *Resistance and Contradiction: Miskitu Indians and the Nicaraguan State, 1894–1987*. Stanford, CA: Stanford University Press.

Hall, S. (1977). Culture, Media, and the Ideological Effect. In *Mass Communications and Society*, J. Curran and M. Gurevitch, eds. London: Arnold.

Hall, S. (1992a). "Race, Culture, and Communications: Looking Backward and Forward at Cultural Studies." *Rethinking Marxism* 5 (1): 10–18.

Hall, S. (1992b). What Is This "Black" in Black Popular Culture? In *Black Popular Culture*, G. Dent, ed. Seattle: Bay Press.

Hall, S. (1996a). *Race: The Floating Signifier*. Northampton: Media Education Foundation.

Hall, S. (1996b). The New Ethnicities. In *Stuart Hall: Critical Dialogues in Cultural Studies*, D. Morley and K.-H. Chen, eds. London: Routledge.

Hall, S. (1997). What Is This Black in Black Popular Culture? In *Stuart Hall: Critical Dialogues in Cultural Studies*, D. Morley and K.-H. Chen, eds. London: Routledge.

Hall, S. and T. Jefferson, eds. (1977). *Resistance Through Rituals: Youth Subcultures in Post-war Britain*. London: Hutchinson & Co.

Hamilton, J. P. (1827). *Travels Through the Interior Provinces of Colombia*. London: John Murray.

Hamm, L. (1996). Soul Food Queen Takes World-Famous Restaurant Nationwide. *The Network Journal*.

Handelman, D. (1977). Play and Ritual: Complementary Frames of Meta-Communication. In *It's a Funny Thing, Humour*, A. Chapman and H. Foot, eds. London: Pergamon, 185–192.

Handler, R., and E. Gable. (1997). *The New History in an Old Museum: Creating the Past at Colonial Williamsburg*. Durham: Duke University Press.

Harris, H. R. (1991). With Christmas Past, Kwanzaa Gives Many a Chance to Stay in Holiday Spirit. *The Washington Post*, D26, M3.

Harris, J. (1995a). Good Food Fast: Celebrating Kwanzaa. *Food & Wine* 18: 6, D1.

Harris, J. B. (1995b). *A Kwanzaa Keepsake: Celebrating the Holiday with New Traditions and Feasts*. New York: Simon & Schuster.

Harrison, F. (1997). The Gendered Politics and Violence of Structural Adjustment: A View from Jamaica. In *Situated Lives: Gender and Culture in Everyday Life*, L. Lamphere, H. Ragone, and P. Zavella, eds. New York and London: Routledge.

Harrison, K. (1989). Kwanzaa Reflects African "Sense of Spirit." *The Washington Post*, D27, B4:1.

Hasenbalg, C. (1979). *Discriminação e desigualdades raciais no Brasil*. Rio de Janeiro: Graal.

Hasenbalg, C. A., and N. V. e Silva. (1992). *Relações Raciais no Brasil Contemporânea*. Rio de Janeiro: Rio Fundo Editora e IUPERJ.

Hazael-Massieux, M.-C. (January 1989). La Langue de Chamoiseau. *Antilia Spécial*, 35–36.

Helms, M. (1977). Negro or Indian? The Changing Identity of a Frontier Population. In *Old Roots in New Lands: Historical and Anthropological Perspectives on Black Experiences in the Americas*, A. Pescatéllo, ed. Westport, CT: Greenwood Press.

Henriques, F. (1953). *Family and Colour in Jamaica*. London: MacGibbon and Kee.

Henriques, F. (1957). *Jamaica: Land of Wood and Water*. London: MacGibbon and Kee.

Hernandez-Reguant, A. (1995). *God Is Black in Washington DC. Afrocentric Identity and Politics*. Meeting of the American Anthropological Association, Washington, DC.

Herskovits, M. (1930). "The Negro in the New World: The Statement of a Problem." *American Anthropologist* 32 (1): 145–155.

Herskovits, M. (1938a). *Dahomey: An Ancient West African Kingdom*. New York: J. J. Augustin.

Herskovits, M. (1938b). Les noirs du nouveau monde: Sujet de recherches Africanistes. *Journal de la Société des Africanistes* 8: 65–82.

Herskovits, M. (1966). Problem, Method and Theory in Afroamerican Studies. In *The New World Negro*, F. Herskovits, ed. Bloomington: Indiana University Press, 43–61.

Heuman, G. (1981). *Between Black and White: Race Politics and the Free Colored in Jamaica, 1792–1865*. Westport, CT: Greenwood Press.

Hill, J. D., ed. (1996). *History, Power, and Identity: Ethnogenesis in the Americas, 1492–1992*. Iowa City: University of Iowa Press.

Hill, R. (1991). The Feasts of Kwanzaa: African-American Ways. *The Washington Post*, D22, M1.

Hill, R. (1994). What's Cooking for Kwanzaa? *The Washington Post*, D21, E1.

Hobsbawm, E. (1983). Introduction: Inventing Traditions. In *The Invention of Tradition*, E. Hobsbawm and T. Ranger, eds. London: Cambridge University Press.

Horne, G. (1995). *Fire This Time: The Watts Uprising and the 1960s*. Charlottesville: University Press of Virginia.

Hughes-Crowley. (1990). Kwanzaa, a Cultural Tribute. *The Washington Post*, D26, E1.

Hulme, P., and N. L. Whitehead, eds. (1992). *Wild Majesty: Encounters with Caribs from Columbus to the Present Day*. Oxford: Oxford University Press.

Hunter, C. (1971). Spirit of Kwanzaa: A Time of Giving. *The New York Times*, D24, A28: 1.

Hurault, J. (1965). *La vie matérielle des noirs réfugis boni et des indiens wayana de Haut-Maroni (Guyane-Française)*. Paris: Orstom.

Hyatt, V. L., and R. Nettleford, eds. (1995). *Race, Discourse, and the Origin of the Americas: A New World View*. Washington, DC: Smithsonian Press.

Ianni, O. (1968). *O colapso do populismo no Brasil*. Rio de Janeiro: Civilzação Brasileira.

Jácome, N. (1978). Un Modelo diferente de vinculación al Mercado Mundial: El Caso de Esmeraldas. *Segundo Encuentro de Historia y Realidad Económica y Social del Ecuador*. Vol. 3. Cuenca: Universidad de Cuenca y Banco Central del Ecuador.

Jácome, N., and J. V. Zevallos. (1979). "La Formación del estrato popular de Esmeraldas en el contexto del desarrollo provincial." *Revista Ciencias Sociales (Quito)* 10–11: 89–144.

Jaramillo Uribe, J. (1963). "Esclavos y señores en la sociedad colombiana del siglo XVIII." *Anuario Colombiano de Historia Social y de la Cultura* 1 (1): 3–62.

Jones, L. (1993). Dreaming of a Black Christmas. *Ebony* 49: 94.

Jurado Noboa, F. (1995). *Historia social de Esmeraldas: indios, negros, mulatos, espaoles y zambos del siglo XVI al XX*. Quito: Editorial y Imprenta Delta.

Justus, J. B. (1976). West Indians in Los Angeles: Community and Identity. In *Caribbean Immigration to the United States*, R. S. Bryce-Laporte and D. M. Mortimer, eds. Washington, DC: Research Institute on Immigration and Ethnic Studies, Smithsonian Institution.

Kahn, J. S. (1995). *Culture, Multiculture, Postculture*. London: Sage.

Kane, S. (1994). *The Phantom Gringo Boat: Shamanic Discourse and Development in Panama*. Washington, DC: Smithsonian Press.

Karenga, M. (1977). *Kwanzaa: Origins, Concepts, Practice*. Los Angeles: Kawaida Publications.

Karenga, M. (1988). *The African American Holiday of Kwanzaa*. Los Angeles: University of Sankofa Press.

Kasinitz, P. (1988). "From Ghetto Elite to Service Sector: A Comparison of Two Waves of West Indian Immigrants in New York City." *Ethnic Groups* 7: 173–204.

Kasinitz, P. (1992). *Caribbean New York: Black Immigrants and the Politics of Race.* Ithaca, NY: Cornell University Press.

Katzin, M. F. (1959). "The Jamaican Country Higgler." *Social and Economic Studies* 8 (4): 421–440.

Kaufman, M. T. (1992). For Lubovitch Rappers, Harmony Breeds Peace. *The New York Times*, D 30, B3: 1.

Keith, M. C., and S. Pile, eds. (1993). *Place and the Politics of Identity.* New York: Routledge.

Kundera, M. (1991). *Beau comme une rencontre multiple.* Paris: L'Infini.

Kuznesof, E. (1989). A History of Domestic Service in Spanish America, 1492–1980. In *Muchachas No More: Household Workers in Latin America and the Caribbean*, E. Chaney and M. Garcia Castro, eds. Philadelphia: Temple University Press.

Lawson, C. (1995). The Debate on Holiday Diversity. *The New York Times*, D21, C1.

Leach, E. (1976). *Culture and Communication: The Logic by Which Symbols Are Connected.* New York: Cambridge University Press.

Leach, E. (1982). *Social Anthropology.* New York: Oxford University Press.

Leopoldi, J. S. (1978). *Escola de samba, ritual e sociedade.* Petrópolis: Vozes.

Levitt, B. (1994). Habari Gani? Kwanzaa. *Detroit News*, D20, C1: 1.

Liechty, M. (1995). Media, Markets and Modernization. Youth Identities and the Experience of Modernity in Kathmandu, Nepal. In *Youth Cultures: A Cross Cultural Perspective*, V. Amut and H. Wulff, eds. London: Routledge.

Light, K. (1993). Kwanzaa. *Black Enterprise* 24: 107.

Losonczy, A.-M. (1997). *Les saints et la forêt: rituel, société et figures de l'échange avec les Indiens Emberá chez les Négro-Colombiens du Chocó.* Paris and Montreal: L'Harmattan.

Lovelace, E. (1981). *The Dragon Can't Dance.* London: Longman.

Lucena Salmoral, M. (1992). Nuevas observaciones sobre los waunamá del Chocó. *Revista Colombiana de Antropología* 11: 137–142.

Luna, E. L., and P. Amaringo. (1991). *Ayahuasca Visions: The Religious Iconography of a Peruvian Shaman.* Berkeley: North Atlantic Books.

Mandle, Jay R. (1996). *Persistent Underdevelopment: Change and Economic Modernization in the West Indies.* Amsterdam: Gordon and Breach Publishers.

Manning, F. (1983). *The Celebration of Society: Perspectives on Contemporary Cultural Performance.* Bowling Green, OH: Bowling Green University Popular Press.

Manning, P. (1982). *Slavery, Colonialism, and Economic Growth in Dahomey, 1640–1960.* Cambridge and New York: Cambridge University Press.

Marcus, R. (1984). Coming Back for Hanukkah: Many Jews Return to Their Spiritual Traditions. *The Washington Post*, D26, C1a.

Marriott, M. (1991). New Tradition for Kwanzaa: Marketing, American Style. *The New York Times*, D25, 1–25: 1.

Marriott, M. (1995). Afrocentric in the Mainstream. *The New York Times*, D24, 1–30.

Marriott, M. (1996). New Symbol of the Holidays Has a Mission, Not a Belly. *The New York Times*, D29, 1–30.

Martin, D. (1993a). Ideas & Trends. Will Success Spoil Kwanzaa? *The New York Times*, D26, 4–4: 4.

Martin, D. (1993b). The Marketing of Kwanzaa. Black American Holiday Earns Dollars, Causing Concern. *The New York Times*, D20, B1: 2.

Mason-Draffen, C. (1986). In Kwanzaa, Two Festive Traditions. *The New York Times*, D24, C3: 2.

Massey, D. (1985). New Directions in Space. In *Social Relations and Spatial Structures*, D. Gregory and J. Urry, eds. New York: St. Martin's Press.

Matos, C. (1982). *Acertei no milhar: samba e malandragem no tempo de Getúlio.* Rio de Janeiro: Paz e Terra.

McCallum, C. (1996). "Resisting Brazil: Perspectives on Local Nationalisms in Salvador da Bahia." *Ethnos* 61 (3–4): 207–229.

McClester, C. (1985). *Everything You Always Wanted to Know but Didn't Know Where to Ask.* New York; Gumbs & Thomas.

McFarlane-Gregory, D., and T. Ruddock-Kelly. (1993). *The Informal Commercial Importers.* Macro Policy Conference, Kingston, Jamaica.

McLarin, K. J. (1993). Holiday Dilemma at Schools: Is That a Legal Decoration? *The New York Times*, D 16, A1: 5.

Medearis, A. S. (1994). *The Seven Days of Kwanzaa.* New York: Scholastic.

Medearis, A. S. (1995). *A Kwanzaa Celebration: Festive Recipes and Homemade Gifts from an African-American Kitchen.* New York: Dutton.

Meeks, B. (1997). "The Political Movement in Jamaica: The Dimensions of Hegemonic Dissolution." *Race and Reason* 3: 39–47.

Merelman, R. M. (1995). *Representing Black Culture: Racial Conflict and Cultural Politics in the United States.* New York: Routledge.

Meyer, E. L. (1986). Kwanzaa Reaffirms Roots. *The Washington Post*, D26, C1d.

Middleton, D. (1997). Reconnaissance of Africa. In *Oxford Atlas of Exploration*. London: Reed International Books Limited, George Philip Limited, 34–35.

Miller, E. (1988). "The Rise of the Matriarchy in the Caribbean." *Caribbean Quarterly* 34 (3–4): 1–21.

Mintz, S. W. (1996). *Tasting Good, Tasting Freedom.* Boston: Beacon Press.

Mintz, S. W., and R. Price. (1992). *The Birth of African-American Culture: An Anthropological Perspective.* Boston: Beacon Press.

Morales, A. (1988). O afoxé Filhos de Gandhi pede paz. In *Escravidao e Invencao da liberdade. Estudos Sobre o Negro no Brasil*, J. J. Reis, ed. São Paulo: Editora Brasiliense, 264–274.

Moreno, I. (1981). "Control político, integración ideológica e identidad étnica: el sistema de cargos en las comunidades indígenas américanas como adaptación de las cofradías étnicas andaluzas." *Primeras Jornadas de Andaluzía y America* 1: 249–265.

Moreno, I. (1982). *La semana santa de Sevilla: Conformación, mixtificación y significaciones.* Seville: Servicio de Publicaciones del Ayuntamiento de Sevilla.

Moreno, I. (1983). *Los cuadros del mestizaje.* Madrid: Jose Porrua Editoriales.

Moreno, I. (1985). *Cofradías y hermandades andaluzas, estructura, simbolismo e identidad.* Seville: Editoriales Andaluzas Unidas.

Moreno, I. (1997). *La Antigua hermandad de los negros de Sevilla: Etnicidad, poder y sociedad en 600 años de Historia.* Seville: Universidad de Sevilla and Consejería de Cultura de la Junta de Andalucía.

Morgan, T. (1978). Kwanza: Stressing Afro-American Heritage. *The Washington Post*, D27, C10b.

Mota, C. G. (1994). *Ideología da Cultura Brasileira.* São Paulo: Ed. Ática.

Muñoz, A. G. (1996). "Handling Hungry Spirits: Shamanic Rituals of the Emberá." *Shamans Drum* (Fall): 36–48.

Naranjo, M. (1987). *La Cultura popular en el Ecuador.* Vol. 4. Esmeraldas, C.I.D.A.P.

Nash, M. (1996). The Core Elements of Ethnicity. In *Ethnicity,* J. Hutchinson and A. D. Smith, eds. New York: Oxford University Press.

Needell, J. D. (1987). *A Tropical Belle Epoque: Elite Culture and Society in Turn-of-Century Rio de Janeiro.* Cambridge: Cambridge University Press.

Nettleford, R. (1972). *Identity, Race and Protest in Jamaica.* New York: Morrow Books.

Nguyen, L. (1996). The Affirming Quality of Kwanzaa. *The Washington Post,* D29, B1.

Noguera-Devers, A. (1991). "The Factors Responsible for the Economic Success of West Indian Migrants." Senior thesis, African American Studies Department. University of California, Berkeley.

Nuñez Cabeza de Vaca, A. (1963 [1542, 1555]). *Castaways: The Narrative of Alvar Núñez Cabeza de Vaca.* E. Pupo-Walker, ed., F. M. López-Morillas, trans. Berkeley: University of California Press.

Nunley, J. W. (1987). *Moving with the Face of the Devil: Art and Politics in Urban West Africa.* Urbana: University of Illinois Press.

Nunley, J. W., and J. Bettleheim, eds. (1988). *Caribbean Festival Arts.* Seattle: University of Washington Press.

Ogren, K. (1989). *The Jazz Revolution: Twenties America and the Meaning of Jazz.* New York: Oxford University Press.

Ortiz, A. (1943). *Juyungo: Historia de un negro, una isla y otros negros.* Buenos Aires: Editorial Americal.

Ortiz, F. (1920–21). *Los cabildos y la fiesta afrocubana del Día de Reyes.* Havana: Revista Bimestre Cubana.

Ortiz, F. (1960). *La Antigua Fiesta Afrocubana del Día de Reyes.* Havana: Ministerio de Relaciones Exteriores, Dpto. de Asuntos Culturales.

Ortiz, R. (1985). *Cultura brasileira e identidade nacional.* São Paulo: Ed. Brasiliense.

Ortiz de Zúñiga. (1677). *Anales eclesiásticos y seculares de la Muy Noble y Muy Leal Ciudad de Sevilla, metropoli de Andalucia, que contienen sus más principales memorias desde el año de 1246, en que emprendió conquistarla del poder de los Moros en el gloriosísimo Rey Fernando III del Castilla y León, hasta el de 1671 en que la Católica Iglesia le concedió el culto y título de Bienaventurado.* Seville.

Owusu, M. (1996). *Inside of History: Roots and Redemption: Reflections on the Paradoxes of Synthetic Nationalism in Jamaica.* International Conference on Caribbean Culture in Honour of Professor the Hon. Rex Nettleford OM, University of the West Indies at Mona, Kingston.

Pacini, D. (1993). "The Pico Phenomenon in Cartagena, Columbia." *America Negra* 6: 69–115.

Page, H. E. (1997). " 'Black Males' Imagery and Media Containment of African American Men." *American Anthropologist* 99(1): 99–111.

Parker, R. G. (1991). *Bodies, Pleasures and Passions: Sexual Culture in Contemporary Brazil.* Boston: Beacon Press.

Peiss, K. (1984). "Charity Girls" and City Pleasures: Historical Notes on Working Class Sexuality, 1880–1920. In *Desire: The Politics of Sexuality,* A. Snitow, C. Stansell, and S. Thompson, eds. London: Virago, 127–139.

Peñas Galindo, D. (1988). *Los bogas de Mompox: historia del zambaje.* Bogotá: Tercer Mundo Editores.

Perdomo Escobar, J. I. (1963). *La historia de la música en Colombia*. Bogotá: Editorial ABC.

Pérez, B. (1997). "Pantera Negra: An Ancestral Figure of the Aripaeños, Maroon Descendants in Southern Venezuela." *History and Anthropology* 10(2–3): 219–240.

Pérez, B. (1998). Pantera Negra: A Messianic Figure of Historical Resistance and Cultural Survival Among Maroon Descendants in Southern Venezuela. In *Blackness in Latin America and the Caribbean: Social Dynamics and Cultural Transformations*, N. E. Whitten, Jr. and A. Torres, eds. Vol. 1. Bloomington: Indiana University Press.

Phelan, J. L. (1967). *The Kingdom of Quito in the Seventeenth Century: Bureaucratic Politics in the Spanish Empire*. Madison: University of Wisconsin Press.

Pierce, P., and B. F. Williams. (1997). And Your Prayers Shall be Answered Through the Womb of a Woman: Insurgent Masculine Redemption and the Nation of Islam. In *Woman Out of Place: The Gender of Agency and the Race of Nationality*, B. Williams, ed. New York and London: Routledge.

Polyani, K. (1996). *Dahomey and the Slave Trade: An Analysis of an Archaic Economy*. Seattle: University of Washington Press.

Price, R., ed. (1979). *Maroon Societies: Rebel Slave Communities in the Americas*. Baltimore, MD: Johns Hopkins University Press.

Price, R. (1983). *First-Time: The Historical Vision of an Afro-American People*. Baltimore, MD: Johns Hopkins University Press.

Price, R., and S. Price. (1993). Collective Fictions: Performance in Saramaka Folktales. In *Imagery and Creativity: Ethnoaesthetics and Art Worlds in the Americas*, D. Whitten and N. Whitten, eds. Tucson: University of Arizona Press, 235–288.

Queiroz, M. I. P. de. (1992). *Carnaval brésilien: Le vécu et le mythe*. Paris: F. Gallimard.

Quintero Rivera, A. (1996). The Somatology of Manners: Class, Race and Gender in the History of Dance Etiquette in the Hispanic Caribbean. In *Ethnicity in the Caribbean*, G. Oostindie, ed. London: Macmillan.

Quiroga, D. (1994). Saints, Virgins, and the Devil: Witchcraft, Magic, and Healing in the Northern Coast of Ecuador. Ph.D. dissertation, Department of Anthropology, University of Illinois.

Rahier, J. (1987). *La décima. Poesía oral Negra del Ecuador*. Quito: Ediciones Abya Yala and Centro Cultural Afro-Ecuatoriano.

Rahier, J. (1991). "El juego de los cucuruchos Afro-Esmeraldeño." *Antropología. Cuadernos de Investigación del departamento de Antropología de la PUCE-Quito* 5: 125–146.

Rahier, J. (1994). La Fête des Rois Afro-Esméraldienne (en République de l'Equateur). *Département de Sociologie*. Nanterre: Université de Paris X.

Rahier, J. (1998). "Blackness, the 'Racial'/Spatial Order, Migrations, and Miss Ecuador 1995–1996." *American Anthropologist* 100(2): 421–430.

Ramos, M., and R. Savoia. (1993). *Semana santa de las comunidades negras*. Quito: Centro Cultural Afroecuatoriano & Departamento de Pastoral Afroecuatoriano.

Reckler, N. (1990). Kwanzaa Taps African Roots. *The Washington Post*, D7, WW63a.

Reichel-Dolmatoff, G. (1960). "Notas etnográficas sobre los indios del Chocó." *Revista Colombiana de Antropología* 11: 75–158.

Reid, P. (1991). Letting Christmas Reflect a Black Identity. *The New York Times*, D15, 12WC31.

Reif, R. (1974). For the Holidays, Museums Offer Festive Banquets. *The New York Times*, D17, 39.

Report. (1996). Kwanzaa Culture. *US News & World Report*, D30, 17.

Restrepo Duque, H. (1991). *Las 100 mejores canciones colombianas y sus autores*. Bogota: RCN, Sonolux.

Richardson, M. (1989). Place and Culture: Two Disciplines, Two Concepts, Two Images of Christ, and a Single Goal. In *The Power of Place*, J. Agnew and J. Duncan, eds. Boston: Unwin Hyman.

Riotur. (1991). *Memórias do Carnaval*. Rio de Janeiro: Oficina do Livro.

Riserio, A. (1981). *Carnaval ijexa. notas sobre afoxés e Blocos de Novo Carnaval Afrobaiano*. Salvador: Corrupio.

Rivera, F., ed. (1986). *Campesinado y organización en Esmeraldas*. Quito: Centro Andino de Acción Popular (CAAP) y Organización Campesina Muisne-Esmeraldas (OCAME).

Robertson, L. (1996). *Kwanzaa Fun*. New York: Kingfisher.

Robinson, D. (1989). The Language and Significance of Place in Latin America. In *The Power of Place*, J. Agnew and J. Duncan, eds. Boston: Unwin Hyman.

Rodney, W. (1969). *The Grounding with My Brothers*. London: Bogle-Loverture Publications.

Rodrigues, A. M. (1984). *Samba negro, espoliação branca*. São Paulo: Editora Hucitec.

Rogers, P. D. (1992). Gift Ideas for a Spirited Holiday. *The Washington Post*, D17, T12.

Ronen, D. (1971). "On the African Role in the Trans-Atlantic Slave Trade in Dahomey." *Cahiers D'Etudes Africaines* 11 (41): 5–13.

Rosaldo, R. (1995). Foreword. In *Hybrid Cultures: Strategies for Entering and Leaving Modernity*, Nancy García Canclini, ed. Minneapolis: University of Minnesota Press: xi–xvii.

Rose, D. (1997). Restaurant Tours: Shark Bar's New-Wave Soul. *Chicago Reader*, Al, 1–39.

Rose, T. (1994). *Black Noise: Rap Music and Black Culture in Contemporary America*. Hanover, NH: Wesleyan University Press of New England University Press.

Ross, A. (1998). *Real Love: In Pursuit of Cultural Justice*. New York: New York University Press.

Russell-Wood, A. J. R. (1995). Before Columbus: Portugal's African Prelude to the Middle Passage and Contribution to Discourse on Race and Slavery. In *Race, Discourse, and the Origin of the Americas*, V. Lawrence Hyatt and R. Nettleford, eds. Washington, DC: Smithsonian Press, 134–168.

Safa, H. I. (1986). "Economic Autonomy and Sexual Equality in Caribbean Society." *Social and Economic Studies* 35 (3): 1–19.

Safran, W. (1991). "Diasporas in Modern Societies: Myths of Homeland and Return." *Diaspora* 1 (1): 83–99.

Sahlins, M. (1993). "Goodbye to Tristes Tropes: Ethnography in the Context of Modern World History." *Journal of Modern History* 65: 1–25.

Said, E. (1984). "Reflections on Exile." *Granta* 13: 159–172.

Salomon, F. (1981). Killing the Yumbo: A Ritual Drama from North Quito. In *Cultural Transformations and Ethnicity in Modern Ecuador*, N. Whitten, ed. Urbana: University of Illinois Press, 162–208.

Salomon, F. (1983). "Shamanism and Politics in Late Colonial Ecuador." *American Ethnologist* 10 (3): 413–428.

Salomon, F. (1986). *Native Lords of Quito in the Age of the Incas: The Political Economy of North Andean Chiefdoms*. New York: Cambridge University Press.

Samper, J. M. (1980). Un viaje completo. In *Crónica grande del rio de la Magdalena*, A. Noguera Mendoza, ed. Vol. 2. Bogotá: Sol y Luna, 87–100.

Sanchez, J. (1992). Sevilla barroca (1581–1700). In *Historia de la Iglesia en Sevilla*, C. Ros, ed. Seville: Editorial Castillejo.

Sandroni, P. (1982). La proletarización de la mujer en Colombia después de 1945. In *Debate sobre la mujer en America Latina y el Caribe*, M. de Leon, ed. Bogotá: ACEP.

Santos, M. (1998). Mangueira e Império: A Carnavalização do Poder Pelas Escolas de Samba. In *Um Século de Favela*, A. Zaluar and M. Alvito, eds. Rio de Janeiro: Fundaçao Getúlio Vargas Editora.

Sapir, J. D. (1977). The Anatomy of Metaphor. In *The Social Use of Metaphor: Essays on the Anthropology of Rhetoric*, J. D. Sapir and J. C. Crocker, eds. Philadelphia: University of Pennsylvania Press, 3–32.

Sargent, E. D. (1980). ''Alternative Festival,'' Kwanzaa Celebrates Spirit of Community and Heritage. *The Washington Post*, D25, DC4.

Sargent, E. D. (1982). Kwanzaa Observed Here: Festive Week Celebrates African Heritage. *The Washington Post*, D27, D3a.

Saunders, A. C., and C. M. Saunders. (1982). *A Social History of Black Slaves and Freedmen in Portugal, 1441–1555*. Cambridge: Cambridge University Press.

Savoia, P. R. (1988). El negro Alonso de Illescas y sus descendientes (entre 1553–1867). *El negro en la historia de Ecuador y del sur de Colombia. Actas del Primer Congreso de Historia del Negro en el Ecuador y Sur de Colombia*. Quito: Centro Cultural Afro-Ecuatoriano, 29–60.

Sayer, A. (1985). The Difference That Space Makes. In *Social Relations and Spatial Structures*, D. Gregory and J. Urry, eds. New York: St. Martin's Press.

Scheller, U. (1972). *El mundo de los Salasacas*. Guayaquil: Fundación Antropología Ecuatoriana.

Schmidt, L. E. (1995). *Consumer Rites: The Buying and Selling of American Holidays*. Princeton, NJ: Princeton University Press.

Schrauf, R. (1997). ''¡Costalero Quiero Ser! Autobiographical Memory and the Oral Life Story of a Holy Week Brother in Southern Spain.'' *Ethos* 25 (4): 428–453.

Schwegler, A. (1996). *''Chi ma nkongo'': Lengua y rito ancestrales en El Palenque de San Basilio (Colombia)*. Frankfurt and Madrid: Vervuet Verlag and Iberoamericana.

Scott, J. (1990). *Domination and the Arts of Resistance: Hidden Transcripts*. New Haven, CT: Yale University Press.

Scott, J. W. (1995). Multiculturalism and the Politics of Identity. In *The Identity in Question*, J. Rajchman, ed. New York: Routledge.

Scott, M. (1852). *Tom Cringle's Log*. Edinburgh: William Blackwood.

Sentaurens, J. (1984). Seville et le theatre: De la fin du Moyen Age à la fin du XVIIe siècle. Lille, France.

Sevcenko, N. (1983). *Literatura como Missão: Tensões Sociais e Criação Cultural na Primeira República*. São Paulo: Ed. Brasiliense.

Sheriff, R. E. The Theft of Carnaval: National Spectacle and Racial Politics in Rio de Janeiro. Unpublished manuscript.

Silva, E. (1995). *Los mitos de la ecuatorianidad. Ensayo sobre la identidad nacional.* Quito: Abya-Yala.

Silva, M. B., and L. Santos. (1980). *Paulo da Portela, traço de união entre duas culturas.* Rio de Janeiro: MEC/Funarte.

Skidmore, T. E. (1974). *Black into White: Race and Nationality in Brazilian Thought.* New York: Oxford University Press.

Slesin, S. (1993). An Exhibit of Festivals. *The New York Times*, D23, C3:1.

Small, G. (1995). *Ruthless: The Global Rise of Yardies.* London: Warner Books.

Smith, M. G. (1957). The African Heritage in the Caribbean. In *Caribbean Studies: A Symposium*, V. Rubin, ed. Jamaica: Institute of Social and Economic Research, University College of the West Indies.

Smith, M. G. (1982). "Ethnicity and Ethnic Groups in America: The View from Harvard." *Ethnic and Racial Studies* 5 (1): 1–22.

Smith, T. W. (1992). "Changing Racial Labels: From 'Colored' to 'Black' to 'African American.' " *Public Opinion Quarterly* 56: 496–514.

Smith-Colin, M. (1994). Holiday Food for the Soul. *Chicago Defender*, D29, 13:1.

Smith-Colin, M. (1995). Foods to Help You Celebrate the "Fruits of the Harvest." *Chicago Defender*, D28, 11:1.

Soas, N. (1992, March 15). Mourning as Spectator Sport. *Daily Gleaner.*

Soas, N. (1993). Fashion of the Times. *Lifestyle Magazine* (Jamaica).

Softky, E. (1995). A Kwanzaa Memory; Growing Up with Dr. Karenga. *The Washington Post*, D20, E1.

Sonenshein, R. (1993). *Politics in Black and White: Race and Power in Los Angeles.* Princeton, NJ: Princeton University Press.

Sowell, T. (1978). Three Black Histories. In *American Ethnic Groups*, T. Sowell and L. D. Collins, eds. Washington, DC: Urban Institute, 37–64.

Spear, T. (1995). Penser la Créolité. In *Penser la Créolité*, M. Hage and M. Condé, eds. Paris: Karthala.

Speiser, S. (1986). Misionero y Antropólogo en el Contexto Afro-Esmeraldeño. *Antropólogos y Misioneros. Posiciones Incompatibles?* Quito: Abya Yala.

Speiser, S. (1987). "Pasión y Muerte de Jesucristo en Esmeraldas." *Cuadernos de Investigación (PUCE, Departamento de Antropología)* 4: 41–63.

Spottswood, R. K. (1990). *Ethnic Music on Record: A Discography of Ethnic Recordings Produced in the United States, 1893 to 1942.* Urbana and Chicago: University of Illinois Press.

Stam, R. (1988). "Carnaval, Politics and Brazilian Culture." *Studies in Latin American Popular Culture* 7: 255–264.

Stam, R. (1989). *Subversive Pleasures: Bakhtin, Cultural Criticism and Film.* Baltimore: Johns Hopkins University Press.

Steinberg, S. (1981). *The Ethnic Myth: Race, Class and Ethnicity in America.* Boston: Beacon Press.

Stevens, J. (1979). Kwanzaa Holiday Helps Preserve African Cultural Heritage. *The Washington Post*, D20, DC3.

Stevens, J. (1979). A Lifestyle Called Kwanzaa. *The Washington Post*, D27, MD3a.

Stocking, G. (1966). "Franz Boas and the Culture Concept in Historical Perspective." *American Anthropologist* 68 (4): 867–882.

Stocking, G. (1968). *Race, Culture, and Evolution: Essays in the History of Anthropology.* New York: Free Press.

252   Bibliography

Streicker, J. (1997). Spatial Reconfigurations, Imagined Geographies, and Social Con-
    flicts in Cartagena, Colombia. *Cultural Anthropology* 12 (1): 109–128.
Sturtevant, W. (1971). Creek into Seminole: North American Indians. In *Historical Per-
    spective*, E. Leacock and N. Lurie, eds. New York: Random House, 92–128.
Stutzman, R. (1981). El Mestizaje: An All-Inclusive Ideology of Exclusion. In *Cultural
    Transformations and Ethnicity in Modern Ecuador*, N. Whitten, ed. Urbana: Uni-
    versity of Illinois Press, 45–94.
Sullivan, B. (1991). Kwanzaa Potluck. *The Chicago Tribune*, D19, 7, 12:1.
Sweets, E. (1996). Kwanzaa. It's a Feast for the Body and the Soul. *Florida Today*, D26,
    E1: 1.
Taussig, M. (1980a). *The Devil and Commodity Fetishism in South America*. Chapel
    Hill: University of Northern Carolina Press.
Taussig, M. (1980b). "Folk Healing and the Structure of Conquest in Southwest Colom-
    bia." *Journal of Latin American Lore* 6 (2): 217–278.
Taussig, M. (1986). *Shamanism, Colonialism and the Wild Man: A Study in Terror and
    Healing*. Chicago: University of Chicago Press.
Terrell, A. (1972). Reaping the Fruits of Kwanzaa. *The Washington Post*, D19, B3:1.
Thornton, J. (1995). Perspectives on African Christianity. In *Race, Discourse, and the
    Origin of the Americas*, V. L. Hyatt and R. Nettleford, eds. Washington, DC:
    Smithsonian Press, 169–198.
Torres, A., and N. E. Whitten, Jr. (1998). *Blackness in Latin America and the Caribbean:
    Social Dynamics and Cultural Transformations, Volume II: Eastern South Amer-
    ica and the Caribbean*. Bloomington: Indiana University Press.
Tousignant, M. (1993). Joy to Everyone's World. Students Cloak Pageant in Many Col-
    ors. *The Washington Post*, D22, B1.
Trouillot, M.-R. (1990). *Haiti State Against Nation*. New York: Monthly Review Press.
Trouillot, M.-R. (1992). "The Caribbean Region: An Open Frontier in Anthropological
    Research." *Annual Review of Anthropology* 21: 19–42.
Turner, V. (1983). Carnaval in Rio: Dionysian Drama in an Industrializing Society. In
    The Celebration of Society: Perspectives on Contemporary Cultural Performance,
    F. Manning, ed. Bowling Green, OH: Bowling Green University Popular Press,
    103–124.
U.S. Bureau of Census. (1990). *The United States Census*. Washington, DC: U.S. Gov-
    ernment Printing Office.
U.S. Office of Immigration. (1984). *Statistical Yearbook, 1980*. Washington, DC: U.S.
    Government Printing Office.
Van Debury, W. J. (1992). *New Day in Babylon: The Black Power Movement and Amer-
    ican Culture, 1965–1975*. Chicago: University of Chicago Press.
Van den Bergue, P. (1984). "Ethnic Cuisine: Culture in Nature." *Ethnic and Racial
    Studies* 7 (3): 387–397.
Vasco, L. G. (1985). *Jaibanás: los verdaderos hombres*. Bogotá: Banco Popular.
Vasconcelos, J. (1925). *La raza cósmica—misión de la raza iberoamericana—notas de
    viaje a América del Sur*. Barcelona: Agencia Mundial de Librería.
Verger, P. (1990). *Retratos da Bahia, 1946 a 1952*. Salvador da Bahia: Corrapa.
Verger, P. (1993). The Orishas of Bahia. In *Os deuses africanos no Candomblé da Bahia/
    African Gods in the Candomblé of Bahia*. Salvador: Bigraf, 235–261.
Wade, P. (1993). *Blackness and Race Mixture: The Dynamics of Racial Identity in Co-
    lombia*. Baltimore, MD: Johns Hopkins University Press.

Wade, P. (1995a). Black Music and Cultural Syncretism in Colombia. In *Slavery and Beyond: The African Impact on Latin America and the Caribbean*, D. J. Davis, ed. Wilmington, DE: Scholarly Resources Books, 121–146.

Wade, P. (1995b). "The Cultural Politics of Blackness in Colombia." *American Ethnologist* 22 (2): 342–358.

Wade, P. (1997). *Race and Ethnicity in Latin America*. London; Pluto Press.

Wade, P. (1998). "Blackness, Music and National Identity: Three Moments in Colombian History." *Popular Music* 17 (1): 1–19.

Wall Street Journal. (1992). Kwanzaa Bonanza? The African Celebration Flourishes and So Do Sales. *The Wall Street Journal*, A1: 5.

Wall Street Journal. (1994). Christmas Plus Kwanzaa Prompts Holiday Marketing Directed At Blacks. *The Wall Street Journal*, A1: 5.

Walter, R. (1969). *The Grounding with My Brothers*. London: Bogle-Louverture Publications.

Walters, R. W. (1993). *Pan Africanism in the African Diaspora*. Detroit, MI: Wayne State University Press.

Washburn, D. K., Ed. (1980). *Hopi Kachina: Spirit of Life*. The California Academy of Sciences in Conjunction with the Exhibition Hopi Kachina. Seattle: University of Washington Press.

Waters, A. (1985). *Race, Class and Political Symbols: Rastafari and Reggae in Jamaican Politics*. New Brunswick, NJ: Transactions Books.

Waters, M. C. (1990). *Ethnic Options: Choosing Identities in America*. Berkeley: University of California Press.

Waxer, L. (1997). Salsa, Champeta, and Rap: Black Sounds and Black Identities in Afro-Colombia. Pittsburgh: Society for Ethnomusicology.

Weffort, F. C. (1978). *O Populismo na Política Brasileira*. Rio de Janeiro: Paz e Terra.

West, R. (1957). *The Pacific Lowlands of Colombia: A Negroid Area of the American Tropics*. Baton Rouge: Louisiana State University Press.

Whitehead, N. L. (1988). *Lords of the Tiger Spirit: A History of the Caribs in Colonial Venezuela and Guyana, 1498–1820*. Dordrecht-Holland: Foris Publications.

Whitten, D. S., and N. E. Whitten, Jr., eds. (1993) *Imagery and Creativity: Ethnoaesthetics and Art Worlds in the Americas*. Tucson: University of Arizona Press.

Whitten, N. E., Jr. (1994 [1974]). *Black Frontiersmen: Afro-Latin American Culture of Ecuador and Colombia*. 4th ed. Prospect Heights, IL: Waveland Press.

Whitten, N. E., Jr., ed. (1981). *Cultural Transformations and Ethnicity in Modern Ecuador*. Urbana: University of Illinois Press.

Whitten, N. E., Jr. (1985). *Sicuanga Runa: The Other Side of Development in Amazonian Ecuador*. Urbana: University of Illinois Press.

Whitten, N. E., Jr. (1988). Historical and Mythic Evocations of Chthonic Power in South America. In *Rethinking History and Myth: Indigenous South American Perspectives on the Past*, J. D. Hill, ed. Urbana: University of Illinois Press, 282–306.

Whitten, N. E., Jr. (1996). The Ecuadorian Levantamiento of 1990 and the Epitomizing Symbol of 1992: Reflections on Nationalism, Ethnic-Bloc Formation, and Racialist Ideologies. In *Culture, Power, and History: Ethnogenesis in the Americas, 1492–1992*, J. D. Hill, ed. Iowa City: University of Iowa Press.

Whitten, N. E., Jr, with M. Naranjo, M. Santi Simbaña, and D. S. Whitten. (1976). *Sacha Runa: Ethnicity and Adaptation of Ecuadorian Jungle Quichua*. Urbana: University of Illinois Press.

Whitten, N. E., Jr., and D. Quiroga, with assistance from P. R. Savoia. (1995). Ecuador. In *Afro-Latin Americans Today. No Longer Invisible*, Minority Rights Group, ed. London: Minority Rights Publications.

Whitten, N. E., Jr., and D. Quiroga. (1998). "To Rescue National Dignity": Blackness as a Quality of Nationalist Creativity in Ecuador. In *Blackness in Latin America and the Caribbean: Social Dynamics and Cultural Transformations*, N. E. Whitten, Jr., and A. Torres, eds. Vol. 1. Bloomington: Indiana University Press.

Whitten, N. E., Jr., and J. Szwed, eds. (1990). *Afro-American Anthropology*. New York: Free Press.

Whitten, N. E., Jr., and A. Torres. (1992). "Blackness in the Americas." *NACLA: Report on the Americas* 25: 16–22, 45–46.

Whitten, N. E., Jr., and A. Torres. (1998a). To Forge the Future in the Fires of the Past. In *Blackness in Latin America and the Caribbean: Social Dynamics and Cultural Transformations*. Vols. 1 and 2. Bloomington: Indiana University Press.

Whitten, N. E., Jr. and A. Torres. (1998b). *Blackness in Latin America and the Caribbean: Social Dynamics and Cultural Transformations*: Vol. 1. Bloomington: Indiana University Press.

Whitten, N. E., Jr., D. S. Whitten, and A. Chango. (1997). "Return of the Yumbo: The Indigenous *Caminata* from Amazonia to Andean Quito." *American Ethnologist* 24 (2): 355–391.

Wilk, R. (1996). Connections and Contradictions: From the Crooked Tree Cashew Queen to Miss World Belize. In *Beauty Queens on the Global Stage*. C. B. Cohen, R. Wilk, and B. J. Stoeltje, eds. New York: Routledge, 217–232.

Williams, B. F. (1989). "A Class Act: Anthropology and the Race to Nation Across Ethnic Terrain." *Annual Review of Anthropology* 18: 401–444.

Williams, M. (1995a). Beyond Sylvia's: A Designer Soul Scene. *The New York Times*, J4, 13–14.

Williams, M. (1995b). The Comfort Zones of the Young, Black Professional. *The New York Times*, A 20.

Willis, W. S., Jr. (1996). Divide and Rule: Red, White, and Black in the Southeast. In *Red, White, and Black: Symposium on Indians in the Old South*, C. M. Hudson, ed. Athens: University of Georgia Press, 99–115.

Wilson, P. (1973). *Crab Antics*. New Haven, CT, and London: Yale University Press.

Wright, B. (1977). *Hopi Kachinas: The Complete Guide to Collecting Kachina Dolls*. Flagstaff, AZ: Northland Press.

Wright, J. (1994). Muslims Celebrate December Holiday. *The Washington Post*, D10, B7.

Wright, J. (1995). It's Kwanzaa! A Week from Today, the Week-Long Rites Begin. *The Washington Post*, D19, B5.

Wynter, S. (1995). 1492: A New World View. In *Race, Discourse, and the Origin of the Americas*, V. L. Hyatt and R. Nettleford, eds. Washington, DC: Smithsonian Press, 169–198.

Young, R. (1995). *Colonial Desire: Hybridity in Theory, Culture and Race*. London: Routledge.

Young, Y. (1997). A Grand Procession. *Daily Gleaner*, March 19.

Zuluaga R. F. U. (1988). Cimarronismo en el sur-occidente del antiguo virreinato de Santa Fe de Bogotá. In *El negro en la historia de Ecuador y del sur de Colombia. Actas del Primer Congreso de Historia del Negro en el Ecuador y Sur de Colombia*, P. R. Savoia, ed. Quito: Cultural Afro-Ecuatoriano, 227–261.

Index

Abrahams, Roger, 150
Acculturation process, 5
Afoxé, xxi, 49–66
African Americans (U.S.), 101–122, 124–
  132, 134–136, 139, 141–145, 158, 196,
  207, 214
African diaspora, in general, xv–xxvi, 50,
  51, 103, 163, 195, 198, 207, 231
Africanisms, xvi
Africans, 134, 137, 153, 154
Afro-Andalusians (or black Andalusians),
  xxi, 3–17
Afro-Brazilians, 49–66
Afrocentrism, xx, 108, 110, 113
Afro-Colombians, 173–191, 219
Afro-Cubans, 4, 8
Afro-Esmeraldians (black Esmeraldians),
  xix, xxi, 19–47, 216, 220, 224, 229,
  231; Festival of the Kings, 44–47
Afro-Jamaicans, 137, 147–172, 179, 184;
  Afro-Jamaican women as Informal
  Commercial Importers (ICIs), xxiii,
  xxv, 147, 148, 150, 151, 156–160,
  167, 168
Afro-Venezuelans, 217
Aja people, 195
Alfaro, Eloy, 221–224

Allada, king of, 196, 197
Allen, Walter, 124, 125
Anderson, Benedict, 110
Appadurai, Arjun, 115, 116
Arawak, 218
Arens, William, 229
Árvelo de Jiménez, Nelly, 230
Ashé, 49–66
Auca, 224

Bakhtin, Mikhail M., xxii, 77, 78, 81, 91,
  92
Bambuco, 180, 181
Beauty pageants, 147, 152–156, 162
Behar, Ruth, 148
Béké, 92
Belafonte, Harry, 124
Belize, 214
Benin, 195–211, 231
Bennett, Louise, 165
Bermúdez, Egberto, 175
Bernabé, Jean, xviii, 95
Black confraternities and brotherhoods.
  See Cabildos
Black nationalism (black nationalists),
  101

Black Panther Party, 104
Black Power movement (Jamaica), 154
Black Power movement (U.S.), 104, 112
Blackness and national identity, 21–23,
    76, 101–122, 154, 179–185
Blacks and homophobia, 158
Blacks, mulattos and "hypersexuality"
    and/or "oversexualization," 148, 161,
    162
Blacks, mulattos and sexuality/erotism:
    "obscenity" and "X-ratedness," 93,
    95, 158, 160–162; representations, im-
    ages of, performances of, xxi–xxiii,
    xxv, 49, 55, 69, 70, 78, 80, 81, 84–88,
    93–96, 159, 161, 163–166, 182–184,
    223
Blanqueamiento (and whitening), 22, 23,
    76, 154, 230
Blue blacks (negros azules), 22, 23
Boas, Franz, xv
Bogas, xxiii, 175–178, 189
Boleros, 180
Bourdieu, Pierre, 150
Boyce Davies, Carole, xx, xxi, 80, 163
Bozales, 11, 13
Brandon, George, xviii
Brazil, 49–89, 173
Bruner, Edward, 207
Butcher, Kristin, 124
Butler, Judith, 149, 167

Cabildos, 3–17, 27, 44, 53, 174, 189, 231
Calypso, 131
Canada, 157
Candomblé, xxii, 50, 52, 53, 56, 63–66,
    80
Canelos Quichua (Ecuador), 216, 224,
    227, 229
Caribbean peoples. See West Indians
Carmichael, Stokely, 104, 124
Carnival, 91–94; Carnivalization, 91–97;
    Jamaica, 164; Rio de Janeiro, 49, 69–
    89, 188; Salasacan (Andean Ecuador),
    223; Salvador-Bahia, 49–66
Césaire, Aimé, 93, 94, 96, 97
Chachi, 216, 220, 224, 227, 229, 232
Chamoiseau, Patrick, xxii, 92, 94–97
Champeta, 187, 188

Chisholm, Shirley, 124
Chocó (Colombia), 218–220
Chude-Sokei, Louis, 158
Cimarronaje, cimarrones, 215–233
Civil Rights movement, 103, 104, 107,
    111, 130
Civrieux, Marc de, 216
Clark, Kenneth, 124
Clifford, James, 210
Colombia, 173–191, 216, 218, 228, 230
Colón, Cristobal, 214, 227
Color constructs and blackness, 147–
    172
Communitas, concept of, 84
Condé, Maryse, 79
Confiant, Raphaël, xxii, 92–97
Coplas, 177
Córdoboa, Juan, 219
Corpus Cristi (Inti Raymi), 216, 220
Corr, Rachel, 195
Cotonou, 200, 201
Créolité (Creoleness), xxii, 95, 96
Creolization, xviii
Cricket, 137, 138, 141, 142
Cuba, 4, 17, 50, 173
Cumbia, 180, 187, 188, 190
Currulao, 177, 178, 189

Dahomey, 195, 198, 208
DaMatta, Roberto, 49, 87
Dancehall, xxiii, xxv, 147, 148, 156, 158,
    159, 161, 162, 165, 166, 169
Danzón, 180
Dayan, Joan, 207
Décimas, xiii, xiv, 19, 177
Deculturation process, 5
Deleuze, Gilles, 21
Dexoten, 205, 206
Diablo (the Devil), El Diablo, Satan, In-
    fierno, Hell, 24, 40–47, 200, 201, 222,
    223
DJs (disc jockeys), 151, 157, 158, 161,
    166
Dodoo, Francis, 125
"The Door of No Return," 196, 205
Douglass, Frederick, 107
Douglass, Lisa, 150, 151, 167
Dunn, Christopher, 50

Ecuador, 19–47, 216, 221–225, 228, 230

Elmina Castle, 196, 207

Emberá, 216, 218, 219, 225, 227, 229, 230, 232

Esmeraldas, 19–47, 216, 218

Estudiantinas, 181

Eurocentrism, xx

Fandango, 180

Fared, Grant, 157

Farley, Reynolds, 124, 125

Fon, 198

Foucault, Michel, xiv, xix, 21, 87

Foxtrot, 180

Freyre, Gilberto, 89

Friedemann, Nina de, 218

Gaita, 177, 180

Gandhi, Mahatma, 52

Ganja (marijuana), 157

Garifuna (Garinagu), 214, 228, 229

Garvey, Marcus, 103, 108, 118, 124, 153

Geertz, Clifford, 215

Gender constructs, and blackness, 49–66, 76, 80, 85, 86, 147–172

Ghana, 109, 154, 196, 207

Gilroy, Paul, xxiv, 85, 105, 117, 197, 207–209

Glazer, Nathan, 124

Glissant, Edouard, xviii, 21, 92, 96

Goose Race, Festival of the, 13–16

Gorée Island, 195, 196

Guadeloupe, 95, 97

Guarachas, 180, 181

Guss, David, 216

Guyana, 137, 218

Habanera, 180

Hackett, Rosalind, 201

Haiti, 50

Haley, Alex, 104

Hall, Stuart, xiv, xx, 105, 110, 159

Hamer, Fannie Lou, 50

Hamilton, James, 175

Harlem Renaissance, 103, 118

Harrison, Faye, 148, 166

Henry the Navigator, Prince, 214

Hernandez-Reguant, Ariana, 126, 127

Herskovist, Melville Jean: research approach, xv, xvi, xxvi, 207; scale of intensity of New World Africanisms, xvii

Hintzen, Percy, xxii, xxiii, 114, 117, 119, 162

Hobsbawm, Eric, 105

Holy Week (*Semana Santa*): Andalusía, 9–12, 16; Esmeraldas, 19–47, 231

Honduras, 214, 228

Hou, 199, 205, 206

Hounon, Daagbo, 196, 198, 199, 201, 203, 204, 205, 206, 207, 209

Ilê Aiyê, 50, 56

Ile-Ife, 206

Indio, 225, 226, 227

Jackson, Jesse, 105, 117

Jews, *Judíos*, Jewish, Jewishness, xxi, 5, 11, 18, 21, 26, 27, 30, 33–36, 38–44, 105

Johnson, James Weldon, 124

Juan of Valladolid (*Conde Negro*), 6, 7, 17

Justus, Joyce, 127

Karenga, Maulana Ron, 104, 106, 107, 109, 114

Karp, Ivan, 229

Kasinitz, Philip, 124

Kenya, 154

Kérékou, Mathieu Ahmed, 200, 201, 202

Ketou, 200

King, Martin Luther, Jr., 50

Konpa, 187

Kroeber, Alfred, xvi

Kundera, Milan, 97

Kwanzaa, xxii, 101–122, 126, 127; and food, 114–117

Leach, Edmund, 215

Liminality, 24, 25, 40, 42, 46, 70, 79, 81, 84, 91

Losonczy, Anne-Marie, 219

Lowie, Robert, xvi

Magi Kings, folklore of, 7, 8, 44–47, 223
Malawi, 154
Malcolm X, 50, 124
Mama Negra, 223
Manley, Michael, 154, 164
Mapalé, 177, 189
Marches, 180
Marley, Bob, 154
Marley, Rita, 161
Martinique, 91–93, 97; literature of, 93
McKay, Claude, 124
Merengue, 184
Middle Passage, 196, 202, 207–209
Mintz, Sidney, 116, 208
Miskitu, 214, 229
"Model minority," 123, 124, 131, 136,
    138–140
Morand, Paul, 96
Moreno, Isidoro, 174, 214, 231
Morenos, 222
Morgan, Louis, xv
Moynihan, Daniel Patrick, 124
Mulattos (mulatos), 9–12, 22, 23, 86–88,
    149, 150, 174, 175, 180, 183, 215–233
Multiculturalism, 101, 102, 104, 110,
    113, 117, 118, 135
Muñoz, Arturo, 219
Música africana, 187
Música tropical, 184
Mustee, 150
Musteffino, 150

Naipaul, V. S., 93
Native Americans (South America), 214–
    233
Negreros, 214
Negritos, 13, 16
Négritude, 93, 104, 217, 232
Nettleford, Rex, 157
Nicaragua, 214, 228
Nigeria, 154, 206
Nkrumah, Kwame, 107
Noanam, 216, 218, 219, 224, 227, 230,
    230
Nyerere, Julius, 104

Orishas (from Candomblé's Pantheon), 49–
    66

Ortiz, Fernando, 4
Owusu, Maxwell, 152

Palenquismo and palenques, 215–233
Pan-Africanist movement, 104
Panamá, 216
Pasillo, 180
Pastaza Province (Ecuador), 225
Patterson, P. J., 166
Poitier, Sidney, 124
Polkas, 180
Porro, 180, 181, 187, 188, 190
Price, Richard, 208, 216
Price, Sally, 218
Proposition 187 (California), 129
Protestant missionaries, 200, 201

Quadroon, 150
Quiroga, Diego, 25, 41, 45
Quito Runa, 216, 219, 220, 227, 229

Rabelais, François, 97
Race mixing, mestizaje, mestizos and
    mulattos, 17, 21, 22, 41, 80, 147–172,
    179, 217, 220, 225–228, 230, 232
Racial/spatial order, concept of, xxiii, 21,
    22, 40, 45, 46, 149
Rahier, Jean Muteba, 216, 231
Rancheras, 180
Rap music, 134, 187–190
Rastafarians, 154, 157, 158, 188
Reggae, 131, 132, 151, 154, 157, 161, 187
Reichel-Dolmatoff, Gerardo, 219
Risério, Antonio, 50
Rodney, Walter, 155
Roumain, Jacques, 93

Sahlins, Marshal, 174
Salasaca Quichua (Ecuador), 216, 221–
    223, 225, 227, 229
Salsa, 186
Salsa romántica, 187
"Samba" (child of mulatto and black),
    150
Sambistas, 71–74, 75, 79
Saramaka (Surinam), 229
Sauer, Karl, xvi
Segalen, Victor, 96

Seminole, 214
Senegal, 196
Sepúlveda dos Santos, Myrian, xxii, 49, 174, 188, 189
"Slackness," 158, 160
Slavery, 3, 4, 9, 13, 44, 80, 91, 196, 197, 202, 204, 207–209, 213, 214
Smith, M. G., xvii, xviii
Soca, 131, 187
Social classes and blackness: black masses, 156; low income, 187; lower class, 125, 127, 147–149, 157, 158, 166, 168, 173, 175; lumpen proletariat, underclass, black poor, 16, 71–83, 111; middle-class, 107, 110, 111, 115, 117, 119, 124, 126, 127, 129, 130, 137, 147, 148, 151, 152, 157, 161–169; upper class, 115, 147, 148, 152, 157, 165, 167–169; upper-middle-class, 124; working class, 152, 168
Soglou, President (Benin), 200
Soukous, 187
South Africa, 50
Spear, Thomas, 96
Stam, Robert, 49
Sutherland, Peter, 231
Szwed, John, 150

Tangos, 180, 186
Taussig, Michael, 42, 223
Terapia, 187
Tiple, 180
Toumson, Roger, 93
Trinidad, 61, 63, 137
Tylor, Edward Burnet, xv

Ulysse, Gina, 117, 119, 179, 184
Umbanda, 80

"Undocumented" California migrants, 129
United States, 50, 101–122, 123–145, 157

Vallenato, 182, 185, 186, 188, 189
Van den Bergue, Pierre, 114, 116
Vargas, Getúlio, 74, 89
Vasco, Luis Guillermo, 219
Venezuela, 216, 218, 228
Verger, Pierre, 52
Villancicos, 175
Vodun, 195–199, 202, 204, 207, 210
Voodoo, 198, 199, 203

Wade, Peter, 21, 213
Waltzes, 180
West Indians: Carnaval (in San Francisco), 133, 134–136, 141, 143, 144; food, 132–134; in Los Angeles, 127; in New York, 123, 125, 126, 128; in San Francisco Bay Area, 123–145
White women and sexuality, representations of, 81
Whitten, Norman, xviii, xix, xxi, 195
Whydah, 195–198, 202–204, 208–210, 231
Wilson, Peter J., 167

Yekuana, 216–218, 220, 221, 222, 224, 225, 227, 229, 230, 232
Yoruba, 50–55, 206, 207
Yovotomen, 195

Zambos, 177, 178, 214–233, 226, 228, 230
Zouk, 131

About the Contributors

CAROLE BOYCE DAVIES is Director of African–New World Studies and Professor of English at Florida International University. In addition to numerous scholarly articles, she has co-edited the following critical texts: *Ngambika: Studies of Women in African Literature* (1986); *Out of the Kumbla: Caribbean Women and Literature* (1990); a two-volume collection of critical and creative writing, *Moving Beyond Boundaries* (volume 1) and *International Dimensions of Black Women's Writing* (volume 2); *Black Women's Diasporas* (1995); and *The African Diaspora: African Origins and New World Self-Fashionings* (1999), co-edited with Isidore Okpewho and Ali Mazrui. She has also authored *Migrations of the Subject: Black Women Writing Identity* (1994).

MARYSE CONDÉ, renowned writer from Guadeloupe, has written a series of novels that have been translated into several languages (including *Segu*; *The Children of Segu*; and *I, Tituba, Witch of Salem*). She has taught at the University of California, Berkeley, the University of Virginia, and Harvard University and is currently the chair of the Center for French and Francophone Studies at Columbia University in New York.

RACHEL CORR specializes in indigenous and other cultures of South America. She is an advanced doctoral student in anthropology at the University of Illinois at Urbana-Champaign. She has extensive research experience in Andean Ecuador, where she is currently completing research on space and time in Salasacan cosmology. Her current funding came from a Fulbright-Hays Fellowship. Previous funding came from a Fulbright Fellowship, a Tinker Foundation Fellowship, FLAS fellowships, and from the University of Illinois at Urbana-Champaign through the Graduate College and the Department of Anthropology.

ARIANA HERNANDEZ-REGUANT is a Ph.D. candidate in anthropology at the University of Chicago. A native of Spain, she has a master's degree in applied anthropology from the University of Maryland and has conducted fieldwork on black churches and the afrocentric movement in the Anacostia neighborhood, in Washington, D.C. Her publications include "Foreign Policy and State Cultural Nationalism in Spain, 1992," in Pauline Turner Strong, ed., *Commemoration and Critique: The Columbus Quincentennary and Other Commemorative Events* (forthcoming); and "The Columbus Quincentenary and the Politics of the 'Encounter' " (1993). Her research interests are mass media, cultural identity, and the state. She is currently conducting her dissertation research on mass media and commercialization in Havana, Cuba.

PERCY C. HINTZEN is Associate Professor and Chairperson of African American studies at the University of California, Berkeley. His teaching and research are concentrated in the areas of political and economic development, Caribbean political economy, comparative race and ethnic relations, and quantitative and qualitative research methods. His current research concentrates on the reproduction of elite domination in underdeveloped countries and on immigrant identity construction in the United States, with a concentration on West Indian migrants. Included among his publications are *The Costs of Regime Survival: Racial Mobilization, Elite Domination*, and *Control of the State in Guyana and Trinidad*; seventy-one biographic entries on Caribbean and Haitian leaders in *Dictionary of Latin American and Caribbean Political Biography*, edited by Robert J. Alexander; and numerous articles in journals and chapters in books on identity and domination in political economy and the causes and consequences of structural adjustment in underdeveloped countries. He also writes articles on politics and economics for major newspapers and for popular magazines and journals.

ISIDORO MORENO is Professor and Director of the Department of Anthropology at the University of Seville, Spain. His fieldwork has focused on Andalusia and Latin America, especially Ecuador. He has directed cross-disciplinary teams of researchers studying sociocultural identities in Spain, the Mediterranean region, and Latin America. Professor Moreno is president of the Andalusian Anthropological Association and contributes to a variety of diverse scientific associations and social science journals throughout the Spanish-speaking world. He studied history of the Americas and majored in anthropology. His doctoral dissertation, the first anthropological study by an Andalusian about rural Andalusia, "Propiedad, clases sociales y hermandades en la Baja Andalucía," was published in 1972. Among his other publications are *Los cuadros del mestizaje americano: Estudio antropológico*; *Cultura y modos de pro-*

ducción; *La Semana Santa de Sevilla: conformación, mixificación y significaciones*; *Antropologia de los Pueblos de España*; *Andalucía: Identidad y Cultura*; and *La antigua hermandad de los negros de Sevilla: Ethnicidad, poder y sociedad en 600 años de historia.* In addition to his theoretical, methodological, and ethnohistorical studies, he is interested in the dynamics of globalization and localization and their consequences upon ethnicities, sociopolitical nationalist movements, gender identity, working culture and the symbols and contexts of reproduction and redefinition of social identities.

JEAN MUTEBA RAHIER was born in the Belgian Congo (Democratic Republic of Congo) from a Congolese mother and a Belgian father. He grew up in Belgium. He studied at the University of Brussels (Belgium) and the Université de Paris X, at Nanterre (France), where he obtained his Ph.D. His research interest focuses on African diaspora identity processes. He has published on Afro-Esmeraldian (Ecuador) oral tradition and festivities and on Louisiana plantation narratives. His recent publications include "Blackness as a Process of Creolization: The Afro-Esmeraldian *Décimas*" (1998), "Blackness, the Racial/Spatial Order, Migrations, and Miss Ecuador 1995–1996" (1998); and "Gone with the Wind Versus the Holocaust Metaphor: Louisiana Plantation Narratives in Black and White" (1999). He is currently Associate Professor of Anthropology and African–New World Studies at Florida International University in Miami.

MYRIAN SEPÚLVEDA DOS SANTOS is Associate Professor of Sociology and Culture in the Graduate and Undergraduate Schools of the Faculty of Social Sciences at the Universidade do Estado do Rio de Janeiro (UERJ), Brazil. Her current work focuses on modern forms of official and popular culture and involves investigating policies and politics of both carnival festivities and museum exhibitions.

PETER SUTHERLAND teaches in the Department of Philosophy and Religious Studies at Louisiana State University, Baton Rouge. He began his recent field research in Benin in 1997, while completing his D.Phil. in cultural anthropology for Oxford University on the ethnohistory of power in a former Himalayan Hindu state.

GINA ULYSSE is a Ph.D. candidate in anthropology at the University of Michigan. She is currently writing her dissertation, entitled "That Cunning Woman: Government, Informal Economies and the Micropolitics of Class and Color." Her other research interests include the body, economic development, feminisims, gender, and popular culture.

PETER WADE received his Ph.D. in social anthropology at Cambridge University, focusing on the black population of Colombia. He was a research fellow at Queen's College Cambridge before becoming a lecturer in geography and Latin American studies at the University of Liverpool. He is currently a senior lecturer in social anthropology at the University of Manchester. His publications include *Blackness and Race Mixture* (1993), *Race and Ethnicity in Latin America* (1997) and ''Music, Blackness and National Identity: Three Moments in Colombian History'' (1998).

NORMAN E. WHITTEN, JR., specializes in indigenous cultures and African Latin-American cultures of South America. He is Professor of Anthropology and Latin American Studies, Affiliate of Afro-American Studies, and Curator of the World Heritage Museum at the University of Illinois at Urbana-Champaign. He obtained his Ph.D. in anthropology at the University of North Carolina–Chapel Hill in 1964. He is past editor of the *American Ethnologist* and past Head of the Department of Anthropology at the UIUC, where he is a Senior University Scholar. His major publications, based on extensive field research in North and South America, include *Class, Kinship, and Power in an Ecuadorian Town: The Blacks of San Lorenzo; Black Frontiersmen: Afro-Hispanic Culture of Ecuador and Colombia; Sacha Runa: Ethnicity and Adaptation of Ecuadorian Jungle Quichua; Cultural Transformations and Ethnicity in Modern Ecuador; Sicuanga Runa: The Other Side of Development in Amazonian Ecuador*; and, with John F. Szwed, *Afro-American Anthropology: Contemporary Perspectives*; with Dorothea S. Whitten, *From Myth to Creation: Art from Amazonian Ecuador* and *Imagery and Creativity: Ethnoaesthetics and Art Worlds in the Americas*. With Arlene Torres he has a two-volume book: *Blackness in Latin America and the Caribbean: Social Dynamics and Cultural Transformations.* His research has been funded by grants from the National Science Foundation, the National Endowment for the Humanities, the Social Science Research Council, the Wenner-Gren Foundation, the Ford Foundation, and a John Simon Guggenheim Memorial Foundation Fellowship, among many others.

ISBN 0-89789-606-8

90000>

EAN

9 780897 896061

HARDCOVER BAR CODE